Critical Care Medicine

Associate Chief of Staff
Cleveland Clinic Foundation
Cleveland, OH
USA

Clinical Specialist
Respiratory Therapy Services
Regional Health Authority Four
Edmundston, New Brunswick
Canada

JAY P. GOLDSMITH
MD
Professor of Pediatrics
Tulane University
Chairman
Department of Pediatrics
Ochsner Clinic
Co-Director of Nurseries
Ochsner Foundation Hospital
New Orleans, Louisiana
USA

ALLAN I. FIELDS
MD
Professor of Pediatrics,
Anesthesiology, and
Critical Care Medicine
Director
Pediatric Critical Care Services
University of Texas
MD Anderson Cancer Center
Houston Texas
USA

SUSAN P. PILBEAM
MS, RRT, FAARC
Clinical Application Specialist
St. Augustine, Florida
USA

SCOT N. JONES
BA, RRT
Respiratory Therapist
Eastern Maine Medical Center
Bangor, Maine
USA

GREGORY M. SUSLA
PharmD, FCCM
Associate Director
Medical Information
MedImmune
Gaithersburg, MD
USA

NICK WIDDER
RRT-NPS, CPFT, RCP
Respiratory Therapist
Hemby Children's Hospital
Charlotte, NC
USA

1 Ventilator Need / Indications

Chapter Contents

Indications for Ventilatory Support

Indications	Description	Examples
Apnea	Absence of breathing	Cardiac Arrest
Acute Respiratory Failure (ARF)	Inability of a patient to maintain adequate PaO_2, $PaCO_2$, and potentially pH.	Two types - see next page
Impending Respiratory Failure	Respiratory failure is imminent in spite of therapies. ***Commonly defined as:*** Patient is barely maintaining (or experiencing gradual deterioration) of normal blood gases but with significant WOB.	Neuromuscular Disease (N-M) Status Asthmaticus
Prophylactic Ventilatory Support	Clinical conditions in which there is a high risk of future respiratory failure. Ventilatory support is instituted to ↓ WOB, minimize O_2 consumption and hypoxemia, reduce cardiopulmonary stress, +/or control airway with sedation.	Brain injury, heart muscle injury, major surgery, shock (prolonged), smoke injury
Hyperventilation Therapy	Ventilatory support is instituted to control and manipulate $PaCO_2$ to lower than normal levels.	Acute head injury

Contraindications to Ventilatory Support

Absolute Contraindications	Relative Contraindications
Untreated tension pneumothorax (PPV) Patient's informed refusal	Medical futility * Patient pain/suffering
* *Medical futility*: Consider non-invasive ventilation (NPPV) as an interim measure until ethical considerations are determined.	

Two Types of Acute Respiratory Failure

Hypoxemic Respiratory Failure	Hypercapnic Respiratory Failure
Known as: Type I ARF, Lung Failure, Oxygenation Failure, Respiratory Insufficiency	***Known as:*** Type II ARF, Pump Failure, Ventilatory Failure
Definition: The failure of lungs and heart to provide adequate O_2 to meet metabolic needs	***Definition:*** The failure of the lungs to eliminate adequate CO_2
Criteria: PaO_2 < 60 mmHg on $FiO_2 \geq .50$ or PaO_2 < 40 mmHg on any FiO_2 SaO_2 < 90	***Criteria:*** Acute ↑ in $PaCO_2$ > 50 mmHg or Acutely above normal baseline in COPD with concurrent ↓ in pH < 7.30
Basic Causes: R-L shunt V/Q mismatch Alveolar hypoventilation Diffusion defect Inadequate FIO_2	***Basic Causes:*** Pump failure (drive, muscles, WOB) ↑ CO_2 production R-L shunt ↑ Deadspace

Signs and Symptoms of Acute Respiratory Failure

(Hypoxemia and/or Hypercarbia)

See Ch 5: Trouble-Shooting/ABG's

Indications for Invasive Ventilation in Adults with Acute Respiratory Failure

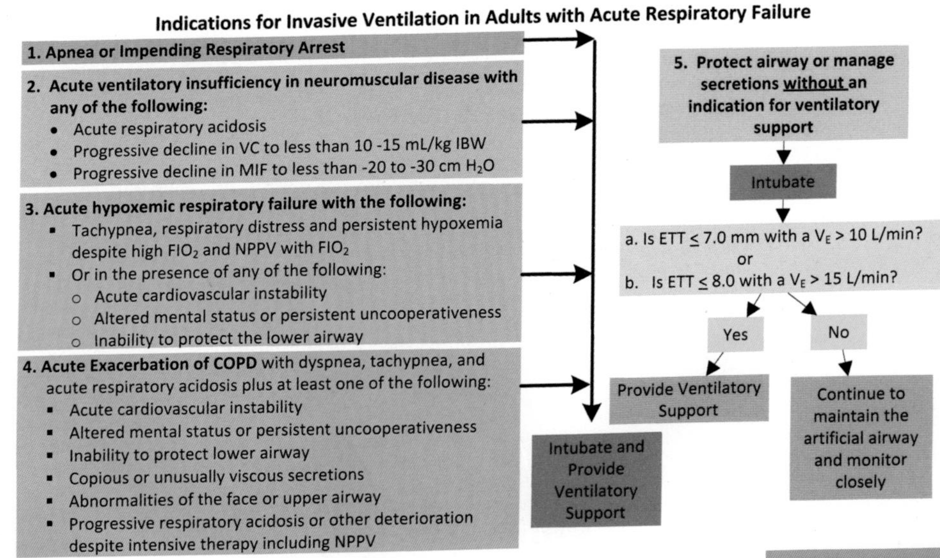

1. Apnea or Impending Respiratory Arrest
2. Acute ventilatory insufficiency in neuromuscular disease with any of the following:
• Acute respiratory acidosis
• Progressive decline in VC to less than 10 -15 mL/kg IBW
• Progressive decline in MIF to less than -20 to -30 cm H_2O
3. Acute hypoxemic respiratory failure with the following:
▪ Tachypnea, respiratory distress and persistent hypoxemia despite high FIO_2 and NPPV with FIO_2
▪ Or in the presence of any of the following:
o Acute cardiovascular instability
o Altered mental status or persistent uncooperativeness
o Inability to protect the lower airway
4. Acute Exacerbation of COPD with dyspnea, tachypnea, and acute respiratory acidosis plus at least one of the following:
▪ Acute cardiovascular instability
▪ Altered mental status or persistent uncooperativeness
▪ Inability to protect lower airway
▪ Copious or unusually viscous secretions
▪ Abnormalities of the face or upper airway
▪ Progressive respiratory acidosis or other deterioration despite intensive therapy including NPPV
Intubate and Provide Ventilatory Support
5. Protect airway or manage secretions without an indication for ventilatory support
Intubate
a. Is ETT ≤ 7.0 mm with a V_E > 10 L/min?
or
b. Is ETT ≤ 8.0 with a V_E > 15 L/min?
Yes
No
Provide Ventilatory Support
Continue to maintain the artificial airway and monitor closely

(Modified from Pierson DJ: *Respiratory Care* 47:3, 249-262, 2002)

Acute Respiratory Failure: A Differential Checklist of Potential Causes

Pulmonary	Chest Wall	CNS Depression	Neuromuscular	Cardiovascular
Acute airway obstruction: Aspiration Bronchoconstriction Edema/inflammation Epiglottitis Foreign objects Secretions, etc. Smoke/chemicals ***Asthma, COPD:*** Acute exacerbation Late stages ***Decreased functioning of lung tissue (severe):*** ARDS, Atelectasis, Fibrosis, Pneumonia, Pulmonary edema, Pulmonary embolism ***Sleep apnea*** (obstructive)	***Restrictive disorders (severe):*** Flail chest Kyphoscoliosis Obesity Rib fracture Severe burns **Intrathorax** Empyema Hemothorax Pleural disease/ effusion Pneumothorax	Cerebral ischemia CVA (infarcts) ***Drugs***: alcohol intoxication, anesthetics, barbiturates, cocaine/heroin, methadone, morphine/ sedatives, narcotics, propoxyphene, tranquilizers Increased ICP (hypoxic brain) Infection Lesions/tumors Metabolic alkalosis (CSF) Pickwickian syndrome Primary hypoventilation (Ondine's curse) Sleep apnea (central) Trauma	ALS ***Drugs***: antibiotics, Ca channel blockers, anticholinesterase, curare/ non-depolarizers, dexamethonium, methyl alcohol, nerve gases, succinylcholine Electrolyte imbalance Guillian-Barré syndrome High spinal injury/disease Multiple sclerosis Muscular dystrophy Myasthenia gravis Myotonia Phrenic nerve injury ***Poisons/toxins***: botulism, mushrooms, paraquat, petroleum distillates Poliomyelitis, Polymyositis Rabies, SLE, Status epilepticus, Tetanus	Cardiac arrest (↓ CO) CHF with pulmonary edema Congenital heart disease Hypovolemia Shock Thromboemboli **Other** Anxiety Hypothyroidism Malnutrion / fatigue MV (air-trapping) Metabolic acidosis Post-op complications

Clinical Parameters Commonly Used to Determine Ventilatory Need

Parameter*	Normal	MV Indicated
Ventilation		
$PaCO_2$	35-45 mmHg	50-55 mmHg or acute ↑ from pt. baseline (e.g., COPD)
pH	7.35-7.45	< 7.25
V_D/V_T	25-40%	> 60%
Oxygenation		
PaO_2	75-100 mmHg (air)	< 50 mmHg (air) < 60 mmHg (50% O_2) < 200 mmHg (100% O_2)
SaO_2	> 95%	< 75%
$PA\text{-}aO_2$	10-25 mmHg (air)	> 350 mmHg on 100% O_2
$PaO_2\text{-}PAO_2$	0.8-0.9	< 0.15
PaO_2/FiO_2	350-400 mmHg	< 200 mmHg
Q_S/Q_T (shunt)	< 5%	> 20%
Mechanical Capabilities		
V_T (ideal)	5-8 mL/kg	< 5 mL/kg
f	12-20	< 10 or > 35
f/V_T (RSBI)	< 105	> 105
$\dot{V}_E$	5-6 L/min	> 10 L/min
VC (ideal)	60-75 mL/kg	< 15 mL/kg
FEV_1 (ideal)	50-60 mL/kg	< 10 mL/kg
FRC	80-100% pred.	< 50% pred.
MVV	120-180 L/min	< 20 L/min or 2 x $\dot{V}_E$
P_I max (MIP, NIF)	-80 to -100 cmH_2O	> -20 cmH_2O
Breathing pattern	Normal	Abnormal / Irregular
Intracranial Pressure		
ICP (hyperventilation)	12-15 cmH_2O	> 20 cmH_2O, impending brainstem herniation, inability to control ↑ ICP's using other methods

* No one parameter or set of parameters has been proven to be an absolute indication of MV. Clinical judgment is to take precedence over objective parameters; trends are far more important than absolute values.

Objectives of Mechanical Ventilation *

I. Physiological Objectives

A. Support or Manipulate Pulmonary Gas Exchange

Alveolar Ventilation ($\dot{V}_A$) (e.g., $PaCO_2$, pH)

In most cases, normalize $\dot{V}_A$.

To reduce ICP, $\dot{V}_A$ > normal.

For permissive hypercapnia and acute-on-chronic respiratory failure use adequate, but < normal $\dot{V}A$.

Arterial Oxygenation (e.g., PaO_2, SaO_2, CaO_2)

Achieve acceptable level using acceptable F_IO_2.

In most cases, SaO_2 > 90% or PaO_2 > 60 mmHg.

Seldom used as the only indication for mechanical ventilation, given other techniques available.

B. Increase Lung Volume

End-Inspiratory Lung Inflation

Achieve sufficient lung expansion with every breath (or intermittently)

Used to prevent or treat atelectasis

End-Expiratory Lung Inflation (FRC)

When indicated, achieve, maintain, or ↑ FRC using PEEP therapy.

C. Decrease or Manipulate Work Of Breathing (WOB)

Unload the ventilatory muscles burdened by ↑ Raw or ↓ C_{LT}

II. Clinical Objectives

Reverse Hypoxia (↑PaO_2 and SaO_2 by: ↑ $\dot{V}_A$, ↑ lung volume, and ↓ oxygen consumption)

Reverse Acute Respiratory Acidosis (life threatening)

Relieve Respiratory Distress (intolerable discomfort)

Prevent or Reverse Atelectasis

Reverse Ventilatory Muscle Fatigue (unload ventilatory muscles)

Permit Sedation and/or Neuromuscular Blockade

Decrease Systemic or Myocardial Oxygen Consumption

Reduce Intracranial Pressure (ICP)

Stabilize Chest Wall

Adapted from ACCP Consensus Conference: Mechanical Ventilation; ***Respiratory Care***, Vol. 38, #12, 1993.

2 Ventilator Operation

Chapter Contents

Operations

Types of Mechanical Ventilation

	Full Ventilatory Support	Partial Ventilatory Support
Definition	Ventilator does all the WOB necessary to maintain effective alveolar ventilation.	Patient and ventilator share the WOB necessary to maintain effective alveolar ventilation.
Goals	Achieve total control of the patient's ventilatory pattern – patient does not breathe spontaneously or trigger the ventilator.	Achieve only partial control of the patient's ventilatory pattern – allow the patient to breathe either spontaneously or trigger the ventilator.
Indications	Initial ARF – Allowing respiratory muscles to rest, ↓O_2 consumption Need for hyperventilation Patient's disease process (e.g., quadriplegic) Pharmacologic therapy (e.g., paralysis)	*Allow patients to*: Maintain respiratory muscle tone Improve patient comfort Weaning (discontinuation)
Clinical Notes	Full support may quickly lead to muscle wasting or atrophy, hence some clinicians opt for partial support, even from the beginning.	In the majority of ventilator modes, the clinician decides on the balance of WOB provided by the patient vs. the ventilator. The exception is A/C where the ventilator provides most of the WOB.

Operations

Two Types of Positive Pressure Ventilation

	Volume Ventilation (VV)	Pressure Ventilation (PV)
Other Names	Volume-limited, targeted, controlled, or cycled ventilation.	Pressure-limited, targeted, or controlled ventilation.
Definition	Airflow is delivered by a mechanical ventilator that terminates the inspiratory phase of the respiratory cycle after a preset volume is reached	Airflow is delivered by a mechanical ventilator that terminates the inspiratory phase of the respiratory cycle when a preset time is reached.
Main Charac.	Volume is set and always the same, whereas pressure varies.	Pressure is set and always the same, whereas volume varies.
Main Advantage	A constant V_T (and/or $\dot{V}_E$) is delivered regardless of changes in patient C or Raw, or ventilator PIP or Pplat.	A constant inflation pressure is delivered regardless of V_T delivery (limits inflation pressure to ↓ risk of alveolar distension). Also has a true decelerating flow.
Major Disadvan.	Alveolar over-distension → ↑ PIP and Pplat if lung condition worsens (i.e., ↑ Raw and/or ↓ C)	Volume delivery (V_T and $\dot{V}_E$ varies as lung condition changes (i.e., either ↑ or ↓ Raw and/or C)
In General	Use VV if precise $PaCO_2$ regulation is more important than overdistension protection or patient-ventilator synchrony.	Use PV if overdistension protection or patient-ventilator synchrony is more important than precise $PaCO_2$ regulation (e.g., ARDS).

Volume Ventilation vs. Pressure Ventilation

VV	PV
V_T (set); PIP (variable)	PIP (set); V_T (variable)
↑ V_T → ↑ PIP + Pplat	↑ PIP → ↑ V_T
↓ V_T → ↓ PIP + Pplat	↓ PIP → ↓ V_T
↑ C → same V_T (↓ PIP + Pplat)	↑ C → same PIP (↑V_T)
↓ C → same V_T (↑ PIP + Pplat)	↓ C → same PIP (↓V_T)
↑ Raw → same V_T (↑ PIP)	↑ Raw → same PIP (↓V_T)
↓ Raw → same V_T (↓ PIP)	↓ Raw → same PIP (↑V_T)

Ventilator Parameters

Parameter *(normal range)*	Definition	Mechanics	Ventilation Effects	Oxygenation
Volumes				
Minute Volume ($\dot{V}_E$) *(5 – 10 L/m)*	The amount of air moved in and out of the lungs in a minute period.	$\dot{V}_E = f \times V_T$ (PIP in PV)	$\dot{V}_E \approx \dot{V}_A \approx 1/PaCO_2$	$\dot{V}_E \approx \dot{V}_A \approx PaO_2$
Tidal Volume (V_T) *(4 – 12 mL/kg)*	Volume of air delivered to the patient for a single inspiratory breath.	$V_T = \dot{V}_E / f$ $V_T = \dot{V}_I \times T_I$ V_T is commonly set (VV) or approximated (PV) according to IBW or disease state. In PV, V_T is variable depending on PIP, PEEP, $\dot{V}_I$, T_I, and patient CLT and Raw.	$V_T \times f = \dot{V}_E \approx \dot{V}_A \approx 1/PaCO_2$ ($\uparrow V_T \rightarrow \downarrow PaCO_2$) Rate changes, rather than V_T changes, are more commonly employed to regulate $PaCO_2$.	$\uparrow V_T \rightarrow \uparrow Paw \rightarrow \uparrow PaO_2$

$\dot{V}_E$ Precautions –
Too small a $\dot{V}_E \rightarrow$ hypoventilation and possible hypoxemia, Too large a $\dot{V}_E \rightarrow$ hyperventilation

V_T Precautions - Small V_T may result in atelectasis, hypoventilation, and hypoxemia. Large V_T may result in volutrauma, hyperventilation, and ↓CO. The V_T inspired by the patient is usually less than the V_T delivered by the ventilator due to compressible volume loss (unless ventilator compensated). Smaller V_T s (with higher rates) now are generally preferred (esp. in ARDS patients), due to less volutrauma.

Parameter *(normal range)*	Definition	Mechanics	Ventilation Effects	Oxygenation
Rate				
Ventilator Rate (f) *(8-12 breaths/ min)*	Number of breaths per minute delivered by the ventilator.	$f \times V_T = \dot{V}_E$ Rate is the main parameter adjusted to change $\dot{V}_E$ and $PaCO_2$ (↑ rate → ↓ $PaCO_2$). "Normal" rate is highly disease-variable. Faster rates (and smaller V_T's) are commonly used in restrictive disease (short TC). Slower rates are used in obstructive disease (long TC).	$f \times V_T = \dot{V}_E \approx 1/PaCO_2$ TC = time constants (See Ch 7 – Ventilation Dynamics)	Affects PaO_2 by providing adequate ventilation to the lungs.
Pressures				
Peak Inspiratory Pressure (PIP or Ppeak)	Highest (peak) proximal airway pressure reached during	Keep PIP < 35 cm H_2O In VV – machine V_T, $\dot{V}_I$, PEEP, and patient C_{LT} and Raw determines PIP.	↑ PIP (V_T) → ↓ $PaCO_2$	↑ PIP (Paw) → ↑ PaO_2

Rate Precautions -
Slow rates may lead to hypoventilation, hypoxemia, and patient-ventilator asynchrony.
Fast rates may lead to hyperventilation and/or inadequate T_I and/or T_E, resulting in hypoventilation and/or air-trapping (auto-PEEP) and its accompanying effects.

Parameter *(normal range)*	Definition	Mechanics	Ventilation Effects	Oxygenation
(< 35 cm H2O)	inspiration.	In PV – PIP is a set pressure limit; PIP + C_{LT} + Raw = V_T ↑ PIP → ↑ V_T, Paw, and Palv (except in high Raw where the ↑ pressure is lost to the airway and may not reach the alveoli) PIP is used to calculate Cdyn and Raw.		

PIP Precautions -
Too low a PIP may result in hypoventilation and atelectasis.
Too high a PIP can increase the risk of barotrauma, compromise both ventilation and oxygenation effects, and significantly compromise hemodynamics.

Clinical Note: In VV, PIP is different than the pressure limit (P/L). P/L is an inspiratory pressure limit that is set 5–10 cmH_2O above PIP and acts as a safety mechanism that will immediately terminate T_I.
In PV, PIP is a pressure limit that may vary or be set, depending on ventilator and/or mode.

Parameter *(normal range)*	Definition	Mechanics	Ventilation Effects	Oxygenation
Mean Airway Pressure ($\overline{P}aw$)	The mean (average) proximal airway pressure during the entire respiratory cycle.	$\overline{P}aw$ is a function of PIP, PEEP, T_I, T_E, $\dot{V}_I$, and $\dot{V}_I$ waveform. It may be a set parameter on newer ventilators.	$\overline{P}aw \rightarrow V_T \approx \frac{1}{PaCO_2}$ ↑ Paw → ↓ $PaCO_2$	$\overline{P}aw$ is perhaps the major determinant of oxygenation ↑Paw → ↑ PaO_2

$\overline{P}aw$ Precautions: Too low a $\overline{P}aw$ may result in hypoventilation and atelectasis.
Too high a $\overline{P}aw$ can increase the risk of barotrauma, compromise both ventilation and oxygenation effects, and significantly compromise hemodynamics.

Parameter *(normal range)*	Definition	Mechanics	Ventilation Effects	Oxygenation
Plateau Pressure (Alveolar Pressure) (Pplat or Palv) *(< 30 cmH_2O)*	The average alveolar pressure during the inspiratory phase.	Pplat is the proximal airway pressure measured during an inspiratory hold. It is then assumed to approximate the average (overall) Palv and is used to determine Cstat and Raw. Palv is not directly measured.	Generally approximates the effects of PIP.	Generally approximates the effects of PIP.
PEEP *(3-5 cmH_2O is minimum to maintain FRC)* *(5-14 cmH_2O is considered "therapeutic")*	Positive end expiratory pressure applied during MV	PEEP increases FRC by stabilizing open alveoli to prevent collapse. ↑ FRC leads to: 1) ↓ atelectasis → ↓ shunt → ↑ V/Q 2) ↑ C_L → ↓ WOB 3) Minimizes shear force lung injury. PEEP → ↑ Paw → ↑ gas exchange	↑ PEEP may ↑V/Q → ↓$PaCO_2$	↑ PEEP →↑ Paw → ↑ V/Q → ↑ PaO_2

PEEP Precautions - Too low a PEEP when needed may lead to alveolar collapse and ↓ FRC (opposite of mechanics above). Too high a PEEP may lead to over-distension. Over-distension → 1) Air-trapping (auto-PEEP) → volutrauma (and other accompanying effects); 2) ↓C_L →↑WOB; 3) ↓ venous return → ↓ CO, ↓ UO, and ↓ ICP; 4) ↑ PVR → ↓ lung perfusion→ ↓ gas exchange; 5) In PV; ↓ (PIP – PEEP) difference → ↓ V_T and ↑ $PaCO_2$

<table>
<tr><th>Parameter
(normal range)</th><th>Definition</th><th>Mechanics</th><th>Ventilation Effects</th><th>Oxygenation</th></tr>
<tr><td colspan="5">Types of PEEP
<u>$PEEP_E$</u> (extrinsic or applied PEEP) = PEEP that is purposely applied by the mechanical ventilator.
<u>$PEEP_I$</u> (intrinsic, inadvertent, occult, or auto-PEEP) = PEEP that is inadvertently applied by the mechanical ventilator (fast rates/short T_E) and/or patient airway obstruction when flow does not return to zero before the next inspiration starts. Most commonly called auto-PEEP, air-trapping or dynamic hyperinflation. It is PEEP at the alveolar level (intrinsic) and is unintentional and undesirable. (see Chapter 11, Ventilator Effects)
<u>Total PEEP</u> = PEEPE + PEEPI
<u>Optimal PEEP</u> = PEEP level at which obtain maximal oxygenation (increased CaO_2) with minimal hemodynamic compromise (↓CO) (i.e., O_2 transport = CaO_2 x CO). Also called best PEEP.</td></tr>
<tr><td>Inspiratory Time
(T_I)
(0.5 – 1.2 sec)</td><td>Time duration of the inspiratory phase.</td><td>$T_I = T_{tot} - T_E$; $T_I = V_T / \dot{V}_I$
T_I = the I part of the I:E ratio
In VV, T_I is commonly the result of $V_T/\dot{V}_I$.
In PV, T_I is commonly a set parameter.
<u>Short T_I's</u> are commonly used in patients with ↓ C_{LT} (short TC).
<u>Longer T_I's</u> are commonly used in patients with ↑ Raw (long TC). See TC.</td><td>A sufficient T_I is necessary for adequate V_T delivery and, therefore, adequate gas exchange.

See T_I Precautions, Next Page</td><td>Long <u>TI's</u> are used to ↑ $\overline{P}aw$ (↑ T_I → ↑ $\overline{P}aw$ → ↑PaO_2).
The longer the T_I, the more time available to deliver the V_T, hence ↑ alveolar distension and ↑ gas exchange.</td></tr>
</table>

Parameter (normal range)	Definition	Mechanics	Ventilation Effects	Oxygenation
	T_I Precautions - *Short T_I* (and slow $\dot{V}_I$) may cause ↓ V_T resulting in hypoventilation and hypoxemia. *Long T_I* may cause patient discomfort, patient-ventilator asynchrony and hypoventilation. The longer the T_I the greater the $\overline{P}aw$ and effects on the heart and lungs (see $\overline{P}aw$).			
Expiratory Time (T_E) *(1.0 - 5.0 sec)*	Time duration of the expiratory phase. Short T_E = faster rate and larger I:E ratio. Long T_E = slower rate and smaller I:E ratio.	$T_E = Ttot - T_I$ T_E = the E part of I:E ratio T_E may be a set parameter, but is more commonly the result of a set T_I (PV), V_T (VV) and rate (f). The longer the T_E the more time available for lung emptying (esp. important in patients with ↑ Raw).	An adequate T_E is necessary for complete emptying of the lung V_T, and therefore, gas exchange.	Little to no effect on PaO_2 unless T_E inadequate for lung emptying.
	T_E Precautions - Short T_E may result in inadequate emptying of the lung (esp. in patients with ↑ Raw) resulting in air-trapping (auto-PEEP) and its accompanying effects. Long T_E may result in hypoventilation and hypoxemia.			
I:E Ratio (I/E; Duty Cycle) *(1:1.5 to 1:4)*	Ratio of inspiratory time to expiratory time.	$I:E = 1 / (T_E/T_I)$ (see T_I and T_E) I:E ratio may be determined by: 1) T_I and f 2) V_T, $\dot{V}_I$, and f 3) Set I:E	An adequate I:E is necessary for complete filling and emptying of the lung and, therefore, gas exchange.	Larger I:E ratios (larger T_I) →↑ $\overline{P}aw$ and allow greater time for gas distribution, thereby

Parameter *(normal range)*	Definition	Mechanics	Ventilation Effects	Oxygenation
		$I + E = \dot{V}_I / \dot{V}_E$ $\dot{V}_I = \dot{V}_E \times I + E$ $T_I = T_{tot} / I + E$ $T_I \% = 1 / I + E$		↑ PaO_2. Inverse ratios ($T_I > T_E$), to ↑ PaO_2, are generally reserved for patients in severe respiratory failure (high PIP and high F_IO_2) due to the ↑ risks associated with them.
Inspiratory Pause (Inflation Hold or Plateau) (*0.5 to 3 sec*)	A delay in the onset of expiration after inspiration is complete.	Inspiratory pause prolongs T_I and ↑ $\overline{P}aw$. It may improve gas distribution within the lung. Its primary use is to measure static lung compliance or Pplat. It may be applied either by an inspiratory pause control on the ventilator or by temporarily occluding the expiratory port at end-inspiration.	Little to no effect. See Pause Precautions, Next Page	Inspiratory pause → ↑ $\overline{P}aw$ and gas distribution, hence may ↑ PaO_2 in certain disease states. It is no longer a recommended use to improve oxygenation - PEEP is used instead.

I:E Precautions - I:E ratios change with the adjustments of many other parameters. Beware of choosing a desired I:E ratio to the exclusion of T_I, $\dot{V}I$, and *f*. Equal or inverse ratios (1:1, 2:1, 3:1, etc.) may cause significant ↑ $\overline{P}aw$, patient discomfort, patient-ventilator asynchrony, air-trapping (auto-PEEP), and hemodynamic compromise.

Parameter *(normal range)*	Definition	Mechanics	Ventilation Effects	Oxygenation
Pause Precautions - Prolonged T_I and/or prohibiting exhalation may cause patient discomfort, patient-ventilator asynchrony, and possible ↑ $PaCO_2$. Do not use in COPD or patients with expiratory flow limitations. Short T_E may result in air-trapping (auto-PEEP) and its accompanying effects.				
Expiratory Hold (End Expiratory Pause) *(0.5 – 2.0 sec)*	A delay in the onset of inspiration and the prevention of any further exhalation.	At the end of the exhalation time period (just prior to inspiration), the exhalation valve is occluded – preventing any further expiratory airflow and delaying inspiration.	**Note:** The primary use of the expiratory hold is to measure auto-PEEP, but is only accurate if no spontaneous efforts by the patient.	
Flow				
Inspiratory Flow ($\dot{V}_I$) *(40 – 100 L/m)*	The rate at which gas is delivered to the patient during the inspiratory phase.	$\dot{V}_I = V_T / T_I$ Used to provide the desired T_I, I:E ratio, and inspiratory pattern. Goal = $\dot{V}_I \geq$ peak inspiratory demand. Proper $\dot{V}_I = \dot{V}_E \times (I + E)$ Slower $\dot{V}_I$ is generally used in patients with ↑Raw and/or poor gas distribution. Slow $\dot{V}_I$ may ↓ PIP and risk of	An adequate and appropriate $\dot{V}_I$ is necessary for proper ventilation and gas exchange.	$\dot{V}_I$ affects T_I and $\overline{P}aw$ which in turn affects PaO_2.

Parameter *(normal range)*	Definition	Mechanics	Ventilation Effects	Oxygenation
		barotrauma in certain disease states. Fast $\dot{V}_I$ may ↓ WOB and improve patient comfort in patients with high inspiratory demand.		

Flow Precautions - Slow $\dot{V}_I$ may not meet the patient's demand (flow-starvation), resulting in ↑WOB, patient discomfort, and possibly hypoventilation. Slow $\dot{V}_I$ results in long T_I and short T_E, leading to patient discomfort and/or air-trapping (auto-PEEP). Fast $\dot{V}_I$ may cause ↑Raw, ↑ PIP, and/or ↓ distribution of ventilation.

Parameter *(normal range)*	Definition	Mechanics	Ventilation Effects	Oxygenation
Inspiratory Flow Waveform ($\dot{V}_I$ waveform)	The flow pattern in which inspiratory flow is delivered.	Much debate exists concerning the clinical benefits of one waveform over another.		
Rise Time	The time required to reach the pressure target (PIP) in PV.	↓ the rise time by ↑ $\dot{V}_I$. ↑ the rise time by ↓ $\dot{V}_I$. Rise time is generally adjusted to "soften" (slow) the initial rapid $\dot{V}_I$.		

Rise Time Precautions -
Patient may need a "softer" (slower) rise time for patient-ventilator synchrony. Too slow a rise time may ↑ WOB

Parameter *(normal range)*	Definition	Mechanics	Ventilation Effects	Oxygenation
Oxygen				
F_IO_2 Whatever is necessary to maintain PaO_2 60 – 100 mmHg and/or $SaO_2 \geq$ 90%.	The fraction of inspired oxygen delivered to the patient by the ventilator.	Determining factors are target PaO_2 or SaO_2, PEEP, $\overline{P}aw$, and hemodynamic status.	None	F_IO_2 determines PAO_2 which in turn affects PaO_2.
Adjuncts				
Sensitivity (Inspiratory Trigger Sensitivity)	The level of spontaneous effort (pressure or flow) needed to trigger a machine inspiratory breath.	Sensitivity directly affects patient-ventilator synchrony and interaction. Flow sensitivity is generally preferred due to less WOB required. May need to readjust following changes in PEEP.	Note: Pressure sensitivity: 0.5 to 2.0 cm H_2O below baseline Flow sensitivity: 1 to 3 L/m below baseline	None

F_IO_2 Precautions -
Low F_IO_2 leads to hypoxemia and hypoxia.
High F_IO_2 may cause O_2 toxicity (lung damage) and intrapulmonary shunting (absorption atelectasis).

Note: Expiratory Trigger Sensitivity = % of peak $\dot{V}_I$ at which the ventilator cycles off (I → E). Used in pressure support and is generally a ventilator specific value.

Sensitivity Precautions - Auto-PEEP will affect the patient's ability and effort to trigger the ventilator and must be either eliminated or adjusted for (see Ch 11).
Too sensitive leads to self-cycling (auto-triggering), air-trapping, and potential hyperventilation. Too insensitive promotes increased WOB, atelectasis, patient discomfort, and patient-ventilator asynchrony.

Parameter *(normal range)*	Definition	Mechanics	Ventilation Effects	Oxygenation
Sigh [Periodic Hyperinflation] *(1.5 to 2 x normal V_T, q 6-10 minutes)*	The periodic delivery of a larger than normal V_T.	Its clinical benefit has not been proven. A low level of PEEP is commonly recommended instead. Use only when indicated: Small V_T (< 7 mL/kg) during controlled ventilation Reexpansion of collapsed lung Extubation (before and during) Suctioning (before and after) CPT (during) Bronchoscopy (during and after)	Its use will insignificantly affect $\dot{V}_E$, $PaCO_2$, or PaO_2	

Sigh Precautions -
Sighs are not recommended when using large V_T (> 7 mL/kg) when Pplat > 30 cmH_2O, or for spontaneous breathing patients on CPAP.

Parameter *(normal range)*	Definition	Mechanics	Ventilation Effects	Oxygenation
Humidification 100% humidity at body temperature; 30 mg H_2O/L absolute humidity; *32 – 34 °C*	The delivery of a heated and humidified gas to the patient.	Prevents water loss from the airway. HMEs may be used except when: Secretions are thick, copious and/or bloody. $\dot{V}_E$ > 10 L/m Body temperature < 32°C Expired V_T < 70% delivered V_T During aerosol treatment via patient circuit (see CPG in Appendix).		
Mechanical Deadspace (VD_{mech}) *50 to 300 mL of circuit tubing added in 50 mL increments*	Artificial deadspace added between the patient's ET tube and the circuit wye.	Used to keep $PaCO_2$ normal in hyperventilating patients when rate is not controlled. Usually preferable to decreasing V_T.	Added to maintain $PaCO_2$ > 30 mmHg.	

Humidity Precautions - Humidity systems should be servo-controlled with temperature readout and alarm (37 ° C). ↓ humidity may result in dried secretions and plugging. Changes in H_2O level of reservoir will change compliance of circuit.

VDmech Precautions -
Watch for hypoventilation as patient rate ↓.
Usually not tolerated well above 300 mL.

Basic Operating Principles of Volume-Controlled Ventilation

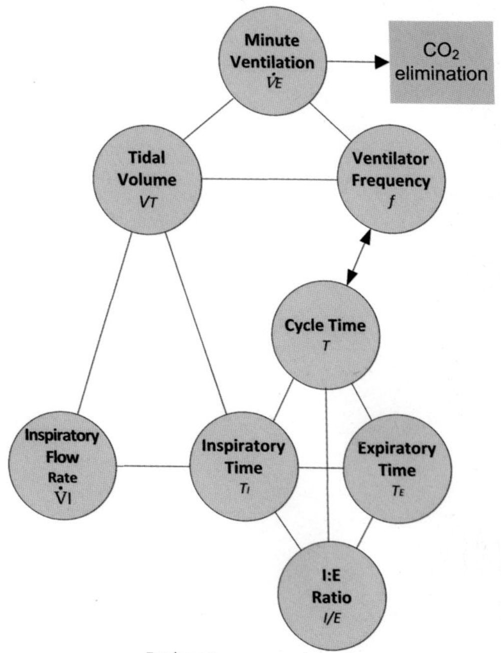

Explanations on next page

Only three parameters are directly adjusted by any one ventilator (this varies with the individual ventilator design). All other factors will be indirectly altered by manipulation of one of those known factors. See ***Oakes' Ventilator Management Study Guide*** for a more complete discussion.

Adapted from Chatburn, R.L. and Lough, M.D.: Mechanical Ventilation. In Lough, M.D. et al: ***Pediatric Respiratory Therapy***, copyright 1985 by Mosby Yearbook.

Operations

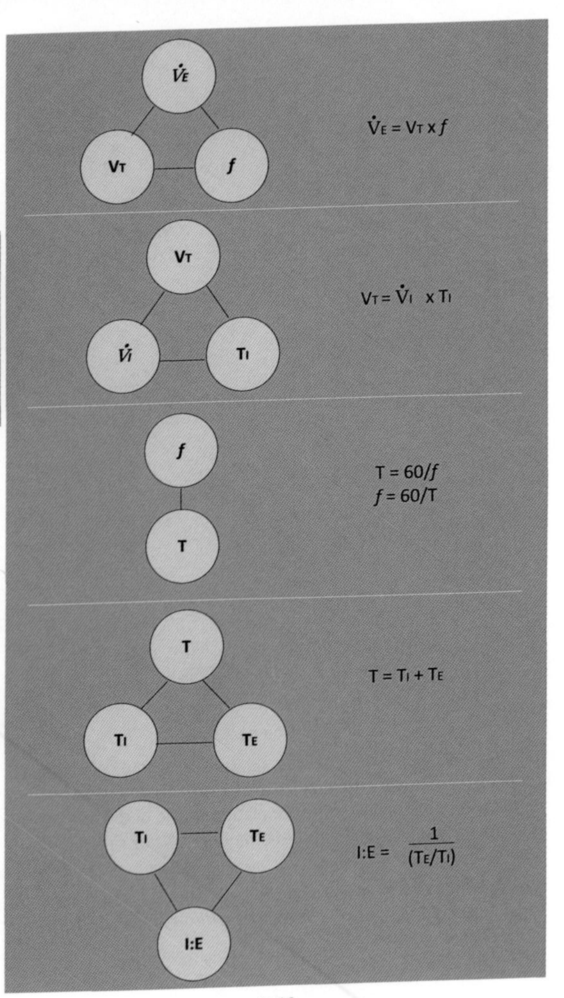

$\dot{V}_E$
V_T
f
$\dot{V}_E = V_T \times f$
V_T
$\dot{V}_I$
T_I
$V_T = \dot{V}_I \times T_I$
f
T
$T = 60/f$
$f = 60/T$
T
T_I
T_E
$T = T_I + T_E$
T_I
T_E
I:E
$I:E = \frac{1}{(T_E/T_I)}$

Basic Operating Principles of Pressure-Controlled Ventilation

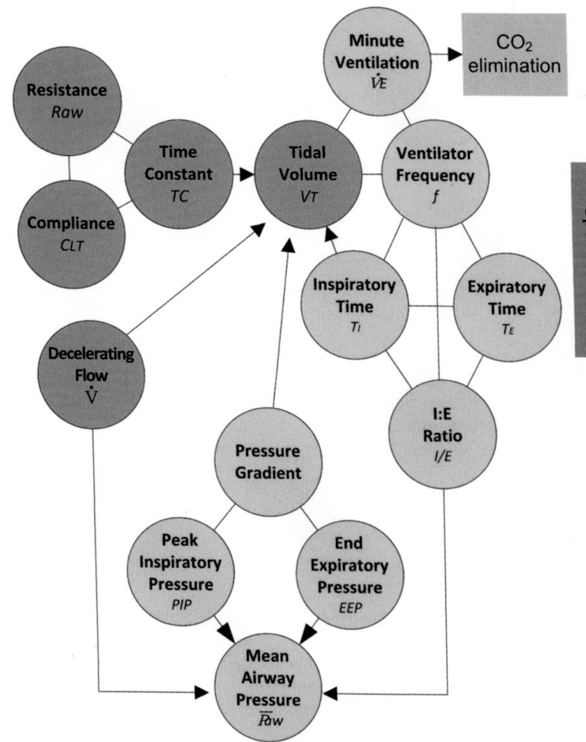

Arrows indicate non-quantifiable, complex relationships.

Orange circles represent variables that are controlled directly by ventilator settings.

Blue circles are controlled indirectly.

Adapted from Chatburn, R.L. and Lough, M.D.: Mechanical Ventilation. In Lough, M.D. et al: ***Pediatric Respiratory Therapy***, copyright 1985 by Mosby Yearbook

Determinants of Oxygenation

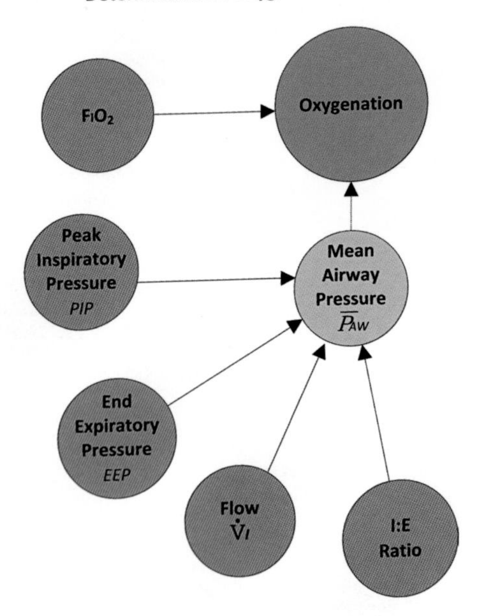

Red circles represent variables that are controlled directly by ventilator settings.

Solid arrows represent the relationships that determine mean airway pressure ($\overline{P}aw$) and oxygenation.

The dashed arrow represents relationships that can't be quantified ($\overline{P}aw$'s impact on oxygenation).

Adapted from Carlo, W.A., Greenough, A. Chatburn, R.L.: Advances in mechanical ventilation. In Boynton B.R., Carlo W.A., Jobe A.H. [Eds.]:***New Therapies for Neonatal Respiratory Failure: A Physiologic Approach***. Cambridge, Cambridge University Press, 1994, p. 134

3 Modes of Ventilation

Chapter Contents

See Page 3 - 2: Each Mode is found by the numerical order on the Mode Chart (next page).

Mode Definition: How a ventilator ventilates a patient (i.e., breath types given or allowed).

Mode Classification: A ventilator mode is classified by:

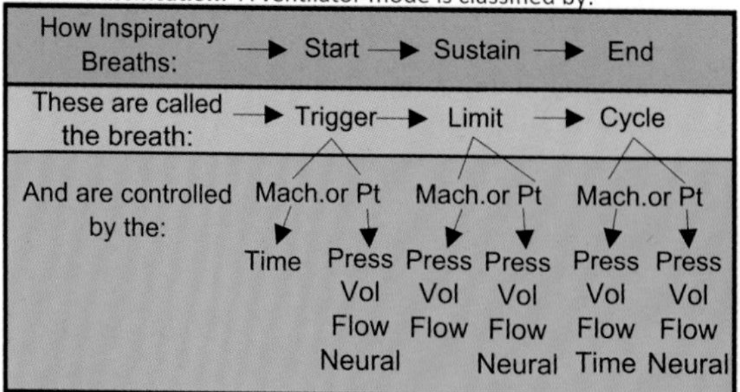

Breath Types

	Inspiratory Phase Variables		
	Trigger	Limit	Cycle
Machine-Cycled Breaths			
Mandatory (control) breath	MT	ML	MC
Assisted breath	PT	ML	MC
Patient-Cycled breath:			
Supported breath	PT	ML	PC
Spontaneous breath	PT	PL	PC

MT = machine-triggered
ML = machine-limited
MC = machine-cycled

PT = patient-triggered
PL = patient-limited
PC = patient-cycled

Modes of Ventilation[1]

(see mode chart key, page 3-5)

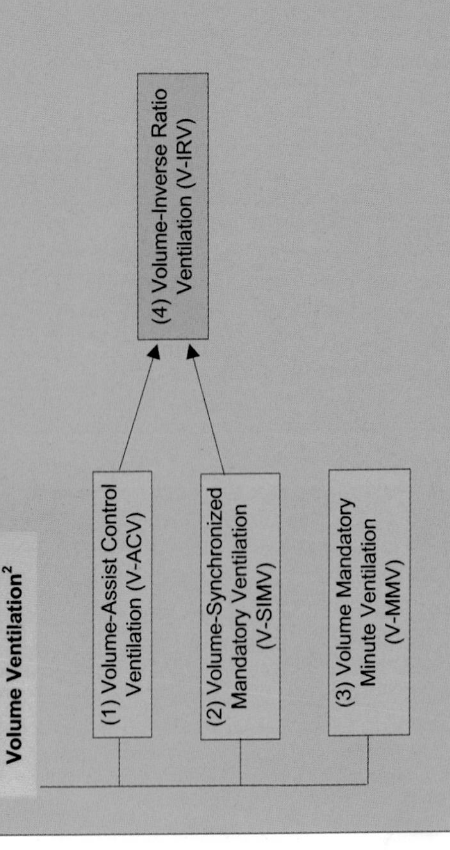

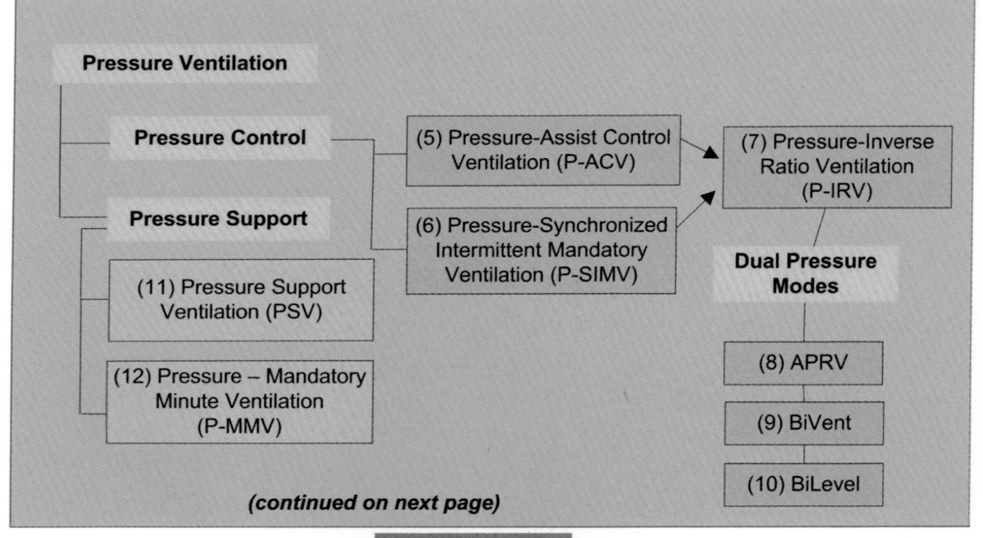
Pressure Ventilation
Pressure Control
(5) Pressure-Assist Control Ventilation (P-ACV)
(6) Pressure-Synchronized Intermittent Mandatory Ventilation (P-SIMV)
(7) Pressure-Inverse Ratio Ventilation (P-IRV)
Dual Pressure Modes
(8) APRV
(9) BiVent
(10) BiLevel
Pressure Support
(11) Pressure Support Ventilation (PSV)
(12) Pressure – Mandatory Minute Ventilation (P-MMV)

(continued on next page)

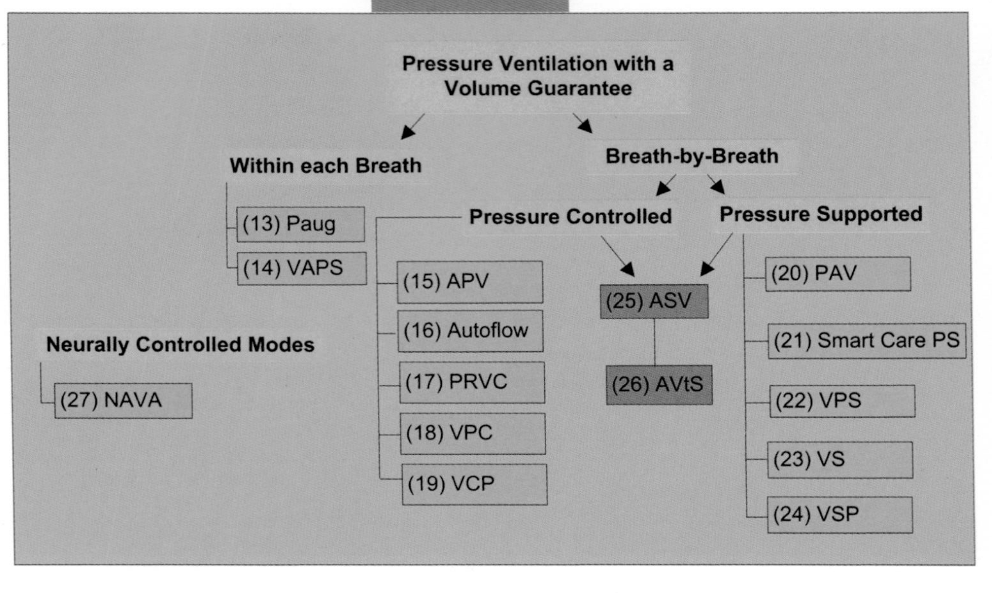
Pressure Ventilation with a Volume Guarantee
Within each Breath
Breath-by-Breath
(13) Paug
(14) VAPS
Pressure Controlled
Pressure Supported
(15) APV
(16) Autoflow
(17) PRVC
(18) VPC
(19) VCP
(25) ASV
(26) AVtS
(20) PAV
(21) Smart Care PS
(22) VPS
(23) VS
(24) VSP
Neurally Controlled Modes
(27) NAVA

Mode Chart Key

- *Volume Ventilation*
  - (1) V-ACV: Volume-Assist Control Ventilation
  - (2) V-SIMV: Volume-Synchronized Intermittent Mandatory Ventilation
  - (3) V-MMV: Volume-Mandatory Minute Ventilation
  - (4) V-IRV: Volume-Inverse Ratio Ventilation

- *Pressure Ventilation*
  - *Pressure-Control*
    - (5) P-ACV: Pressure-Assist Control Ventilation
    - (6) P-SIMV: Pressure-Synchronized Intermittent Mandatory Ventilation
    - (7) P-IRV: Pressure-Inverse Ratio Ventilation
      - Dual Pressure Modes of Ventilation
        - (8) APRV: Airway Pressure Release Ventilation
        - (9) Bivent
        - (10) Bilevel
  - *Pressure Supported*
    - (11) PSV: Pressure Support Ventilation
    - (12) P-MMV: Pressure-Mandatory Minute Ventilation

- *Pressure Ventilation with a Volume Guarantee (Combination Modes)*
  - Within Each Breath
    - (13) Paug: Pressure Augmentation
    - (14) VAPS: Volume Assured Pressure Support
  - Breath-by-Breath (over several breaths)
    - Pressure-Controlled
      - (15) APV: Adaptive Pressure Ventilation
      - (16) AutoFlow
      - (17) PRVC: Pressure Regulated Volume Control
      - (18) VPC: Variable Pressure Control
      - (19) VCP: Volume Control Plus
    - Pressure-Supported
      - (20) PAV: Proportional Assist Ventilation
      - (21) Smart Care PS
      - (22) VPS: Variable Pressure Support
      - (23) VS: Volume Support

(continued on next page)

-(24) VSP: Volume Support Plus
- o Both pressure controlled and pressure supported
  - (25) ASV: Adaptive Support Ventilation
  - (26) AVtS: Adaptive Tidal Volume Support

- *Neural Control Modes*
  - o (27) NAVA

- *Other "Modes"* (Not true modes, but rather adjuncts, not listed in chart)
  - o (28) ATC: Automatic Tube Compensation
  - o (29) Automode
  - o (30) CPAP: Continuous Positive Airway Pressure

1- The various ventilator mode names, combinations, and classification terms used today are absolutely baffling! In an attempt to bring some clarity and ease of understanding amidst all the inconsistencies and confusion, we present the following simplified, quick reference approach to current "modes of ventilation".

Unfortunately, most of the newer modes have minimal clinical outcome studies to prove their effectiveness over the more traditional modes. Choice of mode is still today based on clinical experience, familiarity with particular ventilators, and personal and institutional preferences and biases.

Finally, the new microprocessor-controlled ventilators incorporate software that manufacturers are continually updating. These changes may result in significant operational differences from those described herein.

2 - Volume ventilation can also be called volume-controlled, -cycled, -limited or -targeted ventilation.

Flow-limited or flow-controlled is synonymous with volume-limited or volume-controlled.

1	V-ACV	Volume-Assist/Control Ventilation

Note: Assist/Control Ventilation is a combination of two older methods of ventilation—Assist Mechanical Ventilation (AMV) and Control Mechanical Ventilation (CMV). Today neither AMV nor CMV is used purely alone, but rather in combination together for safety and proper ventilation.

Volume assisted ventilation refers to V-ACV with the rate turned to zero. This should be done cautiously and only with a back-up ventilation safety mode activated.

Pure volume control ventilation should never be used alone in case of spontaneous patient effort (i.e., the assist sensitivity should never be turned down or off). An appropriate sensitivity is always used for safety. Clinicians may "control" ventilation in obtunded or paralyzed patients, but the mode is still assist/control.

Other Names for Volume-Assist/Control	
Volume Control Volume Assist Mechanical Ventilation Continuous Mechanical Ventilation (CMV) Assist/Control Volume Ventilation (A/C-Vol)	
Other Names for Assist	**Other Names for Control**
Assisted Ventilation (AV)	Control Mode
Assisted Mechanical Ventilation (AMV)	Controlled Mechanical Ventilation (CMV)
	Controlled Mandatory Ventilation (CMV)
Volume Assist (VA)	Volume Control Ventilation (VCV)
Volume Cycled Ventilation (VCV)	Volume Cycled Ventilation (VCV)

Technical Description:

- A combination of assisted and/or controlled (mandatory) ventilation.
- All breaths are delivered at a set V_T and $\dot{V}_I$
- In between the controlled breaths, a patient can trigger a full machine (assisted) breath at the same parameters as the controlled breath (i.e., V_T and $\dot{V}_I$).

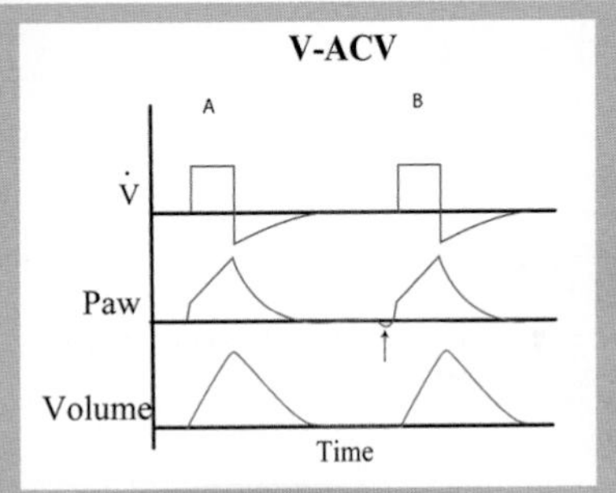

Breath A is Controlled + Machine-Triggered
Breath B is Assisted + Patient-Triggered
Each Breath is a Full Machine-Pressure Breath

	Classified By:		
Breath Type	**Trigger**	**Limit**	**Cycle**
Mandatory ***(Controlled)***	MT *(Time)*	ML *($\dot{V}$ or Vol)*	MC *(Vol)*
Assisted	PT *(Press or $\dot{V}$)*	ML *($\dot{V}$ or Vol)*	MC *(Vol)*

Indications:

- Patients requiring full ventilatory support
  - A. For those who make inadequate or no respiratory effort due to: drugs, cerebral malfunction, spinal cord or phrenic nerve injury, or motor nerve paralysis.
  - B. To control the patient's ventilatory activity
    1. Tetanus or other seizure activity that interrupts MV
    2. Complete rest for a prolonged period of time (>24 hr)
    3. Crushed chest injury with paradoxical chest wall movement associated with spontaneous inspiratory efforts.
- Used in patients with stable respiratory drives who are able to trigger the ventilator.

Advantages:

- Full ventilatory support
- Guaranteed V_T and a minimum $\dot{V}_E$
- Minimal patient WOB (if parameters are properly adjusted)
- Allows some patient control of *f* and $\dot{V}_E$

Disadvantages:

- High pressure limit must be set appropriately to minimize the risk of volutrauma/barotrauma.
- Excessive patient WOB if flow and sensitivity are not set correctly.
- The flow is fixed, which inhibits the patient who has a ↑ $\dot{V}_I$ or volume demand.
- Possible alveolar hyperventilation and respiratory alkalosis
  Due to:
  1. Inappropriate sensitivity setting (auto-cycling)
  2. Rapid (assisted) breathing rate
- High risk of cardiovascular compromise
- May be poorly tolerated in awake, nonsedated patients
- May cause or worsen auto-PEEP (dynamic hyperinflation)
- Possible respiratory muscle atrophy

2	V-SIMV	Volume-Synchronized Intermittent Mandatory Ventilation

Technical Description:

- A combination of spontaneous and mandatory ventilation.
- The ventilator will deliver a set number of mandatory (controlled) breaths per minute.
- These mandatory breaths will be at a preset V_T and $\dot{V}_I$
- The patient may breathe spontaneously in between the mandatory machine breaths from the baseline pressure. The breath may be assisted with PS.
- If the patient begins to inspire just prior to the time triggered mandatory (control) breath, a full machine-assisted breath will be delivered.

Indications:

- Full to partial ventilatory support
- Used after a period of full ventilatory support to begin the transfer of work to the patient (i.e., weaning).
  (See Disadvantages & Risks)

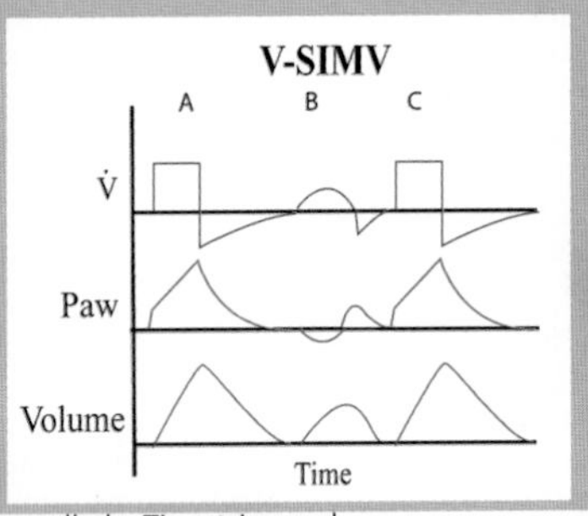

Breath A is Controlled + Time triggered

Breath B is a spontaneous breath

Breath C is synchronized and assited

Breaths A + C are both full machine volume breaths

	Classified By:		
Breath Type	**Trigger**	**Limit**	**Cycle**
Mandatory ***(Controlled)***	MT *(Time)*	ML *($\dot{V}$ or Vol)*	MC *(Vol)*
Assisted	PT *(Press or $\dot{V}$)*	ML *($\dot{V}$ or Vol)*	MC *(Vol)*
Spontaneous	PT *(Press or $\dot{V}$)*	PL *(Press)*	PC *(Press or $\dot{V}$)*

Advantages:

- Guaranteed volume with each mandatory breath.
- Security of a safe minimum $\dot{V}_E$.
- Maintains respir. muscle strength and avoids muscle atrophy.
- Lowers $\overline{P}aw$
- May reduce respiratory alkalosis associated with A/C.
- Synchronization of spontaneous and machine breaths
- The spontaneous breaths may be supported with PS if the clinician chooses. (See PSV Mode)
- Spontaneous breathing generally produces better gas distribution and less CO compromise.

Disadvantages & Risks:

- No control over maximum distension of the lung.
- High pressure limit must be set appropriately to minimize the risk of volutrauma/barotrauma.

- Excessive patient WOB if flow rate and sensitivity are not set correctly.
- Possible tachypnea with fatigue and hypercapnia, if mandatory (control) rate is set too low (i.e., inadequate ventilatory support or weaning too rapidly).
- ↑ patient WOB with demand valves on older ventilators
- ↑ patient WOB for spontaneous breaths unless PSV is added
- Studies suggest that SIMV weaning is associated with the poorest outcomes (longer weaning times). *

* Hess D. Ventilator modes used in weaning. ***Chest*** 2001; 120:6 Supp. 474S-476S

3	V-MMV	Volume-Mandatory Minute Ventilation

Other names and abbreviations:

- Minimum Mandatory Ventilation (MMV)
- Augmented Minute Ventilation (AMV)
- Extended Mandatory Minute Ventilation (EMMV)

Ventilator Specific: Drager dura 2 & Evita 4, Bear 1000, Bear 5
**Refer to the manufacturer's manual

Technical Description:

- Volume ventilation which guarantees a minimum $\dot{V}_E$.
- A set minute volume is guaranteed by monitoring the patient's spontaneous minute volume. The ventilator will add supplemental breaths as needed to achieve the set $\dot{V}_E$.

How it works:

- If the patient's spontaneous ventilation does not equal or exceed the set $\dot{V}_E$ ($V_T \times f$), the ventilator delivers the difference between the actual and set target $\dot{V}_E$.
- The difference is provided by the ventilator changing its mandatory rate.
- If the patient exceeds the set minute volume, no ventilator support is added.

Indications:

- Any patient who is spontaneously breathing and is deemed ready to wean.
- Patients with unstable ventilatory drive.

Modes

	Classified By:		
Breath Type	Trigger	Limit	Cycle
Mandatory *(Controlled)*	MT *(Time)*	ML *($\dot{V}$ or Vol)*	MC *(Vol)*
Assisted	PT *(Press or $\dot{V}$)*	ML *($\dot{V}$ or Vol)*	MC *(Vol)*
Spontaneous	PT *(Press or $\dot{V}$)*	PL *(Press)*	PC *(Press or $\dot{V}$)*

Advantages:
- Full to partial ventilatory support
- Allows spontaneous ventilation with a safety net
- Patient's $\dot{V}_E$ remains constant
- Prevents hypoventilation

Disadvantages and Risks:
- An adequate $\dot{V}_E$ may not equal an adequate $\dot{V}_A$ (e.g., rapid shallow breathing).
- The high rate alarm must be set low enough to alert clinician of rapid shallow breathing.
- Variable PIP
- A PS level should be used to support the patient's spontaneous breaths (by ↓ the resistance of the ET tube)
- An inadequate set $\dot{V}_E$ (< spontaneous $\dot{V}_E$) can lead to inadequate support and patient fatigue
- An excessive set $\dot{V}_E$ (> spontaneous $\dot{V}_E$) with no spontaneous breathing can lead to total support

Modes

4 V-IRV Volume-Inverse Ratio Ventilation

**Warning: IRV is safer and easier to manipulate in P-IRV

Other names:
- Volume Control Inverse Ratio Ventilation (VC-IRV)

Technical Description:
- Volume ventilation with inverse ratio
- V-ACV with a $T_I > T_E$ (1:1, 2:1, 3:1, etc.)
- An extended T_I is achieved by lowering the $\dot{V}_I$ or by adding an inspiratory pause or both.

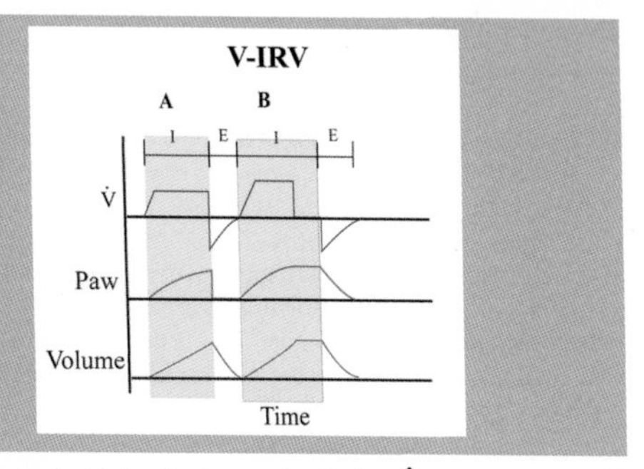

Breath A's extended I-time is the result of a low $\dot{V}_I$
Breath B's extended I-time is the result of an inspiratory hold

	Classified By (depending on mode used *):		
Breath Type	**Trigger**	**Limit**	**Cycle**
Mandatory *(Controlled)*	MT *(Time)*	ML *($\dot{V}$ or Vol)*	MC *(Vol or Time)*
Assisted	PT *(Press or $\dot{V}$)*	ML *($\dot{V}$ or Vol)*	MC *(Vol or Time)*
Spontaneous	PT *(Press or $\dot{V}$)*	PL *(Press)*	PC *(Press or $\dot{V}$)*

*See Indications, Advantages, Disadvantages and Risks for type and mode used.

Modes

Indications:

- ALI/ARDS
- High F_IO_2 and PEEP requirements
- V/Q mismatch/shunting

Advantages:

- Recruits alveoli
- Improves oxygenation by ↑ and maintaining the $\overline{P}aw$
- Guaranteed V_T and $\dot{V}_E$

Disadvantages and Risks:

- Auto-PEEP will occur which is dangerous in volume ventilation. P-IRV is recommended with fewer complications (should be monitored closely)

- Sedation and paralysis are nearly always required.
- Settings must be set appropriately
- More difficult to set stable T_I than P-IRV
- Requires careful monitoring of variable PIP and P_{plat}
- Barotrauma due to high alveolar pressure secondary to auto-PEEP
- ↓ BP and/or CO due to ↑ $\overline{P}aw$
- Caution should be used with hemodynamically unstable patients
- Requires the use of an inspiratory plateau (pause), which may not be available on all ventilators. Furthermore, the inspiratory plateau may not be sufficient to inverse the ratio with lower rates.

5	P-ACV	Pressure-Assist Control Ventilation

(See note as for V-ACV)

Note: Pressure assist refers to the P-ACV with the rate turned to zero. This should be done cautiously and only with a back-up ventilation safety mode activated.

**Caution: Some ventilators have the pressure control parameter as the pressure control level above PEEP while others have the parameter as the true PIP.

Other Names for Pressure-Assist/Control	
Pressure Control Pressure Assist Mechanical Ventilation	
Other Names for Assist	**Other Names for Control**
Pressure Assist (PA) Pressure Control Ventilation (PCV) Assisted Ventilation (AV) Assisted Mechanical Ventilation (AMV)	Control Mode Controlled Mechanical Ventilation (CMV) Pressure Control Ventilation (PCV)

Technical Description:

- A combination of assisted and/or controlled (mandatory) ventilation
- All breaths are delivered at a preset PIP and T_I
- In between the controlled breaths a patient can trigger a full machine (assisted) breath at the same parameters as the controlled breath (i.e., PIP and T_I).

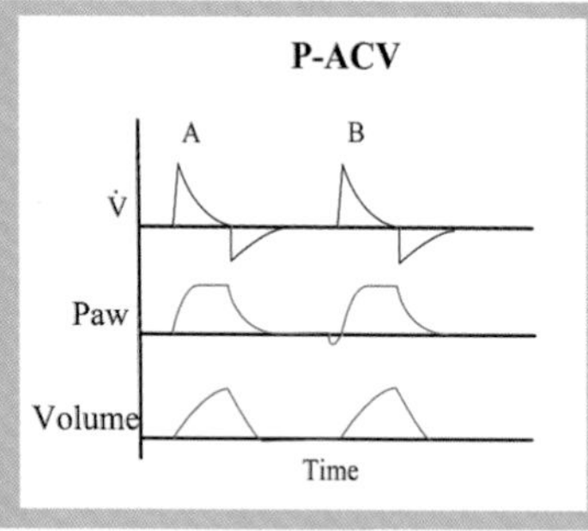

Breath A is controlled and time-triggered
Breath B is assisted and patient-triggered
Each breath is a full machine pressure breath

	Classified By:		
Breath Type	**Trigger**	**Limit**	**Cycle**
Mandatory ***(Controlled)***	MT *(Time)*	ML *(Press)*	MC *(Time)*
Assisted	PT *(Press or $\dot{V}$)*	ML *(Press or Vol)*	MC *(Time)*

Modes

Indications:

- Patients requiring full ventilatory support
  - A. For those who make inadequate or no respiratory effort due to: drugs, cerebral malfunction, spinal cord or phrenic nerve injury, or motor nerve paralysis.
  - B. To control the patient's ventilatory activity
    1. Tetanus or other seizure activity that interrupts MV
    2. Complete rest for a prolonged period of time (>24 hrs)
    3. Crushed chest injury with paradoxical chest wall movement associated with spontaneous inspiratory efforts.
- Patients with stable respiratory drives who are able to trigger the ventilator.
- Patients requiring a preset pressure limit and variable inspiratory flow.

Advantages:

- Full ventilatory support
- Guaranteed pressure limited breaths (to minimize PIP and Pplat)
- Minimal patient WOB (if parameters are properly adjusted)
- Allows patient control of rate and $\dot{V}_E$
- Variable $\dot{V}_I$ may be more comfortable for patients.
- Delivers volume early in the breath which may improve gas distribution.

Disadvantages:

- No guaranteed V_T (as in volume ventilation)
- Low exhaled V_T and $\dot{V}_E$ alarms must be set properly
- Excessive patient WOB if sensitivity is not set correctly
- Possible alveolar hyperventilation and possible respiratory alkalosis due to:
  1. Inappropriate sensitivity setting (auto-cycling)
  2. Rapid breathing rate
- High risk of cardiovascular compromise
- May cause or worsen auto-PEEP (dynamic hyperinflation)
- Possible respiratory muscle atrophy

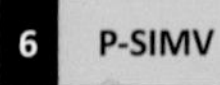

6	P-SIMV	Pressure-Synchronized Intermittent Mandatory Ventilation

**Caution: Some ventilators have the pressure control parameter as the pressure control level above PEEP, while others have the parameter as the true PIP.

Technical Description:

- A combination of spontaneous ventilation and P-ACV.
- The ventilator will deliver a set number of mandatory (controlled) breaths per minute
- These mandatory breaths will be at a preset PIP and T_I.
- The patient may breathe spontaneously in between the mandatory machine breaths from the baseline pressure. The breath may be assisted with PS
- If the patient begins to inspire just prior to the time-triggered mandatory (control) breath, a full machine-assisted breath will be delivered

	Classified By:		
Breath Type	**Trigger**	**Limit**	**Cycle**
Mandatory ***(Controlled)***	MT *(Time)*	ML *(Press)*	MC *(Time)*
Assisted	PT *(Press or $\dot{V}$)*	ML *(Press)*	MC *(Time)*
Spontaneous	PT *(Press or $\dot{V}$)*	PL *(Press)*	PC *(Press or $\dot{V}$)*

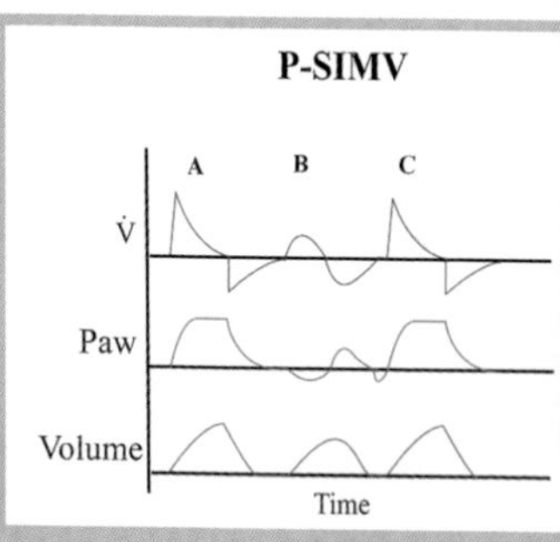

Breath A is controlled and time-triggered
Breath B is a spontaneous breath
Breath C is synchronized and assisted
Breaths A and C are full machine pressure breaths

Indications:

- Full to partial ventilatory support
- Used after a period of full ventilatory support to begin the transfer of work to the patient (i.e., weaning)

(See Disadvantages & Risks)

- Patients requiring a preset PIP and variable $\dot{V}$

Advantages:

- Guaranteed pressure-limited breaths
- Maintains respiratory muscle strength and avoids muscle atrophy
- Lowers $\overline{Paw}$
- May reduce respiratory alkalosis associated with A/C
- Synchronization of spontaneous and machine breaths

Modes

- The spontaneous breaths may be supported with PS if the clinician chooses. (See PSV Mode)
- Delivers volume early in the breath, which may improve gas distribution.

Disadvantages & Risks:
- No guaranteed V_T. Low exhaled V_T and $\dot{V}_E$ alarms must be set properly.
- Excessive patient WOB if the sensitivity is not set correctly
- Possible tachypnea with fatigue and hypercapnia, if mandatory rate is set too low (i.e., inadequate ventilatory support or weaning too rapidly).
- ↑ patient WOB with demand valves on older ventilators
- ↑ patient WOB for spontaneous breaths unless PSV is added
- Studies suggest that SIMV weaning is associated with the poorest outcomes. *

*Hess D. Ventilator modes used in weaning. ***Chest*** 2001; 120:6 Supp. 474S-476S

7	P-IRV	Pressure-Inverse Ratio Ventilation

**The preferred method of administering IRV (over V-IRV)

Other names:
- Pressure Control Inverse Ratio Ventilation (PC-IRV)

Technical Description:
- Pressure ventilation with inverse ratio
- P-ACV with $T_I > T_E$ (1:1, 2:1, 3:1, etc.) An extended T_I is achieved by setting the T_I accordingly, coupled with the set *f*

	Classified By (depending on mode used *):		
Breath Type	**Trigger**	**Limit**	**Cycle**
Mandatory *(Controlled)*	MT *(Time)*	ML *(Press)*	MC *(Time)*
Assisted	PT *(Press or $\dot{V}$)*	ML *(Press)*	MC *(Time)*

* See Indications, Advantages, Disadvantages and Risks for type and mode used.

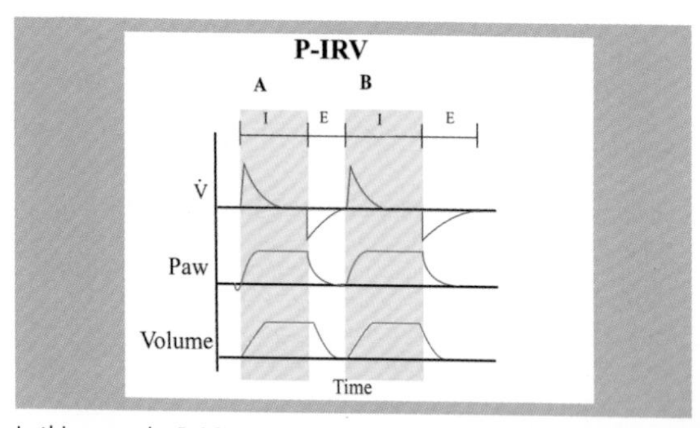

In this example, P-ACV is combined with P-IRV where the I-time is longer than the E-time. The breaths are full machine pressure breaths. Note that the pressure is held constant throughout the entire I-time. Breath B I-time is slightly longer than Breath A.

Indications:

- ALI/ARDS
- High FiO_2 and PEEP requirements
- V/Q mismatch/shunting

Advantages:

- Recruits alveoli.
- Improves oxygenation by ↑ and maintaining the $\overline{P}aw$.
- Maintains a set PIP.

Disadvantages and Risks:

- Sedation and paralysis are nearly always required
- Settings must be set appropriately
- Requires careful monitoring of the variable V_T and $\dot{V}_E$
- Auto-PEEP may occur and should be monitored (V_T will ↓ as a result)
- Barotrauma due to high P_{alv} secondary to auto-PEEP
- ↓ BP and/or CO due to ↑ $\overline{P}aw$.
- Caution should be used with hemodynamically unstable pts.
- Not available on all ventilators

8	APRV	Airway Pressure Release Ventilation

Other names:
- Bilevel Positive Airway Pressure (BIPAP)
- Variable Positive Airway Pressure (VPAP)
- Intermittent CPAP
- CPAP with release

Ventilator Specific: Drager Medical Evita 2,4,XL; Viasys Avea,Vela; BiLevel-Puritan Bennett 840; Bivent-Maquet Servo I (with BiLevel and Bivent, PS breaths can augment spontaneous breaths if the clinician desires), Hamilton Galileo (Duo-PAP)
Note: Each specific ventilator handles spontaneous breaths in its own way. Refer to the manufacturer's manual.

Technical Description:
- Inverse ratio ventilation (IRV) using two levels of CPAP (P high and P low)
- Same as P-IRV if spontaneous breaths are absent

Modes

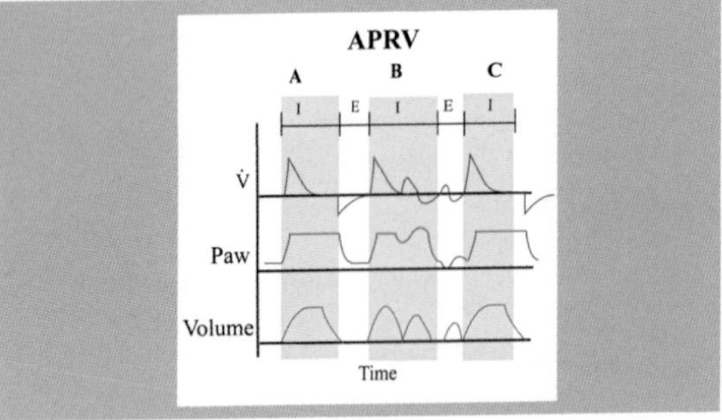

Breath A and C are machine breaths without any spontaneous efforts. Breath B has spontaneous breaths in the I + E phase.

How it works:
- Allows spontaneously breathing patients to breathe at a high CPAP level, but drop briefly (approximately 1 second) and periodically to a low CPAP level for extra CO_2 elimination (airway pressure release)

- Mandatory breaths (Pressure Level) occur when the pressure limit rises from the lower CPAP to the higher CPAP level.

	Classified By:		
Breath Type	**Trigger**	**Limit**	**Cycle**
Mandatory ***(Controlled)***	MT *(Time)*	ML *(Press)*	MC *(Time)*
Assisted	PT *(Press or $\dot{V}$)*	ML *(Press)*	MC *(Press or $\dot{V}$)*

Indications:

- Partial to full ventilatory support
- Patients with ALI/ARDS
- Patients with refractory hypoxemia due to collapsed alveoli
- Patients with massive atelectasis
- May use with mild or no lung disease

Advantages:

- Allows IRV with or without spontaneous breathing (less need for sedation or paralysis).
- Improves patient-ventilator synchrony if spontaneous breathing present.
- Improves $\overline{P}aw$
- Improves oxygenation by stabilizing collapsed alveoli
- Allows patients to breathe spontaneously while continuing lung recruitment.
- Lowers PIP
- May decrease physiologic deadspace

Disadvantages and Risks:

- Variable V_T
- Could be harmful to patients with high expiratory resistance (i.e., COPD or asthma).
- Auto-PEEP is usually present.
- Caution should be used with hemodynamically unstable patients.
- Asynchrony can occur if spontaneous breaths (if present) are out of sync with release time.
- Requires the presence of an "active exhalation valve"

Modes

9 Bivent

Ventilator Specific: Maquet Servo I (optional)
**Refer to the manufacturer's manual
***Similar to APRV. See APRV (#8) for Technical Description, Indications, Advantages and Disadvantages and Risks

10 BiLevel

Ventilator Specific: PB 840
**Refer to the manufacturer's manual

Other names:
- BiPAP
- Biphasic

Technical Description:
- A mixed mode that combines mandatory and spontaneous breathing in which a patient can breathe spontaneously at two levels of CPAP (PEEP).
- A variation of APRV (which is a form of inverse ratio ventilation). See APRV (#8).
- There are two ventilating strategies with Bilevel, distinguishable by the time allowed at the lower PEEP level (PEEP L):

BiPAP: Conventional I:E ratios
The time spent at both levels of PEEP is long enough to allow spontaneous breathing at both levels.

APRV: Inverse ratio ventilation

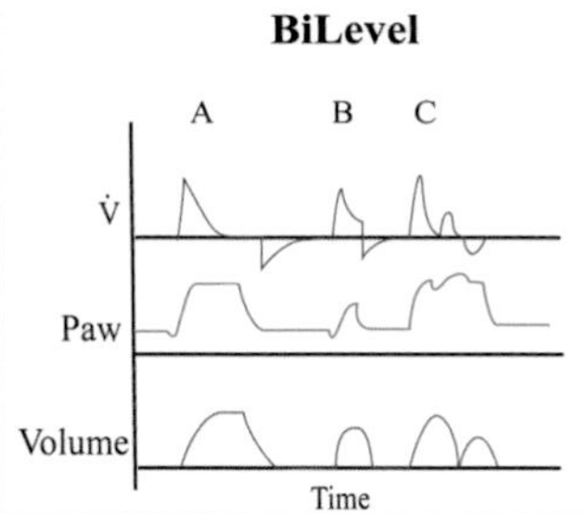

Breath A is a synchronized assisted patient-triggered breath. Breath B is a spontaneous pressure-supported breath at the low PEEP level. Breath C is a time-triggered controlled breath with a spontaneous breath at the high PEEP level.

How it works:

- The clinician selects a high CPAP level ($PEEP_H$) and a low CPAP level ($PEEP_L$) and a set time for the two levels. This sets the mandatory rate.
- The patient may breathe spontaneously at both CPAP levels. These breaths can be pressure supported using the following rules:
  - o Pressure support can assist spontaneous breaths at $PEEP_L$ and $PEEP_H$ (provided there is adequate time at $PEEP_L$)
  - o Pressure support is always relative to PEEP. Target pressure level = $PEEP_L$ + pressure support
  - o Spontaneous breaths at $PEEP_H$ are not supported unless the PS level > ($PEEP_H$-$PEEP_L$). All spontaneous breaths are supported with at least 1.5 cmH_2O.
  - o If (pressure support + PEEPL) > (PEEPH + 1.5 cmH_2O), all of the spontaneous breaths at PEEPL are assisted by PS setting and all spontaneous breaths at PEEPH are assisted by PS - ($PEEP_H$-$PEEP_L$).
- If the patient does not breathe spontaneously, the mode acts like P-ACV.
- The mandatory breaths occur when the pressure limit rises from the lower PEEP level to the higher PEEP level.

See APRV for complete Technical Description, Indications, Advantages and Disadvantages and Risks

11	PSV	Pressure Support Ventilation

Other names:

- Inspiratory assist (IA)
- Inspiratory Pressure Support (IPS)
- Spontaneous Pressure Support (SPS)
- Inspiratory Flow Assist (IFA)

Technical Description:

- Spontaneous ventilation with all of the patient's spontaneous breaths supported or augmented by the ventilator.

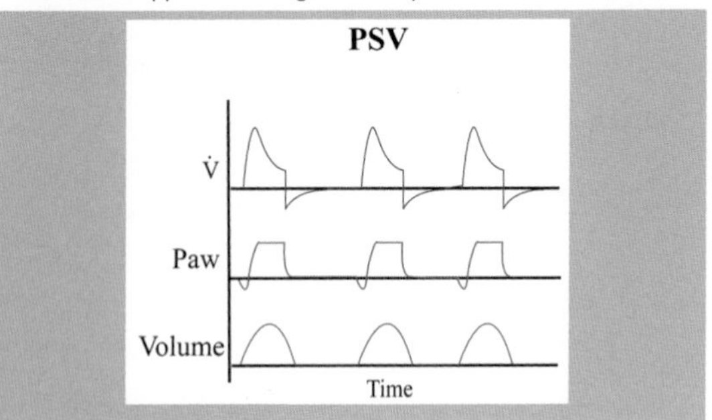

All of the breaths are patient-triggered and flow-cycled

How it works:

- The patient's inspiratory effort is augmented by the ventilator up to a set level of inspiratory pressure.
- Inspiratory phase ends when the inspiratory flow rate reaches a set minimum flow rate or percentage of the patient's peak flow (ventilator specific). Some newer ventilators have variable cycling criteria known as "expiratory sensitivity" and "inspiratory cycle off". There are also pressure and time cycling criteria as back up measures available on some ventilators.

	Classified By:		
Breath Type	**Trigger**	**Limit**	**Cycle**
Supported	PT *(Press or $\dot{V}$)*	PL *(Press)*	PC *(P, Time or $\dot{V}$)*

Modes

Indications:

- Spontaneously breathing patients who require additional ventilatory support to help overcome:
  ↑ WOB (↓ C or ↑ Raw) or respiratory muscle weakness
- Weaning

Advantages:

- Full to partial ventilatory support
- Augments the patient's spontaneous V_T
- Decreases the patient's spontaneous RR
- Decreases patient WOB by overcoming the resistance of the artificial airway, vent circuit and demand valves.
- Allows patient control of the T_I, $\dot{V}_I$, f and V_T
- Set peak pressure
- Prevents respiratory muscle atrophy
- Lowers $\overline{P}aw$
- Facilitates weaning
- Improves patient comfort and reduces need for sedation
- May be applied in any mode that allows spontaneous breathing (e.g., V-SIMV, P-SIMV)

Disadvantages & Risks:

- Requires consistent spontaneous ventilation
- Patients in stand-alone mode should have back-up ventilation
- V_T variable and dependant on lung characteristics and synchrony
- Low exhaled $\dot{V}_E$ (V_T & high f alarms should be set properly)
- The expiratory cycling criteria vary depending on the ventilator used. Cycling asynchrony could occur. Refer to the manufacturer's manual.
- Fatigue and tachypnea if PS level is set too low (If patient using sternocleidomastoid muscles consider ↑ the PS level.)
- Auto-PEEP if PS level is set too high (If the PS level is decreased and there is no change in the V_T or accessory muscle use, consider leaving at the new level.)

12	P-MMV	Pressure-Mandatory Minute Ventilation

Other names and abbreviations:

- Minimum Mandatory Ventilation (MMV)
- Augmented Minute Ventilation (AMV)
- Extended Mandatory Minute Ventilation (EMMV)

Ventilator Specific: Hamilton Veolar

**Refer to the manufacturer's manual

Technical Description:

- Pressure ventilation which guarantees a minimum $\dot{V}_E$.
- A form of PSV where the PS is not set, but rather variable according to the patient need.

How it works:

- If the patient's spontaneous ventilation does not equal or exceed the set $\dot{V}_E$ ($V_T \times f$), the ventilator delivers the difference between the actual and set target $\dot{V}_E$.
- The difference is provided by the ventilator changing the PS of the spontaneous breaths.
- If the patient exceeds the set $\dot{V}_E$, no ventilator support is added.

	Classified By:		
Breath Type	**Trigger**	**Limit**	**Cycle**
Supported	PT *(Press or $\dot{V}$)*	PL *(Press)*	PC *(P, Time or $\dot{V}$)*

Indications:

- Any patient who is spontaneously breathing and is deemed ready to wean.
- Patients with unstable ventilatory drive.

Advantages:

- Full to partial ventilatory support
- Allows spontaneous ventilation with a safety net
- Patient's $\dot{V}_E$ remains stable
- Prevents hypoventilation

Disadvantages and Risks:

- An adequate $\dot{V}_E$ may not equal sufficient $\dot{V}_A$ (e.g., rapid shallow breathing)
- The high rate alarm must be set low enough to alert clinician of rapid shallow breathing.
- Variable $\overline{P}aw$
- An inadequate set $\dot{V}_E$ (< spontaneous $\dot{V}_E$) can lead to inadequate support and patient fatigue.
- An excessive set $\dot{V}_E$ (> spontaneous $\dot{V}_E$) with no spontaneous breathing can lead to total support.

13 | Paug | Pressure Augment or Pressure Augmentation

Ventilator Specific: Bear 1000
**Refer to the manufacturer's manual

Technical Description:
Same as VAPS, except patient must be able to initiate a breath and have a regular RR.

See VAPS (# 14) for complete Technical Description, Indications, Advantages and Disadvantages and Risks

14 | VAPS | Volume Assured Pressure Support

Ventilator Specific: T-Bird AVS III and Bird 8400Ti
**Refer to the manufacturer's manual

Other names: Volume-Assisted Pressure Support

Technical Description:

- The ventilator delivers a PS breath that can switch to a volume breath
- Used with ACV, SIMV, or CPAP (VAPS is only active in apnea ventilation while in CPAP Mode)
- In whichever mode is used, the mandatory (controlled) or assisted breaths of that mode become VAPS breaths.
- VAPS breaths can be patient or machine-triggered, depending on the mode used (i.e., ACV)
- This mode is similar to Pressure Augmentation (P_{aug}) available on the Bear 1000 ventilator, except with Paug, the patient must have a consistent respiratory effort

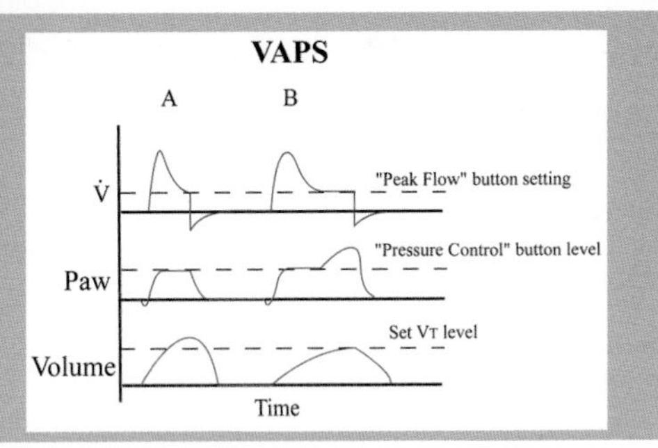

Breath A: Depicts a PS-like breath that has been terminated at the set "Peak Flow" after the minimum V_T has been delivered.

Breath B: Depicts a transition from a PS-like breath to a volume assured (controlled) breath. Transition occurs when flow has decelerated to the set "Peak Flow" and the set V_T has not been delivered. The I-time is extended until the set V_T is delivered.

Modes

How it works:

- When a VAPS breath is delivered, the breath is delivered using whatever pressure level is set ("Pressure Control" button on the front panel).
- If the set minimum V_T is achieved by the time the flow ↓ to the set flow-cycle value ("Peak Flow" button on the front panel), the ventilator cycles into exhalation. In this case, the breath acts as a normal PS breath. The V_T could be exceeded.
- If the set V_T is not achieved, the flow is maintained as a constant flow pattern at the set "peak flow" value until the set V_T is achieved. The breath then acts as a volume-cycled breath.
- If the breath becomes a volume-cycled breath, the resulting pressure will be higher than the set pressure support level

Note: Setting the correct pressure level is difficult and no studies have been done to show the best settings.

	Classified By:		
Breath Type	**Trigger**	**Limit**	**Cycle**
Mandatory *(Controlled)*	MT *(Time)*	PL *(Press or Vol)*	PC *(Vol or $\dot{V}$)*
Assisted	PT *(Press or $\dot{V}$)*	PL *(Press or $\dot{V}$)*	PC *(Vol or $\dot{V}$)*
Supported	PT *(Press or $\dot{V}$)*	PL *(Press)*	PC *($\dot{V}$)*

Indications:

- Spontaneous breathing patients who require minimum V_T
- Patients who are asynchronous with the ventilator
- Used as a back-up safety net for pressure support ventilation (to assure a minimum V_T for each breath).

Advantages:

- Volume guaranteed with every breath
- High variable flow for better synchrony
- Pressure-limited breath for improved gas mixing/oxygenation. *
- Decreased patient WOB

* When the ventilator switches to a volume ventilation breath, the pressure limiting advantage is lost

Disadvantages and Risks:

- Choosing the appropriate pressure and flow settings are crucial for successful and safe operation. *Examples*:
  - o If the "peak flow" (flow-cycle value) is set too high, all the breaths will switch from pressure to volume-cycled, which will defeat the purpose of the mode.
  - o If the "peak flow" is set too low, the inspiratory time could be too long to achieve the desired set V_T.
  - o If the pressure is set too high, the volume back-up will never be needed.
  - o If the pressure is set too low and/or the V_T is set too low, the patient could become distressed and/or under-ventilated.
- Varying $\overline{P}aw$
- A sudden ↑ in RR and demand may result in a ↓ in ventilator support.

Adaptive Pressure Ventilation

Ventilator Specific: Hamilton Galileo
**Refer to the manufacturer's manual

Technical Description:
- Pressure ventilation with a guaranteed volume; similar to PRVC
- Used in conjunction with P-ACV or P-SIMV

See PRVC (# 17) for graphic

How it works:
- The ventilator continuously calculates system and patient C, and volume delivery
- If the exhaled V_T is less or more than the set V_T, the inspiratory pressure level is regulated until the preset volumes are delivered. Pressure changes are made in 1 cmH_2O increments
- Maximum available inspiratory pressure level is 10 cmH_2O below the set upper pressure limit
- The amount of pressure cannot be set lower than 5 cmH_2O above the baseline pressure (PEEP)
- The patient will receive a minimum number of time-triggered mandatory breaths per minute. (Set back-up rate)

See Indications, Advantages, Disadvantages and Risks for P-ACV and P-SIMV

	Classified By:		
Breath Type	**Trigger**	**Limit**	**Cycle**
Mandatory	MT *(Time)*	ML *(Press or Vol)*	MC *(Time)*
Assisted	PT *(Press or $\dot{V}$)*	ML *(Press or Vol)*	MC *(Time)*

Indications:
- Patients who require the lowest possible pressure and a guaranteed V_T
- ALI/ARDS
- Patients requiring high and/or variable $\dot{V}_I$
- Patients not breathing spontaneously and not triggering the ventilator
- Patients with the possibility of workload changes (C and Raw)
- Patients requiring Full (A/C) or Partial (SIMV) ventilation

Advantages:

- Guaranteed V_T and $\dot{V}_E$
- Patient has very little work of breathing requirement (P-ACV)
- Patient can breathe above the set *f*
- Allows patient control of RR and $\dot{V}_E$
- Variable $\dot{V}_I$ to meet patient demand
- Decelerating flow waveform for improved gas distribution

Disadvantages and Risks:

- Upper pressure limit must be set appropriately
- Excessive patient work of breathing if sensitivity is not set correctly.
- Possible respiratory atrophy (P-ACV)
- May cause or worsen auto-PEEP
- A sudden increase in RR and demand may result in a ↓ in ventilator support.

16 Autoflow

Modes

Ventilator Specific: Drager Evita 2 dura, 4, XL, and Savina
**Refer to the manufacturer's manual

Technical Description:

- PV with a guaranteed volume delivery over the course of several breaths.
- This mode automatically optimizes inspiratory flow (autoflow) for the volume modes and changes the breath to a pressure control breath.
- Patient flow is variable and in proportion to patient demand
- Similar to PRVC and VS on the Siemens ventilators and Variable Pressure Control on the Cardiopulmonary Corporation Venturi ventilator.

See PRVC (#17) for graphic

How it works:

- On the first breath, a volume-targeted breath is delivered.
- During that first breath, plateau pressure is measured automatically, which becomes the starting pressure for Autoflow.
- System compliance and resistance is calculated with each subsequent breath and the minimum pressure needed to deliver the set V_T is established.

- If the delivered V_T is less than or greater than the set V_T, delivered pressure is ↑ or ↓ respectively up to 3 cmH_2O.
- Maximum available pressure level is 5 cmH_2O below the preset upper pressure limit (alarm will sound at this point and the breath will switch into exhalation).
- Volume delivery may be ↑ if the patient actively inspires.

	Classified By:		
Breath Type	**Trigger**	**Limit**	**Cycle**
Mandatory	MT *(Time)*	ML *(Press + Vol)*	MC *(Time)*
Assisted	PT *(Press or $\dot{V}$)*	ML *(Press +/or $\dot{V}$)*	MC *(Time)*
Spontaneous	PT *(Press or $\dot{V}$)*	PL *(Press)*	PC *(Press)*

Indications:

- Patients who require the lowest possible pressure and a guaranteed V_T
- ALI/ARDS
- Patients requiring high and/or variable $\dot{V}_I$
- Patients with the possibility of workload changes (C and Raw)

Advantages:

- Guaranteed V_T and $\dot{V}_E$
- Patient has very little work of breathing requirement
- Patient can breathe above the set f
- Allows patient control of RR and $\dot{V}_E$
- Variable $\dot{V}_I$ to meet patient demand
- Decelerating flow waveform for improved gas distribution
- Breath by breath analysis
- May be used with any VV mode (V-ACV, V-SIMV, and V-MMV), but changes VV to PV with volume target
- The expiratory valve is floating, which allows the patient to cough or breathe during the inspiratory time of the mandatory breath while maintaining the achieved inspiratory pressure without a significant drop or overshoot

Disadvantages and Risks:

- Upper pressure limit must be set appropriately (start with 5-10 cmH_2O above Pplat, then readjust).
- May cause or worsen auto-PEEP
- Varying $\overline{P}aw$

- If inspiration ends before the flow drops to zero, the volume may be delivered at higher pressure. In this case T_I should be ↑ to ↓ the pressure.
- A sudden ↑ in RR and demand may result in a ↓ in ventilator support.

17	PRVC	Pressure Regulated Volume Control

Ventilator Specific: PRVC-Maquet Servo I; Servo 300/300A **Viasys Avea and Viasys Vela
**Refer to the manufacturer's manual (algorithms slightly different)

Technical Description:
PV with a guaranteed volume delivery over the course of several breaths. Is more of a breath type than a mode.

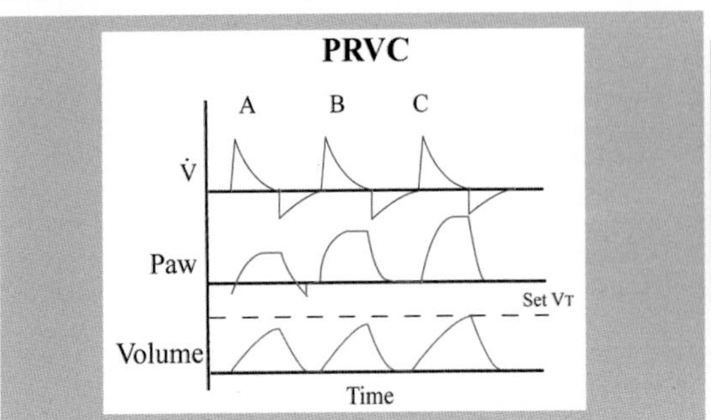

As the breaths advance from A to C, the pressure is automatically increased to achieve the set V_T.

How it works:

- Ventilator gives a test volume breath with a pause (plateau)
- The second breath will be a pressure breath (square) at that plateau pressure from the previous breath
- The ventilator will not change the inspiratory pressure more than 3 cmH_2O from one breath to the next.
- Maximum available pressure level is 5 cmH_2O below the preset upper pressure limit (alarm will sound at this point and the

breath will switch into exhalation).

- The minimum inspiratory pressure limit is the baseline setting (PEEP)
- The patient will receive a minimum number of time-triggered mandatory breaths per minute (as in P-ACV)
- PRVC can be done with SIMV
- The beginning breath sequence is different. The patient is given 1 volume breath at the set volume. An automatic 10% inspiratory pause is put on the breath resulting in a plateau pressure. The volume is achieved from then on as in PRVC with the Servo 300/300A

	Classified By:		
Breath Type	**Trigger**	**Limit**	**Cycle**
Mandatory	MT *(Time)*	ML *(Press or Vol)*	MC *(Time)*
Assisted	PT *(Press or $\dot{V}$)*	ML *(Press or Vol)*	MC *(Time)*

Modes

Indications:

- Patients who require the lowest possible pressure and a guaranteed consistent V_T
- ALI/ARDS (if patient is adequately sedated, if not consider V-AC)
- Patients requiring high and/or variable $\dot{V}_I$
- Patients not breathing spontaneously and not triggering the ventilator
- Patients with the possibility of workload changes (C and Raw)

Advantages:

- Maintains a minimum PIP
- Guaranteed V_T and $\dot{V}_E$
- Patient has very little WOB requirement
- Patient can trigger additional breaths above the set *f*
- Allows patient control of RR and $\dot{V}_E$
- Variable $\dot{V}_I$ to meet patient demand
- Decelerating flow waveform for improved gas distribution
- Breath by breath analysis

Disadvantages and Risks:

- Upper pressure limit must be set appropriately (start with 5-10 cmH_2O above P_{plat}, then readjust).
- Only available in A/C (SIMV is an option on the Servo Inspiration ventilator) .

- May cause or worsen auto-PEEP
- Varying $\overline{P}aw$
- When patient demand is ↑, pressure level may diminish when support is needed. Pressure waveform should be square – if not ↑ set V_T or switch to an alternative mode of ventilation.
- May be tolerated poorly in awake nonsedated patients, especially if low V_T are used.
- A sudden ↑ in RR and demand may result in a ↓ in ventilator support.

18	VPC	Variable Pressure Control

Ventilator Specific: Cardiopulmonary Corporation Venturi
**Refer to the manufacturer's manual

***Similar to PRVC. See PRVC (#17) for Technical Description, Indications, Advantages and Disadvantages and Risks

19	VCP	Volume Control Plus

Ventilator Specific: Puritan Bennett 840 Ventilator
**Refer to the manufacturer's manual

***Similar to PRVC. See PRVC (#17) for Technical Description, Indications, Advantages and Disadvantages and Risks

20	PAV	Proportional Assist Ventilation

Ventilator Specific: Drager Evita 4 and XL, Puritan Bennett 840 (PAV+)
**Refer to manufacturer's manual

Other names: Proportional Pressure Support (PPS), PAV +

Technical Description:
- Patient-triggered breaths that are provided proportionately to the patient during inspiration.
- Incorporates both a "flow assist" and a "volume assist" in proportion to patient demand.
- The greater the patient effort, the higher the flow, volume, and pressure.

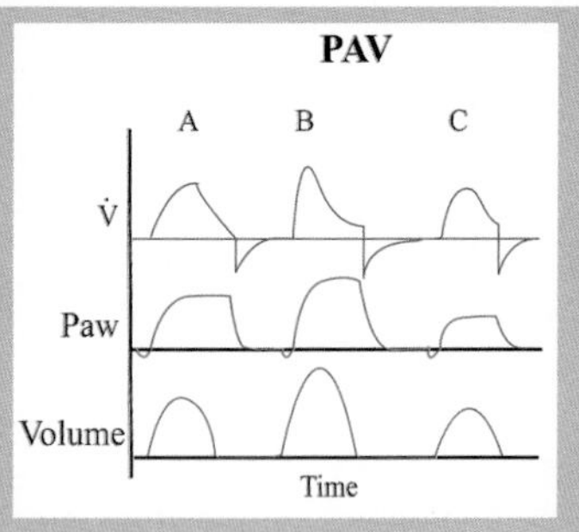

The effort and pressure are increased in Breath B compared to Breath A. The effort and pressure are decreased in Breath C.

How it works:

- Set the ventilator's volume and flow assist at approximately 80% of the patient's elastance and resistance (↓ as the condition improves)
- Used with assisted breaths only
- The ventilator then senses the patient's effort to breathe (both flow and volume)
- The ventilator then generates proportional flow and volume assist pressures to augment the patient's own effort
- The greater the patient effort, the greater the pressures the machine generates
- The delivered volume or pressure then varies according to the patient's inspiratory effort. (The % of the patient WOB {20%} remains the same regardless of changes in C or Raw.)
- Determination of pattern of breathing is shifted to the patient

	Classified By:		
Breath Type	**Trigger**	**Limit**	**Cycle**
Assisted	PT *(Press or $\dot{V}$)*	ML *(Press)*	MC *($\dot{V}$)*

Indications:

- Pts who have WOB problems with worsening lung characteristics
- Asynchronous patients who are stable with an inspiratory effort
- Ventilator-dependent patients with COPD

Advantages:

- The patient controls the ventilatory variables ($\dot{V}_I$, PIP, T_I, T_E, V_T)
- Trends the changes of ventilatory effort over time
- When used with CPAP, inspiratory muscle work is near that of a normal subject and may decrease or prevent muscle atrophy
- Lowers airway pressures

Disadvantages and Risks:

- Patient must have adequate spontaneous respiratory drive
- Variable V_T and/or PIP
- Excessive assist ("Runaway") by the ventilator may occur (High V_T and pressure alarms must be set appropriately)
- Air leak could cause excessive assist or automatic cycling
- Trigger effort may increase with auto-PEEP
- Backup mode required in case of apnea
- Correct determination of C and Raw is essential, yet difficult. Both under and over estimates of C and Raw (or changes in C and Raw, such as repositioning) may significantly impair proper patient-ventilator interaction

21 Smart Care Pressure Support

Modes

Ventilator Specific: Drager Evita XL (optional)

** Refer to manufacturer's manual

Technical Description:

- An automated weaning technique that automatically adjusts pressure support levels, to comfortably maintain a patient's breathing frequency, tidal volume and end-tidal CO_2 parameters within predetermined ranges.
- Weight range 15-200 kg

How It Works:

- There are three sets of values based on actual body weight of the patient
- Each body weight range (15-35kg, 26-55kg, and over 55kg) has different criteria for acceptable tidal volume and frequency.
- Based on the patient's initial frequency, tidal volume and $etCO_2$, Smartcare assigns the patient's ventilation to one of eight

categories: normal ventilation, insufficient ventilation, hypoventilation, central hypoventilation, tachypnea, severe tachypnea, hyperventilation, or unexplained hyperventilation.

- The clinician also may select COPD or Neurological disorder to allow different acceptable parameters (eg., higher PETCO2)
- Ventilation other than normal will initiate an increase or decrease of PS by 2-4 cmH_2O within a period of time depending which parameter is violated.
- Smartcare assesses the patient's RR, V_T and $etCO_2$ every 10 seconds and analyzes ventilation every two minutes if there was no PS change or every 5 minutes if there was a PS change.
- When the target pressure is obtained, a spontaneous breathing test is performed and if predetermined weight-based values are met a message "SC-Consider Separation" is displayed suggesting to the clinician that liberation may be possible.

Modes

Indications:
- Spontaneously breathing patients with weights between 15 and 200 kg
- Patients who are screened for the ventilator weaning process

Advantages:
- Ability to have patient frequently assessed mechanically.
- Possibly improved weaning times

Disadvantages & Risks:
- Clinician must still use bedside assessment and judgment
- $EtCO_2$ results will be off if any V/Q mismatch present

22	VPS	Variable Pressure Support

Ventilator Specific: Cardiopulmonary Corporation Venturi
**Refer to the manufacturer's manual

Other name: Volume Pressure Support

****Similar to Volume Support. See VS (# 23) for Technical Description, Indications, Advantages and Disadvantages and Risks***

23	VS	Volume Support

Ventilator Specific: Maquet Servo I

** Refer to the manufacturer's manual

** Volume Support algorithm will be different for the Servo 300A ventilator.

** VS on the Servo 300/300A is $\dot{V}_E$ based.

Technical Description:

- PSV with a guaranteed volume delivery over the course of several breaths
- This mode is similar to VPS.

	Classified By:		
Breath Type	**Trigger**	**Limit**	**Cycle**
Supported	PT *(Press or $\dot{V}$)*	PL *(Press or Vol)*	PC *($\dot{V}$ or Time)*

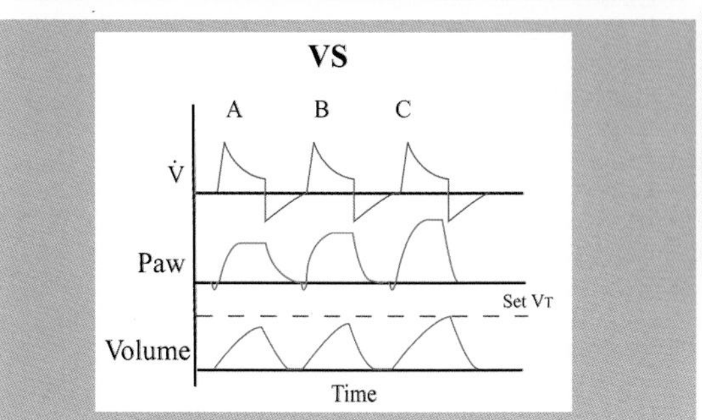

In this example, as the breaths advance from A to C, the pressure is automatically increased to achieve the set V_T. All breaths are patient-triggered breaths.

How it works:

- The ventilator gives a test breath with an inspiratory pressure of 10 cmH_2O above PEEP (5 cmH_2O in earlier software versions).
- It measures the volume delivered and calculates system C.
- For each subsequent breath, the ventilator calculates compliance of the previous breath and adjusts the inspiratory pres-

Modes

sure level to achieve the set V_T on the next breath.

- The ventilator will not change the inspiratory pressure more than 3 cmH_2O from one breath to the next
- Maximum available inspiratory pressure level is 5 cmH_2O below the preset upper pressure limit (alarm will sound at this point and the breath will switch into exhalation)
- The minimum pressure limit is the baseline setting (PEEP)
- If apnea occurs, back up pressure support is activated and an alarm sounds
- If Automode is on and patient becomes apneic, the mode will automatically switch to PRVC. (See Automode)

Indications:

- Spontaneous breathing patients who require minimum V_T
- Patients who have inspiratory efforts who need added support
- Patients who are asynchronous with the ventilator
- Used for patients who are ready to wean

Advantages:

- Guaranteed V_T and $\dot{V}_E$
- Pressure supported breaths using the lowest required pressure
- Decreases the patient's spontaneous RR
- Decreases patient WOB
- Allows patient control of I:E time
- Breath by breath analysis
- Variable $\dot{V}_I$ to meet the patient's demand

Disadvantages and Risks:

- Spontaneous ventilation required
- Upper pressure limit must be set appropriately
- Low minute volume alarm should be set properly
- V_T selected may be too large or small for patient
- Varying $\overline{P}aw$
- Auto-PEEP may affect proper functioning
- A sudden ↑ in RR and demand may result in a ↓ in ventilator support.

24	VSP	Volume Support Plus

Ventilator Specific: Puritan Bennett 840 Ventilator
**Refer to the manufacturer's manual

***Similar to Volume Support. See Volume Support (#23) for Technical Description, Indications, Advantages and Disadvantages and Risks

25	ASV	Adaptive Support Ventilation

Ventilator Specific: Hamilton Galileo, G5
** Refer to the manufacturer's manual

Technical Description:

- A dual control mode that uses PV (both PC and PS) to maintain a set minimum $\dot{V}_E$ (volume target) using the least required settings for minimal WOB depending on the patient's condition and effort
- It automatically adapts to patient demand by ↑ and ↓ support, depending on the patient's elastic and resistive loads

How It Works:

- The clinician enters the patient's IBW, which allows the ventilator's algorithm to choose a required $\dot{V}_E$.
- The ventilator delivers 100 mL/min/kg (200 mL/min/kg in pediatric patients)
- This can be adjusted from 20% - 200%, depending on the ventilatory goal and patient's condition
- A series of test breaths measures the system C, resistance, and auto-PEEP
- If no spontaneous effort occurs, the ventilator determines the appropriate *f*, V_T, and pressure limit delivered for the mandatory breaths
- The I:E ratio and T_I of the mandatory breaths are continuously being "optimized" by the ventilator to prevent auto-PEEP.
- If the patient starts having inspiratory effort, the number of mandatory breaths ↓ and the ventilator switches to PS at the same pressure level
- The pressure limit for both the spontaneous and mandatory breaths is then always being automatically adjusted

- The spontaneous and mandatory breaths are combined to meet the $\dot{V}_E$ target
- The more the spontaneous (PS) breathing, the less the mandatory (PC) breaths
- The ventilator also calculates the expiratory time constant and adjusts the I:E of mandatory breaths to prevent auto-PEEP

	Classified By:		
Breath Type	**Trigger**	**Limit**	**Cycle**
Mandatory	MT *(Time)*	ML *(Press)*	MC *(Time)*
Supported	PT *(Press or $\dot{V}$)*	PL *(Press)*	PC *($\dot{V}$, P, Time)*

Indications:
- Full or partial ventilatory support
- Patients requiring a lowest possible PIP and a guaranteed V_T
- ALI/ARDS
- Patients requiring high and/or variable $\dot{V}$
- Patients not breathing spontaneously and not triggering the ventilator
- Patients with the possibility of work load changes (C and Raw)
- Facilitates weaning

Modes

Advantages:
- Guaranteed V_T and $\dot{V}_E$
- Minimal patient WOB
- Ventilator adapts to the patient
- Weaning is done automatically and continuously
- Variable $\dot{V}$ to meet patient demand
- Decelerating flow waveform for improved gas distribution
- Breath by breath analysis

Disadvantages and Risks:
- Inability to recognize and adjust to Δ in alveolar V_D
- Possible respiratory atrophy
- Varying $\overline{P}aw$
- In patients with COPD, a longer T_E may be required
- A sudden ↑ in RR and demand may result in a ↓ in ventilator support.

26 AVtS Adaptive Tidal Volume Support

Ventilator Specific: Hamilton Galileo, G5
** Refer to the manufacturer's manual

***Similar to Adaptive Support Ventilation with greater clinician control over selected values. See ASV (# 25) for Technical Description, Indications, Advantages and Disadvantages and Risks

27 NAVA Neurally Adjusted Ventilatory Assist

Ventilator Specific: Maquet Servo I (optional)

Technical Description:

- NAVA is a mode of ventilation based on neural respiratory input from the respiratory center
- NAVA is a patient initiated breathing mode in which the breathing support is triggered by the Edi (electrical activity of the diaphragm)
- NAVA ventilation delivers ventilatory assist in proportion and synchronized to the patient's Edi. The Edi waveform is also made available in other modes as a monitoring tool to monitor the patient's neural breathing efforts and the subsequent Edi.
- Electrical activity in the diaphragm precedes the mechanical contraction of the diaphragm muscle

How It Works:

- A special functioning NG/Feeding tube with an array of measuring electrodes (Edi catheter) is positioned in the esophagus so that the set of measuring electrodes span the path of movement of the diaphragm
- A calculation based on physical landmarks and the Edi positioning screen assist the clinician on the proper placement of the Edi catheter
- The ventilator receives signals from the Edi catheter and uses those signals for ventilatory monitoring and regulation
- The clinician can set the level of support proportional to the Edi.
- Inspiration is triggered by activation of the Edi signal (neurally)
- The patient can also pneumatically trigger (pressure or flow) the

ventilator as well, on a first-come, first-served basis

- Back-up systems include a back up pressure support if the neural respiratory rate and timing differs from the pneumatic rate and time. This may be caused by an Edi catheter that has moved. The clinician sets a backup PS level with a trigger and cycle off criteria.
- If case of an apnea (resulting in a permanently low Edi signal and no pneumatic trigger), the ventilator will switch to NAVA backup (pressure control) after the adjustable apnea limit is reached.

Steps necessary to transform central respiratory drive into an inspiration at which technology able to control a ventilator could be implemented.

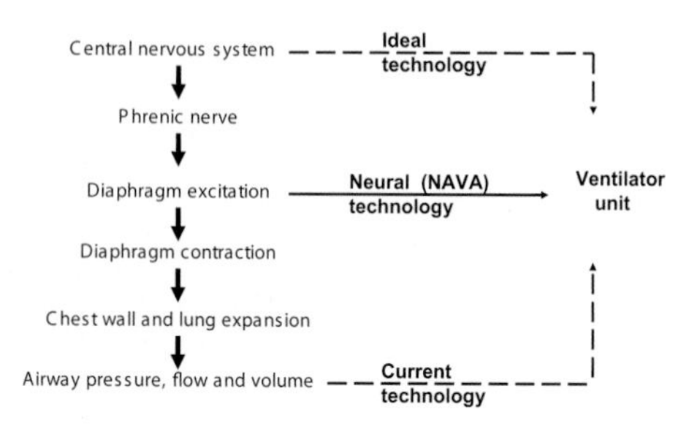

Indications:

- Mode is used in the neonatal thru the adult populations
- NAVA monitoring (Edi) alone may be done on any patient in any mode of ventilation
- Intubated patients only, NIV use is pending FDA approval.
- The NAVA mode is primarily designed for spontaneously breathing patients
- Patients who are dys-synchronous on conventional modes of ventilation

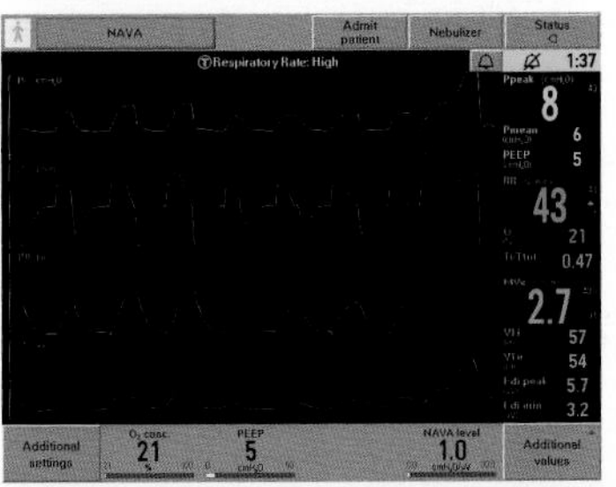

Breath Type		Classified By: Trigger	Limit	Cycle
NAVA	Spontaneous	PT *(Neurally, Press or $\dot{V}$)*	PL *(Neurally)*	PC *(Neurally)*
NAVA (PS)	Spontaneous	PT *(Press or $\dot{V}$)*	PL *(Press)*	PC *($\dot{V}$, P, Time)*
NAVA BACKUP	Mandatory	MT *(Time)*	ML *(Press)*	MC *(Time)*
NAVA BACKUP	Assisted	PT *(Press or Vol)*	ML *(Press)*	MC *(Time)*

Advantages:

- Reduced work of breathing—less missed patient trigger efforts. Intrinsic PEEP will not affect triggering in NAVA
- Improved synchrony—the patient's neural and diaphragmatic electrical activity control onset, breath delivery and cycling off of the breath. Synchrony with the ventilator is an important part of unloading the work of the diaphragm, during both inspiration and expiration
- Reduced need for sedation and/or paralysis – by allowing the patient to control his breathing pattern, less sedation may be required
- Improvement in ventilation, compared to standard methods, by allowing neural triggering, cycling and neurally-adjusted ventilator assistance, particularly in patients with severe airflow impairment

Disadvantages & Risks:

- Can not be used if the respiratory center, phrenic nerve and neuromuscular junction are not intact
- The Edi signal may not be present if patient is over ventilated. This may be a result of too high of a pressure support level or NAVA level if in NAVA mode

28	ATC	Automatic Tube Compensation

Ventilator Specific: Drager Evita 4 and XL and PB 840 (Tube Compensation), Viasys Avea and Hamilton Galileo

**Refer to the manufacturer's manual

Technical Description:

- Not a mode, but rather a component of ventilatory support
- An adjunct that overcomes the WOB created by the resistance of the artificial airway, by compensating for the pressure differential between the two ends of the ET tube
- Flow-proportional pressure support
- Airway pressure is automatically regulated at the tracheal level in proportion to the ventilator flow rate
- May be used in all modes

Modes

How it works:

- The airway pressure (PS) is ↑ during I and ↓ during E to overcome the resistance (the expiratory portion can be disabled).
- The pressure assists in expiration of mandatory breaths and both phases of all spontaneous breaths
- The pressure can be as high as 5 cmH_2O below the upper pressure limit and as low as 0 cmH_2O.
- The clinician sets the percentage of compensation desired (1%-100%).

Indications:

- Any mechanically ventilated patient with an artificial airway

Advantages:

- Addresses the ventilatory support needed for compensation of the artificial airway only, separate from the support needed to ventilate the patient.
- Superior to PSV for compensation of resistance of artificial airway (i.e., ↓WOB and ↑patient comfort).

- Supports expiration as well as inspiration if desired

Disadvantages and Risks:

- Incomplete compensation may occur with kinks or bends in the artificial airway and secretions in the inner lumen
- In patients with COPD, small airways may be kept open by PEEP and ETT resistance; therefore ATC may need to be inactive for the expiratory portion
- Adding ATC to another mode may result in over assist, in which case, the primary support level may need to be reduced

29 Automode

Ventilator Specific: Maquet Servo 300A, Servo I
**Refer to the manufacturer's manual

Technical Description:

- A ventilator control switch that automatically switches modes
- Allows patient to switch from a control (limit) mode (Volume Control, Pressure Control, Pressure Regulated Volume Control) to a support mode (Volume Support, Pressure Support) and vice versa

How it works:

- While in a control mode, if the patient has two consecutive triggering efforts, the ventilator will switch to a support mode. If the patient becomes apneic*, the ventilator will switch back to the control mode

*Apnea times with Automode only (300A)

Adult	12 seconds
Pediatric	8 seconds
Neonatal	5 seconds

(Apnea times are clinician set with the Servo I by setting "Trigger Timeout")

Control modes partner with support modes as follows:

Control Mode		Support Mode
Volume Control	⟷	Volume Support
Pressure Control	⟷	Pressure Support
Pressure Reg. Volume Control	⟷	Volume Support

Modes

- If switching to VS, the ventilator uses the following formula to determine the inspiratory pressure:
  Set P={(PIP-PEEP) x 0.5 + PEEP}

See the following Modes for complete descriptions:
- Volume Control on Maquet 300A and Servo I is V-ACV
- Pressure Control on Maquet 300A and Servo I is P-AVC
- Pressure Regulated Volume Support
- Volume Support

Indications:
- Used to adapt the ventilator status to the patient's breathing efforts
- Used to facilitate weaning (discontinuation)

See indications for the separate control and support modes.

Advantages:
- Shifts work to patient when ventilator detects two consecutive patient efforts (one breath with the Servo Inspiration)
- Shifts the work to ventilator if patient becomes apneic

See advantages for the separate control and support modes

Disadvantages and Risks:
- Possibility of ↑ WOB
- No alarm is activated when shift occurs (light signal only)
- Shouldn't be used in patients with neuromuscular block or a drug that severely depresses the respiratory drive.
- Switching from time-cycled to flow cycle ventilation may drop $\bar{P}aw$
- Settings must be set appropriately for both the control and support mode being utilized
- Trigger sensitivity must be set appropriately. Auto-triggering would be sensed as patient-triggered breaths, causing it to switch to the support mode

See disadvantages and risks for the separate control and support modes.

30	CPAP	Continuous Positive Airway Pressure

Intubated patients only

Other names:
- Continuous Distending Pressure (CDP)
- Continuous Positive Pressure Breathing (CPPB)

Technical Description:
- Spontaneous ventilation with an elevated end-expiratory pressure above atmospheric pressure
- All breaths are spontaneous and unsupported

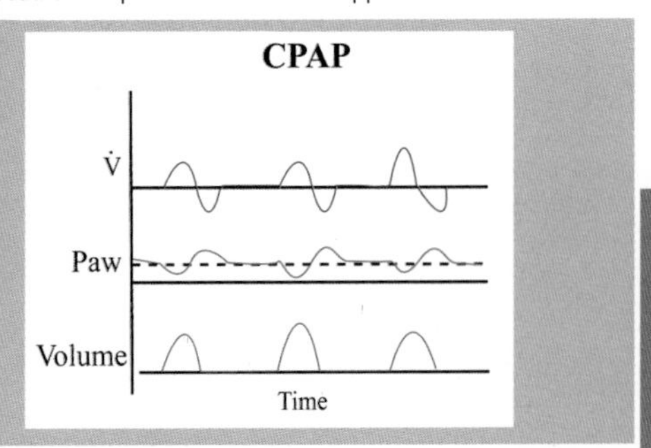

Modes

	Classified By:		
Breath Type	**Trigger**	**Limit**	**Cycle**
Spontaneous	PT *(Press or $\dot{V}$)*	PL *(Press)*	PC *(Press or $\dot{V}$)*

Indications:
- Adequate spontaneous breathing with ↓ FRC and ↓CL
- Adequate spontaneous breathing with an intrapulmonary shunt and refractory hypoxemia (PaO_2 < 60 on 60% FiO_2)
- Used in spontaneous breathing trials (SBT) during the discontinuation (weaning) process

Advantages:

- Increases FRC while patient remains intubated
- Improves oxygenation if hypoxemia is secondary to ↓ lung volume
- It may recruit collapsed lung units and minimize the WOB
- It may reduce WOB in patients with dynamic hyperinflation and auto-PEEP
- Serves as a technique for the spontaneous breathing trial during the ventilator discontinuation process

Disadvantages & Risks:

- No ventilatory support (patients must support own $\dot{V}_E$)
- Low exhaled $\dot{V}_E$ (low exhaled V_T and high respiratory rate) may go undetected if alarms are not set properly)
- May ↑ WOB if patient unable to maintain adequate $\dot{V}_E$
- Hyperinflation and ↑. expiratory work may result if excessive levels are used
- Does not compensate for resistance of artificial airway
- High levels not recommended in patients with ↑ FRC.

4 Initial Settings

Chapter Contents

Ordering Mechanical Ventilation

Remember that there is alot of variance between settings, modes, institutions and individual physicians as to the approach of MV, and changes to those settings once they are initially set.

Possible Approaches:

Approach	Example
Individual ventilator parameters *rigid settings which the practitioner likely needs to gain specific new orders to make a change*	Set F_IO_2 @ 0.50, PEEP 5
Specified Outcomes *Practitioners can independently adjust degree/form of support within established order*	Adjust F_IO_2 to maintain $SpO_2 \geq 93\%$.
Protocol *Institution-established guidelines, tailored to specific clinical situations. This has really become the practice-of-choice today.*	Wean F_IO_2/PEEP per protocol

Initial Settings

Clinicians rarely know the precise initial ventilatory requirements of any patient; selection of initial settings is usually based upon: 1) rough predictions and 2) clinical experience. Careful consideration should be given to underlying pulmonary pathophysiology, pulmonary mechanics, patient size, age, and interaction with the ventilator (see Chapter 10: Specific Disease Management, and Chapter 14: Neonatal and Pediatric Ventilation, for other initial settings).

Initial Settings Overview

$\dot{V}_E$	5-10 L/min	PIP	15 cmH20	$\dot{V}_I$	40-100 LPM
V_T	4-12 mL/kg	PEEP	0-5 cmH20	$\dot{V}_I$	Waveform Constant
f	8-12 bpm	T_I	0.8 - 1.2 sec	F_IO_2	100%

Volumes

Minute Ventilation ($\dot{V}_E$)

Initial Setting: 5 – 10 L/m	Clinical Notes
$\dot{V}_E$ is the major determinant of $\dot{V}_A$ which determines $PaCO_2$ ($\dot{V}_E \approx 1/PaCO_2$): ↑ $\dot{V}_E$ to ↓ $PaCO_2$ ↓ $\dot{V}_E$ to ↑ $PaCO_2$ *Total Ventilatory Support*: $\dot{V}_E = \dot{V}_E$ mach *Partial Ventilatory Support*: $\dot{V}_E = \dot{V}_E$ mach + $\dot{V}_E$ spont *In VV*, $\dot{V}_E = V_T \times f$ *In PV*, $\dot{V}_E \approx (PIP - PEEP) \times f$	Determining factors for selecting appropriate $\dot{V}_E$ include target pH, $PaCO_2$, spontaneous ventilation, and disease state Use total ventilatory support if patient is hypercapneic. May use partial ventilatory support if patient is hypoxemic with effective spontaneous ventilation It is often recommended that the initial phase of MV provide full ventilatory support to ensure that the patient's total ventilatory drive is satisfied

Calculation of Normal $\dot{V}_E$

Males: $\dot{V}_E = 4 \times BSA$

Females: $\dot{V}_E = 3.5 \times BSA$ *See Dubois BSA Table in Appendix*

Tidal Volume (V_T)

Initial Setting: 4 – 12 mL/kg IBW

V_T Based on Lung Characteristics

	V_T (mL/kg)	*f* (bpm)
Normal Lungs	6-12	8-12
Obstructive disease	8-10	8-12
Restrictive Disease	4-8	15-25
Adolescents (8-16 yrs)	6-10	20-30
Children (1-8 yrs)	6-8	25-30

Low V_T (6 mL/kg; range 4-8 mL/kg) is now recommended for ARDS patients to minimize airway pressures and barotrauma. This commonly results in permissive hypercapnia.

Other conditions that may benefit from low V_T (5-10 mL/kg) are pulmonary edema, emphysema, status asthmaticus, and/or pneumonectomy.

Clinical Notes

Determining factors for selecting appropriate V_T include target $PaCO_2$, pH, PIP, P_{plat}, PEEP, auto-PEEP, $\dot{V}_I$, T_I, disease state, C_L, Raw, over-distension, oxygenation, tubing compliance, V_D/V_T, spontaneous ventilation, and patient comfort

In VV, V_T is a set parameter. Some vents deliver V_T as $\dot{V}_E$ (set) / *f* (set). In most, $V_T = \dot{V}_I \times T_I$

In PV, $V_T \approx$ PIP – PEEP (includes any auto-PEEP)

Always adjust to ensure Pplat < 30 cmH_2O (lower V_T to 4 mL/kg if needed). V_T > 12 mL/kg is not recommended

Calculation of IBW (Ideal Body Weight) – See Equations Chapter 4

Factors Affecting Delivered VT during Volume Ventilation

1) Tubing Compliance

V_T (delivered to patient) = V_T (set) – CCV (circuit compressible volume)

CCV = volume loss to tubing compliance
= CF (compliance factor of tubing) x $P_{gradient}$
= CF (mL/cm H_2O) x (PIP – PEEP)

Determining CF

Set ventilator V_T to 100-200 mL, set pressure limit as high as possible, completely occlude patient wye connection, manually cycle ventilator, record expired V_T (mL) and PIP (cm H_2O);
CF = V_T /PIP.

Clinical Notes

CCV may then be added to V_T (set) to achieve V_T (desired), if different from V_T (delivered). (Newer ventilators automatically

Initial Settings

compensate for this tubing loss). Correcting for tubing compliance loss is especially important in infants, children and very small patients when V_T is < 300 mL.

2) Mechanical Deadspace

VD_{mech} (mechanical deadspace) is usually insignificant: HME's add ≈ 20 - 90 mL. Wye connectors add ≈ 75 mL and ET tubes deduct ≈ 75 mL (1 mL/kg) so these two cancel each other out.

Determining VT Delivery during Pressure Ventilation

How To Set Pressure

Option 1	Option 2
1) Volume ventilate with desired V_T to find P_{plat} and EEP. 2) Set PIP at Pplat and baseline pressure at EEP. 3) Adjust PIP as needed to obtain desired V_T.	1) Start at low PIP (10-15 cm H_2O) and check V_T. 2) Adjust PIP as needed to obtain desired V_T.

V_T ≈ PIP - PEEP (PEEP includes any auto-PEEP)

$P_{plat} = P_{alv}$ ≈ peak Palv *It is recommended that a maximum Pplat of 30 cm H_2O is not exceeded.*

Factors Affecting Delivered V_T during Pressure Ventilation

Pressure Gradient (PIP - PEEP)	Patient's Lungs	T_I
↑ PIP – PEEP → ↑ V_T ↓ PIP – PEEP → ↓ V_T ↑ auto-PEEP → ↓ V_T	↓ CL → ↓ V_T ↑ CL → ↑ V_T ↓ Raw → ↑ V_T ↑ Raw → ↓ V_T	↑ T_I → ↑ V_T (with active flow) ↓ T_I → ↓ V_T

Rate

Ventilator Rate (f)

Initial Setting: 8-12 breaths/min

f Based on Lung Characteristics

	f (bpm)	V_T (mL/kg)
Normal Lungs	8-12	6-12
Obstructive disease	8-12	8-10
Restrictive Disease	15-25	4-8
Adolescents (8-16 yrs)	20-30	6-10
Children (1-8 yrs)	25-30	6-8

Adjusting rate:

$$\text{New Rate} = \frac{\text{Current Rate} \times PaCO_2}{\text{Desired } PaCO_2}$$

Clinical Notes

$f = \dot{V}_E / V_T$

$f = 60 / T_I + T_E$

Rate is the primary control for altering pH and $PaCO_2$:

↑ f to ↑pH and ↓$PaCO_2$

↓ f to ↓pH and ↑ $PaCO_2$

Determining factors for selecting appropriate rate include target $PaCO_2$, pH, V_T, PIP, $\dot{V}_I$, PEEP, auto-PEEP, mode, C_L, Raw, V_D/V_T, metabolic rate, spontaneous ventilation, and patient comfort.

Oxygen

F_IO_2

Initial Setting

<u>If baseline ABG is not available</u>

Start with 50-100% O_2, then titrate down as soon as able to

<u>If baseline ABG is available</u>

If PaO_2 is in the desired range prior to MV, use the same F_IO_2.

If PaO_2 is below desired range:

$$\text{New } FIO_2 = \frac{PaO_2\text{ (desired)} \times F_IO_2}{PaO_2\text{ (known)}}$$

Clinical Notes

Initial F_IO_2 must be evaluated by ABG after patient stabilization, and adjusted.

Any further adjustment needed is most likely due to MV effects on cardiopulmonary function.

↓ to < 0.5 ASAP. If F_IO_2 > 0.65 is required, consider PEEP.

Determining factors for selecting appropriate F_IO_2 include target PaO_2, PEEP, $\overline{P}aw$, and hemodynamic status.

P_AO_2 Targets

Normal lung	≥ 80 mmHg	Moderate lung injury	≥ 60 mmHg
Mild lung injury	≥ 70 mmHg	Severe lung injury	≥ 55 mmHg

Pressures

Peak Inspiratory Pressure (PIP or P_{Peak})

Initial Setting	Clinical Notes
15 cmH_2O Adjust to desired V_T	Permissive hypercapnia may be needed in some disease states (e.g., ARDS) to keep distending pressure (PIP – PEEP) < 30 - 35 cm H_2O.

Positive End-Expiratory Pressure (PEEP)

Initial Setting: 0-5 cmH_20	Clinical Notes
Indications: $PaO_2 \le 60$ mmHg -or- $SaO_2 \le 90$ mmHg on $F_IO_2 \ge 0.5$ *Maintain FRC:* physiological PEEP (3-5 cmH_2O) *Contraindications*: Excessive PIP, Pplat > 30 cm H_2O, hypotension, untreated pneumothorax, ↑ICP, large B-P fistula, and possibly unilateral lung disease or COPD	Determining factors for selecting PEEP include: F_IO_2, target PaO_2, CL, and hemodynamic response. Subsequent changes are based on ABGs, F_IO_2 needs, PEEP tolerance, auto-PEEP, trigger asynchrony, and hemodynamic response.

Times

Inspiratory Time (T_I)

Initial Setting: 0.8 - 1.2 sec

Clinical Notes

Determining factors for selecting appropriate T_I include oxygenation, rate, auto-PEEP, hemodynamic status, CL, Raw, patient-ventilator synchrony, and lung recruitment.

In VV, T_I is usually the result of $V_T/\dot{V}_I$.

In PV, T_I is set.

Short T_I's are commonly used in patients with ↓C_L (short TC).

Longer T_I's are commonly used in patients with ↑Raw (long TC).

Expiratory Time (T_E)

Initial Setting: $T_E > T_I$

Usually a function of T_I and *f*.

$T_E = (60 / f) - T_I$

Initial Settings

I:E Ratio

Initial Setting: 1:3 (usually a function of other set parameters)

Clinical Notes

I:E ratio is determined by $\dot{V}_I$, T_I, T_I%, *f*, and/or $\dot{V}_E$ (V_T x *f*).

Determining factors for selecting appropriate I:E ratio include hemodynamic response to MV, oxygenation status, patient-ventilator synchrony.

Small I:E ratios (longer T_E: 1:4, 1:6) may be used for patients requiring longer exhalation to avoid air-trapping and auto-PEEP (e.g., asthma, COPD).

Large I:E ratios (longer T_I: 1:1, 1:2) may be used for patients requiring ↑ $\overline{P}$aw and ↑ gas distribution time.

Inverse I:E ratios should not be used until traditional MV strategies have failed to improve patient's ventilation and oxygenation.

Adjusting I:E Ratio

$\dot{V}_I$:	↑ $\dot{V}_I$ → ↓T_I →smaller I:E ratio ↓ $\dot{V}_I$ → ↑T_I → larger I:E ratio
V_T:	↑ V_T → ↑ T_I → larger I:E ratio ↓ V_T → ↓ T_I → smaller I:E ratio
f :	↑ RR → ↓ T_E → larger I:E ratio ↓ RR → ↑ T_E → smaller I:E ratio
T_I %:	↑ TI% → larger I:E ratio (see →→→

T_I%	I:E Ratio
14.3%	1:6
16.7%	1:5
20.0%	1:4
25.0%	1:3
33.3%	1:2
50.0%	1:1
60.0%	1.5:1
66.7%	2:1

Caution: When an I:E ratio is ordered (e.g., IRV), the I:E ratio will change in PV (constant set I time) when the patient's breath rate (patient-triggered) increases.

Flow

Inspiratory Flow ($\dot{V}_I$)

Initial Setting: 40-100 LPM (VV)	Clinical Notes
Goal Set $\dot{V}_I \geq$ patient's peak inspiratory demand and deliver an I:E ratio of 1:1.5 to 1:4 (usually with initial T_I of 1.0 sec) 1:4 to 1:6 may be required for COPD Assess airway pressure-time waveform and V-P loop to insure goal is met *Minimum* $\dot{V}_I = \dot{V}_E \times (I + E)$	In VV, $\dot{V}_I$ is usually either preset or limited, and determines T_I (rate determines T_E) In PV, $\dot{V}_I$ is variable and determined by the patient Some vents allow adjusting of $\dot{V}_I$ during PS (see rise time) Determining factors for selecting appropriate $\dot{V}_I$ include disease state, spontaneous inspiratory effort (volume-targeted), WOB, patient-ventilator synchrony

$\dot{V}_I$ based on lung characteristics

ARDS: slow $\dot{V}_I$ (T_I of 3-4 time constants)

COPD: fast $\dot{V}_I$ (T_E of 3-4 time constants) (avoid too high a flow)

	Potential Advantages	Potential Disadvantages
Slower $\dot{V}I$	↑ T_I ↓ PIP → ↓ risk of barotrauma Improved gas distribution	↓ T_E→ air trapping (auto-PEEP) ↑ $\overline{P}aw$ → CV effects May not meet pt. demand → flow starvation
Faster $\dot{V}I$	↓ T_I, Meets pt. demand ↓ WOB, ↓ auto-PEEP	↑ PIP Poor gas distribution

Inspiratory Flow Waveform

Initial Setting: Constant (Square) Flow Pattern

The main advantage of an initial constant flow pattern is to obtain baseline measures of C and Raw (peak flow = mean flow).

Adjustment of flow pattern may be made after pt. stabilization – with main focus for selection being desired PIP and $\overline{P}aw$.

Optimal flow pattern is highly variable and dependent on the individual patient's lung and airway conditions. Pattern variation usually has insignificant effects on normal lungs.

VV with a decelerating waveform may provide similar results to PV. PV has a true decelerating flow, but in VV, the decelerating flow is algorithm-driven, which can lead to "flow starvation".

Changing flow patterns may affect peak $\dot{V}_I$, T_I and/or T_E, depending on the ventilation type.

Adjuncts

Sensitivity: Inspiratory Trigger Sensitivity

Initial Setting	Clinical Notes
Pressure triggering: 0.5 to 2.0 cmH_2O below baseline (EEP) *Flow triggering*: 1 – 3 LPM below baseline	Fine-tune the setting to prevent auto-triggering, ↑ WOB, and/or patient-ventilator asynchrony Observe patient's inspiratory efforts, pressure manometer, and graphics display Avoid using mechanical demand valves May need to readjust after Δ in PEEP

If auto-PEEP (PEEPI) is present:

Pressure triggering = $PEEP_I$ + (- 0.5 to - 2.0 cm H_2O)

Adjust $PEEP_E$ (set PEEP) to equal and cancel out $PEEP_I$

Example: If auto-PEEP is 10 cm H_2O, the pt. must generate - 11 to - 12 cm H_2O to trigger ventilator. ↑ $PEEP_E$ until pt. effectively triggers the ventilator (up to 80% of auto-PEEP) (e.g., 8 cm H_2O).

See Ventilator Graphics Ch 6: trigger asynchrony and auto-PEEP.

Measuring auto-PEEP (PEEPI):

1) *Measure*: See Ch 11.
2) *Estimate*:
   a) ↑ $PEEP_E$ until PIP begins to rise
   b) ↑ $PEEP_E$ until accessory muscle use decreases
   c) ↑ $PEEP_E$ until each inspiratory effort triggers the ventilator

Note: If sensitivity is too sensitive, the ventilator will self-cycle.

If sensitivity is too insensitive, there will be an ↑ WOB.

(The pressure needle should not dip significantly below end-expiratory pressure at the beginning of inspiration).

Sensitivity: Expiratory Sensitivity (Inspiratory Cycle Off)

Used in PSV to assist patient in terminating the I phase.

Begin @ 25%, depending on graphics and patient comfort. Adjust down to 10% for Restrictive; up to 40% for obstructive disorders

Humidification

Initial Setting	Clinical Notes
HME: start with HME (unless contraindicated) *Heated: 31 –35 C (38-40 C for patient rewarming)*	Replace HME q1-5 days and PRN (>5 days; use heated). Switch to heated humidification if: > 4 HMEs used in 1 day Body temp < 32 Secretion problem $\dot{V}_E$ > 10 L/min Airleaks > 30% of V_T

Alarm Limits

Initial Settings

Alarm	Setting
Apnea	< 20 sec
High/Low $\dot{V}_E$	10-15% +/- set $\dot{V}_E$
High/Low V_T	10-15% +/- set V_T
High/Low PIP	10 cmH_2O +/- avg. PIP
High/Low PEEP	3-5 cmH_2O +/- set PEEP
High/Low F_IO_2	5% +/- set F_IO_2
High/Low Rate	10-15 bpm +/- set rate
I:E Ratio	when I>E
Temp	2° above/below set temp.

Clinical Notes

There are no predetermined levels for setting some alarm parameters. Operators must use their judgment when setting alarms to indicate possible changes in the patient's condition. Don't set alarms so sensitive as to cause constant triggering

Initial Settings for Specific Modes

Few studies have reported optimal initial settings for specific modes of ventilation (esp. the newer modes). Below are a few generalizations. The only initial settings mentioned are those specific to the individual mode. See above for the other settings.

Pressure Support Ventilation (PSV)

Initial Settings	Clinical Notes
Normal lungs ≈ 5 cmH_2O *Diseased lungs* ≈ 8 – 12 cmH_2O **Goals** Overcome Raw of the artificial airway to ↓ WOB. ↓ Accessory muscle use to a minimum (esp. sternocleidomastoid)	Determining Initial PS level 1) PS level = PIP – Pplat or 2) PS level = $\frac{PIP - Pplat}{\dot{V}_I \text{ (constant)}}$ *Note*: Volume ventilate with desired V_T to find PIP and Pplat. adjust as needed to achieve desired V_T (4–12 mL/kg) and *f* (< 20 breaths/min).

Pressure (Controlled) Ventilation (P-ACV, P-SIMV)

Initial Settings

1) Set pressure level at Pplat (P_{plat} determined by desired V_T with VV) or
2) Set pressure level at 10 - 15 cmH_2O

   Then, adjust pressure level as needed to achieve desired V_T.

   Set *f*, T_I, and I:E as with VV.

Pressure-Inverse Ratio Ventilation (P-IRV)

Initial Settings	Clinical Notes
Same as Pressure (Controlled) Ventilation except I:E ratio is started at 1:2 and then progressively ↑ to ≥ 2:1 (per patient assessment). *Ratios > 2:1 need to be used with caution because of auto-PEEP effect on CV system.*	***Indication*** Severe hypoxemic respiratory failure (esp. ARDS) when VV requires: PIP ≥ 50 cmH_2O P_{plat} ≥ 30 - 35 cmH_2O PEEP ≥ 15 cmH_2O F_IO_2 = 1.0 *f* ≥ 16 breaths/min

Initial Settings

Airway Pressure Release Ventilation (APRV)

Initial Settings
P high (APRV pressure): ≥ optimal PEEP or $\overline{P}aw$ during conventional ventilation.
P low (release pressure): set to allow exhalation of V_T that permits adequate removal of CO_2 ($V_T \approx$ P high – P low).
f: set to allow for the shortest release time (T low) possible for adequate ventilation. $T_{tot} = T_I$ (T high) + T_E (T low)

Initial Settings for Normal or Mildly Decresed Compliance	Initial Settings for Severe Lung Injury
P high ≈ 10 – 12 cm H_2O P low ≈ 0 - 2 cmH_2O	P high ≈ 20 – 30 cmH_2O (5 – 10 cmH_2O above optimal PEEP) P low ≈ 0 - 2 cm H_2O
T high to establish *f* < 15 bpm ≥ 4 sec T low ≈ 0.5 – 1.0 sec*	T high ≈ 2 – 6 sec (*f* = 10 – 20) T low ≈ 0.5 – 1.0 sec*

Note: Set IPAP below Upper Inflection Point (UIP) and EPAP above Lower Inflection Point (LIP) on V-P curve, if available.

*T low is highly variable and set according to lung compliance

BiPAP

Initial Settings	Clinical Notes
IPAP ≈ *5 – 10 cmH_2O* ↑ *in increments of 3 - 5 cm H_2O until: V_T ≥ 7 mL/kg, f ≤ 25 breaths/min* *(6 mL/kg in ARDS/ALI)* ***EPAP*** ≈ *2 - 5 cm* H_2O ↑ *in increments of 3 - 5 cmH_2O.*	In COPD patients with auto-PEEP, use EPAP of 80 - 90% of auto-PEEP (usually 3 - 10 cmH_2O). In patients with hypoxemic respiratory failure, if no improvement after 2 hrs of BiPAP, a more aggressive mode of ventilation is indicated.

Pressure Augmentation (PAug) - or -
Volume-Assured Pressure Support (VAPS)

Initial Settings

Set PIP = P_{plat} - PEEP

No studies have reported the best method for selecting initial appropriate pressure-support level.

Peak flow must be adjusted for appropriate T_I and allowing sufficient T_E to prevent auto-PEEP. Pressure-time and flow-time graphics should be used to optimize patient comfort.

Pressure-Regulated Volume Control (PRVC)

Initial Settings

1) Set desired V_T ($V_T = \dot{V}_E / f$)
   Note: Must be set high enough to keep up with flow demand.
2) Set baseline pressure (PEEP) and maximum pressure limit

Volume Support (VS)

Initial Settings

This is purely a spontaneous mode. The patient establishes his own RR and V_T. Set minimum backup V_T and f, similar to PRCV.

5 Patient-Ventilator Assessment/Troubleshooting

Chapter Contents

Signs of Sudden Patient Distress

Patient	***Vital Signs***	***Cardiovascular Assessment***
	Tachypnea	Arrhythmias
	Tachycardia	
	Hypotension	
	Respiratory Assessment	
	Accessory muscle use	Diaphoresis
	Change in BS/percussion	Nasal flaring
	Paradoxical chest /abdomen movements	
	Retractions	
Ventilator	↑↓ PIP (VV)	
	↑↓ VT (PV)	
	Graphic waveform changes	

See next page for Sudden Patient Distress Algorithm

Differential Diagnosis of Sudden Respiratory Distress

Patient-Related Causes

Airway problems:
- Bronchospasm/edema
- ET tube dislocation (pharynx, esophagus, carina, Rt mainstem)
- ET tube kink (bending or biting)
- ET tube cuff (leak, rupture, herniation)
- Secretions/obstructions
- T-E fistula

Lung problems:
- Atelectasis
- Auto-PEEP
- B-P fistula
- Pleural effusion
- Pneumothorax

Cardiovascular problems:
- CHF, MI
- Fluid imbalance
- Innominate artery rupture
- Pulmonary edema
- Pulmonary embolism

Altered respiratory drive:
- Anxiety, Delirium, Drugs
- Excessive carbohydrate load
- Fear, Fever
- Inadequate nutritional support
- Pain, Stress, Neuro disorders

Other Causes:
- Abdominal distension
- Altered patient position
- Drug-induced problems
- Electrolyte imbalance

Ventilator-Related Causes

Inadequate or altered settings:
- Inadequate F_IO_2 (↓ PaO_2)
- Inadequate ventilatory support (↑ $PaCO_2$, ↑WOB)
- Improper sensitivity setting
- Leak/disconnection
- Malfunction (ventilator, circuit, humidifier, valves)
- Patient-ventilator asynchrony (See below)

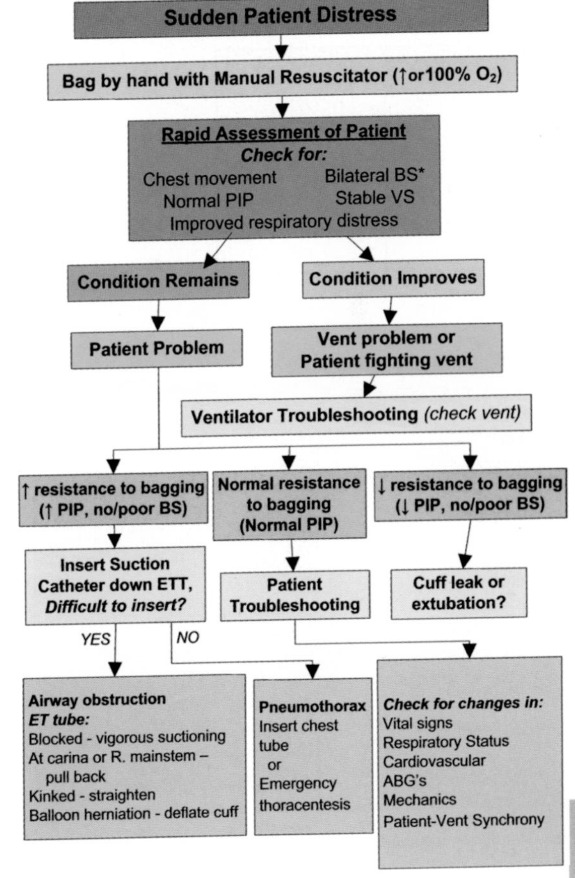
Sudden Patient Distress
Bag by hand with Manual Resuscitator (↑or100% O_2)
Rapid Assessment of Patient
Check for:
Chest movement
Bilateral BS*
Normal PIP
Stable VS
Improved respiratory distress
Condition Remains
Condition Improves
Patient Problem
Vent problem or Patient fighting vent
Ventilator Troubleshooting (check vent)
↑ resistance to bagging (↑ PIP, no/poor BS)
Normal resistance to bagging (Normal PIP)
↓ resistance to bagging (↓ PIP, no/poor BS)
Insert Suction Catheter down ETT, Difficult to insert?
Patient Troubleshooting
Cuff leak or extubation?
YES
NO
Airway obstruction
ET tube:
Blocked - vigorous suctioning
At carina or R. mainstem – pull back
Kinked - straighten
Balloon herniation - deflate cuff
Pneumothorax
Insert chest tube
or
Emergency thoracentesis
Check for changes in:
Vital signs
Respiratory Status
Cardiovascular
ABG's
Mechanics
Patient-Vent Synchrony

Assess/Troubleshoot

Respiratory Rate

Age	Normal RR
Adult	12-16
5 - 12 yrs	16-20
Preschool	20-30
1 yr	25-40
Newborn	30-60

Changes in Respiratory Rate

Tachypnea - Causes of	*Bradypnea - Causes of*
Artificial airway problems Atelectasis Auto-PEEP Bronchospasm CHF, Drugs Fear/anxiety Fever Hypercapnia Hypoxemia ↑ metabolism Metabolic acidosis MV (altered settings or problems) Pain, Pneumonia Pneumothorax Pulmonary edema WOB ↑ (↓ C, ↑ Raw)	Diabetic coma Drugs (sedation/paralysis, etc.) Head injury Hyperoxia in chronic respiratory acidosis Hypocapnia Hypothermia ↑ ICP Metabolic alkalosis MI (severe) MV (altered settings) Neurologic disease Respiratory muscle fatigue Sleep Uremia WOB ↓ (↑ C, ↓ Raw)

See Ventilator Trouble-Shooting for ventilator-induced rate changes.

Heart Rate

Age	Normal RR
Adult	60-100
5 - 12 yrs	70-110
Preschool	80-120
1 yr	80-160
Newborn	90-180

Strength/Amplitude

4 bounding
3 full
2 normal
1 diminished
0 absent

Compare equality of strength between:

I vs E
Rside vs Lside
Upper vs Lower

Heart Rhythms

Pulsus Alternans	Regular alteration of weak and strongpulses
Pulsus Corrigans	Strong or bounding with ↑PP
Pulsus Parvus	Weak pulse with ↓PP
Pulsus Paradoxus	↓pulse strength during inspiration; ↑during expiration (> 10 mmHg is signif., > 20 is needed to feel the difference)
Reverse Pulsus Paradoxus	Reverse of above during PPV

Changes in Heart Rate

Tachycardia - Causes of		*Bradycardia - Causes of*	
Alkalosis/ acidosis Anxiety/ stress/fear Drugs Fever Hypovolemia	Hypoxemia MI Pain Shock	Arrhythmias (drugs, anxiety) Coronary blood flow decrease ↓ venous return Drugs Heart block	Hypothermia Hypoxemia (sudden) SA node abnormality Sleep Vagal stimulus

Blood Pressure

Age	Normal BP	Systolic / Diastolic
Adult	120/80	100-140 / 60-80
5 - 12 yrs	110/70	100-120 / 60-80
Preschool	100/60	95-105 / 50-65
1 yr	95/60	85-105 / 50-65
Newborn	70/45	40-90 / 20-60

Pulse Pressure =	BPsys - BPdia	Normal = 40 mmHg (range = 20-80 mmHg)
Mean BP =	BPsys + 2BPdia/3	Normal = 93 mmHg (range = 70-105 mmHg)

Changes in Blood Pressure

Hypertension (> 140/90) - Causes of		*Hypotension (< 90/60) - Causes of*
Anxiety/ stress CHF CV disease Drugs	Fluid overload Hypocapnia Hypoxia Pain	Absolute hypovolemia (blood loss, dehydration) Relative hypovolemia (↓ CO, sepsis, shock) Drugs PPV (↓ venous return: high pressures, auto-PEEP, pneumothorax) Pump failure (e.g., CHF)

Temperature

Type	Normal
Oral	97.7 - 99.5° F
	36.5 - 37.5° C
Axillary	96.7 - 98.5° F
	35.9 - 36.9° C
Rectal Tympanic (ear)	98.7 - 100.5° F
	37.1 - 38.1° C

Cool or heated aerosol by face may affect oral temperature

Changes in Temperature

Hyperthermia - Causes of		*Hypothermia - Causes of*
Asynchrony CNS problem High humidification temperature ↑ metabolic rate Infection Hyperthyroidism	Late stage carcinoma Leukemia Tissue necrosis WOB ↑ (↓ C, ↑ Raw)	CNS problem Drugs Hypothyroidism Induced (CABG, head injury) Metabolic disorders Toxins

Inspection

Inspection	
Head	*Face*: Color, expression, alertness, distress, fear, mood, pain *Nose*: Nasal flaring *Lips*: Color, pursed lip breathing *Neck*: Accessory muscle use, JVD, tracheal position
Skin	*Color*: Pale, cyanosis (peripheral vs. central), rudy or flushed Capillary refill (3 sec) Diaphoresis *Edema*: Legs/ankles Subcutaneous emphysema *Temperature*: Hot/cold/normal
Chest	*Breathing*: Rate (spont, mech), Depth (spont, mech) *Pattern -Abnormal*: patient-ventilator asynchrony, fighting, abdominal, paradoxical, abdominal paradox, respiratory alternans, inability to trigger ventilator Accessory muscle use I/E ratio Retractions, location, bulging, splinting, clavicular lift Symmetry (unilateral, bilateral) WOB (dyspnea, fatigue)

Abnormal Breathing Patterns - Causes of

Breathing Asymmetry	Retractions	Patient-Ventilator Asynchrony
Atelectasis (massive) Flail chest Lobar consolidation Misplaced ET tube Mucous plugging of bronchus Pleural effusion Splinting Tension pneumothorax	Decreased $\dot{V}I$ Patient-ventilator asynchrony (inappropriate settings) Obstructed airway (bronchospasm, mucous plugging, etc.) Misplaced tracheostomy tube	*Patient*: Acidosis Artificial airway problem Bronchospasm Change in body position Fear/anxiety Hypercapnia Hypoxemia Pain Pneumothorax Pulmonary edema

Palpation

Palpation
Chest and diaphragm excursion (depth, symmetry) PMI (5th IC space, mid-clavicular) Subcutaneous emphysema / Tracheal position Tenderness / Vocal (tactile) fremitus (↑or ↓)

Changes in Palpation

Abnormal Palpation - Causes of

Abnormal Expansion	*Bilateral* ↓: COPD, neuromuscular disease *Unilateral* ↓: Atelectasis, lobar consolidation, pleural effusion, pneumothorax
Abdominal (Gastric) Distention	Air-swallowing, E-T tube in esophagus, excessive negative pressure, leak around cuff, T-E fistula
Bulging Intercostal Spaces	Tension pneumothorax
Jugular Vein Distension	RHF Hypervolemia
Subcutaneous Emphysema	Dissection of air around tracheostomy Pneumomediastinum, pneumothorax
Tracheal Position Shift	*Shifts towards*: unilateral upper lobe collapse *Shifts away from*: lung tumor, pleural effusion, tension pneumothorax

Clinical Notes

Subcutaneous Emphysema	Pneumomediastinum
Diagnosis – Skin crepitus/auscultation Treatment – Tends to clear without treatment and usually occurs without complications, but watch for accompanying pneumothorax.	Diagnosis – CXR Treatment – treat if cardiac tamponade is present

Pneumothorax	
Simple Pneumothorax	***Tension Pneumothorax***
Rapid or slow rise in PIP or Pplat	High PIP and Pplat
↓ BS on affected side	Absent BS on affected side
Hyperresonant percussion on affected side	Tympanic percussion on affected side
Tracheal deviation away from affected side	Tracheal deviation away from affected side
CXR	CXR

Note: A simple pneumothorax can rapidly develop into a tension on MV.

Treatment: Chest tube/emergency thoracentesis (needle decompression)

Emergency Thoracentesis:

Insert 14 –18 gauge needle into 2nd – 3rd intercostal space, midclavicular line.

Remove patient from ventilator, bag manually with 100% O_2, and as low a PIP as possible.

Percussion

Percussion
Resonance over normal lung Dull over heart

Changes in Percussion

Note	Normal Examples	Abnormal Causes
Flat	Thigh, muscle	Massive atelectasis, massive pleural effusion, pneumonectomy
Dull	Heart, liver	Atelectasis, consolidation, enlarged heart, fibrosis, neoplasm, pleural effusion or thickening, pulmonary edema
Resonance	Normal lung	
Hyper-resonance	Abdomen	Acute asthma, emphysema, pneumothorax
Tympany	Large gastric air bubble	Large pulmonary cavity, tension pneumothorax

Auscultation

Breath Sounds		
Normal	Vesicular (over most of lungs) Bronchovescicular (over carina, between upper scapulae) Bronchial (over manubrium) Tracheal (over upper trachea)	
Other	*Abnormal*: Decreased or increased	*Adventitious*: Crackles (fine, coarse) Wheeze, Stridor, Rub

Changes in Auscultation

↓ *Breath Sounds*	↑ *Breath Sounds*
↓ *air movement*: Bronchospasm, obstruction, restriction, secretions ET tube malposition *Insulation*: Air – pneumothorax Fat – obesity Fibrosis – pleural thickening Fluid – effusion	*Consolidation*: Atelectasis, fibrosis, infarct, pneumonia, tumor

Distinguishing Between Air, Solid and Fluid in the Chest Cavity

		↑ Presence of:		
Method	**Sign**	**Air**	**Solid**	**Fluid**
Palpation	Fremitus	↓	↑	↓
Percussion	Resonance	↑	↓	↓
Auscultation	Breath sounds	↓	↑	↓

Adventitious Breath Sounds - Causes of

	Type*	Description	Probable Location	Common Cause
Crackle (Rale)	Fine (subcrepitant)	Discontinuous, high-pitched crackling, at end-inspiration	Alveoli- atelectasis or excessive fluid	Atelectasis, fibrosis, pneumonia, pulmonary edema
	Medium (crepitant)	Wetter and louder, any part of inspiration	Bronchioles - air moving through fluid	Bronchitis, emphysema, pneumonia, pulmonary edema
	Coarse	Loud low-pitched bubbling, usually during expiration	Larger airways - air moving through fluid, often clears with cough	Bronchitis, emphysema, pneumonia, pulmonary edema
Wheeze	High pitch- lower airway squeak	Musical, continuous vibration, usually occurs on expiration (maybe inspir.)	Lower airway narrowing	Asthma, bronchitis, CHF, emphsema, foreign body, mucous plug, stenosis, tumor
	Low pitch - upper airway snore		Thick secretions (may disappear with cough)	
Stridor		Loud, high-pitched crowing in upper airway, usually during inspir.	Usually due to tracheal narrowing. Can be found with partial plugging of artificial airway	Epiglottitis, croup, foreign body, tracheal stenosis, tumor, vocal cord edema, plugging
Rub	*Grating vibration, loud and harsh*			
	Pleural	Inspiration and Expiration	Pleural membranes	Peripheral pneumonia, pleurisy, pulmonary emboli, TB
	Pericardial	Associated with heartbeat	Pericardial sac	Pericarditis

As recommended by ACCP - ATS Joint Committee on Pulmonary Nomenclature, 1975 and updates.

Arterial Blood Gases

	Arterial		Mixed Venous	
	Norm	Range	Norm	Range
pH (pHa, pH$\bar{v}$), units	7.40	7.35-7.45	7.36	7.31-7.41
PCO_2 ($PaCO_2$, $P\bar{v}CO_2$), mmHg	40	35-45	46	41-51
PO_2 (PaO_2, $P\bar{v}O_2$), mmHg*	100	80-100	40	35-42
O_2 Sat (SaO_2, $S\bar{v}O_2$), %	97%	95-100%	75%	68-77%
HCO_3, mEq/L	24	22-26	24	22-26
TCO_2	25	23-27	25	23-27
BE, mEq/L	0	+/- 2	0	+/- 2
O_2 content (CaO_2, $C\bar{v}O_2$), mL/dL	20	15-24	15	12-15

See Oakes' ***ABG Pocket Guide*** for differential diagnosis of ABG disorders.

Signs and Symptoms of:

Acute Hypoxemia/Hypoxia ***(relative order of appearance)***		**Hypercarbia** ***(relative order of appearance)***
Tachypnea Dyspnea Pallor Tachycardia Hypertension Headache Anxiety Cyanosis Arrhythmias Blurred or tunnel vision Impaired judgment	Confusion Euphoria Bradycardia Hypotension Nausea/vomiting Loss of coordination, Lethargy/ weakness Tremors/hyperactive reflexes Stupor Coma Death	Tachypnea Dyspnea Tachycardia Hypertension Vasodilation (diaphoresis, flushing) Headache Bradypnea Hypotension Drowsiness Hallucination Convulsions Coma Death

Note: Hypoxemia and hypercarbia usually occur together (unless patient is on O_2 therapy. See Chapter 8 for strategies to improve.

Types and Causes of Hypoxemia/Hypoxia:
See Oakes' ***Clinical Practitioner's Pocket Guide to Respiratory Care***, for a detailed summary.

Oxygenation at the Lungs (external respiration)			Oxygenation at the Tissues (internal respiration)		
	Norm	Ab-norm		Norm	Ab-norm
Adequacy					
PaO_2*	80-100 mmHg	< 80 mmHg	$P\bar{v}O_2$	35-42 mmHg	< 35 or > 45 mmHg
CaO_2	15-24 mL/dL	↑↓	$C\bar{v}O_2$	12-15 mL/dL	↑↓
SaO_2**	> 95%	< 95%	$S\bar{v}O_2$	60-80%	< 60%
SpO_2	> 95%	< 95%	$Ca\text{-}\bar{v}O_2$	4.5-5.0 mL/dL	↑↓
Efficiency					
$PA\text{-}aO_2$	10-25 mmHg (air) 30-50 mmHg (100%)	>25 mmHg	O_{2ER}	25%	↑↓
			$\dot{V}O_2$	200-250 mL/min	↑↓
			$\dot{D}O_2$	750 - 1000 mL/min	↑↓
PaO_2/PAO_2	0.8-0.9	<0.6	VQI	0.8	↑↓
PaO_2/FIO_2	>300	<300			
$PA\text{-}aO_2/PaO_2$	<1.0	>1.0			
Q_S/Q_T phys	2-5%	> 20%			

*Normal Variations: Due to age, FIO_2, or barometric pressure
Age: $PaO_2 \approx 110 - 1/2$ patient's age

**SaO_2 = calculated O_2 saturation from PaO_2
SpO_2 = Peripheral O_2 saturation - measured value of Hgb

Assessment of Ventilation

	Normal	Abnormal		Normal	Abnormal
Adequacy			**Efficiency**		
$\dot{V}_E$	5-7 L/min	↑↓	**V_D phys**	1/3$\dot{V}$E	↑↓
$PaCO_2$	35-45mmHg	↑↓	**V_D/V_T**	0.33-0.45	↑↓
$P_{ET}CO_2$	35-43 mmHg (4.6 - 5.6%)	↑↓			
$Pa\text{-}_{ET}CO_2$	1-5 mmHg	> 6 mmHg			

Changes in Ventilation

Hyperventilation - Causes of	Hypoventilation - Causes of
Anxiety CNS pathology Hypoxia Metabolic acidosis MV	MV Neuropathy N-M blockade (disease, blocking agents) Respiratory center depression (pathologic, iatrogenic) Respiratory muscle weakness (fatigue,disease) Trauma

Assessment of Ventilatory Mechanics

Assessment of Load

	Normal	Abnormal
Adequacy:		
C_{dyn}	40-60 mL/cmH_2O	↓
C_{stat}	70-100 mL/cmH_2O	↓
Raw	0.5 - 2.5 cmH_2O/L/sec @ 0.5 L/sec (4-8 with ET tube)	> 15 cmH_2O/L/sec
RSBI (f/V_T)	< 105	> 105

Assessment of Capacity

	Normal	Abnormal
Respiratory Drive:		
P0.1	< 2 cm H_2O	> 4-6 cmH_2O
Respiratory Muscle Strength		
VC	60-80 mL/kg	< 60 mL/kg
P_{Imax} (MIP, NIF)	< -60 cmH_2O	> -30 cmH_2O
Respiratory Muscle Endurance		
MVV	120-180 L/min	< 20 L/min
$\dot{V}_E$/MVV	< 1:2	> 1:2

Changes in Ventilatory Mechanics

Static Compliance

Conditions Causing ↓ Cstat		Conditions Causing ↑ Cstat
Lung Air-trapping (auto-PEEP), ARDS, atelectasis, bronchial intubation, consolidation, fibrosis, hemothorax, pleural effusion, pneumonia, pneumothorax, position change, pulmonary edema	**Thorax/diaphragm** Abdominal distension Ankylosing spondylitis Kyphoscoliosis Muscle tension Obesity	Improvement in disease state COPD (esp. emphysema) Flail chest Position change

Dynamic Compliance

Conditions Causing ↓ Cdyn	Conditions Causing ↑ Cdyn
↓Cstat (see above) ↑ Raw (see below)	↑ Cstat (see above) ↓ Raw (see below)

Airway Resistance Changes - Causes of

Conditions Causing ↑ Raw

Obstruction of Airway	Collapse of Airway
Condensation in circuit, epiglottis, ET tube (small diameter, plug, kinking, biting), foreign body aspiration, mucosal edema, post intubation swelling, secretions, tumors	Asthma, bronchospasm, bronchitis, bronchiolitis, emphysema, low lung volumes, laryngotracheobronchitis (croup), pneumothorax, pleural effusion, tumors
High $\dot{V}_I$ (turbulence)	

Conditions Causing ↓ Raw

Bronchodilator therapy
Improvement of an ↑ Raw
Suctioning
↓ $\dot{V}_I$

Definitions

Capnography: The continuous measurement and graphic display of CO_2 (FCO_2) at the airway opening

Capnogram: The graphic waveform

Capnometry: The measurement and display of $PetCO_2$ ($ETCO_2$)

Purpose

Monitor the elimination of CO_2 from the lungs

Indications:

Ventilation (elimination of CO_2 from the lungs)

Assess:

Immediate detection of apnea or respiratory crisis

RR and adequacy of ventilation in the critically ill, obtunded or unconscious, or seizing patients, and/or during procedural sedation and analgesia (detects Δ CO_2 before Δ in SpO_2)

Severity of asthma, COPD and acute respiratory distress and the response to treatment

Confirm:

Position of ET tube during intubation (considered the most reliable indicator)

Monitor:

ET tube position (watch for extubation) - useful during patient transport and/or repositioning

Hyper or hypoventilation :

- Use to avoid hyperventilation during CPR in trauma patients
- Use to titrate CO_2 levels in suspected ↑ ICP
- Recommended to achieve eucapnia during ventilation of trauma victims (Brain Trauma Foundation)

Circulation (transport of CO_2 to the lungs)

Assess:

Cardiac arrest (indicator of event and prognosis)

- Monitor effectiveness of CPR (reflection of CO)
- Earliest indicator of ROSC (↑ $ETCO_2$ often occurs before return of palpable pulse or BP) - virtually eliminates the need to stop compressions to check for a pulse.

Monitor:

↑ or ↓ CO (early warning sign of shock)

Hyper or hypotension, hyper or hypovolemia

Ventilation & Circulation (transfer of CO2 from blood to lungs)

Monitor: Prognosis of trauma victims
V/Q mismatch ***(deadspace)***

Metabolism (CO2 production)

Detect: Hyper or hypometabolism,
Metabolic acidosis in diabetic patients

Normal value

$PetCO_2$ = 35-45
< 35 = Hyperventilation / Hypocapnia
> 45 = Hypoventilation / Hypercapnia
Note: Trends are often more useful than single measurements

$PetCO_2$: Pressure of the end-tidal CO_2 at the airway
$Pa\text{-}etCO_2$: Gradient between $PaCO_2$ and $PetCO_2$

Description of End-Tidal CO_2:

- $PetCO_2$ represents alveolar PCO_2 ($PACO_2$)
- $PACO_2$ is determined by V/Q matching
- Normal 35-45 mmHg
- $PaCO_2$ > $PetCO_2$, P(a-et)CO2 is normally small (< 5 mmHg)
- Increase A-a gradient = higher $P(a\text{-}et)CO_2$
- Useful in detection of esophageal intubation ($PetCO_2$ = 0 mmHg)

Increased $PetCO_2$

Ventilation

- Hypoventilation (decreased RR and/or V_T) (altered mental status [drugs, overdose, sedation, stroke, trauma], bronchial intubation, bronchospasm, kinked ET tube, partial airway obstruction, ventilatory muscle fatigue)
- Rebreathing CO_2 or rapid shallow breathing

Circulation (increased perfusion of lungs)

- Increased CO or BP

Metabolism (increased CO_2 production)

- Hyperthermia (fever, sepsis, malignant hyperthermia)
- $NaHCO_3$ administration
- Pregnancy, ↑muscle activity (shivering, seizures, agitation)

Equipment errors

- Exhausted CO_2 absorber
- Inadequate fresh gas flow
- Breathing system leak
- Monitor, valve or ventilator malfunction

Decreased $PetCO_2$

Ventilation

- Hyperventilation (increased RR and/or V_T, anxiety, hypoxemia, pain)
- Absent ventilation (apnea, complete airway obstruction, esophageal intubation, extubation)

Circulation (decreased perfusion of lungs; ↑ deadspace)

- Cardiac arrest or decreased CO or BP
- Hypovolemia
- PEEP
- Pulmonary embolism

Metabolism (decreased CO_2 production)

- Hypothermia, sedation, sleep

Equipment errors

- Circuit disconnect or leak, sampling tube leak, monitor or ventilator malfunction

NORMAL WAVEFORMS

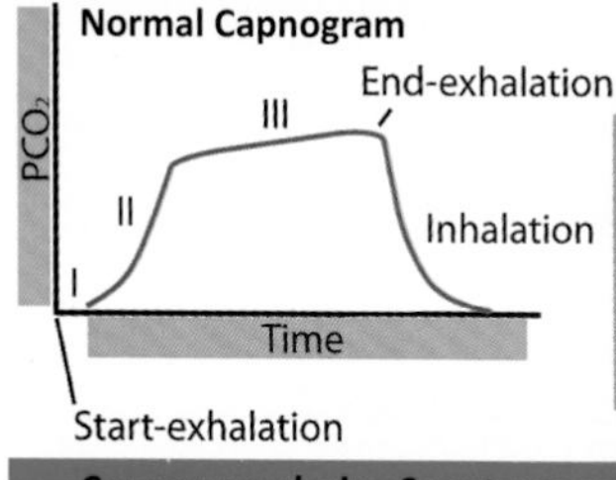

I: Anatomic Deadspace, $PetCO_2 = 0$
II: Alveolar and Deadspace gas mixing
III: Alveolar gas (Alveolar plateau)

Capnogram during Spontaneous Ventilation

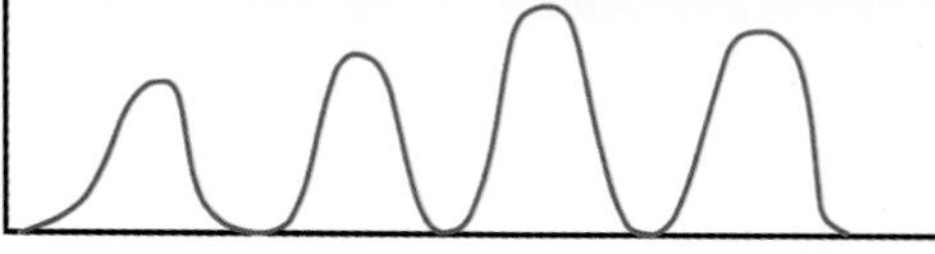

Capnogram during IMV

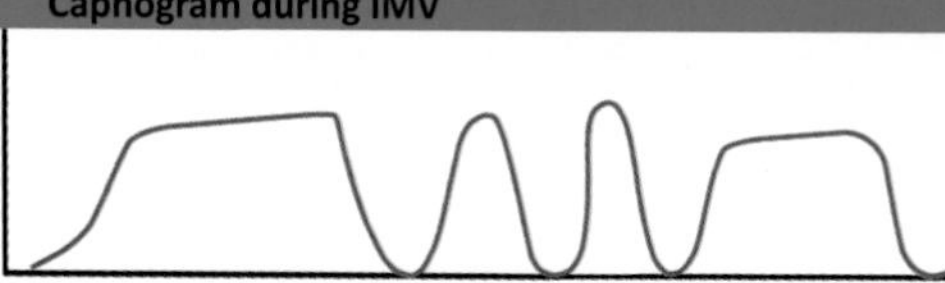

ABNORMAL WAVEFORMS

Spontaneous Breaths during a MV Breath

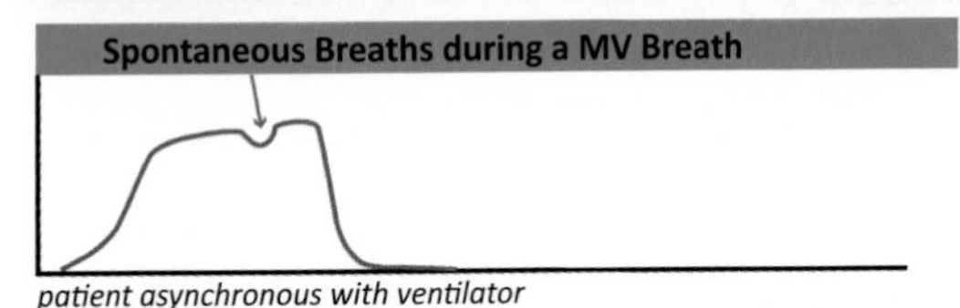

patient asynchronous with ventilator

Low $PetCO_2$ with Good Alveolar Plateau

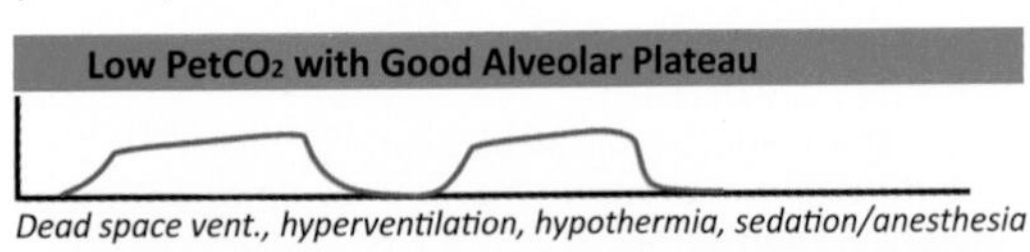

Dead space vent., hyperventilation, hypothermia, sedation/anesthesia

Elevated $PetCO_2$ with Good Alveolar Plateau

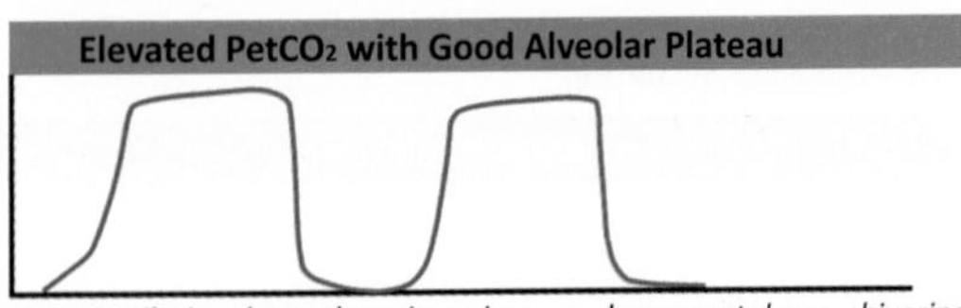

Hypoventilation, hyperthermia, pain, resp. depressant drugs, shivering

Sudden Loss of $PetCO_2$ to Zero or Near-Zero

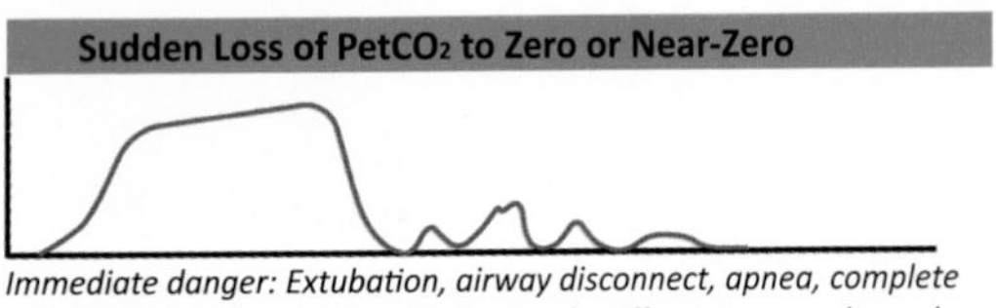

Immediate danger: Extubation, airway disconnect, apnea, complete airway or ET tube obstruction (kinked), cuff rupture, esophageal intubation, equipment malfunction (monitor, tubing, ventilator)

During CPR: cellular death during prolonged cardiac arrest, poor chest compressions

Exponential Decrease in $PetCO_2$

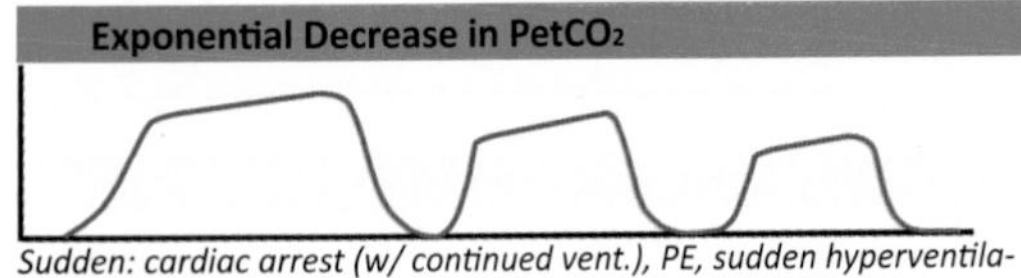

Sudden: cardiac arrest (w/ continued vent.), PE, sudden hyperventilation (changed MV setting), sudden hypotension (blood loss)

Gradual: ET tube in hypopharynx or right mainstem, leak in the airway, sampling to/around cuff, partial circuit disconnect, partial airway obstruct (secretions, spasm)

Exponential Increase in $PetCO_2$

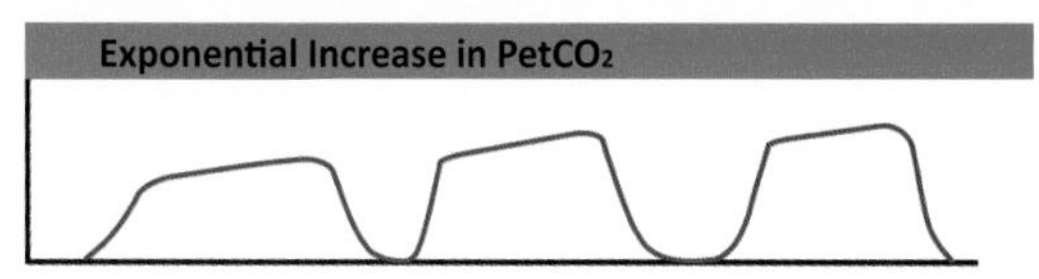

Hypermetabolic state, $NaCO^3$ administration, partial airway obstruction, sudden hypoventilation (changed MV settings), sudden increase in BP or body temperature

Loss of Alveolar Plateau

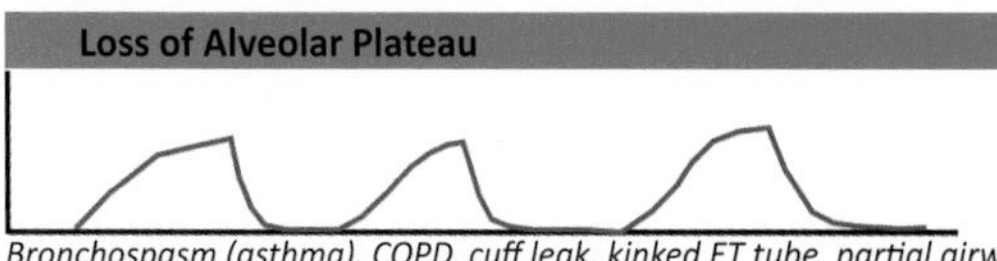

Bronchospasm (asthma), COPD, cuff leak, kinked ET tube, partial airway obstruction, late pregnancy

Note: In mild asthma, hyperventilation causes a decrease in $PetCO_2$. As the asthma attack worsens, $PetCO_2$ will rise to normal levels. When severe, $PetCO_2$ will increase above normal.

Exponential Increase in Baseline

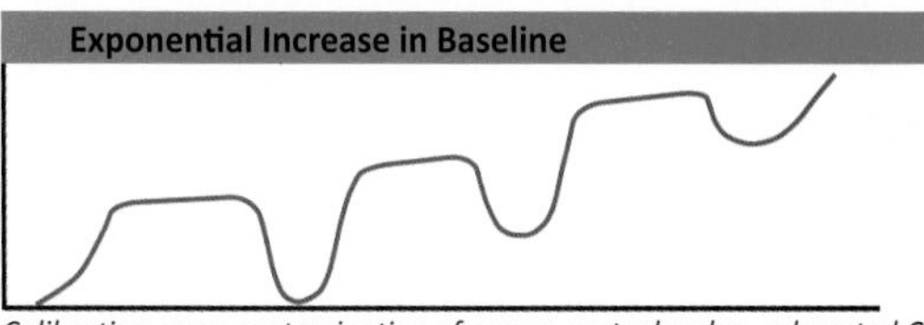

Calibration error, contamination of sensor or stuck valve, exhausted CO_2 absorber, rebreathing CO_2

Downward Slope of Alveolar Plateau

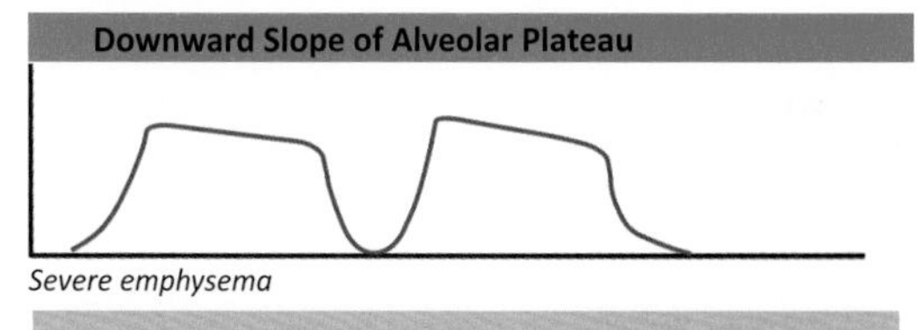

Severe emphysema

See AARC Clinical Practice Guideline, "Capnography/Capnometry during Mechanical Ventilation," in the Appendix

Cardiovascular Assessment

EKG PMI JVD Capillary Refill
Heart sounds and murmurs (see also vital signs)

(See Oakes ***Clinical Practitioner's Pocket Guide to Respiratory Care***, for a detailed references for bedside assessment of EKGs)

Hemodynamic Parameters:

Parameter	Normal	Parameter	Normal
CO	4-8 L/min	PAP:	
CI	2.5-4.4 L/min/m^2	PASP	15-25 mmHg
CVP	0-8 cmH_2O 0-6 mmHg	PADP	8-15 mmHg
		PAMP	10-15 mmHg
		PAWP	3-12 mmHg

A-Line, CVP, and PAP Monitoring
See Oakes' ***Hemodynamic Monitoring: A Bedside Reference Manual*** for a detailed reference guide for bedside hemodynamic assessment and monitoring.

Changes in PMI - Causes of

Intensity	Shift
↓ in COPD	Towards a lobar collapse Away from a tension pneumo or hydrothorax

For Changes in Hemodynamic Parameters in Various Disease States: See Oakes' ***Hemodynamic Monitoring: A Bedside Reference Manual***, for a detailed summary.

Neurological/Psychological Assessment

Check for:

- Mental/emotional status
- Motor activity (movement, posturing, pupil size/reactivity)
- Comfort/complaints

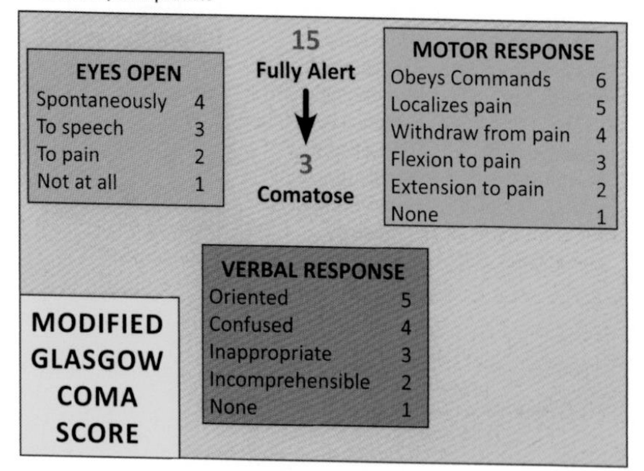

See Oakes' ***Neonatal/Pediatric Respiratory Care: A Critical Care Pocket Guide*** for scoring of infants and children.

Descriptive Terms for Level of Consciousness (LOC)

Alert: Awake, oriented and responds appropriately
Confusion: Inability to think clearly, impaired judgment
Disorientation: Beginning loss of consciousness, disoriented to time/place
Lethargic: Sleepy, arouses easily, responds appropriately
Obtunded: Awakens only with diff.; then responds appropriately
Stuporous: Does not completely awaken, responds only to deep pain, withdraws or pushes you away
Semicomatose: Responds only to deep pain, exhibits reflex
Comatose: No response, flaccid muscle tone

SEE also Chapter 12 – Drug Management for assessment of sedation levels

Patient Comfort / Psychology - Causes of Distress

Anxiety Depression Distended organs Drug response Emotional response to situation ET tube (pain/pulling) Fear of failure of ventilator Fear of future health and abilities	Fear of personnel and incompetence Helplessness Hopelessness/ despair Impending death Loneliness/isolation Loss of control of body functions Loss of privacy/ modesty Loss of speech and mobility	Pain response Poor oral hygiene Positioning Restraints Sleep deprivation Temperature (cold/hot) Thirst Total dependence on others Ventilation inadequate

Fluid and Electrolyte Assessment

Urine Output:

Average 1200 mL/day
male 900-1800
female 600-1600

Normal Electrolyte Values Affecting Ventilatory Muscles:

K^+ (3.5-5.0 mEq/L),
Mg^{++} (1.3-2.5 mEq/L),
$PO_4^{=}$ (1.4-2.7 mEq/L)

Fluid Balance Assessment

Fluid Excess	Fluid Deficit
↑body weight, ↑CO	↓body weight, ↓PAP, CVP, ↑HR ,
↑PAP, CVP	↑Hgb, Hct
↓Hgb, Hct	Poor peripheral pulse
Bounding pulse	Extremities:
Pulmonary edema	cool/pale & trunk: warm/dry
↑UO from overload	↑UO (diuresis)
↑UO (< 0.5 mL/kg/hr x 2 hr)	↓ capillary refill

Changes in Fluid Balance - Causes of

↑ Fluid (Hypervolemia)		↓ Fluid (Hypovolemia)	
↑ Intake	↓ Output	↓ Intake	↑ Output
Iatrogenic	↓ Renal perfusion:	Dehydration	Burns
	Heart failure	Starvation	Diarrhea
	PPV (↓CO, ↑ADH)		Diuresis
	Renal system	*Fluid shift:*	Hemorrhage
	malfunction	Burns, shock	Vomiting
	Blocked Foley		

Other Assessments

Auto-PEEP	See Chapter 11 – Ventilator Effects
Bedside PFTs	See Oakes' ***Clinical Practitioner's Pocket Guide***
Chest X-ray	See Oakes' ***Clinical Practitioner's Pocket Guide***
Lab Data	See Oakes' ***Clinical Practitioner's Pocket Guide***
Patient Position	See Chapter 8 – Ventilator Management
Response to Drug Therapy	See Chapter 12 – Drug Management
Sputum	See Oakes' ***Clinical Practitioner's Pocket Guide***

Airway Assessment
(See also Chapter 8 for Airway Management)

ET Tube Assessment

- Size
- Stability
- Date of Intubation
- Patency
- Presence/Need for bite block
- Cuff Pressure (20-25 mmHg)
- Condition of patient skin at contact
- Placement: cm mark @ mouth or nares (22-24 cm [men], 20-22 cm [women] at incisors), 4-6 cm above carina on CXR (T2-T4).

Endotracheal Tube (ET tube)

Equipment Sizes	ET Tube I.D.(mm)	Trach Tube	Blade	Mask	Sx Catheter (Fr)
Adult Male	8.5-9.5	6	3-4	4	16
Adult Female	8.0-8.5	5	3	4	14

See Oakes' ***Neonatal/Pediatric Respiratory Care: A Critical Care Pocket Guide*** for sizes for neonates and children.

Insertion:

Pulse oximetry and ECG should be monitored continuously during intubation of patient. Interrupt attempt if oxygenation/ventilation is needed.

Successful Intubation Checklist:

- Lungs: BS in both lungs (axilla), Bilateral chest expansion
- Abdomen: ↓ sounds in abdomen, No ↑ abdom. distention
- Warm air exhaled from tube
- Codensation inside of tube
- End Tidal CO_2
- Esophageal detector
- Improved color & SpO_2
- Light wand
- Visualization with scope
- CXR verification

Notes:

No one single confirmation technique is completely reliable, including H_2O vapor, except for direct visualization.

If any doubt: Use larynogoscope to visualize tube passing through vocal cords. If still doubt, remove tube.

Remove tube at once if hear stomach gurgling and see no chest expansion.

End-tidal CO_2 Detector ($P_{ET}CO_2$)

CO_2 detected: Tube is most likely in trachea*

*May rarely detect CO_2 if tube in esophagus and large amounts of carbonated fluid ingested prior. CO_2 will disappear after a few ventilations if in esophagus, it will continue if in trachea.

CO_2 not detected:

1) Tube is in esophagus
2) Tube may be in trachea
    - ↓ CO_2 **in** lungs: poor blood flow to lungs
        - Cardiac arrest
        - Pulmonary embolus
        - IV bolus of epinephrine
    - ↓ CO_2 **from** lungs:
        - Airway obstruction (eg., status asthmaticus)
        - Pulmonary edema

    Use another method to confirm (direct visualization or esophageal detector)
3) Detector contaminated with gastric contents or acidic drug (eg., tracheal admin. epinephrine)

Esophageal Detector Device

May use as one method of confirmation of ET tube placement.

Children: use only if child > 20 kg and has a perfusing rhythm

Caution: may be misleading in morbid obesity, late pregnancy, status asthmaticus, or copious secretions.

Artificial Airway Complications to Watch

Insertion	Cuff	Obstruction
Apnea Arrhythmias/↓BP Aspiration (gag reflex): vomitis, blood, tooth. Bronchospasm Laryngospasm Hypoxia (max 15 sec) Trauma (poor technique): hemorrhage, broken teeth, spinal cord damage. Vagal stimulation **Improper Position** Esophagus, pharynx, right mainstem, beveling at carina.	Leak: not enough air, tube to small, hole in cuff or balloon, ↑ tracheal diameter (malacia). Over-inflation: Necrosis (tracheomalacia), tracheal stenosis, fistula, vessel rupture, cuff herniation. **Improper Care** Contamination, desiccation, oral/nasal necrosis **Accidental Extubation**	Cuff herniation, kinking, secretions. **Body Response** Airway perforation, atelectasis, barotrauma, cord paralysis, edema, granulomas, pneumonia, sepsis, subglottic stenosis. **Additional Complications of Trach Tubes** Hemorrhage, infection, laryngeal nerve damage, pneumothorax, subQ emphysema.

Troubleshooting Airway Emergencies

Tube Obstruction

Signs/Symptoms:

Partial obstruction: ↓ BS and ↓ airflow

Complete obstruction: No BS or airflow, severe distress

If on PPV: ↓ V_T (PV) or ↑ PIP (VV)

Causes	Corrections
Orifice against tracheal wall	Try moving patient's head and neck
Kinking or biting tube	Correct kink or biting, consider a bite block
Mucus plugging	Attempt to pass suction catheter, remove inner cannula if present
Herniation of cuff over tip	Deflate cuff

When all else fails, extubate and reintubate!

Cuff Leak

Signs/Symptoms:

↓ BS and ↓ cuff pressures

If on PPV: ↓ V_T (VV) or ↓ PIP (PV) and feel airflow at mouth

Causes	Corrections
Slow leak: leak in valve or pilot balloon or tube	Reposition tube slightly Attempt to reinflate the cuff
Large leak: blown cuff	Replace tube

Accidental Extubation

Signs/Symptoms

↓ BS and ↓ airflow, no obstruction to passing catheter

If on PPV: ↓ V_T (VV) or ↓ PIP (PV) and feel airflow at mouth or into stomach

Correction: Remove tube, provide ventilatory support as needed, re-intubate with new tube.

Aspiration

Leakage of secretions past the cuff. Check via methylene blue test

T-E fistula Clinical signs – rushing abdominal sounds in synchrony with ventilator, ↑ tracheal secretions, coughing after eating/drinking, gastric distention, or pneumonia.

T-I fistula Clinical signs – visibly pulsating trach tube in synchrony w/ pulse rate, bleeding around trach site, or massive hemoptysis.

Management of Airway Emergencies[1] (AARC CPG)

Indications

Conditions requiring general airway management: airway compromise, protection, respiratory failure.

Conditions requiring emergency tracheal intubation, surgical placement or alternative techniques (see the AARC guideline for a list of numerous specific conditions).

Contraindications

Patient's documented desire not to be resuscitated.

Monitoring

Patient:

Clinical signs – airway obstruction (blood, foreign objects, secretions, vomitus), BS, chest movement, epigastric sounds, LOC, nasal flaring, retractions, skin color, upper airway sounds (snoring, stridor), ventilation ease.

Physiologic variables – ABG, pulse ox., CXR, $PeCO_2$, HR, rhythm, f, V_T, Paw.

Tube positioned in trachea:

Confirmed by – chest x-ray, endoscopic visualization, exhaled CO_2

Suggested by – BS (bilateral), chest movement (symmetrical), condensate upon exhalation, epigastrium (absence of ventilation sounds), esophageal detector devices, visualization of passage through vocal cords.

Precautions/Hazards/ Complications

Emergency Ventilation:

barotrauma, gastric insufflation/rupture, hypo/hyper ventilation, hypotension, O_2 delivery (inadequate), unstable cervical spine, upper airway obstruction, ventilation (prolonged interruption), vomiting, aspiration.

Trans-Laryngeal intubation, Cricothyroidotomy:

Aspiration, bronchospasm, laryngospasm, bradycardia, tachycardia, dysrhythmia, hypo/hypertension.

ET tube problems –

Cuff herniation, perforation, extubation (inadvertent), pilot tube valve incompetence, size inappropriate, tube kinking, occlusion.

Failure to establish patient airway, intubate the trachea

Intubation of bronchi, esophagus

Pneumonia

Trauma – airway, cervical spine, dental, esophagus, eye, nasal, needle cricothyroidotomy (bleeding, esophageal perforation, subcutaneous emphysema), vocal cords.

Ulceration, stenosis, malacia

1) Adapted from the AARC Clinical Practice Guidelines: Management of Airway Emergencies, ***Respiratory Care***, Volume 40, #7, 1995.

Suctioning

Notes:

Natural coughing is the most desirable method of clearing secretions. Manually assisted coughing or mechanical cough assist (see Lung Expansion Therapy, this Chapter) may reduce the need for suctioning.

Routine and frequent suctioning is not recommended. Suction catheters traumatize the airway mucosa potentially increasing secretion production, may cause hypoxemia and/or cardiac arrhythmias, possible atelectasis, as well as the risk of infection.

When suctioning is necessary, perform as gently as possible, keeping the catheter within the tube, if possible.

If suctioning beyond the tube tip is necessary, the catheter should be advanced gently and suction applied only during catheter withdrawal, with suction being applied for no more than 15 sec.

Use the lowest suction pressure possible to obtain the desired result. If suction catheter becomes clogged, quickly clear out obstruction, do not increase suction.

Indications/Need	
Evidence of Secretions	**Alterations in Patient and/or Ventilation**
Visible secretions in tube Audible course, wet, +/or ↓ BS Palpation of wet, course vibrations through chest wall	Patient: ↑ agitation, irritability, restless Ventilator: ↑ Raw VV: ↑ PIP and ↑ high pressure alarms PV: ↓ VT
Alterations in Vital Signs	**Alterations in O_2 and Ventilation**
Change in respiratory pattern: ↑ WOB, tachypnea, retractions Change in cardiac pattern: ↑ or ↓ HR	↓ SpO_2 (< 90%) Skin color changes – pale, dusky, or cyanotic Changes in ABGs - ↑ $PaCO_2$, ↓ PaO_2, respiratory acidosis

Suction Pressures/Catheter Sizes

Suction Pressures	Suction Catheter Size
Adult -100 to –120 mm Hg Child -80 to –100 mm Hg Infant -60 to –80 mm Hg	ET tube size (ID) x 2, then use next smaller size suction catheter E.g.; 6.0 x 2 = 12, use 10 FR

See AARC Clinical Practice Guideline, "Endotracheal Suctioning of Mechanically Ventilated Adults and Children," in the Appendix

Ventilator Assessment

Ventilator Settings		Ventilator Circuit
Orders:	**Sensitivity**:	**Humidifier**:
Settings consistent with orders?	Pressure threshold	Temperature (set, measured)
Verification of changes	Flow threshold	Water level
Current Settings	Patient triggering	
Mode and breath type	Auto-triggering	**Tubing**:
	Times:	Circuit temperature
Oxygenation:	T_I	Condensate
F_IO_2 (set, analyzed)	T_E	Clean, secure
	I/E	Tension on ET tube
Volumes:		Tubing compliance
V_T (set, delivered, expired)	**Flows**:	Last circuit change
V_T (spont)	$\dot{V}_I$	
$\dot{V}_E$ mach (set, delivered)	$\dot{V}_I$ waveform	
$\dot{V}_E$ spont	$\dot{V}_I$ continuous	***Ventilator Circuit Changes*** (see AARC CPG 1994)
$\dot{V}_E$ total		
	Sighs:	
Rate:	Volume	**Other**
f (set, delivered)	Rate	**Location and condition of**:
f (spont)	Frequency	Manual resuscitator with mask, tubing, and flow-meter
		Suction equipment
Pressures:	**Alarms** (set & functioning):	Chest tube apparatus
PIP (Ppeak)	High $\dot{V}_E$	
Pplat (Palv)	Low $\dot{V}_E$	
PTA (PIP – Pplat)	High V_T	
$\bar{P}aw$	Low V_T	
PEEP (set, auto)	High P/L	
CPAP	Low P/L	
PS level	Low PEEP/CPAP	
Pressure limits	F_IO_2	

Ventilator Graphics (See Chapter 6)

Patient-Ventilator System Check (See AARC CPG in Appendix)

Changes in Ventilator Parameters

Changes in Tidal Volume

↓ Inspired Tidal Volume	↑ Inspired Tidal Volume
VV: If corresponding ↓ in PIP: see PIP (↓) If not a corresponding ↓ in PIP = altered settings *PV*: Above, plus ↓ C or ↑ Raw	*VV*: If corresponding ↑ in PIP: see PIP (↑) If not a corresponding ↑ in PIP =altered settings *PV*: Above, plus ↑C or ↓ Raw

↓ Expired Tidal Volume	↑ Expired Tidal Volume
VV: If corresponding ↓ in PIP: See PIP ↓ If not a corresponding ↓ in PIP: Leak in spirometer, between exhalation valve and spirometer/transducer, or from chest tube Malfunction of transducer *PV*: Above, plus ↓ C, ↑ Raw, or ↑ auto-PEEP	*VV*: If corresponding ↑ in PIP: see PIP ↑ If not a corresponding ↑ in PIP = Transducer malfunction External nebulizer flow *PV*: Above, plus ↑C, ↓ Raw, or ↓ auto-PEEP

Changes in Minute Volume

↓or ↑ Minute Volume
Same as ↓ or↑ V_T (above) with the added effect of rate changes.

Changes in Rate (↑/↓ or Apnea)

Machine	Patient
Altered settings Inappropriate sensitivity Malfunction/disconnection	See changes in Vital Signs (above) Patient disconnection from ventilator (↓ or apnea)

Changes in Pressures

Slow Rise of Needle on Pressure Gauge to PIP	Slow Return of Needle on Pressure Gauge to Baseline
Leak	Exhalation tubing or exhalation valve tubing kinked Sticky exhalation valve Expiratory resistance or inflation hold on

↓ PEEP/CPAP		↑ PEEP/CPAP	
Machine	*Patient*	*Machine*	*Patient*
Altered settings ↓ expiratory flow Proximal Paw line occluded	↑ patient inspiratory flowrate	Altered settings ↑ expiratory flow	Auto-PEEP Patient-ventilator asynchrony (see below)

↓ PIP	↑ PIP
Machine: Altered settings Internal leak/power or gas source failure **Circuit**: Disconnection Leak (see below) Proximal Paw line occluded **Patient**: *CL* ↑: improved lung, position change *Raw* ↓: ↓ secretions or bronchospasm Patient-ventilator asynchrony (see below) *Leak at:* ET tube (displaced in pharynx or esophagus) Cuff (deflation/rupture/leak or inadequate inflation) Chest tube T-E fistula	**Machine**: Altered settings Blocked exhalation Internal problem Malfunctioning I or E valves **Circuit**: Tubing kinked H_2O in circuit **Patient**: Auto-PEEP *CL* ↓: abdominal distension, ARDS, atelectasis, hemothorax, pleural effusion, pneumonia, pneumothorax, position change, pulmonary edema *Raw* ↑: bronchospasm, cough, edema, ET tube displaced (in RT mainstem, against carina), kinked, or bitten, ET tube cuff herniation, H_2O in circuit, secretions or mucous plugs. Patient-ventilator asynchrony

Checking for Leaks

1. ***Check Patient***

   Remove patient from ventilator and manually ventilate.
   Listen to breath sounds over trachea.
   ET tube cuff inflated? (see page 5-31).

2. ***Check Ventilator:***

   Obstruct patient wye and manually cycle the ventilator.
   If the high pressure alarm fails to activate, then obstruct the patient circuit at various places starting at the ventilator and working distal to find the leak (until the alarm does not activate).

I:E Ratio (↑ or ↓)

Machine	Patient
Altered settings	Pressure cycling off (↑Raw)
Too sensitive or subtle leak	Fighting the vent

Loss of Power or Low Gas Source - Check:

Electrical power supply:	*Gas supply:*
Power switch on Connection to outlet/battery Fuse/circuit breaker Reset button	50 psi wall connection or air compressor High pressure hose connections (patency of high pressure hoses; not crushed by bed wheels)

Ventilator Inoperative: Turn ventilator off and reset

Operator Settings Incompatible with Machine Parameters: Usually I:E related

I:E Ratio Alarm

Usually I:E > 1:1 (correct settings)
If desired, check flowrate (VV)

F_IO_2 Error

Analyzer: uncalibrated or defective
Blender: source gas failure, tubing kinked, leak or disconnect

Patient-Ventilator Asynchrony ("Fighting the Vent")*

* See Ventilator Management, Chapter 8, for corrective actions

Potential Causes

Machine:

1) Triggering too sensitive
2) ↑ patient WOB:
   - Inadequate $\dot{V}_I$
   - Level of ventilator support inadequate
   - Prolonged T_I (VV) or flow cycle (PV)
   - Triggering too insensitive (setting or demand valve)
   - ↑ $\dot{V}_I$ resistance:
     - Bubble humidifier or water-laden HME
     - ET tube resistance (too small, kinks, secretions)
     - ↑ $\dot{V}_E$ (PEEP valve resistance)

Patient: Auto-PEEP, ↑ patient ventilatory drive, anxiety/stress (see also page 5-8).

Assess/Troubleshoot

6 Ventilator Graphics: Waveform Analysis

Chapter Contents

(Continued on Next Page)

Definition
Waveforms are graphic representations of data collected by the ventilator that reflect patient-ventilator interaction.

Purpose (Indications)

Patient

- Monitor patient's disease pathology (C + Raw)
- Calculate respiratory mechanics (C + Raw)
- Assess patient's response to therapy (e.g., bronchodilators)

Ventilator

- Monitor ventilator function
- Fine tune ventilator parameters and modes to:
  - o Improve patient comfort
  - o Decrease WOB
  - o Optimize ventilation

Patient-Ventilator Interaction

Interpret, evaluate, and troubleshoot patient's response to the ventilator

Clinical Note:

When analyzing graphic waveforms, it is important to first look at the parameters and the scaling of each parameter. It is imperative that the mode is identified. A graphic that appears to be abnormal could be normal depending on the mode and breath type.

Each graphic waveform is idealized. There are a myriad of variations seen in the clinical setting (far beyond the scope of this book).

The goal in understanding and interpreting graphics is not to memorize shapes, but rather to understand how they are created and how they are affected by variables.

See the Equation of Motion: Chapter 4

Types Of Graphic Waveforms

Scalars – Graphic displays of **pressure, volume**, and **flow** over time.

Loops – Graphic displays of two parameters (**Pressure and Volume** or **Flow and Volume**) on a horizontal (x) axis and a vertical (y) axis. Time is not depicted on loops.

Scalars

Pressure -Time Waveform

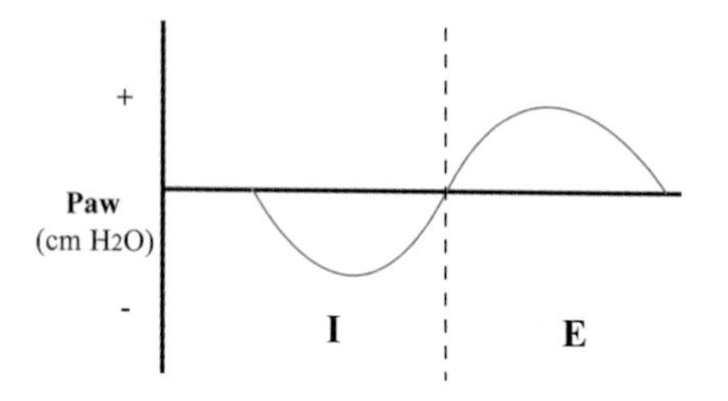

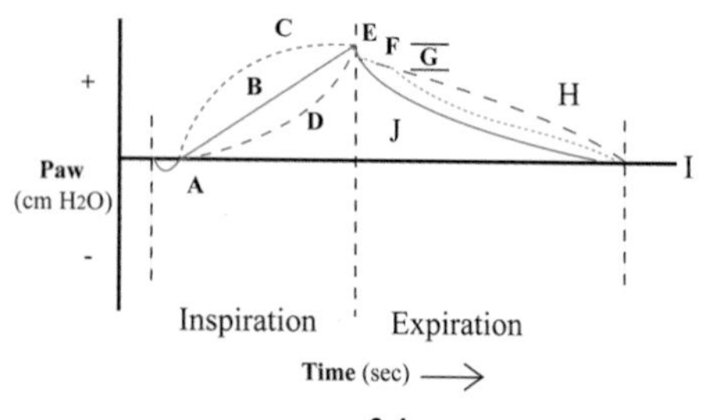

A No negative deflection = machine-triggered (MT) breath (controlled)

Negative deflection = patient-triggered (PT) breath (assisted)

The greater the depth and time below baseline, the greater the patient effort required to trigger the ventilator.

Flow-triggering (flow-by) will virtually eliminate patient effort, resulting in less negative deflection.

B Square wave inspiratory flow pattern

The steeper the slope, the greater the $\dot{V}_I$

C Decelerating inspiratory flow pattern

D Sine wave inspiratory flow pattern

E Peak inspiratory pressure (Ppeak)

Ppeak may rise to a plateau when a breath is pressure-controlled (limited) or pressure-supported. This Ppeak pressure plateau is not to be confused with Pplat.

Used to calculate Cdyn.

F Plateau pressure (Pplat)

Results from an inspiratory hold

Used to calculate Cstat

G Ppeak - Pplat = Raw (Raw is flow dependent)

Pressure required to overcome resistance of airway and ET tube.

H Expiratory retard

Analogous to pursed-lip breathing

May be patient-induced (e.g., COPD) or machine-induced (rarely done)

I Baseline pressure (beginning and end-expiratory pressure)

ZEEP – zero (atmospheric)

PEEP – positive (above zero)

NEEP – negative (below zero) (caution—indicates an abnormal pressure gradient)

Failure of the pressure curve to return to the set baseline pressure before the next inspiration = inadequate TE and may result in air-trapping and auto-PEEP

J Area under the entire curve, including any PEEP, is ≈ average $\overline{P}aw$.

Applications – Pressure-time waveforms are used to analyze:

Patient	Ventilator	Pt-Vent Interaction
• Air-trapping (auto-PEEP) • Airway obstruction • Active exhalation • Bronchodilator response • Respiratory mechanics (C + Raw)	• Breath type • Ppeak • Pplat • PEEP/CPAP • $\dot{V}_I$ • Pressure waveform shape • T_I, T_E, I:E	• Asynchrony • Triggering effort

Volume-Time Waveform

Spontaneous breath:

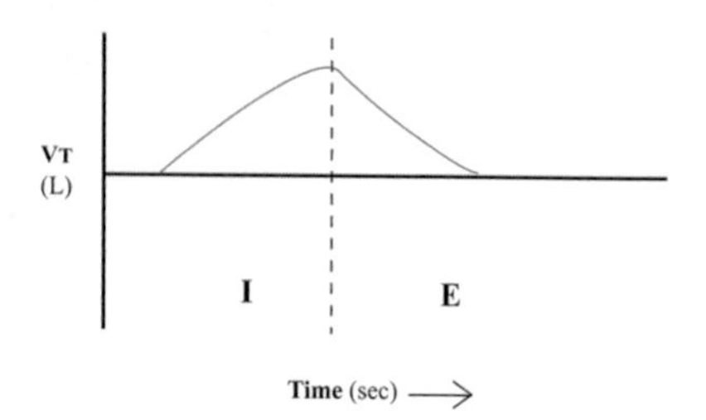

Ventilator breath:

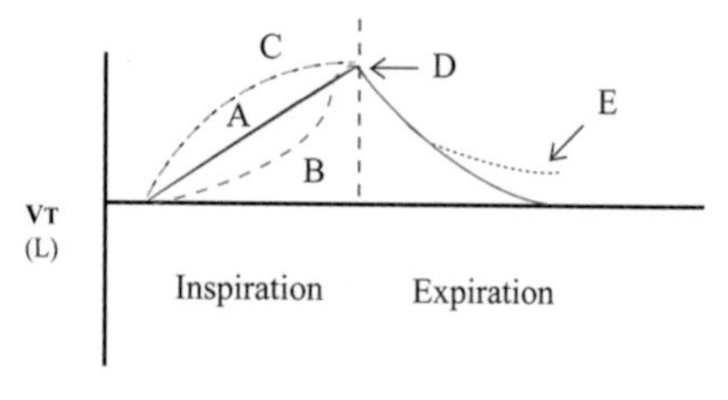

A Square wave inspiratory flow pattern
B Sine wave inspiratory flow pattern
C Decelerating inspiratory flow pattern (or pressure-supported breath)
D Inspiratory V_T (a plateau at this peak of the curve may indicate pressure-controlled or supported breath)
E An exhalation curve that does not return to baseline may indicate leak or air-trapping

Application – Volume-Time waveforms are used to analyze:

Patient	Ventilator	Pt-Vent Interaction
• Air-trapping (auto-PEEP) • Active exhalation	• Breath type • Volume waveform shape • V_T • $\dot{V}_I$ • Leaks	• Asynchrony

Flow-Time Waveform

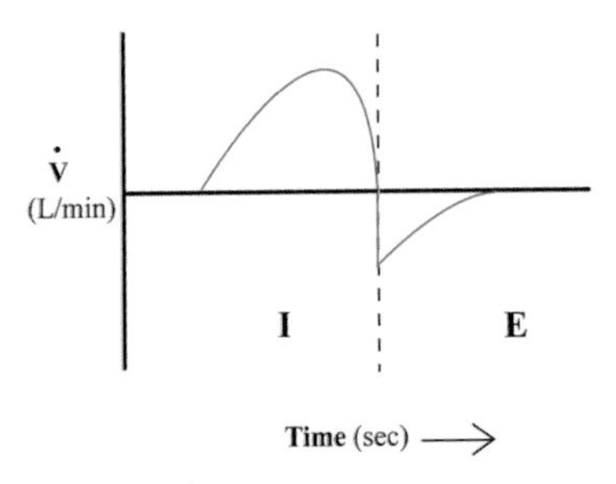

Ventilator Breaths

Ventilator breaths:

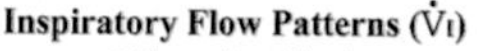

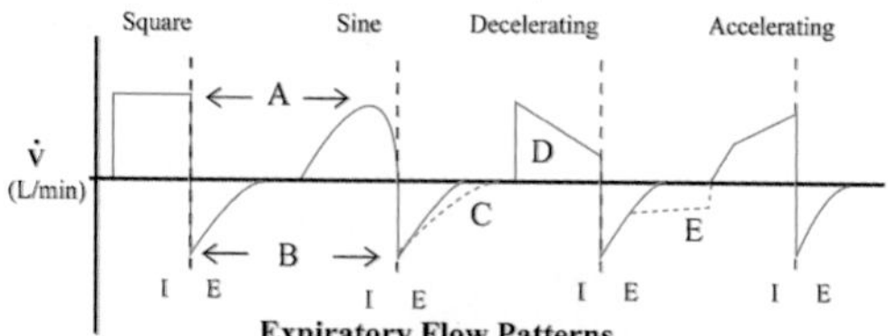

Expiratory Flow Patterns
(Below baseline)
Time (sec) ⟶

A	Peak inspiratory flow (set $\dot{V}_I$)
B	Peak expiratory flow
C	Expiratory retard— Increased resistance to expiratory flow (see H under pressure-time curve)
B&C	May be used to analyze response to bronchodilator therapy
D	Pressure-control and supported breaths have a decelerating flow pattern
E	Expiratory flow patterns have one basic shape and should return to baseline(zero flow) indicating a complete exhalation. Expiratory flow that does not return to zero prior to the next inspiration, indicates inadequate T_E, resulting in air-trapping and auto-PEEP. (The higher the end-expiratory flow, the greater the auto-PEEP) An expiratory flow that returns to above the baseline indicates a leak during flow-by.

Applications – Flow-Time waveforms are used to analyze:

Patient	Ventilator	Pt-Vent Interaction
• Air-trapping (auto-PEEP) • Airway obstruction • Active exhalation • Bronchodilator response • Respiratory mechanics (C + Raw)	• Breath type • Flow waveform shape • Inspiratory flow • Flow starvation (VV) • Adjustment of inspiratory time in PV • Adjustment of rise to pressure time in PV • Leaks	• Asynchrony • Triggering effort

Loops

Volume-Pressure Loop

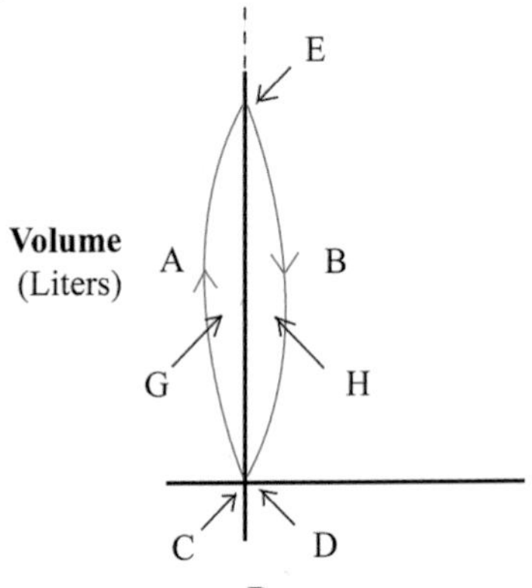

Ventilator Breath (Volume Ventilation)

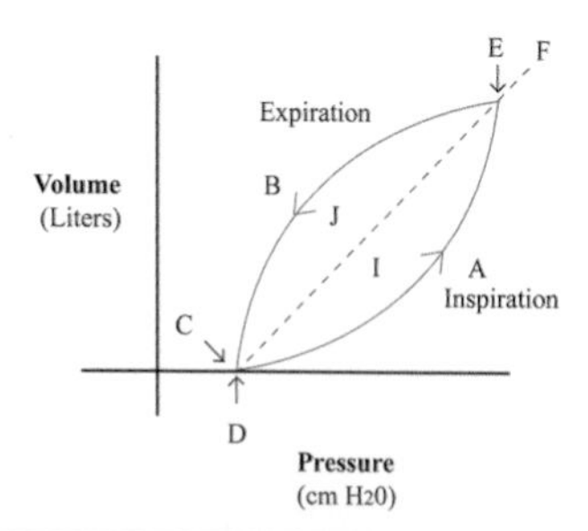

A Inspiratory curve (upward)

B Expiratory curve (downward)

Note: Spontaneous breaths go clockwise; positive pressure breaths always go counter clockwise.

C The bottom point of the loop:

Inspiration begins and expiration ends

D Point on pressure axis where inspiration (I) begins and expiration (E) ends (indicates end-expiratory pressure level)

E The upper point of the loop:

1) Inspiration ends and expiration begins
2) Point of maximal pressure and volume
3) Dynamic compliance ($\Delta V/\Delta P$)

F The imaginary (dashed) line between the 2 points (C & E), (begin I & end I) depicts the slope of the loop.

The slope is indicative of the patient's dynamic compliance ($\Delta V/\Delta P$)

G The area to the left of the vertical line represents patient inspiratory WOB (inspiratory resistance)

H The area to the right of the vertical axis represents patient expiratory WOB (expiratory resistance)

I The area of the curve to the right of the slope line depicts the ventilator WOB required to overcome Raw. (↑ area = ↑ work)

WOB = amount of pressure required to move a certain volume

J The area of the curve to the left of the slope line depicts the WOB required to overcome C_{RS}

Total WOB = area I and area J (↑ area = ↑ work)

Note: These areas show only the mechanical WOB by the ventilator and are only accurate if the patient is not contributing any WOB. Patient WOB can be measured indirectly by plotting the esophageal pressure.

Applications – Volume - Pressure loops are used to analyze:

Patient	Ventilator	Pt-Vent Interaction
• Airway obstruction • Active exhalation • Bronchodilator response • Lung over-distension • Respiratory mechanics • (Cdyn + Raw) • WOB	• Adjusting pressure support levels • Flow starvation (VV) • Leaks	• Triggering effort

Flow-Volume Loop

Spontaneous breath:

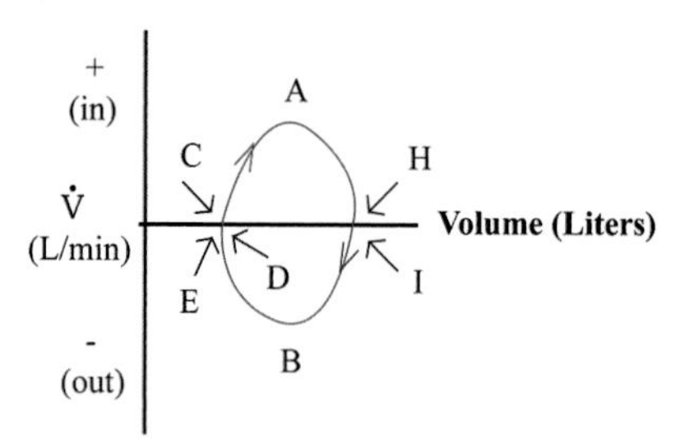

Ventilator breath:
(Volume Ventilation)

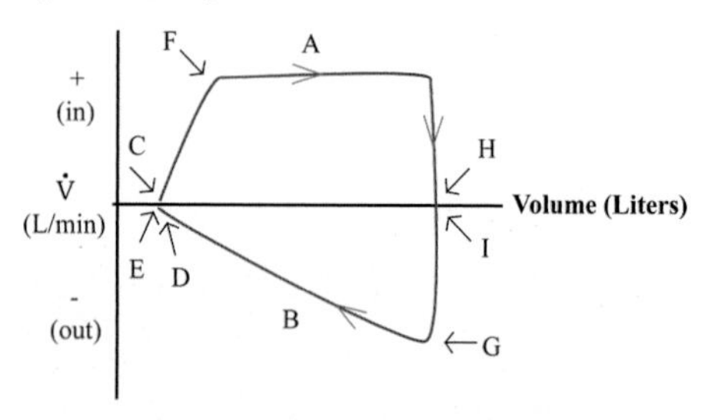

A Inspiratory curve (above the horizontal axis)
On the ventilator breath, the shape of the inspiratory curve will reflect the flow pattern set on the ventilator.

B Expiratory curve (below the horizontal axis)
The shape of the expiratory curve will reflect patient exhalation (usually passive).

C Begin inspiration

D End expiration

E Point on volume axis where I begins and E ends. This indicates end-expiratory pressure level.
Note: C, D, and E should all be the same point. (See abnormal waveforms if not)

F	Peak inspiratory flow rate ($\dot{V}_I$)
G	Peak expiratory flow rate
H	Point on volume axis of maximum V_T and end I (flow rate 0)
I	Begin E
	Note: H and I should be the same point. (See abnormal waveforms if not)

* **Note**:

Pulmonary function flow-volume loops (depicting FVC) traditionally display the inspiratory curve below the horizontal axis and expiration above the axis.

Ventilator flow-volume loops (depicting V_T) most commonly display the inspiratory curve above the horizontal axis and expiration below the axis (to maintain consistency with scalars).

There is, however, no set convention and some ventilators will display the loops like pulmonary function loops. When reading F-V loops, be certain to properly identify the orientation.

This book will display all loops with the inspiratory curve above the axis.

Applications – Flow-volume loops are used to analyze:

Patient	Ventilator	Pt-Vent Interaction
• Air-trapping (auto-PEEP) • Airway obstruction • Airway resistance changes • Active exhalation • Bronchodilator response	• Inspiratory flow • Expiratory flow • Flow starvation (VV) • V_T • Leaks • Water and secretions buildup	• Asynchrony

Normal Graphic Waveforms by Waveform Type

Scalars: Pressure-Time

Spontaneous Ventilation During I, pressure is a negative deflection. During E, pressure is a positive deflection. Pressures are generally much lower than with ventilator breaths. I to E is patient-cycled	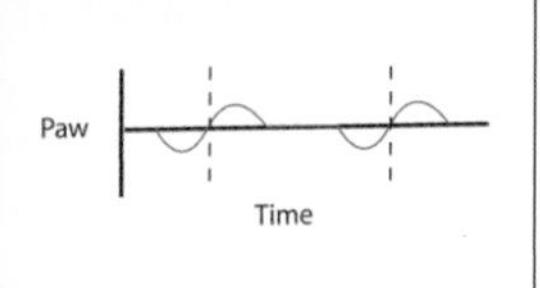

Volume Ventilation – Assist/Control (constant or square flow) The pressure curve generally shows a linear rise to Ppeak. Ppeak is dependent on V_T, $\dot{V}_I$, PEEP, C, and Raw. 1st breath is assisted (patient-triggered). 2nd breath is controlled (machine-triggered). I to E is volume-cycled.	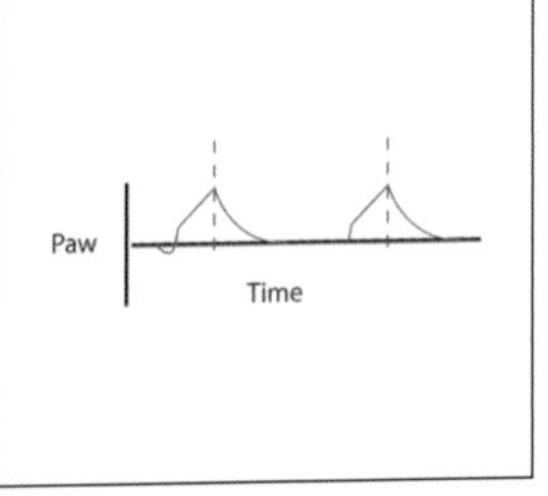

Clinical note: The pressure-time curve is the only scalar that identifies an assisted breath. The depth of deflection and the period of time below the baseline reflect the degree of patient effort to trigger the ventilator. Flow-triggering virtually eliminates all of the patient effort of triggering.

Volume Ventilation – Assist/Control (decelerating flow) Same as square flow (above), except that the upward slope to Ppeak is usually convex.	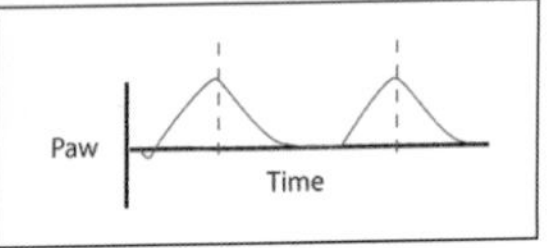

SIMV (square flow) A combination of assisted VV and spontaneous ventilation.	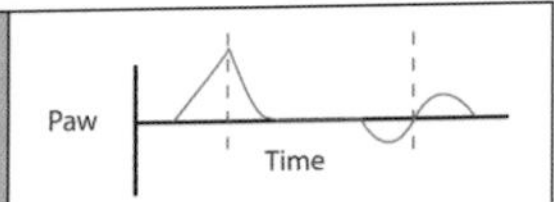

Pressure Ventilation – Assist/ Control

The pressure curve generally shows an immediate rise to Ppeak (set pressure), which is then maintained during the entire inspiratory phase. The speed (slope) in which set pressure is reached is dependent on the ventilator (See rise to pressure time, Chapter 2, Operating Principles). Patient C and Raw generally do not affect the shape of the waveform.

1st breath is assisted (patient-triggered).

2nd breath is controlled (machine-triggered).

I to E is time-cycled (hence T_I is constant).

Clinical note: Ppeak = Pplat, provided there is zero flow at end-inspiration.

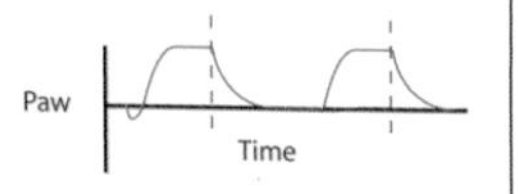

Pressure Support Ventilation Similar to PV (above), with the following differences:

1) Ppeak is usually lower (unless PSmax is set)
2) Every breath is an assisted breath
3) I to E is flow-cycled (hence T_I may vary between breaths)

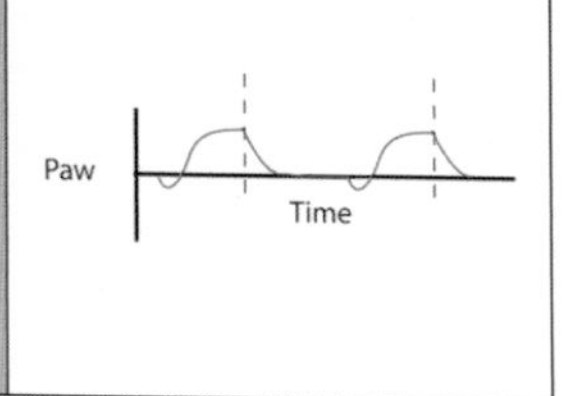

Scalars: Volume-Time

Spontaneous Ventilation The volume achieved is dependent on patient effort, C, and Raw. The rise to achieved volume is generally sinusoidal. I to E is patient-cycled	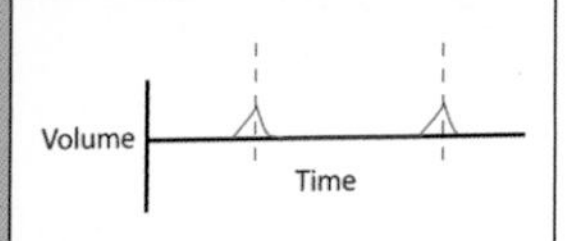
Volume Ventilation – Assist/ Control (constant or square flow) The volume delivered is determined by the set volume. The rise to delivered V_T is linear. 1st breath is assisted (patient-triggered). 2nd breath is controlled (machine-triggered). I to E is volume-cycled.	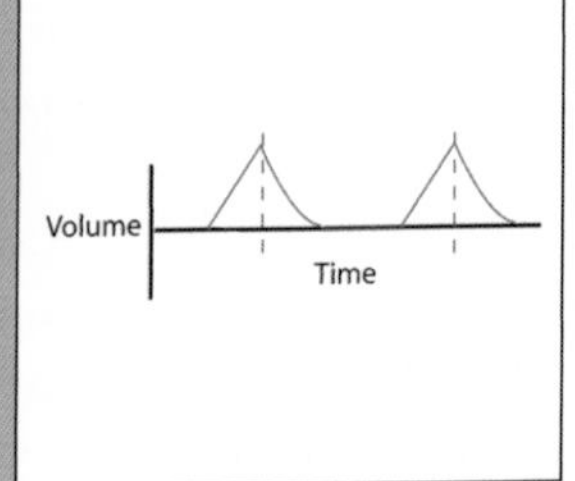
Volume Ventilation – Assist/ Control (decelerating flow) Same as square flow (above), except that the rise to delivered V_T is usually convex.	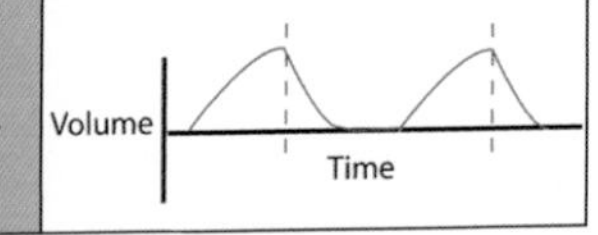
SIMV (constant or square flow) A combination of assisted VV and spontaneous ventilation.	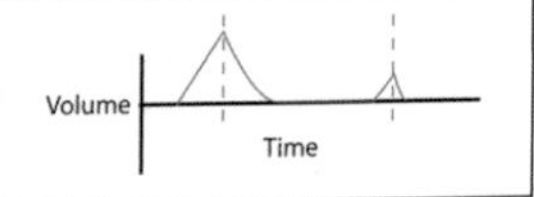

Pressure Ventilation – Assist/ Control The volume delivered is determined by the set pressure level, C, and Raw of the lungs. The rise to deliver the V_T is generally initially rapid, followed by a decrease, and finally a plateau. 1st breath is assisted (patient-triggered). 2nd breath is controlled (machine-triggered). I to E is time-cycled (hence T_I is constant).	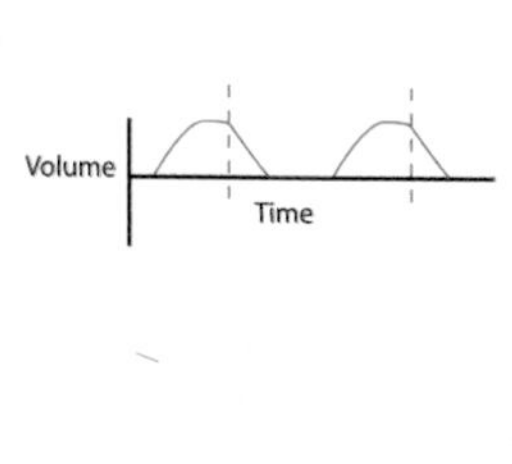

Pressure Support Ventilation Similar to PV (above), with the following differences: 1) The delivered volume (plateau) is usually lower (unless PSmax is set) 2) The delivered volume is dependent on: a) Set pressure support level b) Patient effort, C, and Raw 3) Every breath is an assisted breath 4) I to E is flow-cycled (hence T_I may vary between breaths)	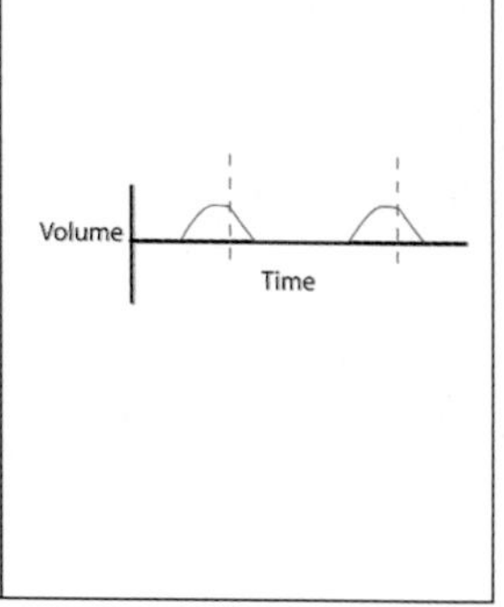

Scalars: Flow-Time

Spontaneous Ventilation
The inspiratory curve is usually sinusoidal in shape, but highly variable, depending on patient effort. Peak flows are generally much lower than with ventilator breaths. I to E is patient-cycled

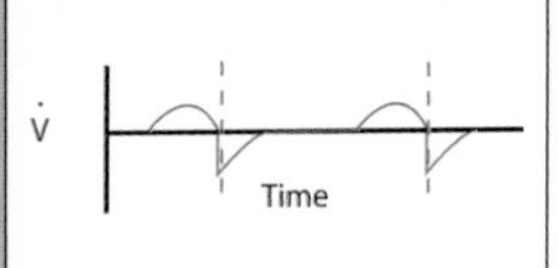

Volume Ventilation – Assist/ Control (constant or square flow)
Flow reaches a maximum at the beginning of I and continues at that maximum during the entire inspiratory phase. 1st breath is assisted (patient-triggered).
2nd breath is controlled (machine-triggered). I to E is volume-cycled.

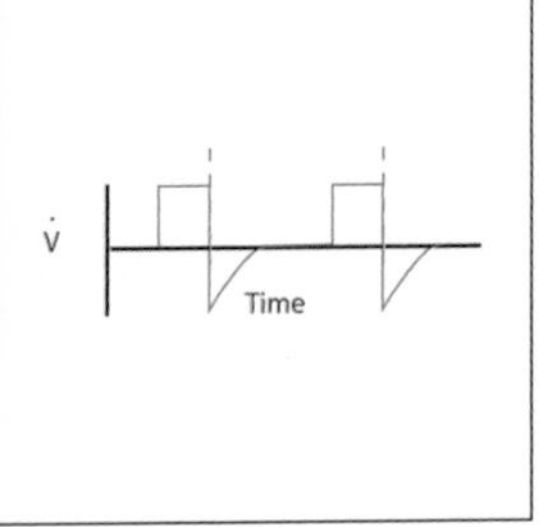

Volume Ventilation – Assist/ Control (decelerating flow)
Same as square flow (above), except that inspiratory flow decelerates during the inspiratory phase. Since I to E is volume-cycled, flow may or may not reach zero before end-inspiration.

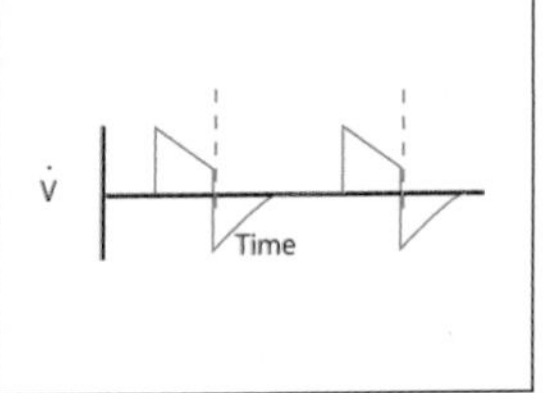

SIMV (square flow)
A combination of assisted VV and spontaneous ventilation.

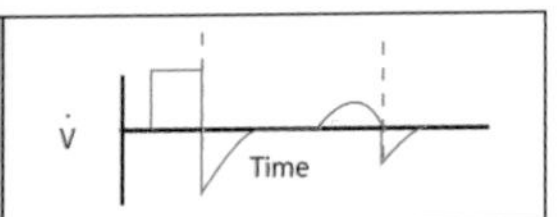

Pressure Ventilation – Assist/ Control	
Inspiratory flow reaches a maximum at the beginning of I and then decelerates during the inspiratory phase. Flow is variable depending on patient's C and Raw. 1st breath is assisted (patient-triggered). 2nd breath is controlled (machine-triggered). I to E is time-cycled (hence T_I is constant). Since I to E is time-cycled, flow may or may not reach zero before end-inspiration. If flow does not reach zero, T_I may be too short.	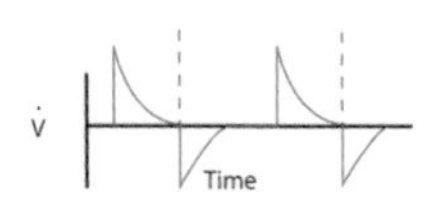

Pressure Support Ventilation	
Inspiratory flow reaches a maximum at the beginning of I and then decelerates during the inspiratory phase. Flow is variable depending on patient's C and Raw. Every breath is an assisted breath. I to E is flow-cycled (hence T_I may vary between breaths). I terminates when $\dot{V}_I$ decreases to a ventilator determined flow (usually 25% of peak flow) (flow never reaches zero) ***Clinical note***: the Flow-Time waveform is the best way to identify a PS breath.	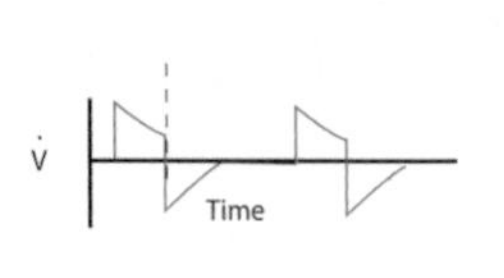

Loops: Volume-Pressure

Spontaneous Ventilation

The loop is clockwise in spontaneous breathing. The inspiratory curve is generally to the left of baseline pressure (vertical axis) due to negative pressure during inspiration. (Negative if ZEEP, less positive if CPAP). The expiratory curve is generally to the right of the baseline pressure due to positive expiratory pressure. The area to the left of the vertical axis represents patient inspiratory WOB (inspiratory resistance). The area to the right of the vertical axis represents patient expiratory WOB (expiratory resistance).

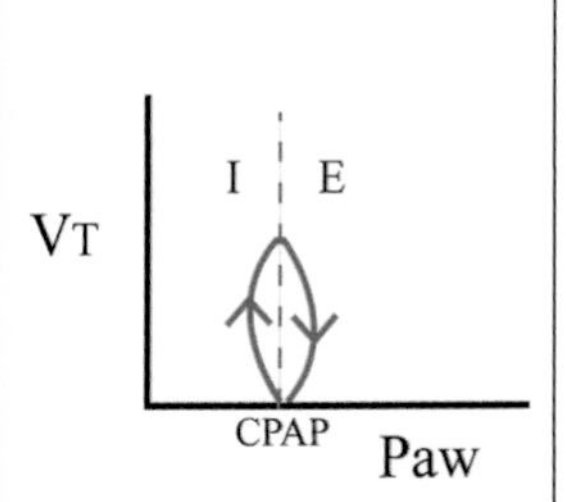

Volume Ventilation – Assist/ Control (constant or square flow)

The loop is counter-clockwise in positive pressure ventilation.

1st breath is assisted (patient-triggered). 2nd breath is controlled (machine-triggered).

During an assisted breath, the inspiratory area to the left of the vertical axis represents the patient WOB required to initiate inspiration. The greater the area, the greater the WOB imposed by the ventilator. Flow-by virtually eliminates imposed WOB. (See enlargement)

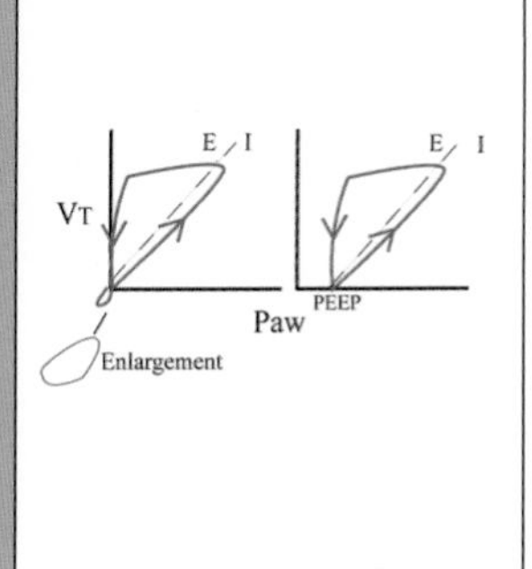

Volume Ventilation – Assist/ Control (decelerating flow) Same as square flow (above), except the inspiratory limb is more convex.	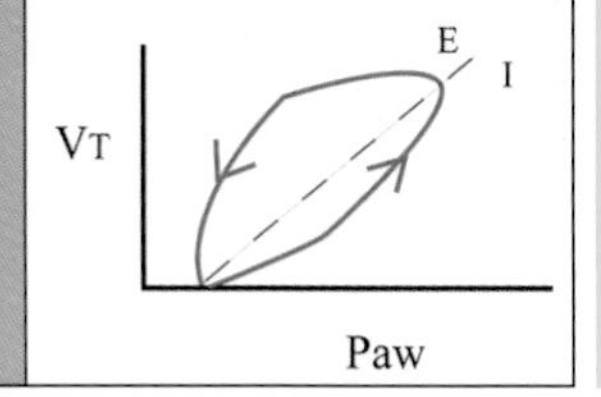
SIMV (constant or square flow) A combination of spontaneous ventilation and assisted VV.	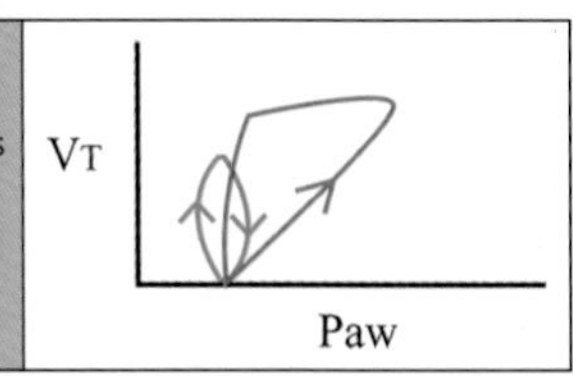
Pressure Ventilation – Assist/ Control The set pressure is reached quickly before the volume has a chance to rise. 1st breath is assisted (patient-triggered). 2nd breath is controlled (machine-triggered).	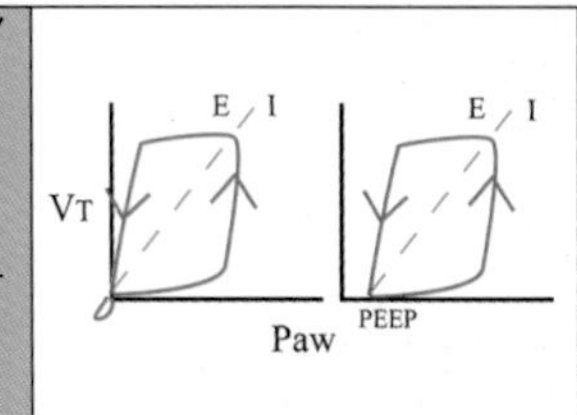
Pressure Support Ventilation Similar to PV, except: 1) Pressure and volume are usually less (unless PSmax). 2) Each breath is assisted.	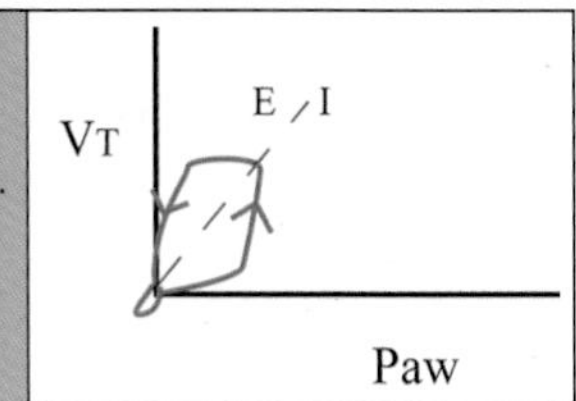

Loops: Flow-Volume

Spontaneous Ventilation
The loop is usually quite circular due to the natural sinusoidal flow rates.

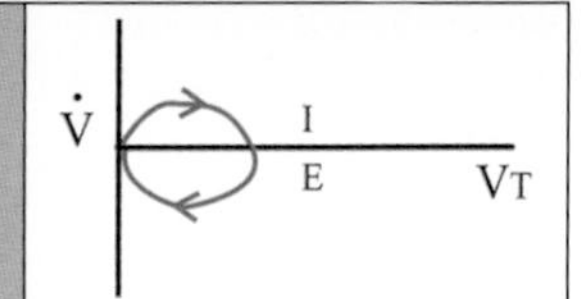

Volume Ventilation – Assist/ Control (constant or square flow)
Flow reaches a maximum at the beginning of I and continues at that maximum during the entire inspiratory phase. VT is peaked as the flow switches from positive to negative (I to E).

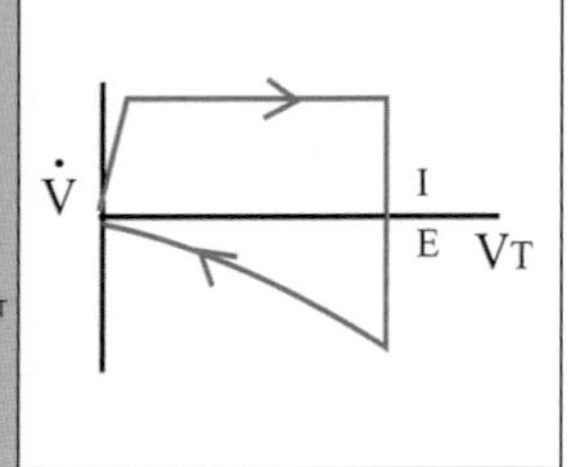

Volume Ventilation – Assist/ Control (decelerating flow)
Same as square flow (above), except inspiratory flow decelerates during the inspiratory phase.

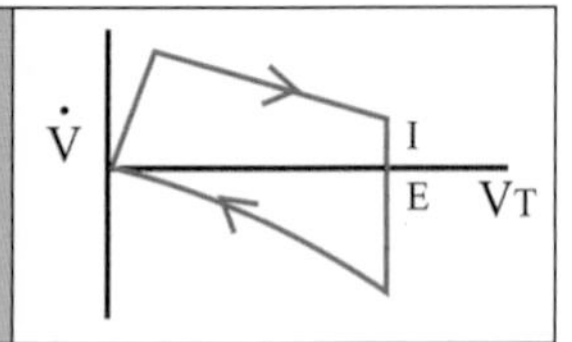

SIMV (constant or square flow)
A combination of spontaneous ventilation and assisted VV.

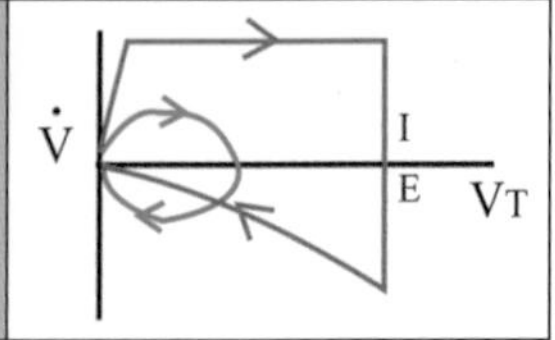

Pressure Ventilation – Assist/ Control Flow reaches a maximum at the beginning of I and then decelerates during the inspiratory phase. V_T is peaked as the flow switches from positive to negative (I to E).	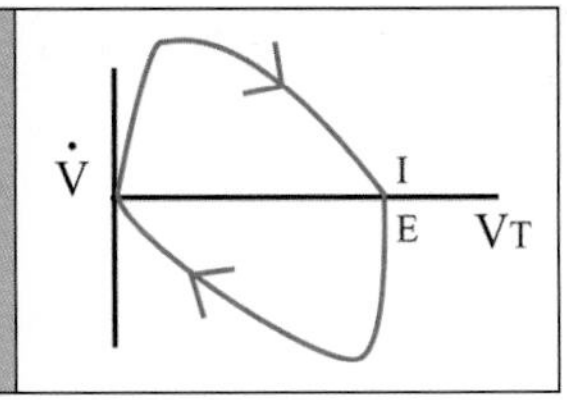
Pressure Support Ventilation Similar to PV, except: 1) Flow and volume are usually less (unless PSmax) 2) The inspiratory phase is terminated when $\dot{V}_I$ decreases to a ventilator determined flow (usually 25% of peak flow) (never reaches zero). 3) Each breath is assisted.	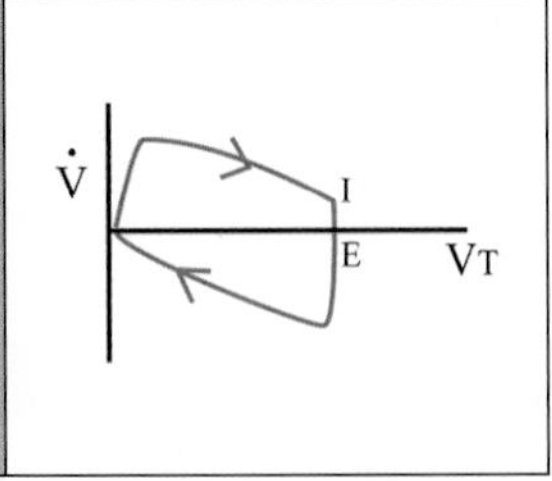

Abnormal Graphic Waveforms by Waveform Type

*** For the description of a particular graph, turn to the Abnormal Graphic Waveform By Problem section and proceed to the particular problem.

All examples are in Volume Ventilation.

Scalars

- Pressure-Time
- Volume-Time
- Flow-Time

Loops

- Volume-Pressure
- Flow-Volume

Scalars: Pressure-Time

Air-trapping (auto-PEEP)

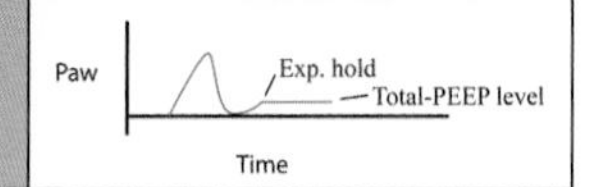

Airway Resistance Changes

↑ PIP-P_{plat}

(5 to 10 cmH_2O)

(Dashed line depicts Pplat)

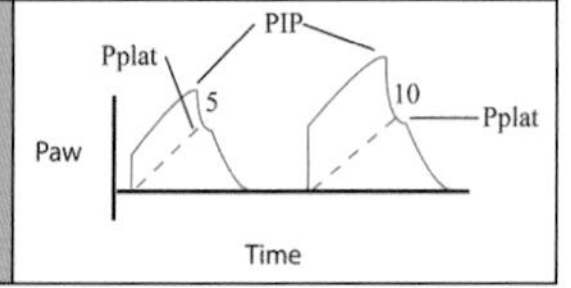

Compliance Changes

↑Pplat

Raw remains the same at 5 cmH_2O

(Dashed line depicts Pplat)

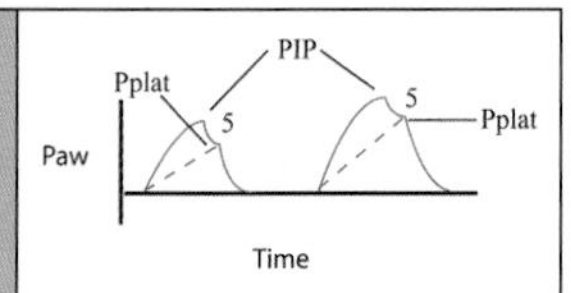

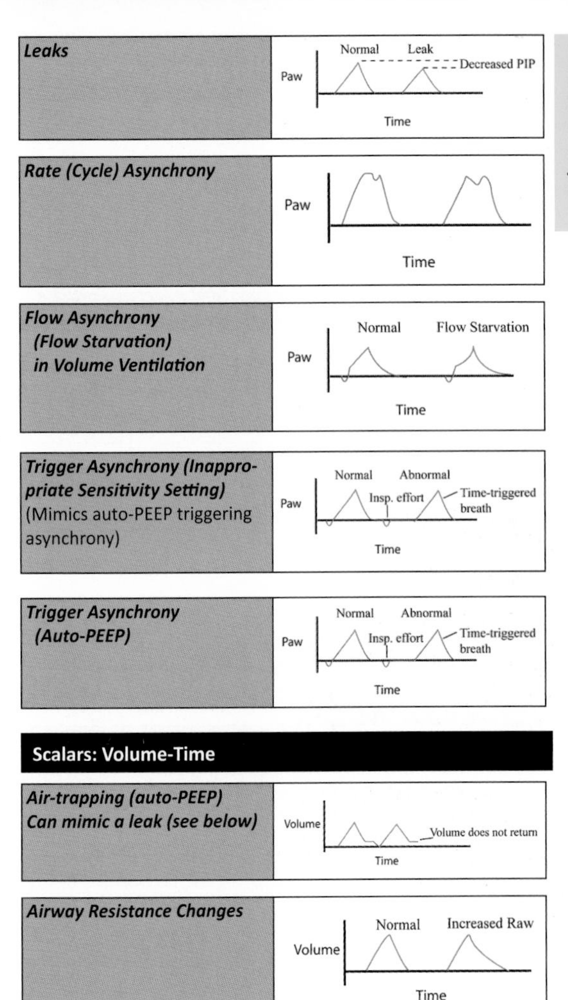
Leaks
Normal
Leak
Decreased PIP
Paw
Time
Rate (Cycle) Asynchrony
Paw
Time
Flow Asynchrony (Flow Starvation) in Volume Ventilation
Normal
Flow Starvation
Paw
Time
Trigger Asynchrony (Inappropriate Sensitivity Setting) (Mimics auto-PEEP triggering asynchrony)
Normal
Abnormal
Insp. effort
Time-triggered breath
Paw
Time
Trigger Asynchrony (Auto-PEEP)
Normal
Abnormal
Insp. effort
Time-triggered breath
Paw
Time
Scalars: Volume-Time
Air-trapping (auto-PEEP) Can mimic a leak (see below)
Volume
Volume does not return
Time
Airway Resistance Changes
Normal
Increased Raw
Volume
Time

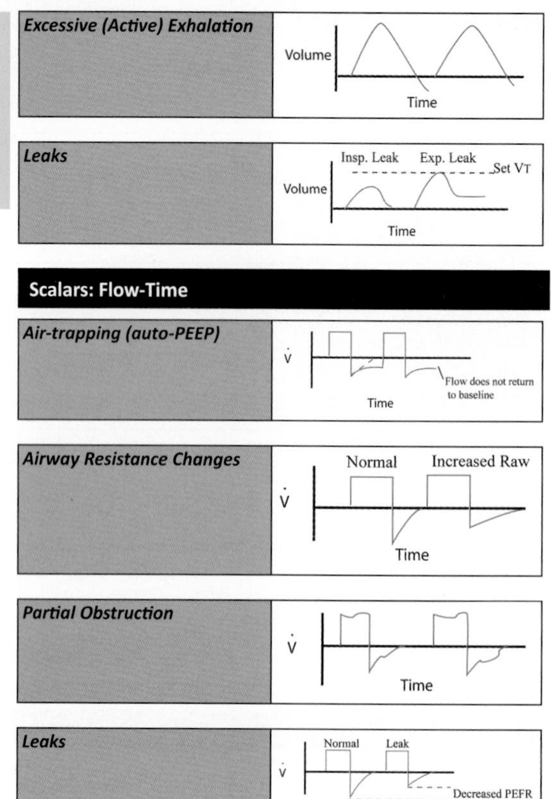
Excessive (Active) Exhalation
Volume
Time
Leaks
Insp. Leak
Exp. Leak
Set VT
Volume
Time
Scalars: Flow-Time
Air-trapping (auto-PEEP)
V
Flow does not return to baseline
Time
Airway Resistance Changes
Normal
Increased Raw
V
Time
Partial Obstruction
V
Time
Leaks
Normal
Leak
V
Decreased PEFR
Time

Rate (Cycle) Asynchrony

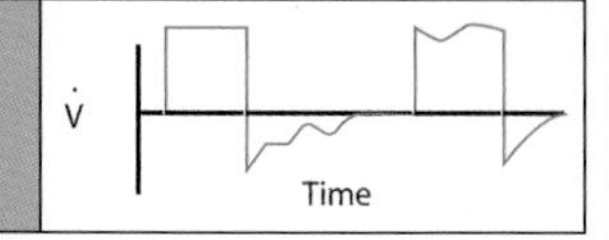

Trigger Asynchrony (Inappropriate Sensitivity Setting)

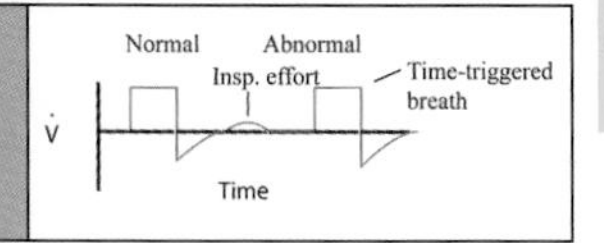

Trigger Asynchrony (Auto-PEEP)

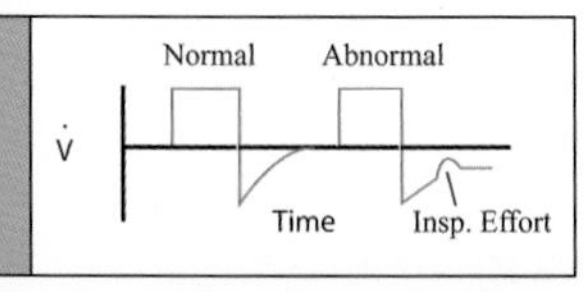

Loops: Volume-Pressure

Air-trapping (auto-PEEP)

Example: Volume Ventilation

VT

Trapped gas from breath stacking

Paw

Airway Resistance Changes (Mechanical Breath)

Dashed lines depicts normal and solid line is ↑ Raw

Example: Volume Ventilation

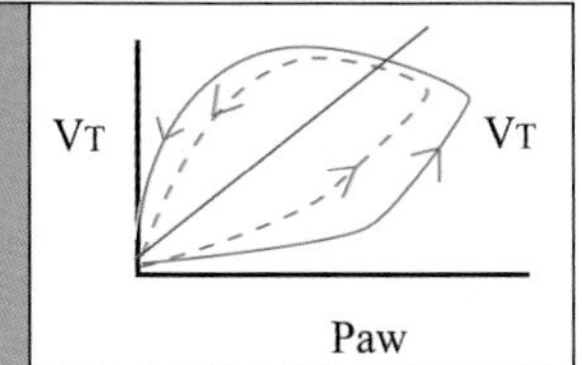

Airway Resistance Changes (Spontaneous Breath)

Dashed lines depicts normal and solid line is ↑ Raw

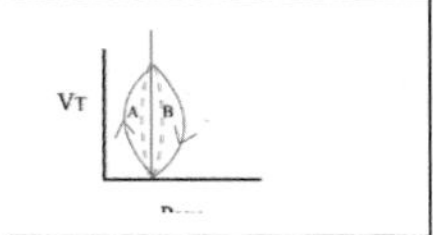

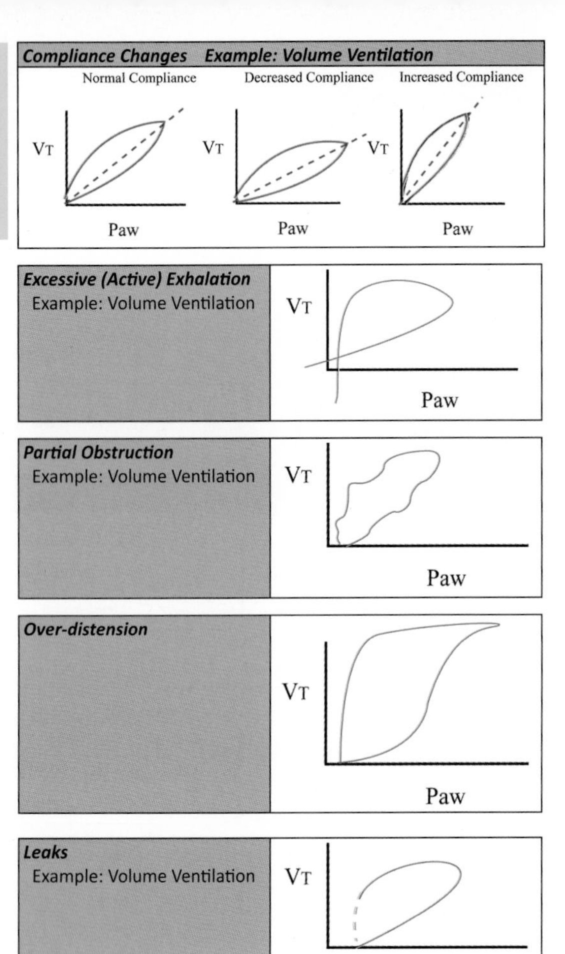
Compliance Changes Example: Volume Ventilation
Normal Compliance
Decreased Compliance
Increased Compliance
VT
Paw
Excessive (Active) Exhalation
Example: Volume Ventilation
VT
Paw
Partial Obstruction
Example: Volume Ventilation
VT
Paw
Over-distension
VT
Paw
Leaks
Example: Volume Ventilation
VT
Paw

Rate (Cycle) Asynchrony

Example: Volume Ventilation

Flow Asynchrony (Flow Starvation)

Example: Volume Ventilation

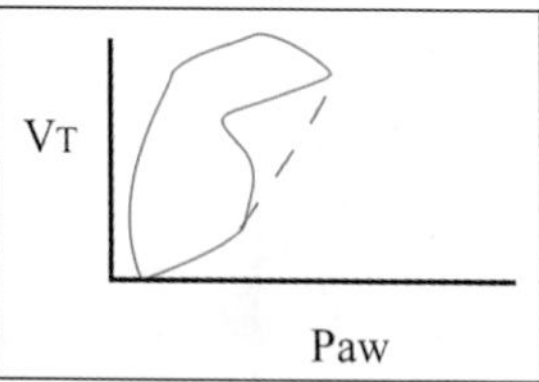

Trigger Asynchrony (Inappropriate Sensitivity Setting)

Example: Volume Ventilation

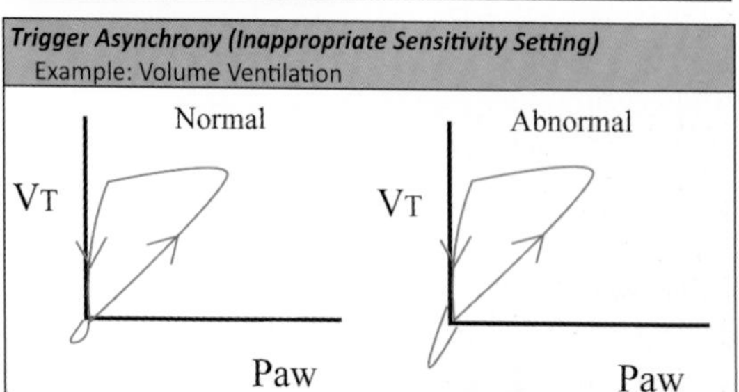

Loops: Flow-Volume

All examples are Volume Ventilation

Air-trapping (auto-PEEP)

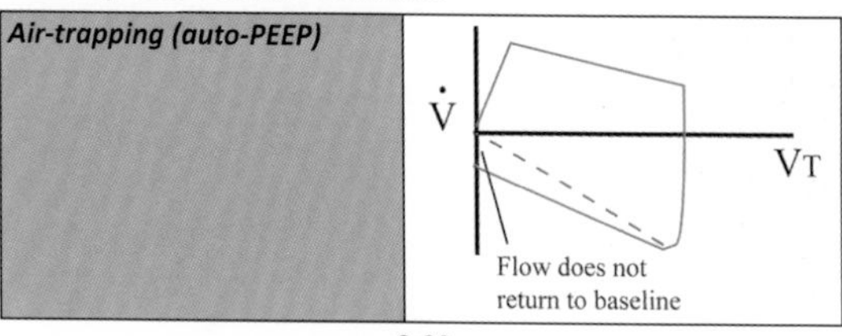

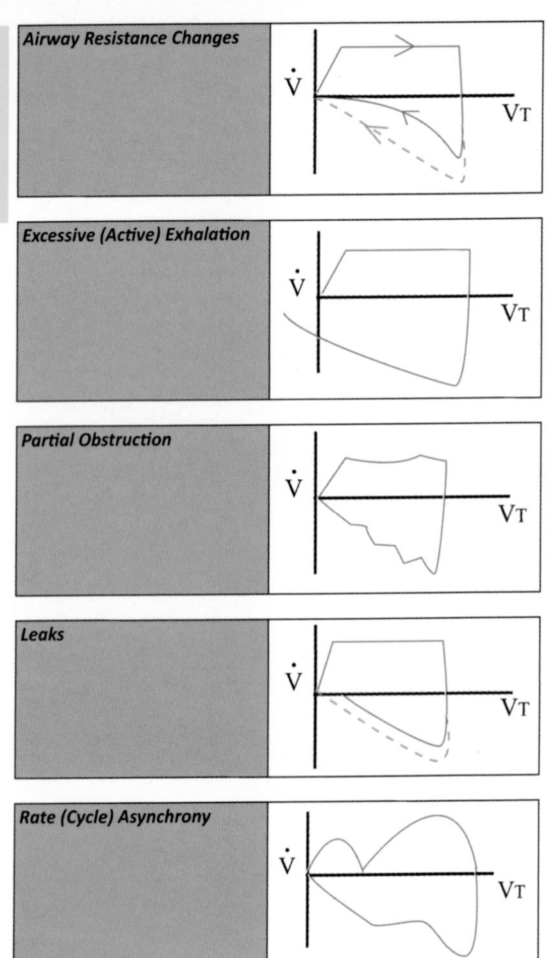
Airway Resistance Changes
V̇
VT
Excessive (Active) Exhalation
V̇
VT
Partial Obstruction
V̇
VT
Leaks
V̇
VT
Rate (Cycle) Asynchrony
V̇
VT

Abnormal Graphic Waveforms by Problem

Section Contents

Patient
- Air-trapping (auto-PEEP)
- Airway resistance changes
- Compliance changes
- Excessive exhalation
- Partial obstruction

Ventilator
- Over-distension
- Leaks

Patient-Ventilator Interaction
- Rate asynchrony
- Flow asynchrony
- Trigger asynchrony (inappropriate sensitivity setting)
- Trigger asynchrony (auto-PEEP)

All examples are in Volume Ventilation.

PATIENT

Air-trapping (auto-PEEP):

Possible Causes

Dynamic hyperinflation (insufficient T_E for complete expiration) due to:

1) Increased expiratory Raw (prolonged expiration)
2) Decreased T_E (insufficient time before next breath)

Early collapse of unstable alveoli during expiration (exhaled air is blocked from flowing out)

Auto-PEEP: Scalars

Pressure-Time

Auto-PEEP can only be identified (and quantified) when an expiratory hold is employed. During the hold, baseline pressure line rises to the auto-PEEP level (depicting pressure still trapped in alveoli). If applied PEEP is employed, the expiratory hold baseline will rise to total PEEP (applied PEEP + auto-PEEP).

Clinical Note: Sufficient hold time must be employed to allow the pressure to reach a plateau, plus there must be not patient respiratory effort during the hold.

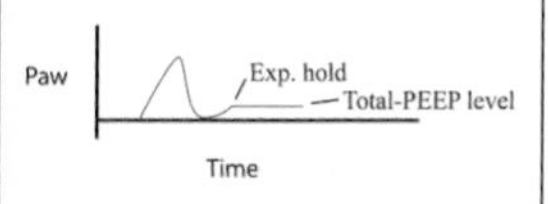

Volume-Time

Volume does not return to baseline (depicting volume still trapped in alveoli). The less the return, the greater the air-trapping. *Note*: this is the same curve as a leak –see Leak.

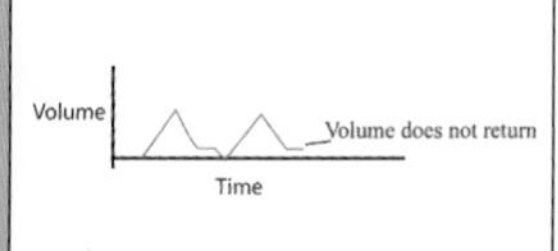

Flow-Time

Expiratory flow does not return to baseline (depicting flow still trapped in alveoli). The less the return, the greater the air-trapping. The dashed line depicts normal flow return to baseline.

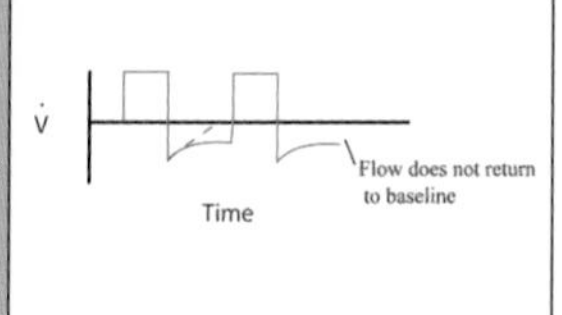

Auto-PEEP: Loops

Volume-Pressure Volume does not return to baseline (depicting volume still trapped in alveoli). The less the return, the greater the air-trapping.	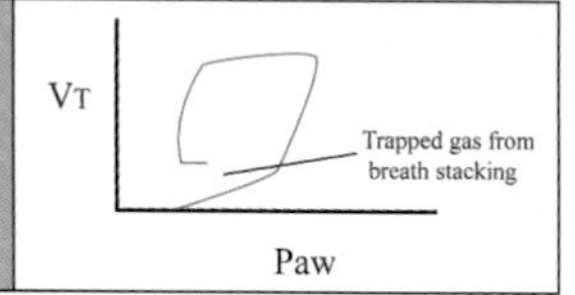
Flow-Volume Expiratory flow does not return to baseline (depicting flow still trapped in alveoli). The less the return, the greater the air-trapping. The dashed line depicts normal flow return to baseline.	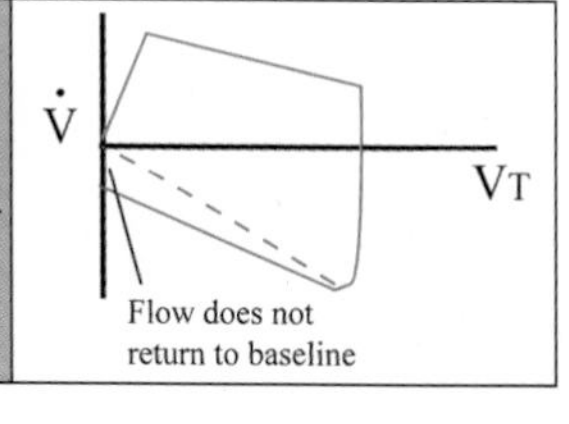

Airway Resistance Changes:

Possible Causes

- Bronchospasm
- Damp or blocked expiratory filter
- ET tube (small size, bitten, kinked, or partially obstructed)
- High $\dot{V}I$
- Secretion buildup (see also water/secretion problem)

Descriptions:
All examples are Volume Ventilation

Raw Δ: Scalars

Pressure-Time Using an inspiratory pause (hold), the difference between Ppeak and Pplat can be visualized and measured. 1st waveform: Ppeak – Pplat = 5 cmH_2O 2nd waveform: Ppeak – Pplat = 10 cmH_2O *Clinical Notes*: An increased Ppeak while Plat remains the same is indicative of an increased Raw. The reverse situation, a decreased Ppeak while Pplat remains the same, is indicative of a decreased Raw (e.g., a positive bronchodilator response). See Compliance Changes, next section.	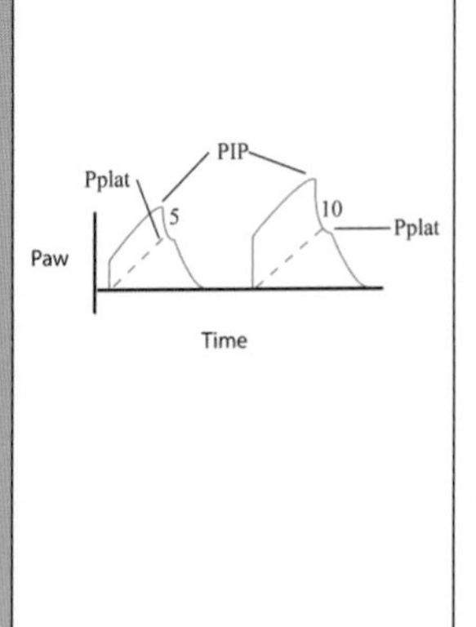
Volume-Time The time for volume emptying is prolonged with increased Raw	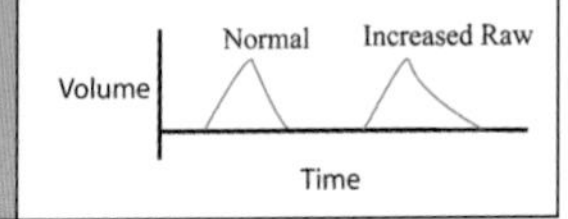

Flow-Time	
A: normal B: ↑ Raw (expiratory): 1) Peak expiratory flow is decreased 2) Expiratory flow is decreased (flatter slope) 3) Time of expiration is prolonged *Clinical Notes*: Bronchodilator response is determined by the degree to which the increased Raw waveform returns to a normal shape. Inspiratory Raw is generally not well depicted on a flow-time scalar because ventilator-driving force is usually sufficient to overcome it.	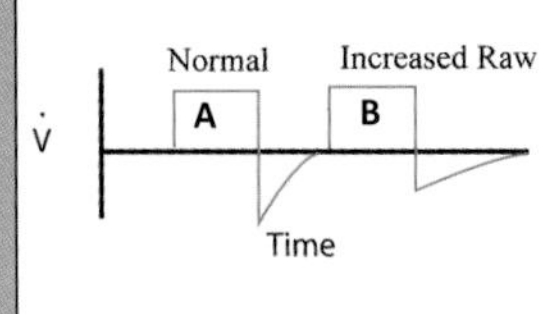

Raw Δ: Loops

Volume-Pressure (mechanical breath)	
The dashed line depicts a normal loop. The solid line depicts increased Raw. The movement of the upward inspiratory slope to the right is indicative of inspiratory resistance. The movement of the downward expiratory slope to the left is indicative of expiratory resistance.	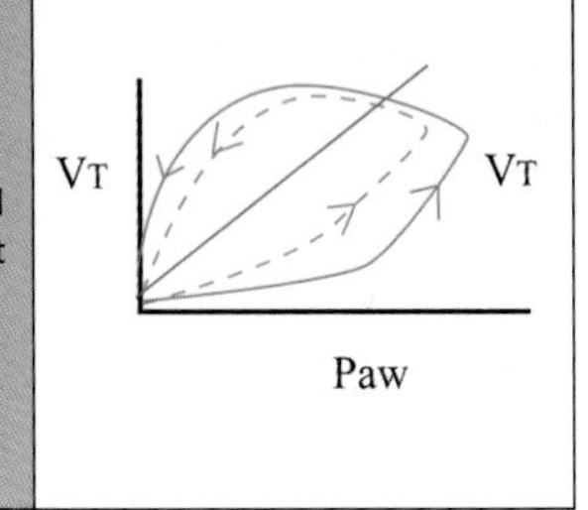

Volume-Pressure (spontaneous breath)
The inspiratory area (A) to the left of the vertical baseline will increase with increased inspiratory Raw. The expiratory area (B) to the right of the vertical baseline will increase with an increase in expiratory Raw.

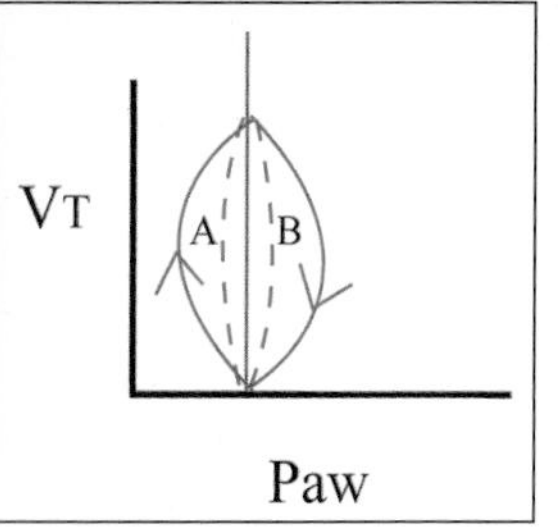

Flow-Volume
The dashed line depicts a normal loop. The solid line depicts increased Raw:

1) Decreased peak expiratory flow
2) Concave mid-expiratory flow curve (theoretically due to resistance in medium and small airways. No concavity suggests the resistance is in the large upper airways).
3) V_T may be reduced in some instances

Clinical Notes: Bronchodilator response is determined by the degree to which the increased Raw waveform returns to a normal shape. Inspiratory Raw is generally not well depicted on a flow-volume loop because ventilator-driving force is usually sufficient to overcome it.

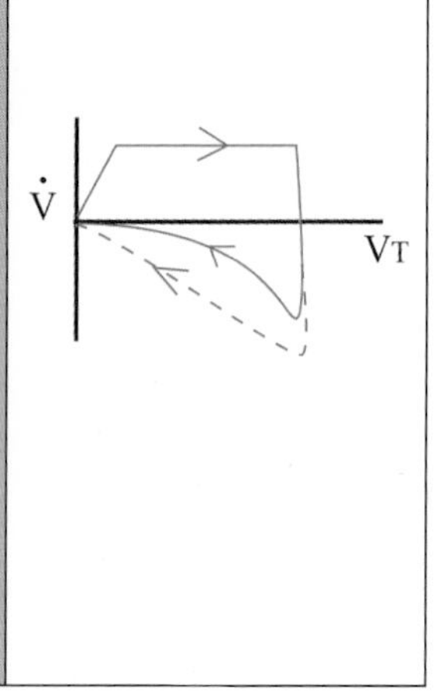

Compliance Changes:

Possible Causes

↓ Compliance (C)	↑ Compliance (C)
ARDS	Emphysema
Atelectasis	Surfactant therapy
Abdominal distention	
CHF	
Consolidation	
Fibrosis	
Hyperinflation	
Pleural effusion	
Right mainstem intubation	
Tension pneumothorax	

Descriptions:

All examples are Volume Ventilation

Compliance Δ: Scalars

Pressure-Time (VV)

Using an inspiratory pause (hold), the difference between Ppeak and Pplat can be visualized and measured.

A: Ppeak – Pplat = 5 cmH_2O

B: Ppeak – Pplat = 5 cmH_2O

Clinical Notes:

If Ppeak and Pplat increase along with the Raw (Ppeak-Pplat), then this in indicative of both a ↓ C and an ↑ Raw.

See airway resistance changes, previous section. Pressure curves remain unchanged in PV. An ↑ Ppeak plus a similar ↑ in Pplat is indicative of ↓ compliance.

The reverse situation, a ↓ Ppeak plus a similar ↓ in Pplat is indicative of an ↑ compliance.

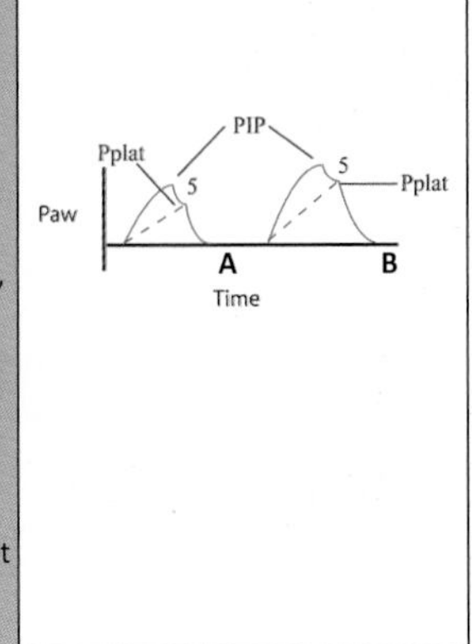

Compliance Δ: Loops

Volume-Pressure

Decreasing compliance: the slope of the imaginary line through the center of the loop moves towards the pressure axis

Increasing compliance: the slope of the imaginary line through the center of the loop moves towards the volume axis.

Clinical Note: Depending on the parameters and scaling, normal compliance curves are conventionally displayed as having a 45° slope

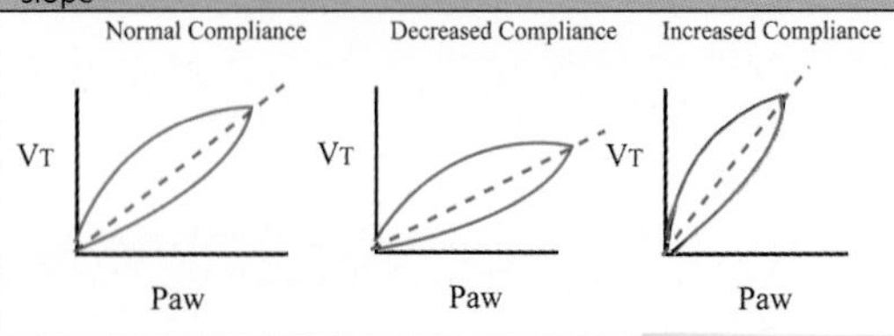

Excessive (Active) Exhalation:

Possible Causes

Patient is exhaling below FRC due to:

Air-trapping (excessive exhalation occurs periodically in an attempt to relieve the trapped volume).

Pain

Positional change

Note: a consistent, regular pattern of excessive exhalation indicates an equipment calibration problem.

Descriptions:

Excessive (Active) Exhalation: Scalars

Volume-Time

Volume curve dips below zero baseline

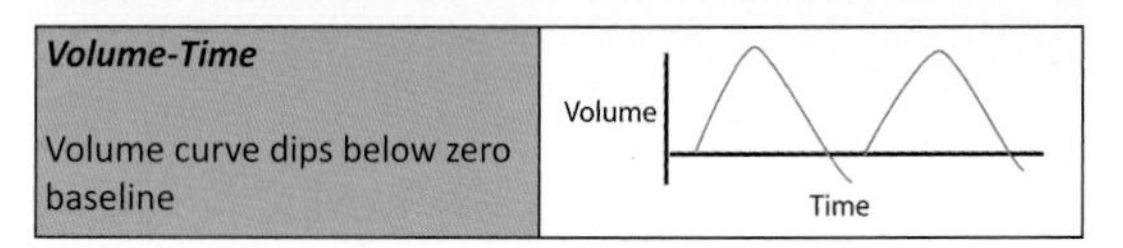

Excessive (Active) Exhalation: Loops

Volume-Pressure Expiration curve continues below the zero volume point.	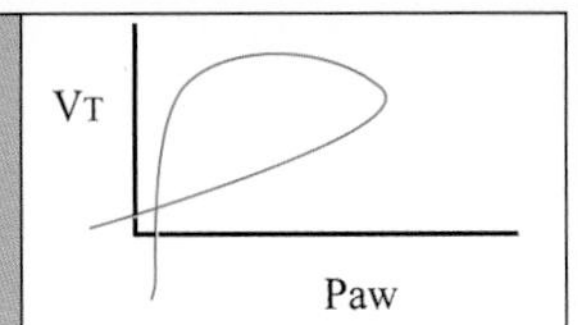
Flow-Volume Expiration curve continues to the left of the zero volume point.	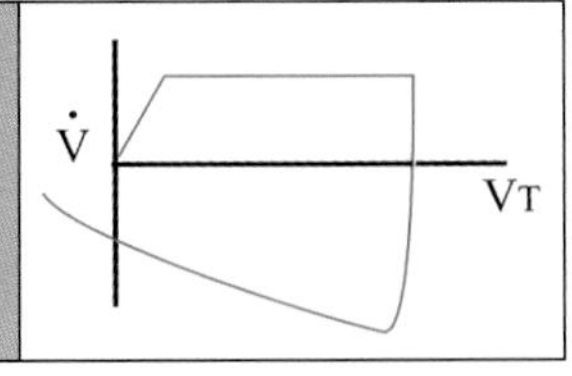

Partial Obstruction:

Possible Causes

Indwelling suction catheter left partially in ET tube
Flap of tissue, Mucous plug
Water/secretions in airways/circuit

Descriptions:

Partial Obstruction: Scalars

Flow-Time The obstruction is moved by flow moving in and out of the airways/circuit resulting in fluctuating flow.	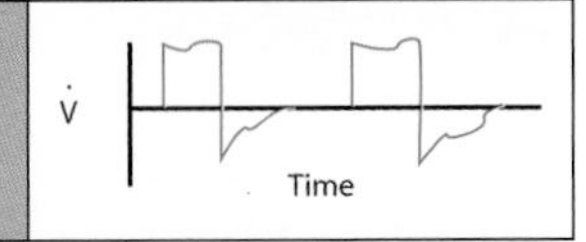

Partial Obstruction: Loops

Volume-Pressure The obstruction is moved by the flow moving in and out of the airways/circuit, resulting in fluctuating pressure.	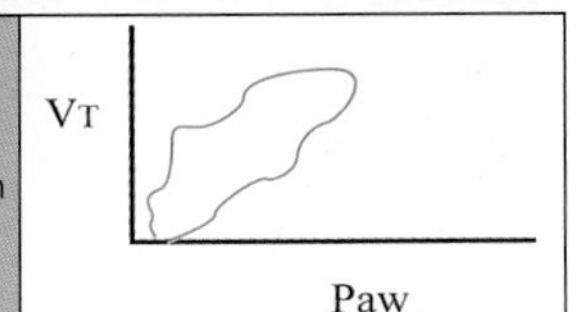

Flow-Volume The obstruction is moved by the flow moving in and out of the airways/circuit, resulting in fluctuating flow. It will have a "saw tooth" appearance if the obstruction is secretions or water.	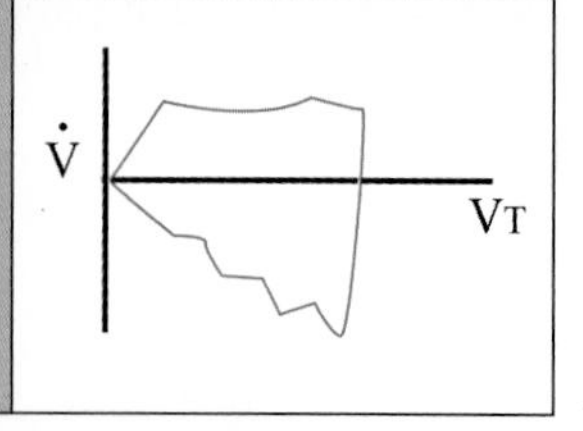

Ventilator

Clinical Note: The static V-P loop is the most accurate way of detecting low and high inflection points. Dynamic loops such as the ones depicted in this book do not quantify these points.

Over-distension

Possible Causes

Too much V_T in Volume Ventilation
Too much pressure in Pressure Ventilation

Description:

Volume-Pressure Loop Increasing volume increases pressure for a very little or no increase V_T causing a "Beaking" at end inspiration. (Example in Volume ventilation) Clinical note: "Beaking" doesn't necessarily indicate overdistention; it may be due to patient-ventilator asynchrony.	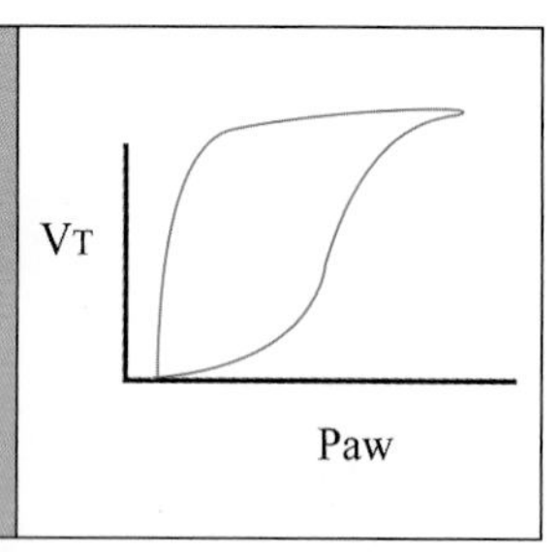

Leaks

Possible Causes

Expiratory	Inspiratory
Air leak through chest tube	Loose connections
BP fistula	Ventilator malfunction
ET tube cuff leak	Faulty flow sensor
NG tube in trachea	

Clinical Note: Leaks are generally expiratory. Set volumes will not be reached if the leak is inspiratory. A leak in the circuit between the ventilator and flow transducer would result in a smaller volume (both I and E); pressure and flow are then set by the ventilator. A volume loss around neonatal cuffless tubes is normal. Lost volume should not exceed 20% of total volume.

Leaks: Scalars

Pressure-Time
Ppeak will be ↓ (esp. VV) due to ↓ returned volume and/or an inspiratory leak.

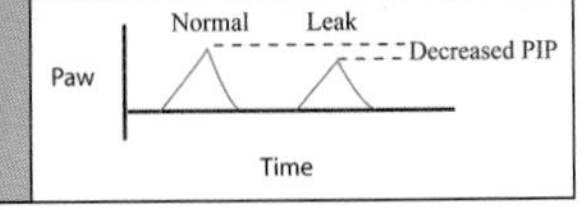

Volume-Time
Set volume is not reached with an inspiratory leak. The returned volume does not return to baseline with an expiratory leak.

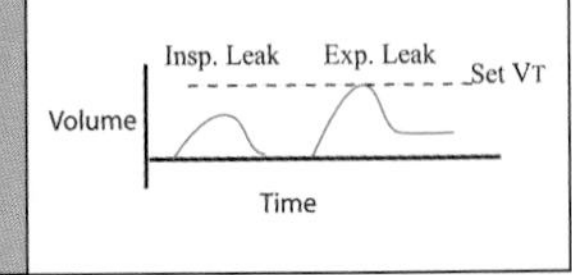

Flow-Time
Peak expiratory flow is ↓ due to ↓ returned volume.

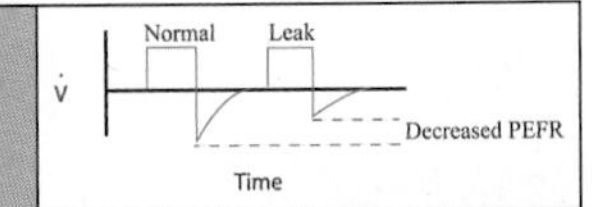

Leaks: Loops

Volume-Pressure
Volume does not return to zero baseline, resulting in an incomplete loop. The dashed line depicts a loop without a leak.

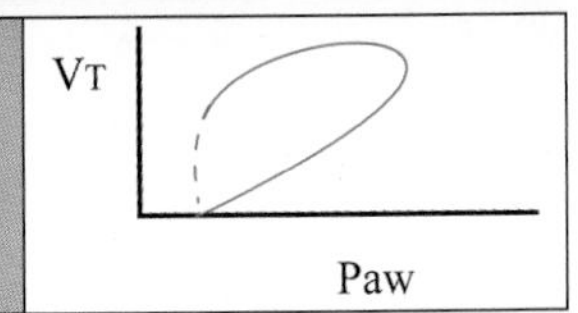

Flow-Volume
Volume does not return to zero baseline, resulting in an incomplete loop. The dashed line depicts a loop without a leak.

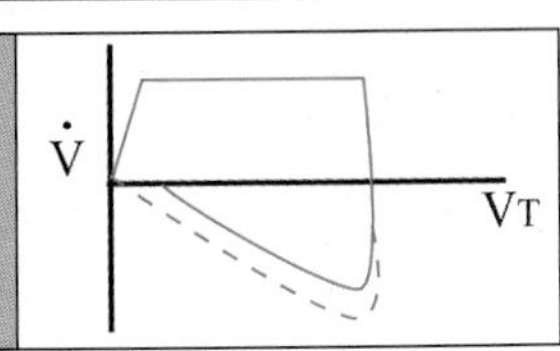

Rate (Cycle) Asynchrony:

Possible Causes
Neurological injury
Patient air-hunger

Descriptions:

Rate (Cycle) Asynchrony: Scalars

Pressure-Time
Erratic inspiratory and/or expiratory phases indicate inspiratory and/or expiratory efforts to inhale or exhale.

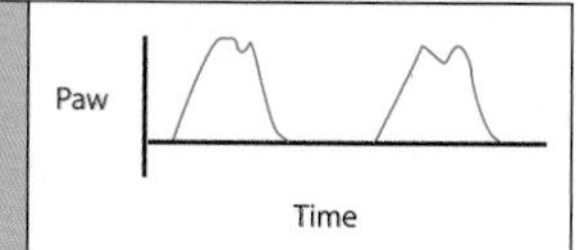

Flow-Time
Erratic inspiratory and/or expiratory phases indicate inspiratory and/or expiratory efforts to inhale or exhale.

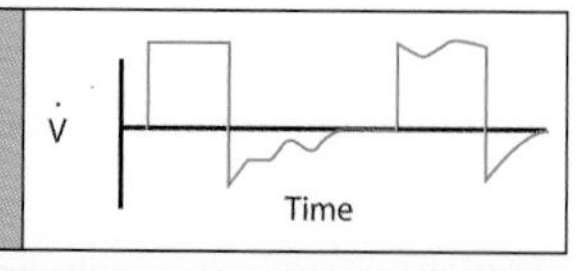

Rate (Cycle) Asynchrony: Loops

Volume-Pressure
Erratic inspiratory and/or expiratory phases indicate inspiratory and/or expiratory efforts to inhale or exhale.

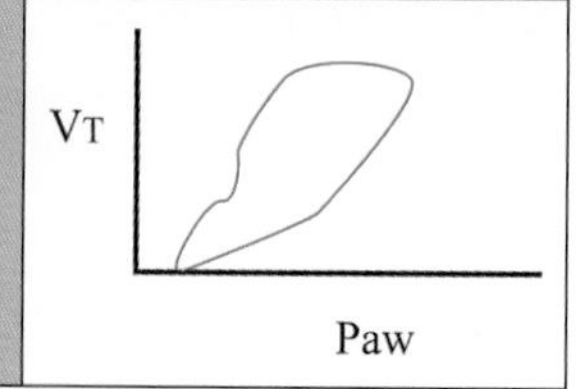

Flow-Volume
Erratic inspiratory and/or expiratory phases indicate inspiratory and/or expiratory efforts to inhale or exhale.

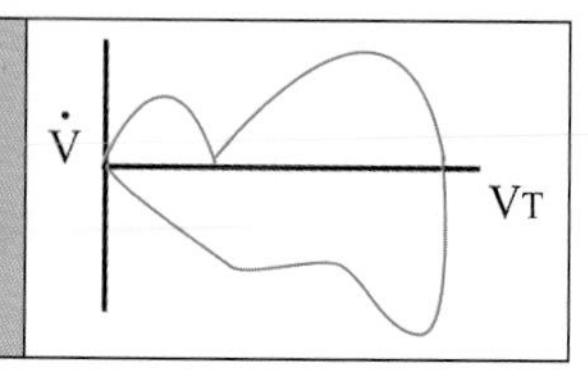

Flow Asynchrony (Flow Starvation)

Descriptions:

Flow Asynchrony (Flow Starvation): Scalars

Pressure-Time The inspiratory limb is concave with a negative pressure deflection due to the patient's attempt to pull more flow. The expiratory curve will be unaffected by flow starvation.	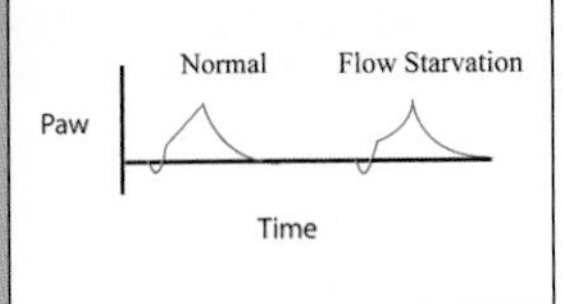

Clinical Note: Adjusting Peak Flow rate:
In VV, the rate of rise in pressure (upward slope) is related to the peak flow setting. An inadequate flow presents as a slow and often concave rise to peak pressure. A high flow will present as a very fast rise to peak pressure (mimicking PV).

Flow Asynchrony (Flow Starvation): Loops

Volume-Pressure The inspiratory limb is concave with a negative pressure deflection due to the patient's attempt to pull more flow. The expiratory curve will be unaffected by flow starvation	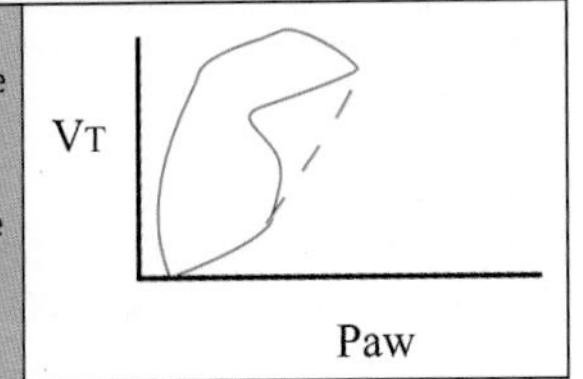

Trigger Asynchrony (Inappropriate Sensitivity Setting)

Descriptions:

Trigger Asynchrony (Sensitivity): Scalars

Pressure-Time Negative inspiratory pressure is applied by the patient, however it is not enough to trigger a machine breath.	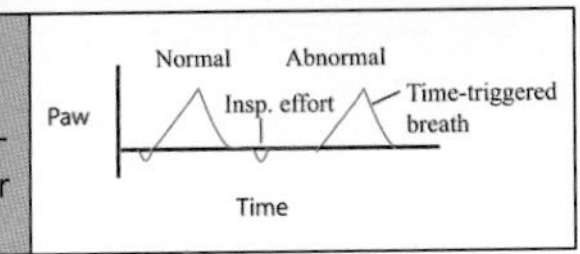

Flow-Time
As the patient attempts to trigger the ventilator, the flow turns slightly positive then negative due to a futile effort.

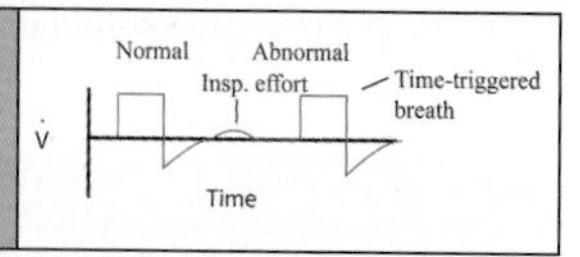

Trigger Asynchrony (Sensitivity): Loops

Volume-Pressure
Normal – the negative deflection is minimal.
Abnormal – the negative deflection is greater. The greater the negative deflection, the greater the effort to trigger.

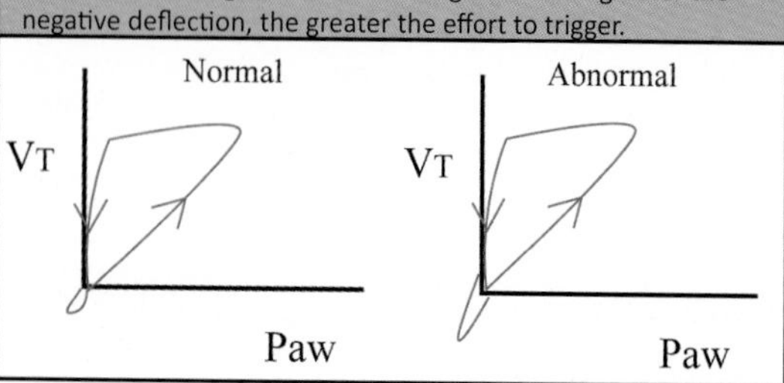

Trigger Asynchrony (Auto-PEEP)

Descriptions:

Trigger Asynchrony (Auto-PEEP): Scalars

Pressure-Time
Normal – the negative deflection is minimal.
Abnormal – the neg. deflection is greater. The greater the negative deflection, the greater the effort to trigger. There is no difference in this graph compared to the "Inappropriate Sensitivity Setting" Pressure-Time Scalar.

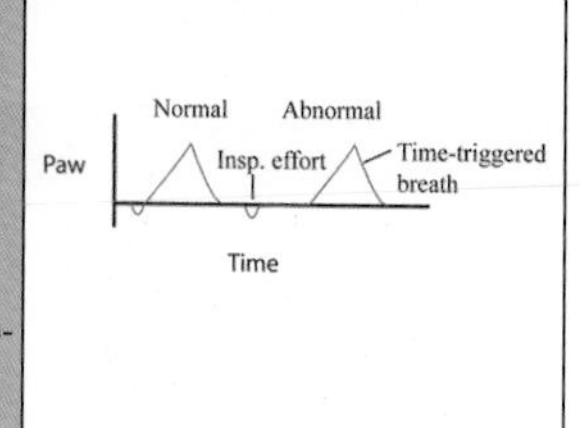

Flow-Time	
As the patient attempts to trigger the ventilator, the expiratory flow curve turns slightly positive then negative due to a futile effort. The difference between this graph and the "Inappropriate Sensitivity Setting" Flow-Time Scalar is that the flow turns + within auto-PEEP area below baseline.	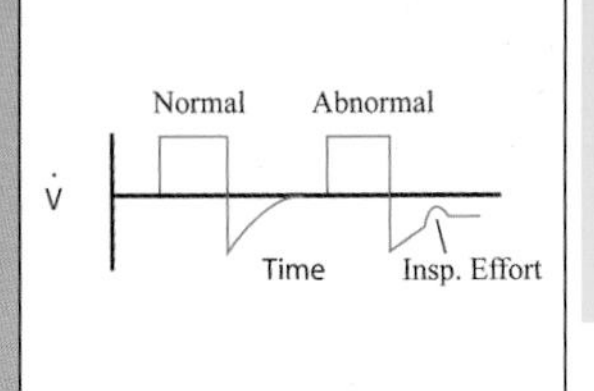

Clinical Note: Inappropriate setting and auto-PEEP trigger asynchrony could be combined.

Other Applications

Pressure-Time Scalars

Determining machine breath types (VV)	
Negative pressure deflection just prior to inspiration indicates an assisted breath.	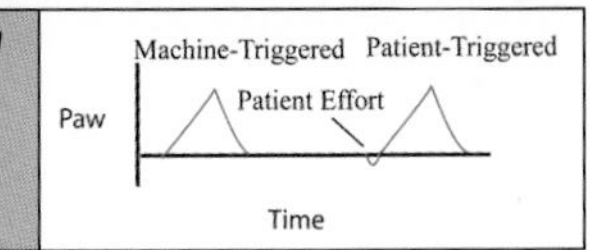

Assessing plateau pressure	
In VV, an inspiratory pause will cause the breath pressure to plateau. The clinician can then separate resistance from compliance to determine the cause of an increase/decrease in Ppeak. • Raw ~ Ppeak – Pplat • Crs ~ Pplat – PEEP See Chapter 7 for Equations to calculate *Clinical Note*: In PV, Ppeak = Pplat, provided zero flow at end-inspiration.	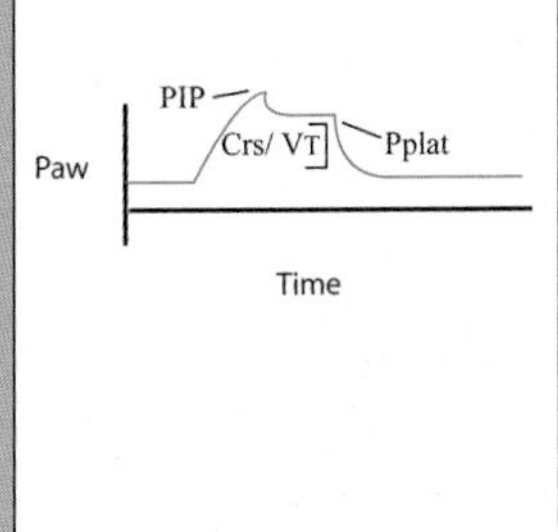

Setting rise-to-pressure time in PV (controlled or supported) The faster the flow, the quicker set pressure is reached in the I phase. This is used in conjunction with the flow-time scalar (see next section). A rise-to-pressure time too fast could cause a spike or "ringing" in the airways and cause the patient to become asynchronous.	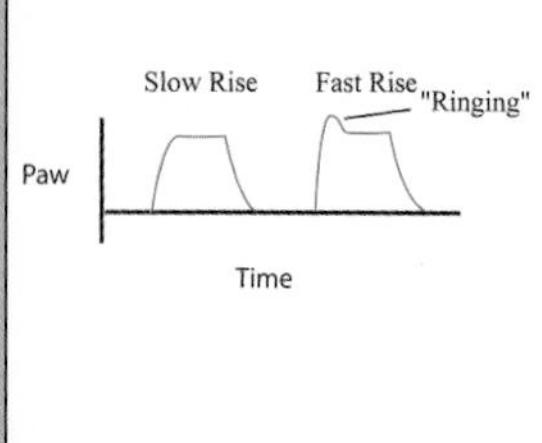

Switching cycling criteria and optimizing inspiratory phase in a pressure support breath. Ventilators have specific flow-cycling criteria for pressure-supported breaths. Some ventilators have backup pressure and time-cycling features that can be adjusted (depending on the ventilator). In the example shown, the first breath is pressure-cycled. Note the pressure spike at the end of inspiration, indicating that the flow-cycling parameter (e.g., 25%) is too low and that the patient is attempting to exhale. Adjusting the expiratory sensitivity or the time-cycling parameter, the clinician can limit the inspiratory phase, which should improve patient comfort.	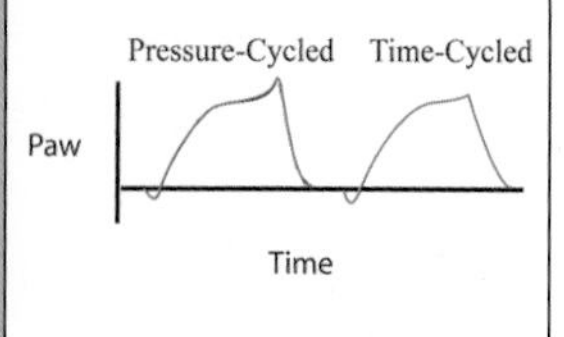

Flow-Time Scalars

Verifying waveform shapes
Some ventilators have flow waveform options in VV. The flow-time scalar is used to verify the waveform selected.

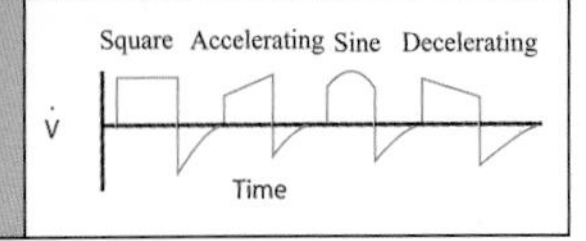

Setting I-time in PV
When lengthening or shortening the inspiratory time, the flow-time scalar should be used to see if there is more flow available for additional volume delivery. Once the V̇I has reached zero (baseline), there will be no volume ↑ with an ↑ I-time (except slight increases due to long TCs).

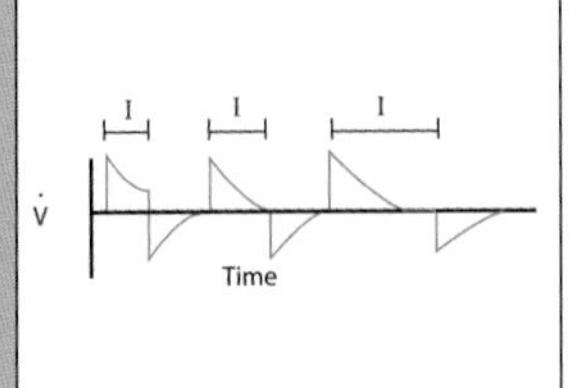

Setting rise-to-pressure time in PV (controlled or supported)
The faster the flow, the quicker set pressure is reached in the I phase. This is used in conjunction with the P-T scalar (see previous section).

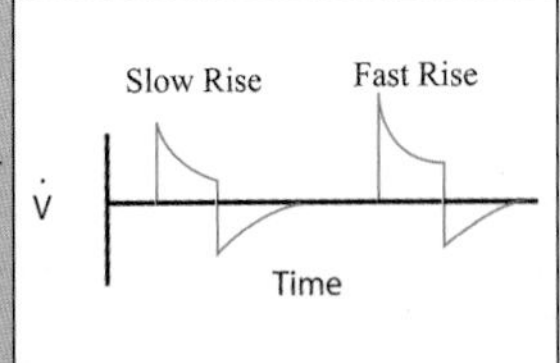

Volume-Pressure Loop

Assessing inspiratory effort
The clockwise loops below the baseline pressure depict patient inspiratory effort in assist ventilation.

- Solid line – increased (inappropriate) trigger effort
- Dashed line – minimum (appropriate) trigger effort

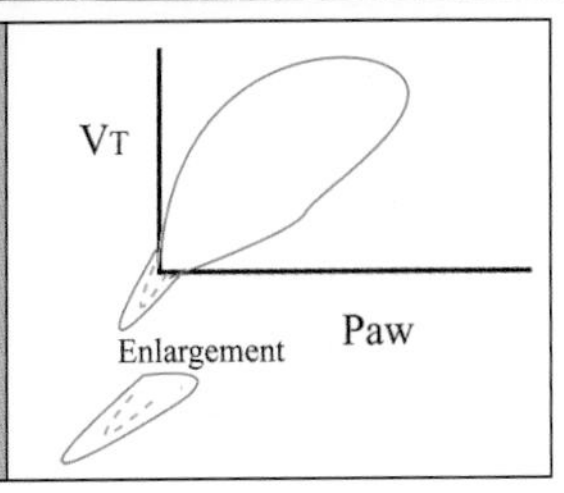

7 Equations

Chapter Contents

Major categories are listed above. All equations are alphabetically listed within each section.

Equation	Comments	Significance
Acid-Base		
Anion Gap 1) $AG = Na^+ - (Cl^- + HCO_3)$ 2) $AG = (Na^+ + K^+) - (Cl^- + HCO_3)$	Normal = 12 (± 4) mEq/L Normal = 20 (± 4) mEq/L AG = the difference between measured cations (+) and anions (–) (ie., unmeasured ions)	Indicates metabolic acidosis due to an increase of acid (rather than a decrease of base) ↑ AG = ↑ unmeasured anions (acid): ↑ **acid production**: lactate (hypoxia), ketones (diabetes) ↑**acid addition**: poisons (methanol, salicylates) ↓ **acid excretion**: renal failure ↓ **AG** = ↓ unmeasured anions: albumin
Note: When an Anion Gap Metabolic Acidosis is present, there are various methods used to calculate for additional or mixed metabolic disorders. See Oakes' ***ABG Pocket Guide: Interpretation and Managemen***t for more details.		
Base Excess (BE) 1) $BE = \frac{\Delta PaCO_2 + \Delta pH \times 100}{2}$ 2) $BE \approx \Delta PaCO_2$ 3) $BE \approx \Delta HCO_3 + 10\ \Delta pH$	$\Delta PaCO_2$ from 40 ΔpH from 7.40 ΔHCO_3 from 24	Base deficit (BD) = - BE Accurate only in ranges of: $PaCO_2$ 30-50, pH 7.30-7.50

Equation	Comments	Significance
Bicarbonate Correction of pH HCO_3 = (0.2)body weight x BD	Corrects to pH 7.40 BD = base deficit	Used to correct for metabolic acidosis.
Henderson-Hasselbach 1) pH = 6.1 + log HCO_3/ H_2CO_3] 2) pH = 6.1 + log [HCO_3/dissolved CO_2] 3) $pH = 6.1 + \frac{\text{total } CO_2 - 0.03PaCO_2}{0.03PaCO_2}$ 4) $PaCO_2 = \frac{\text{total } CO_2}{0.3 \times [1 - \text{antilog}(pH - 6.1)]}$	$\text{Total } CO_2 = \frac{\text{volume \%}}{2.2}$	Calculation of pH or $PaCO_2$.
Rule of 8's At: pH — HCO_3 = 7.6 — 8/8 ($PaCO_2$) 7.5 — 6/8 ($PaCO_2$) 7.4 — 5/8 ($PaCO_2$) 7.3 — 4/8 ($PaCO_2$) 7.2 — 3/8 ($PaCO_2$)	Examples: when pH 7.4, $PaCO_2$ 40, HCO_3 = 5/8 (40) = 25 pH 7.3, $PaCO_2$ 60, HCO_3 = 4/8 (60) = 30	Estimate of HCO_3 in relation to pH and $PaCO_2$.

Equation	Comments	Significance
T40 Bicarbonate $T40 = HCO_3 - \text{expected } \Delta HCO_3$	HCO_3 = standard plasma $\text{Expected } \Delta HCO_3 = \frac{PaCO_2 - 40}{15}$	Used to find a "true" metabolic component in acute hypercapnia.
Winters Formula $PaCO_2 \text{ predicted} = 1.54 \times HCO_3 + 8.36 (\pm 1)$	Measures respiratory compensation for metabolic acidosis.	$PaCO_2$ (actual) > $PaCO_2$ (pred) = mixed acidosis $PaCO_2$ (actual) < $PaCO_2$ (predicted) = respiratory alkalosis
Oxygenation		
A-a Gradient ($PA\text{-}aO_2$) ($A\text{-}aDO_2$) Alveolar- arterial O_2 tension difference 1) $PA\text{-}aO_2 = PAO_2 - PaO_2$	Normal = 10 - 25 mm Hg (air) = 30 - 50mm Hg (100% O_2) Increases with age and FIO_2. PaO_2 is calculated at FIO_2 0.5 breathed x 20 min to get PaO_2 > 150 (100% not used due to ↑ shunt).	Indicates efficiency of gas exchange. Normal values indicate normal shunt. Distinguishes between true shunt and V/Q mismatch. ↑ = shunt, V/Q mismatch, alveolar hypoventilation, or ↓ diffusion. > 350 mm Hg indicative of weaning failure.
2) $PA\text{-}aO_2 = 140 - (PaO_2 + PaCO_2)$	ABG is drawn for $PaCO_2$ and PaO_2.	Less accurate estimate (on 21% only).
3) $PA\text{-}aO_2 / 20$	Estimate of shunt (100% O_2)	See shunt equation.

Equation	Comments	Significance
Alveolar O_2 Tension (Alveolar air equation) (PAO_2) 1) P_AO_2 = ([PB - PH_2O] x FIO_2) – $PaCO_2$ x (FIO_2 + 1 - FIO_2/RE)	Normal =100 mm Hg(air) = 663 mm Hg (100%, sea level) RE = respiratory exchange ratio (normal = 0.8)	Partial pressure of O_2 in alveoli. Used to determine alveolar O_2 tension to calculate PA-aO_2 gradient, a/A ratio, and % shunt.
2) P_AO_2 = ([PB - PH_2O] x FIO_2) – $PaCO_2$ (1.25)	Short form when breathing < 100% O_2	
3) P_AO_2 = PIO_2 - $PaCO_2$ (1.25)	Short form when breathing 100% O_2. PIO_2 = (PB - PH_2O) x FIO_2	
4) P_AO_2 = 150 - $PaCO_2$ (1.25)	Estimate only on room air	
5) P_AO_2 = (FIO_2 x 700) - 50	Estimate only	
Arterial/Alveolar O_2 Tension (a/A Ratio) PaO_2 / P_AO_2	Index of gas exchange function or efficiency of the lungs. Normal = 0.8 - 0.9 (0.75 elderly) at any FIO_2.	More stable than A-a gradient: A-a gradient changes with FIO_2, a/A remains relatively stable with FIO_2 changes. Changes only with $PaCO_2$ or V/Q changes. Low a/A (<0.6) = shunt, V/Q mismatch, or diffusion defect; < 0.35 indicative of weaning failure, <0.15 = refractory hypoxemia.
PaO_2 known / P_AO_2 calculated = PaO_2 desired / P_AO_2 unknown	Useful to predict PaO_2 when changing FIO_2 (See FIO_2 estimation equation)	Can be used to estimate shunt (See shunt equation).

Equation	Comments	Significance
Arterial-(mixed)Venous O_2 Content Difference ($Ca\text{-}\bar{v}O_2$) $CaO_2 - C\bar{v}O_2 = Ca\text{-}\bar{v}O_2$	Difference between arterial and mixed venous O_2 contents. Normal = 4.2 - 5.0 mL/dL (vol%)	Represents O_2 consumption by tissue and estimate of cardiac output. ↑ = ↓CO or ↑ metabolism. ↓ = ↑CO or ↓ metabolism.
Arterial-(mixed)Venous O_2 Tension Difference ($Pa\text{-}\bar{v}O_2$ or $a\text{-}\bar{v}DO_2$) $PaO_2 - P\bar{v}O_2 = Pa\text{-}\bar{v}O_2$	Normal = 60 mm Hg	Difference between arterial and mixed venous O_2 tensions.
Arterial CO_2 tension ($PaCO_2$) **PaCO2** = $\frac{\dot{V}CO_2}{\dot{V}A}$	Normal = 35-45 mm Hg	
FIO2 Estimation 1) Using a/A ratio: $PAO_2 = PaO_2$ desired / a/A ratio	Figured at any FIO_2.	Used to estimate the FIO_2 needed to achieve a desired PaO_2 or the PaO_2 that will be achieved at any given FIO_2.
2)Using alveolar O_2 tension: $FIO_2 = PAO_2 + (PaCO_2 / 0.8) / (PB–H_2O)$	Need ↑ FIO_2 x 20 minutes	$\frac{\text{Current } PaO_2}{\text{Current } FIO_2} = \frac{\text{Desired } PaO_2}{\text{New } FIO_2}$
3)Using A-a gradient: $FIO_2 = PA\text{-}aO_2$ + desired PaO_2 / 760		
4) Using P/F Ratio: PaO_2 should be: $\frac{5\ PaO_2}{1\ FIO_2}$		New $FIO_2 = PaO_2$ desired + $PaCO_2$ desired / (PaO_2/ PAO_2) / $(PB - H_2O)$
5) Estimate: $FIO_2 = PaO_2 / 500$		

Equation	Comments	Significance
O_2 Consumption (Demand) ($\dot{V}O_2$) $\dot{V}O_2 = CO \times (CaO_2 - C\bar{v}O_2) \times 10$ $= CO \times Ca\text{-}\bar{v}O_2 \times 10$	Normal = 200 - 250 mL/min	Volume of O_2 consumed (utilized) by the body tissues per min. Index of metabolic level and CO. $\uparrow\dot{V}O_2$ = ↑metabolism or CO; $\downarrow\dot{V}O_2$ = ↓metabolism or CO
O_2 Consumption Index ($\dot{V}O_2I$) $\dot{V}O_2I = CI \times Ca\text{-}\bar{v}O_2 \times 10$	$\dot{V}O_2I = \dot{V}O_2/BSA$ $= 110\text{-}165$ mL/min/m^2	O_2 consumption per body size.
O_2 Content 1) Arterial $CaO_2 = (Hgb \times 1.36) \times SaO_2 + (PaO_2 \times 0.0031)$ 2) Venous (mixed) $C\bar{v}O_2 = (Hgb \times 1.36) \times S\bar{v}O_2 + (P\bar{v}O_2 \times 0.0031)$ $= \dot{V}O_2/CO$ 3) Pulmonary capillary CcO_2	Normal = 15-24 mL/dL (vol%) Both 1.36 and 1.39 are considered correct. Hgb = gm % Normal = 12-15 mL/dL (vol%) $P\bar{v}O_2$ = pressure in mixed venous blood obtained from pulmonary artery. See shunt equation.	Total amount of O_2 in arterial blood (combined plus dissolved). Total amount of O_2 in mixed venous blood (combined plus dissolved). SaO_2 and $S\bar{v}O_2$ obtained from oximeter or oxyheme dissociation curve.

Equation	Comments	Significance
O_2 Delivery (Supply, Transport) ($\dot{D}O_2$) $\dot{D}O_2 = CO \times CaO_2 \times 10$	Normal = 750-1000 mL/min Quantity of O_2 delivered to the body tissues per minute. Requires CO determination.	↑ O_2 transport = ↑CO +/or ↑ CaO_2 ↓ O_2 transport = ↓CO +/or ↓ CaO_2 10 = conversion factor to mL/min
O_2 Delivery Index ($\dot{D}O_2I$) $\dot{D}O_2I = CI \times CaO_2 \times 10$	$\dot{D}O_2I = \dot{D}O_2 / BSA$ $= 500\text{-}600\ mL/min/m^2$	O_2 delivery per body size.
O_2 Extraction Ratio (O_2 ER) $O_2\ ER = \frac{O_2\ \text{consumption (demand)}}{O_2\ \text{delivery (supply)}}$ $= \frac{\dot{V}O_2 \times 100}{\dot{D}O_2}$ $= \frac{Ca\text{-}\bar{v}O_2}{CaO_2}$	Normal = 25 % Amount of O_2 extracted and consumed by the body tissues, relative to the amount delivered. Estimate = $\frac{Sa\text{-}\bar{v}O_2}{SaO_2}$	Indicator of O_2 supply/demand balance. ↑ratio = ↓ O_2 +/or ↑ O_2 transport ↓ ratio = ↑O_2 +/or ↓ O_2 transport
O_2 Index (OI)	$OI = (\overline{P}aw \times FIO_2 \times 100) / PaO_2$	> 40 = severe respiratory distress with high mortality; 20 - 25 = mortality > 50%
O_2 Reserve $O_2\ Reserve = \dot{D}O_2 - \dot{V}O_2$	Normal = 750 mL/min $= CO \times C\bar{v}O_2 \times 10$	Venous O_2 supply: O_2 supply minus O_2 demand

Equation	Comments	Significance
O2 Saturation (mixed venous) ($S\bar{v}O_2$) $S\bar{v}O_2 = SaO_2 - \dot{V}O_2/\dot{D}O_2$ $= SaO_2 - Sa\text{-}\bar{v}O_2$	Normal = 75 % (60-80 %)	Percent of hemoglobin in mixed venous blood, saturated with O_2.
P/F Ratio (Oxygenation Ratio) PaO_2 / FIO_2	Normal = 400 – 500 (regardless of FIO_2) What PaO_2 Should Be: $\frac{5\ PaO_2}{1\ FIO_2\%}$	< 300 indicative of ALI < 200 = ARDS
Predicted PaO_2 (based on age)	$PaO_2 = 110 - ½$ age	
Respiratory Index (RI) $PA\text{-}aO_2 / PaO_2$	Normal = < 1.0	1.0- 5.0 = V/Q mismatch > 5.0 = refractory hypoxemia due to physiol. shunt
Respiratory Quotient (Exchange ratio) (RQ, RE, RR) 1) $RQ = \frac{\dot{V}CO_2}{\dot{V}O_2}$ 2) $RQ = \dot{V}E \times \frac{F\bar{E}\,CO_2 - F_ICO_2}{F_IO_2 - F\bar{E}\,O_2}$ 3) $RQ = \frac{F\bar{E}\,CO_2}{FIO2 - F\bar{E}\,O_2}$	$\frac{\text{Volume } CO_2 \text{ produced/min}}{\text{Volume } O_2 \text{ consumed/min}}$ Normal = 200 / 250 = 0.8	RQ = ratio of CO_2 produced to O_2 consumed (internal respiration). RE represents the amount of O_2/CO_2 exchange in the lungs per minute (external respiration). RE = RQ in steady state condition.

Equation	Comments	Significance
Ventilation/Perfusion Index (VQI) $VQI = \frac{1 - SaO_2}{1 - S\bar{v}O_2}$	Normal = 0.8	Combines assessment of SaO_2 and $S\bar{v}O_2$ to estimate venous admixture. Correlates well with $\dot{Q}_S/\dot{Q}_T$.
Ventilation		
Alveolar Ventilation ($\dot{V}_A$) 1) $\dot{V}_A = \dot{V}_E - \dot{V}_D$ 2) $\dot{V}_A = (V_T - V_{Dphys}) \times f$ 3) $\dot{V}_A = (\dot{V}_ECO_2/PaCO_2) \times 863$ 4) Ideal $\dot{V}_A = (\dot{V}_ECO_2/ PaCO_2$ desired) x 863 5) $\dot{V}_A \times PaCO_2$ known = $\dot{V}_A \times$ $PaCO_2$ desired	Normal = 4 - 6 L/min $\dot{V}_ECO_2 = \dot{V}_E$ measured x $F\bar{E}\ CO_2$ calculated or measured $F\bar{E}\ CO_2 = P\bar{E}\ CO_2$ measured / $P_B - PH_2O$ 863 = correction factor if in milliliters, (0.863 = if in liters). Estimated $\dot{V}_ECO_2$ = 3mL/kg/min	The volume of inspired air which participates in gas exchange per minute. Used to calculate the ideal alveolar ventilation needed to maintain a desired $PaCO_2$.
Alveolar Volume (V_A) 1) $V_A = \dot{V}_A / f$ 2) $V_A = V_T - V_D$ 3) $V_A = 2 \times IBW$ (lbs) 4) $V_A = 2/3\ V_T$	 Estimate Estimate (normal)	The volume of each breath that participates in gas exchange.

Equation	Comments	Significance
Deadspace Ventilation ($\dot{V}_D$) 1) $\dot{V}_D phys = V_D phys \times f$ 2) $\dot{V}_D phys = \dot{V}_E - \dot{V}_A$ 3) $\dot{V}_D phys = (PaCO_2 - PECO_2 / PaCO_2) \times \dot{V}_E$ 4) $\dot{V}_D phys = \dot{V}_D/V_T \times \dot{V}_E$	Normal = 1/3 $\dot{V}_E$	The volume of wasted air (not participating in gas exchange) per minute.
Deadspace Volume (V_D) 1) $V_D = V_T - V_A$ 2) $V_D = \dot{V}_E - \dot{V}_A / f$ 3) $V_D phys = V_D anat + V_D alv + V_D mech + V_D comp$ = total V_D	Normal = 1/3 V_T $V_D anat$ = anatomical V_D (1 mL/lb IBW; 0.5 mL/lb with ET tube or trach) $V_D alv$ = alveolar V_D $V_D mech$ = mechanical (10mL/inch) VDcomp = tubing compliance loss	The volume of wasted air (not participating in gas exchange) per breath (V > Q). ↑$V_D alv$ = ↓ CO, pulmonary vasoconstriction, pulmonary embolus

Equation	Comments	Significance
Deadspace / Tidal Volume Ratio (V_D/V_T Ratio) 1) Bohr Equation: $\frac{V_{D}phys}{V_T} = \frac{PaCO_2 - P\bar{E}CO_2}{P_ACO_2}$ $\frac{V_{D}anat}{V_T} = \frac{PetCO_2 - P\bar{E}CO_2}{PetCO_2}$	Normal = 0.33 $\frac{(150\ V_D)}{(450\ V_T)}$ $P\bar{E}CO_2$ = mixed expired Normal = 0.33 (no ABG required) Pet = end tidal	Used to measure the portion of V_T not participating in gas exchange (wasted ventilation). $V_D/V_T > 0.5$ is indicative of respiratory failure. Many lung diseases (atelectasis, pneumonia, pulmonary edema, emboli, etc.) can exhibit changes in V_D (i.e., $V_{D}alv$) without corresponding changes in $PaCO_2$.
2) Estimate: $V_{D}phys / V_T = (\dot{V}_E$ actual / $\dot{V}_E$ predicted) x ($PaCO_2$ actual / 40) x 0.33	This equation is quite accurate. No mixed expired sample required.	
Minute Ventilation ($\dot{V}_E$) (Minute Volume) 1) $\dot{V}_E = V_T \times f$ 2) $\dot{V}_E = \dot{V}_A + \dot{V}_D$ 3) $\dot{V}_E \approx 1/PaCO_2$ 4) New $\dot{V}_E = \dot{V}_E$ current x $PaCO_2$ current/ $PaCO_2$ desired 5) $PaCO_2$ desired x $\dot{V}_E$ needed = $PaCO_2$ current x $\dot{V}_E$ current 6) Nomogram (See next page)	Normal = 5 - 7 L/min. Changing f is often preferred to changing V_T (due to altering V_D/V_T ratio). $\dot{V}_A$ = effective alveolar ventilation $\dot{V}_D$ = physiological deadspace	The total air in or out of the lungs in one minute. Used to calculate the $\dot{V}_E$ needed to maintain a desired $PaCO_2$. Change rate to change $\dot{V}_E$, changing V_T may alter the V_D/V_T ratio.

Equation	Comments	Significance
Ventilation/Perfusion Ratio ($\dot{V}/\dot{Q}$ Ratio) $\dot{V}_A/\dot{Q}c = \frac{(C\bar{v}CO_2 - CaCO_2) \times 8.63}{PaCO_2}$	Normal = $\frac{4L/min}{5L/min}$ = 0.8 Ratio of minute alveolar ventilation to minute capillary blood flow. Represents external respiration.	Ratio changes represent the degree and type of respiratory imbalances. ↓ Ratio (↓V/Q) = atelectasis, COPD, pneumonia, pneumothorax, N-M disorders, etc. ↑ Ratio (V/↑Q) = shock, pulmonary emboli, cor pulmonale, PPV.

Nomogram to estimate minute ventilation required to maintain a given PaCO2 when VD/VT is known:
To obtain the require minute ventilation to achieve a given PaCO2, the minute ventilation is plotted against the PaCO2 (measured simultaneously) and the VD/VT ratio is read on the isopleth that corresponds to the intersection. The isopleth is then followed to the desired PaCO2 and the corresponding minute ventilation read off the vertical axis.

For example: A patient with a VE of 5L and a PaCO2 of 60 mmHg has an estimated VD/VT ratio of 0.40. To achieve a desired PaCO2 of 40 mmHg, follow the 0.40 isopleth up to correspond to the PaCO2 of 40 on the horizontal axis. Then read the appropriate minute ventilation of about 8L/min off the vertical axis.

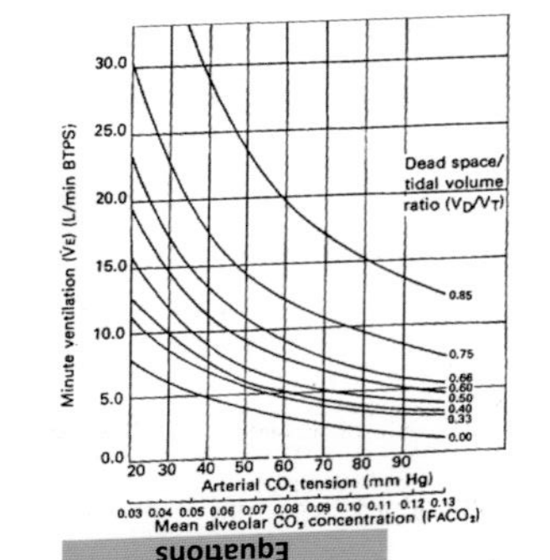

Equation	Comments	Significance
Ventilator Calculations		
Ventilator Flow $\dot{V} = \dot{V}_E \times RFF$ or $\dot{V} = \dot{V}_E \times 1/TI\%$	RFF = ratio flow factor = I + E Example: I:E ratio = 1:3, RFF = 4	Used to calculate proper flow to deliver a V_T in a given T_I.
Ventilator Rate Needed for Desired $PaCO_2$ New rate = $\frac{\text{current rate} \times PaCO_2}{\text{desired } PaCO_2}$	Desired $\dot{V}_E$ = $\frac{\text{present } PaCO_2 \times \text{present } \dot{V}_E}{\text{desired } PaCO_2}$	This equation holds presuming a steady metabolic rate, stable or no spontaneous breathing, and no change in other ventilator parameters, or $V_D$mech.
Mechanics		
Airway Occlusion Pressure (P0.1)	Normal = < 2 cm H_2O Change in airway pressure at 0.1 sec after beginning inspiration against an occluded airway. Used to assess ventilatory drive and demand. Indicative of ventilatory demand.	↑ P0.1 = ↑ patient workload +/or drive (possible inadequate ventilator support). ↓ P0.1 = ↓ patient workload +/or drive (possible excessive ventilator support). > 4 - 6 cm H_2O is indicative of weaning failure. (See PImax) Although actual value is negative, it is reported as a positive.

Equation	Comments	Significance
Airway Resistance (Raw) 1) $R = \Delta P / \dot{V}$ 2) Raw = Pmouth - Palv / $\dot{V}_I$ 3) Raw = PIP - Pplat / $\dot{V}_I$ 4) Raw = Cdyn - Cstat (see below)	Normal = 0.5 - 2.5 cm H_2O/L/sec @ 0.5 L/sec (30 L/min) ET tube = 4 - 8 cm H_2O/L/sec $\dot{V}_I$ = inspiratory flow in L/sec, square wave flow pattern (use 30 L/min if comparing with norm).	Represents frictional resistance of air-flow (80%) and tissue motion (20%). Raw ≈ $1/r^4$ ↑ airflow resistance = airway collapse, edema, bronchospasm, secretions, ET tube etc. ↑ tissue resistance = pulmonary edema, fibrosis, pneumonia, etc. > 5 cm H_2O/L/sec may = wean failure.
Clinical Note: A quick estimate of Raw: = P_{TA} (transairway pressure) = PIP - Pplat ↑P_{TA} = ↑Raw ↓P_{TA} = ↓Raw	↑PIP + ↑Pplat (P_{TA} constant) = ↓Cstat ↑PIP + same Pplat (↑P_{TA}) = ↑Raw ↓PIP + ↓Pplat (P_{TA} constant) = ↑Cstat ↓PIP + same Pplat (↓P_{TA}) = ↓Raw	Pressure support is used primarily to overcome airway resistance of circuit and ET tube. Appropriate PS level can be estimated as PTA (i.e., PIP - Pplat). Note: By convention Raw refers to inspiratory Raw. Expiratory Raw may be determined by PIP - PEEP / $\dot{V}$expir and is typically > inspiratory Raw.

Equation	Comments	Significance
Compliance (C) $C = \Delta V / \Delta P$ $C_{LT} = C_L + C_{CW}$ $= \Delta V / P_{alv} - P_B$ $C_L = \Delta V / P_{alv} - P_{pl}$ $C_{CW} = \Delta V / P_{pl} - P_B$	Normal = 70 - 100 mL/cm H_2O Total compliance is referred to as C_{LT} (lung + thorax) or Crs (respiratory system). C_L = lung compliance C_{CW} = chest wall (thorax) compliance	Represents the ease of distention of the lungs and thorax. Includes elastic, functional, and tissue viscous resistance. Ideal = 100mL/ cm H_2O Lungs and chest wall each = 200 mL/ cm H_2O. P_B = barometric pressure; Ppl = pleural pressure Palv = alveolar pressure

Equation	Comments	Significance
Static Compliance (Cstat) How To Measure Cstat = V_T - Vtubing / Pplat - PEEP Pplat = the pressure needed to maintain lung inflation during zero airflow. It is measured by using either an inspiratory hold or temporarily occluding the exhalation port until pressure stabilizes (approx 1 - 4 sec). PEEP = PEEPE + PEEPI Clinical Note: In VV, a ↓Cstat results in an ↑PIP and ↑Pplat (V_T constant). In PV, a ↓Cstat results in a ↓V_T (PIP and Pplat constant).	Normal = 70 - 100 mL/cm H_2O Vtubing = volume loss in tubing due to circuit compliance Vtubing = CF (tubing compliance factor) x Pgradient (Pplat - PEEP) CF must be determined for each patient-ventilator setup (normals range from 1.5 - 5.0 mL/cm H_2O). It is either calculated by newer ventilators or manually by: setting V_T to 200 mL, triggering the ventilator, occluding the patient wye, and observing PIP. CF = V_T (200) / PIP (Pplat can be used in place of PIP). V_{tubing} = (V_T (200) / PIP) x (Pplat - PEEP)	Represents the combination of lung elasticity and chest wall recoil. Usually measured while on MV. ↓ Cstat = ↓ lung elasticity or ↓ chest wall recoil. ↑ Cstat = ↑ lung elasticity or ↑ chest wall recoil. For conditions causing ↑ or ↓ Cstat, see page 5-18. Trend changes in Cstat and Cdyn are more significant in interpreting lung conditions than single measurements. A Cstat ≤ 25- 33 mL/cm H_2O is indicative of weaning failure. Cstat can also be used to determine optimal PEEP.

Equation	Comments	Significance
Dynamic Compliance (Cdyn) How To Measure Cdyn = V_T - Vtubing / PIP - PEEP Usually measured while on MV.	Normal = 40 - 70 mL/cm H_2O Vtubing = CF x (PIP - PEEP) (See Cstat above to determine CF) PEEP = $PEEP_E$ + $PEEP_I$	Represents the combination of static lung compliance (Cstat) and airway resistance (Raw). For conditions causing ↑ or ↓Cdyn, see Cstat (above) Trend changes in Cstat and Cdyn are more significant in interpreting lung conditions than single measurements.

Clinical Notes:

↑Cdyn (same Cstat) =↓Raw
↓Cdyn (same Cstat) = ↑Raw

In VV, a↓Cdyn results in an↑PIP (V_T constant).
In VV, a ↓PIP (V_T constant) = improved Cstat or Raw or a leak.

↑Cdyn (with same↑ in Cstat) = ↑Cstat
↓Cdyn (with same ↓ in Cstat) = ↓Cstat

In PV, a ↓Cdyn results in a ↓V_T (PIP constant).
In PV, an ↑V_T (PIP constant) = improved Cstat or Raw.

↑Cdyn (with partial ↑ in Cstat) =↓Raw and ↑Cstat
↓Cdyn (with partial ↓ in Cstat) = ↑Raw and ↓Cstat

Equation	Comments	Significance
Equation of Motion Pawo = V/C + (Raw x $\dot{V}$)	Elastic components of respiratory system: P = V/C V = P x C C = V/P Resistive components of respiratory system: P = Raw x $\dot{V}$ $\dot{V}$ = P/Raw Raw = P/ $\dot{V}$	At any moment the airway opening pressure (Pawo) must exactly balance the opposing lung and chest wall expansion forces. P, $\dot{V}_I$, + V can be controlled by the clinician. In VV: Set $\dot{V}$: P varies with Raw Set V: P varies with C In PV: Set P: $\dot{V}$ varies with Raw Set P: V varies with C
Maximal Inspiratory Pressure (PImax) (MIP, NIP) Two methods: Marini #1- total occlusion @ end-exhalation Marini #2- total occlusion @ below FRC	The maximal inspiratory effort (pressure) generated against an occluded airway (approx 20 sec). Normal < 20 cm H_2O (i.e., < - 20 cm H_2O) Although actual value is negative, it is reported as a positive.	Indicative of the capability of the inspiratory muscles. (See P0.1 above) P0.1 / PImax = demand / capability = predictive weaning index ≤ 0.9 indicative of weaning failure Prior to start of test patient should be actively breathing (remove vent support). Remove $PEEP_E$ and $PEEP_I$. Respiratory muscles should not be fatigued.

Equation	Comments	Significance
Mean Airway Pressure ($\overline{P}aw$) $\overline{P}aw = \frac{(T_I \times PIP) + (T_E \times PEEP)}{Ttot}$ $\overline{P}aw = (PIP - PEEP) \times T_I/Ttot + PEEP$	Average airway pressure during several breathing cycles.	$\overline{P}aw = ([P_{TA} + ½ PA] - PEEP) \times T_I/Ttot + PEEP$ Note: Should always be less than CVP (1 cm H_2O = 0.735 mmHg)
Rapid - Shallow Breathing Index (RSBI) RSBI = f / V_T or $f^2 / \dot{V}_E$	Measure f and V_T (in liters) while off the ventilator. Normal = < 100	Has proven to be one of the best predictive indices for weaning. > 105 is indicative of weaning failure
Time Constant (TC) TC = Raw x Cstat $TC = \Delta P/\dot{V} \times \Delta V/\Delta P$ Note: TC generally refers to inspiratory TC. Expiratory TC may be much longer than inspiratory TC in COPD.	1TC = 63% 2TC = 87% 3TC = 95% 4TC = 98% 5TC = 99% % = % of V_T entering lungs within each TC period. Normal TC = 0.2 sec Normal T_I = 3 - 4 TC = 3 or 4 x 0.2 sec = 0.6 – 0.8 sec	TC (inspir) indicates alveolar filling time. ↑ TC (> 0.2 sec) is usually indicative of ↑Raw (but may be ↑C_{LT}). ↓ TC (< 0.2 sec) is usually indicative of ↓C_{LT} (but may be ↓Raw). TC(expir) indicates alveolar emptying time. < 3 TCexpir will generally result in air-trapping. TCexpir may be approximated with a F-V loop.

Equation	Comments	Significance
Vital Capacity (VC)	Normal is 60-80 mL/kg	< 60 mL/kg indicates general restr. process > 10 mL/kg is needed for effective deep breathing and cough. < 10 mL/kg = impending respiratory failure
Work of Breathing (WOB) $W = \int P \times V$ WOB / min (W) = WOB x f WOB / liter = $W / \dot{V}_E$ WOB total = WOB patient + WOB vent	The energy (pressure gradient) required to take a breath. Normal = 0.6 - 1.0 j (1j = 0.1 kg.m) $W / \dot{V}_E$ closely reflects abnormal pulmonary mechanics.	Intrinsic WOB = energy required to overcome patient's elastic and resistive forces. Extrinsic WOB = energy required to overcome added extrinsic systems
Weaning Equations		
CROP CROP = Cdyn x (PaO_2/PAO_2) x PImax / rate	C = compliance R = rate O = oxygenation P = pressure	< 13 mL/breath/min indicative of weaning failure.
Simplified Weaning Index SWI = f (mech) x (PIP - PEEP / PImax) x ($PaCO_2$ / 40)	Normal = < 9 min	Simplified version of weaning index (WI). Less accurate than WI, but quick and easy. > 11 min indicative of weaning failure
P0.1 / PImax and RSBI (f /V_T): See above		

Equation	Comments	Significance
Perfusion/Hemodynamic Monitoring		
Cardiac Index (CI) $CI = CO/BSA$	Cardiac output per body size. Normal = 2.5 - 4.4 $L/min/m^2$ BSA (See Pg 7-28)	More precise measure of pump efficiency than CO. CI 1.8 - 2.5 = moderate cardiac disease CI < 1.8 = severe cardiac disease
Cardiac Output (CO or $\dot{Q}_T$) $CO = SV \times HR$	Normal = 4-8 L/min (at rest) See Fick equation below & Oakes' ***Hemodynamic Monitoring: A Bedside Reference Manual*** for more information.	Amount of blood ejected from heart per minute. Indicator of pump efficiency and a determinant of tissue perfusion.
Coronary Artery Perfusion Pressure (CPP or CAPP) $CPP = MAP - PAWP$ $= BPdia - PAWP$	Normal = 60-80 mm Hg	Driving pressure of coronary blood flow.
Fick Equation $\dot{V}O_2 = CO \times Ca\text{-}\bar{v}O_2$	See Oakes' ***Hemodynamic Monitoring: A Bedside Reference Manual*** for more info.	Method of measuring cardiac output. Fick estimate: $CO = 125 \times BSA / Ca\text{-}\bar{v}O_2$

Equation	Comments	Significance
Left Ventricular Stroke Work (LVSW) LVSW = $(\overline{BP}-$ PAWP) x SV x 0.0136	Normal = 60-80 gm/m/beat	Measure of pumping function of left ventricle (LV contractility).
Left Ventricular Stroke Work Index (LVSWI) LVSWI = $(\overline{BP}-$ PAWP) x SVI x 0.0136	Normal = 40-75 gm/m/beat/m^2	Measure of pumping function of left ventricle (LV contractility) / body size.
Mean Arterial Blood Pressure ($\overline{BP}$, MAP) $\overline{BP}$ = 1/3 PP + BPdia $= \frac{BPsys + 2BPdia}{3}$	Normal = 93 mmHg (70-105)	Average driving force of systemic circulation. Determined by cardiac output and total peripheral resistance.
Mean Pulmonary Artery Pressure ($\overline{PAP}$, PAMP) $\overline{PAP}$= 1/3 pulmPP + PADP	Normal = 10 - 15 mmHg $= \frac{PASP + 2PADP}{3}$	Average driving force of blood from the right heart to left heart.
Pulmonary Vascular Resistance (PVR) PVR = $\frac{PAMP - PAWP}{CO}$ x 80	Normal = 20-250 dynes•sec•cm^{-5} = 0.25-2.5 units (mm Hg/L/min) E.g. $\frac{14\ mm\ Hg - 5\ mm\ Hg}{5\ L/min}$ = 1.8 units	Resistance to RV ejection of blood into pulmonary vasculature. Indicator of RV afterload. mm Hg/L/min x 80 = dynes•sec•cm^{-5}

Equation	Comments	Significance
Pulmonary Vascular Resistance Index (PVRI) $PVRI = \frac{PAMP - PAWP}{CI} \times 80$	Normal = 35-350 dynes•sec•cm^{-5}/ m^2	PVR related to body size.
Pulse Pressure (PP) PP = BPsys - BPdia	Normal = 40 mm Hg (20-80)	Difference between BP systolic and BP diastolic.
Rate Pressure Product (RPP) RPP = BPsys x HR	Normal = < 12,000 mm Hg/min	Indirect determinant of $M\dot{V}O_2$.
Right Ventricular Stroke Work (RVSW) = (PAMP - CVP) x SV x 0.0136	Normal = 10-15 gm/m/beat	Measure of pumping function of right ventricle (RV contractility).
Right Ventricular Stroke Work Index (RVSW) = (PAMP - CVP) x SVI x 0.0136	Normal = 4-12 gm/m/beat/m^2 = RVSW / BSA	Measure of pumping function of right ventricle (RV contractility) / body size.

Equation	Comments	Significance
Shunt Equation ($\dot{Q}_S/\dot{Q}_T$) 1) Classical $\dot{Q}_S/\dot{Q}_T = \frac{CcO_2 - CaO_2}{Cc\text{-}\bar{v}O_2}$	Normal = 2-5% CcO_2 = pulmonary capillary blood O_2 content ("ideal") at 100% saturated with alveolar O_2. Cannot be sampled. $CcO_2 = (Hgb \times 1.34)\ SaO_2 + (PAO_2 \times 0.003)$	Indicates ratio of shunted blood (Q_S) (blood not participating in gas exchange) to total cardiac output (Q_T). $Q_S = Q_T - Q_C$ $Q_S = QS_{phys} = Qs_{anat} + Qs_{cap}$ Indicator or efficiency of pulm system: < 10% = normal lungs 10-20% = minimal effect 20-30% = significant pulm disease > 30% = life-threatening
2) Clinical $\dot{Q}_S/\dot{Q}_T = \frac{PA\text{-}aO_2 \times 0.003}{Ca\text{-}\bar{v}O2 + PA\text{-}aO2 \times 0.003}$	Less accurate/easier. Perform breathing ↑ FIO_2 (50% preferred over 100% due to ↑shunting from alveolar collapse) x 20 minutes.	
3) Estimate $\dot{Q}_S/\dot{Q}_T = \frac{PA\text{-}aO2 \times 0.003}{3.5 + PA\text{-}aO2 \times 0.003}$		Clinical equation assumes Hgb 100% saturated ($PaO_2 > 150$). If $PaO_2 < 150$, then must use classical shunt equation.
4) Estimates $\dot{Q}_S/\dot{Q}_T = \frac{PA\text{-}aO_2}{20}$ $\dot{Q}_S/\dot{Q}_T$ = 5% per every 100 mm Hg below expected	5%/100 mm Hg (2%/50 mm Hg) Most accurate when breathing 100% O_2. Plus normal 2-5%. Estimate good until $PaO_2 < 100$ mm Hg	$Ca\text{-}\bar{v}O_2$ can be assumed if a mixed venous sample cannot be obtained: 4.5 - 5% in patients with good CO and perfusion. 3.5% in critically ill patients. Estimate: PaO_2/FIO_2 > 300 = < 15% shunt 200 - 300 = 15 - 20%; < 200 = > 20% shunt

Equation	Comments	Significance
Stroke Volume (SV) SV = CO/HR x 1000	Normal = 60-120 mL/beat	Amount of blood ejected by either ventricle per contraction.
Stroke Volume Index (SVI) SVI = CO/HR x 1000 / BSA	Normal = 35-75 mL/beat/m^2	Relates SV to body size.
Systemic Vascular Resistance (SVR) $SVR = \frac{\overline{BP} - CVP}{CO} \times 80$	Normal = 800-1600 dynes•sec•cm^{-5} = 10-20 units (mm Hg/L/min) E.g. $\frac{93 \text{ mm Hg} - 3 \text{ mm Hg}}{5 \text{ L/min}} = 18$ units	Resistance to LV ejection of blood into systemic circulation. Indicator of LV afterload. mm Hg/L/min x 80 = dynes•sec•cm^{-5}
Systemic Vascular Resistance Index (SVRI) $SVRI = \frac{\overline{BP} - CVP}{CI} \times 80$	Normal = 1400-2600 dynes•sec•cm^{-5}/ m^2	SVR per body size.
Patient Calculations		
Body Surface Area (BSA) BSA (m^2) = (Ht $(cm)^{0.725}$) x (Wt $(kg)^{0.425}$) x 0.007184	BSA (m^2) = (4 x Kg) + 7 / Kg + 90	Used to determine cardiac index and other hemodynamic parameters. Relates parameters to body size. Kg = 2.2 lbs

Equation	Comments	Significance
Ideal Body Weight (IBW) Hamwi method (see page 10-6 for PBW)	Male: 106 lbs for 5 ft tall. Add 6 lbs/in above 5 ft. 1 Kg = 2.2 lbs	Female: 100 lbs for 5 ft tall. Add 5 lbs/in above 5 ft.
Miscellaneous		
ATPS to BTPS Vol BTPS = Vol ATPS x factor	See Appendix	Correction of lung volumes measured at room temp to body temp.
Fick's Law of Diffusion $\text{Diffusion} = \frac{\text{Area x diffusion coefficient x } \Delta P}{\text{Thickness}}$		Gas diffusion rate across the lung membrane.
Gas Laws Dalton's Law: Total P = P1+P2+P3, etc. Boyle's Law: P1 x V1 = P2 x V2 — P and V are inversely related (T constant) Charles' Law: V1/T1 = V2/T2 — V and T are directly related (P constant) Gay-Lussac's Law: P1/T1 = P2/T2 — P and T are directly related (V constant) Combined Gas Law: P1 x V1 / T1 = P2 x V2 / T2		
Graham's Law of Diffusion Coefficient	Diffusion coefficient = $\frac{\text{solubility coefficient}}{\sqrt{\text{gmw}}}$	Rate of gas diffusion is inversely proportional to the square root of its gram molecular weight.

Equation	Comments	Significance
Helium/Oxygen (He/O_2) Flow Conversion	80% He / 20% O_2: actual flow = flow x 1.8 70% He / 30% O_2 = flow x 1.6 60% He / 40% O_2 = flow x 1.4	Conversion is used when an O_2 flow meter is used to measure Heliox flow. Used in patients with obstructive disorders.
Law of LaPlace	P = 2ST / r	P = pressure (dynes/cm^2); r = radius (cm) ST = surface tension (dynes/cm)
Oxygen Blending Ratios FIO_2 desired ↓ 100 ___ 21 air units ___ O2 units	Select desired FIO_2. Subtract 100 - FIO_2 = air units Subtract FIO_2 - 20 = O_2 units	To find air/O_2 ratio for desired FIO_2. Air units/O_2 units = air/O_2 ratio E.g: 40% O_2 desired $\frac{100 - 40 = 60}{40 - 20 = 20} = \frac{60}{20} = \frac{3}{1}$

Equation	Comments	Significance
Oxygen Duration Times **Duration of a Cylinder** $\text{Time (min)} = \frac{\text{Pcyl} \times \text{CF}}{\text{Flow (L/min)}}$	P_{cyl} = total pressure in cylinder (psi) – 500 psi (reserve) CF = conversion factor (L/psi) $= \frac{(\text{ft}^3 \text{ of cyl}) \times 28.3\ \text{L/ft}^3}{\max P_{cyl}}$	Used to calculate how long a cylinder of O2 gas will last. 500 psi equals reserve. Size / ft^3 / factor: A / 2.7 / 0.035 B / 5.3 / 0.068 D / 12.6 / 0.16 E / 22 / 0.28 G / 186 / 2.41 H/K / 244 / 3.14 M / 128 / 1.65
Duration of a Liquid System	Liquid weight is known: Duration time (min) = $\frac{344\ \text{L/lb} \times \text{liquid weight (lb)}}{O_2 \text{ flow (L/min)}}$ 1 L liquid = 860 L gas Liquid Wt = Total Wt - Cylinder Wt	Gauge fraction is known: Duration time (min) = $\frac{\text{Liquid capacity (L)} \times 860 \times \text{gauge fraction}}{O_2 \text{ flow (L/min)}}$ Note: Does not account for evaporative loss.

Size	ft^3	factor
A	2.7	0.035
B	5.3	0.068
D	12.6	0.16
E	22	0.28
G	186	2.41
H/K	244	3.14
M	128	1.65

Equation	Comments	Significance
Oxygen Entrainment Ratios $TF = O_2 \text{ flow} \times \frac{0.79}{FIO_2 - 0.21}$ $FIO_2 = \frac{0.79}{TF / O_2 \text{ Flow}} + 0.21$	TF = total flow in liters (O_2 + air) Mixture = O_2 + air $(FIO_2)(\text{Flow}) = (1.0)(O_2 \text{ Flow}) + (0.21)(\text{air Flow})$	Determines total flows, entrained flows, or O_2 percent when air and O_2 are entrained together. See O_2 blending ratio above.
Poiseuille's Law $\dot{V} = \frac{\Delta P\, r\, 4\pi}{\mu L 8} = \Delta P\, r^4$	$\dot{V}$ = flow, πP = driving pressure 8 = constant, r = radius of airway π = pi	μ = viscosity of gas L = length of airway
Reynold's Number $Rn = \frac{v \times D \times d}{\mu}$	Rn = Reynold's # v = velocity of fluid D = density of fluid	d = diameter of tube μ = viscosity of fluid $Rn < 2000$ = laminar flow $Rn > 2000$ = turbulent
Temperature Conversion	$F = (C^\circ \times 9/5) + 32^\circ$ $C^\circ = (F^\circ - 32) \times 5/9$	See Appendix $K^\circ = C^\circ + 273$

8 Airway and Ventilator Management

Chapter Contents

Airway Management

Ventilator Management

Management

Artificial Airways

Ventilation **O**bstruction **P**rotection **S**ecretion

Types/Indications

Type	Indications
Oropharyngeal	V (with bag), O, S,
Nasopharyngeal	O, S
Endotracheal	V, O, P, S
Tracheostomy	V, O, P, S

Notes:

Oropharyngeal Airway – Use only in unconscious (unresponsive) patients with no cough or gag reflex.

Incorrect insertion can displace the tongue into hypopharynx.

Nasopharyngeal airway – Useful in patients with (or at risk of developing) airway obstruction (particularly clenched jaw).

May be better tolerated than oropharyngeal in patients not deeply unconscious. Caution in patients with severe cranial facial injury.

Endotracheal Tube (ET tube)

Equipment Sizes	ET Tube I.D.(mm)	Trach Tube	Blade	Mask	Sx Catheter (Fr)
Adult Male	8.5-9.5	6	3-4	4	16
Adult Female	8.0-8.5	5	3	4	14

See Oakes' ***Neonatal/Pediatric Respiratory Care: A Critical Care Pocket Guide*** for sizes for neonates and children.

Insertion:

Pulse oximetry and ECG should be monitored continuously during intubation of patient. Interrupt attempt if oxygenation/ventilation is needed.

Insertion distance: Male: 21-23 cm; female: 19-21 cm

Difficult Airways: Consider use of cricoid pressure, fiberoptic intubation, OR intubation (non-emergent), cricothyrotomy (emergent)

Successful Intubation Checklist:

- Lungs: BS in both lungs (axilla), Bilateral chest expansion
- Abdomen: ↓ sounds in abdomen, No ↑ abdom. distention
- Warm air exhaled from tube
- Codensation inside of tube
- End Tidal CO_2
- Esophageal detector
- Improved color & SpO_2
- Light wand
- Visualization with scope
- CXR verification

Notes:

No one single confirmation technique is completely reliable, including H_2O vapor, except for direct visualization.

If any doubt: Use larynogoscope to visualize tube passing through vocal cords. If still doubt, remove tube.

Remove tube at once if hear stomach gurgling and see no chest expansion.

End-tidal CO_2 Detector ($P_{ET}CO_2$)

CO_2 detected: Tube is most likely in trachea*

*May rarely detect CO_2 if tube in esophagus and large amounts of carbonated fluid ingested prior. CO_2 will disappear after a few ventilations if in esophagus, it will continue if in trachea.

CO_2 not detected:

1) Tube is in esophagus
2) Tube may be in trachea
   - ↓ CO_2 <u>in</u> lungs: poor blood flow to lungs
     - Cardiac arrest
     - Pulmonary embolus
     - IV bolus of epinephrine
   - ↓ CO_2 **<u>from</u>** lungs:
     - Airway obstruction (eg., status asthmaticus)
     - Pulmonary edema

   Use another method to confirm
   (direct visualization or esophageal detector)
3) Detector contaminated with gastric contents or acidic drug (eg., tracheal admin. epinephrine)

Esophageal Detector Device

May use as one method of confirmation of ET tube placement.

Children: use only if child > 20 kg and has a perfusing rhythm

Caution: may be misleading in morbid obesity, late pregnancy, status asthmaticus, or copious secretions

Artificial Airway Complications to Watch

Insertion	Cuff	Obstruction
Apnea Arrhythmias/↓BP Aspiration (gag reflex): vomitis, blood, tooth. Bronchospasm Laryngospasm Hypoxia (max 15 sec) Trauma (poor technique): hemorrhage, broken teeth, spinal cord damage. Vagal stimulation **Improper Position** Esophagus, pharynx, right mainstem, beveling at carina.	Leak: not enough air, tube too small, hole in cuff or balloon,↑ tracheal diameter (malacia). Over-inflation: Necrosis (tracheomalacia), tracheal stenosis, fistula, vessel rupture, cuff herniation. **Improper Care** Contamination, desiccation, oral/nasal necrosis **Accidental Extubation**	Cuff herniation, kinking, secretions. **Body Response** Airway perforation, atelectasis, barotrauma, cord paralysis, edema, granulomas, pneumonia, sepsis, subglottic stenosis. **Additional Complications of Trach Tubes** Hemorrhage, infection, laryngeal nerve damage, pneumothorax, subQ emphysema.

Management

Cuff Care

Pressures	Techniques
Tracheal perfusion pressure = 30 mmHg (arterial) 18 mmHg (venous) Maximum cuff pressure = 20-25 mm Hg (27-33 cm H_2O) Recommended cuff pressure = just enough to seal trachea	***MOV*** (Minimum Occluding Volume) – inflate until hear no leak during PIP. ***MLT*** (Minimum Leak Technique) – inflate until hear no leak during PIP, then release a small amount of air to allow a slight leak at PIP*

Clinical Note: Cuff pressures should be monitored r via a hand-held cuff or pressure manometer. Finger palpation of the pilot balloon to estimate cuffed pressure is not recommended. Cuff volume should also be periodically monitored using a syringe. Volumes should not exceed 6-8 mL. > 10 mL may indicate tracheal injury. Foam cuff seals trachea with atmospheric pressure in cuff, hence cuff pressure and volume does not need to be monitored.

* Note: Minimum Leak Technique (MLT) is no longer commonly recommended, to decrease incidence of VAP.

Caution: Cuffed tubes permit secretions to pool above inflated cuff which may be released upon deflation. Suction well before deflation. VAP may be greatly ↓ by maintaining a 45º head elevation.

Bag & Valve Mask Ventilation

Volumes:

Adult	Infant/Child
500-600 mL (6-7 mL/kg) 1 L Adult Bag: 1/2 - 2/3 vol 2 L Adult Bag: 1/3 vol	Visible Chest Rise Bag size should be at least 450-500 mL

(All volumes must be sufficient for visible chest rise. Do not deliver breaths greater than needed to produce visible chest rise.)

Rates:

Most patients: 10- 12 breaths/min (q 5-6 sec), 1 sec inspiration

COPD, ↑ Raw, and/or hypovolemia: 6- 8 breaths/min (q 7-10 sec) to avoid auto-PEEP, 1 sec inspiration

Notes:

Use O_2 @ 10-15 L/min

Bag – mask ventilation is most effective when two trained and experienced rescuers work together – one opens the airway and seals the mask, while the other squeezes the bag. Both rescuers watch for visible chest rise.

Caution: Avoid hyperventilation! Giving > 12 breaths/min (>q 5 sec) may ↑ PIT, ↓venous return, ↓CO, and ↓ coronary and cerebral perfusion.

Gastric inflation: Giving large or forceful breaths may cause regurgitation, aspiration, elevated diaphragm, ↓ lung movement, and ↓ CL.

Cricoid pressure – May help prevent gastric inflation. Use only if victim is deeply unconscious (no cough or gag reflex). Usually requires third rescuer.

If regurgitation occurs – Turn victim to side, wipe out mouth, return to supine.

Signs of Inadequate Face Mask Ventilation

Absent or ↓: breath sounds, chest movement, expired CO_2	Excessive gas leak
↓ SpO_2	Gastric air entry/dilatation
Cyanosis	Hemodynamic changes (↑HR, ↑ BP, arrhythmias

Management

Suctioning

Notes:

Natural coughing is the most desirable method of clearing secretions. Manually assisted coughing or mechanical cough assist (see Lung Expansion Therapy, this Chapter) may reduce the need for suctioning.

Routine and frequent suctioning is not recommended. Suction catheters traumatize the airway mucosa potentially increasing secretion production, may cause hypoxemia and/or cardiac arrhythmias, possible atelectasis, as well as the risk of infection.

When suctioning is necessary, perform as gently as possible, keeping the catheter within the tube, if possible.

If suctioning beyond the tube tip is necessary, the catheter should be advanced gently and suction applied only during catheter withdrawal, with suction being applied for no more than 15 sec.

Use the lowest suction pressure possible to obtain the desired result. If suction catheter becomes clogged, quickly clear out obstruction, do not increase suction.

Indications/Need	
Evidence of Secretions	**Alterations in Patient and/or Ventilation**
Visible secretions in tube Audible course, wet, +/or ↓ BS Palpation of wet, course vibrations through chest wall	Patient: ↑ agitation, irritability, restless Ventilator: ↑ Raw VV: ↑ PIP and ↑ high pressure alarms PV: ↓ V_T
Alterations in Vital Signs	**Alterations in O_2 and Ventilation**
Change in respiratory pattern: ↑ WOB, tachypnea, retractions Change in cardiac pattern: ↑ or ↓ HR	↓ SpO_2 (< 90%) Skin color changes – pale, dusky, or cyanotic Changes in ABGs - ↑ $PaCO_2$, ↓ PaO_2, respiratory acidosis

Suction Pressures/Catheter Sizes

Suction Pressures	Suction Catheter Size
Adult -100 to –120 mmHg Child -80 to –100 mmHg Infant -60 to –80 mmHg	ET tube size (ID) x 2, then use next smaller size suction catheter E.g.; 6.0 x 2 = 12, use 10 FR

Suctioning Procedure

1. Assess indications/need as above
2. Set up and test suction pressure
3. Explain procedure to patient ("this will make you cough")
4. Position patient: (commonly, unless contraindicated)
   Nasaotracheal and pharyngeal suctioning – Semi-Fowler's position with neck hyperextended
   Endotracheal and tracheostomy – supine
5. Wash and glove both hands – use sterile technique
6. Pre-oxygenate with 100% O_2 for 30 sec (may use same FIO_2 in COPD patients)
7. Note RR, HR, and SpO_2, and monitor throughout procedure
8. Insert catheter as far as possible (until you feel resistance, or until patient begins to cough), then withdraw a few cm. (For ET or trach tubes, advance to just past ET tube tip [shallow sx] or until meet resistance at carina and then withdraw 1 cm [deep sx]
9. Apply suction while withdrawing and rotating the catheter (< 10-15 sec). Do not move catheter up and down. Stop and remove immediately if untoward patient response.
10. Allow patient to rest and re-oxygenate for 1 min
11. Clean secretions from catheter by suctioning sterile water
12. Monitor patient (VS + response)
13. Repeat steps 6-11 as needed
14. Return any continuous O_2 to pre-suction settings

Extubation

Assessment for Removal of the Artificial Airway

- Is the original need for the airway no longer present?
- Is the airway patent?
- Can the patient protect his lower airway? (gag reflex, adequate cough)
- Can the patient pass a cuff leak test?

Cuff Leak Test

Assessing for airflow around a deflated cuff.

Procedure:

- Suction the mouth and upper airway.
- Deflate the cuff

  1. Assess for spontaneous breathing around the cuff by briefly occlude the ET tube, or
  2. Assess for airflow around the cuff during a positive pressure breath.

CUFF LEAK TEST RESULTS

Test Result	Consider . . .
Airflow does occur around the deflated cuff	removing tube
Patient is unable to breathe around the occluded ET tube with the cuff deflated or the positive pressure does not "leak" around the cuff. Laryngeal edema is then suspected.	adminstration of steroids prior to extubation extubate in O.R.?

Management

Extubation Procedure

Equipment needed:

- Manual resuscitation bag with reservoir for 100% F_IO_2
- Oxygen source
- Oxygen mask or cannula
- High-volume suction source and equipment (appropriately sized catheter, large bore oral suction device)
- Oral and pharyngeal airways
- Reintubation equipment (if needed)
- A 10cc syringe (for cuff deflation)

Procedure:

1. Choose an appropriate time of the day (preferably AM) and not during shift change.
2. Explain the procedure to the patient.
3. Monitor patient throughout and after procedure (ECG, SpO_2).
4. Sit patient in semi- or high Fowler's position.
5. Pre-oxygenate patient with 100% FiO_2.
6. Suction the mouth and pharynx.
7. Give large breath with hold as the cuff is being deflated to force secretions above the cuff (repeat until clear).
8. Loosen the tape or ET Tube holder.
9. Deflate the cuff fully.
10. Hyperinflate the patient while withdrawing the ET tube (rapidly and smoothly).
11. Instruct the patient to cough while the ET tube is being removed.
12. Instruct the patient to cough directly after the ET tube is removed.
13. Administer the same (or slightly higher) FiO_2 as prior to extubation.
14. Encourage the patient to take deep breaths and cough.
15. Monitor the patient closely.
16. Obtain ABG after 1 hour (optional).

Parameters to Be Monitored After Extubation

Cyanosis	Paradoxical breathing	Chest pain
Diaphoresis	Stridor	Hemodynamics
Dyspnea	↑ WOB	↓ Mental status

If stridor occurs following extubation, consider:

- Cool aerosol with supplemental oxygen via mask
- Nebulized racemic epinephrine
- Helium-oxygen mixture (60% helium and 40% oxygen) delivered with a non-rebreathing mask
- Steroids?

Consider Re-Intubation or NPPV if:

RR	> 35 breaths/min or </= 6 breaths/min
$\dot{V}_E$	> 10 L/min
HR	Tachycardia (>100 beats/min) Bradycardia (< 60 beats/min)
BP	Hypotension (BPsys < 90 mm Hg) Hypertension (BPsys >170 mm Hg) or ↑ > 20 mm Hg above baseline
ECG	New arrythmias & ischemia

Causes for extubation failure: Upper airway obstruction, inability to protect the airway, inability to remove secretions.

Note: Extubation failure can occur for reasons distinct from discontinuation failure.

See AARC Clinical Practice Guideline, "Removal of the Endotracheal Tube," in the Appendix

Tracheostomy Tubes

Indications

- Patients unable to protect their airways
- Excessive secretions
- Failure of noninvasive methods of cough assist
- Swallowing or cough impairment with chronic aspiration
- Patients requiring invasive ventilation > 21 days
- Contraindications to, failed, or cannot tolerate NPPV
- Need to reduce anatomical deadspace for improved oxygenation and/or ventilation

Types of Tracheostomy Tubes

- Cuffed (with disposable inner cannula (DIC) or permanent inner cannula)
- Uncuffed (with DIC or permanent inner cannula)
- Fenestrated (with fenestrated DIC or permanent inner cannula)
- Foam Cuffed
- Jackson Silver or metal tube
- Custom made (physician indicates specifications such as tube length, diameter, and style)

Management

Speaking Valves

Commonly used speaking valves are Olympic, Passy-Muir, Shiley, and Montgomery. Available in a number of designs depending on the specific need of the patient.

Purpose	Clinical Application	Procedure	Problems
Allows patient communication	Spontaneously breathing or ventilator-dependent patients	1. Deflate cuff 2. Attach speaking valve to trach tube 3. If needed, ↑ V_T on ventilator-dependent patients 4. On initial placement monitor patient for HR, RR, and SpO_2 5. If indicated, attach oxygen tubing to speaking valve	Air-trapping Fatigue Mucus can occlude one-way valve Unable to tolerate valve

Potential Complications of Trach Tubes

Balloon won't stay inflated
Bleeding
Chest pain
Crackling and/or puffiness of skin around tube
Difficulty passing sx catheter
Difficulty replacing inner cannula or tube
Drying of tracheal mucosa
Excessive coughing, gagging, choking, SOB
Increased mucus
Infection: change in secretions (color, consistency, amount), redness of skin around tube, SOB, fever
Tracheal erosion/malacia
Granulation tissue

Tracheostomy Tube Care
Removing and Cleaning of Trach Tube

1. Wash hands vigorously with soap and water
2. Apply gloves
3. Open all packages
4. Suction trach tube before removing
5. Glove each hand
6. Remove inner cannula by unlocking and gently pulling outward or remove single tube or outer cannula by cutting ties, holding tube in place with finger, deflate cuff (if present), pull gently outward and downward.
7. Soap tube in cleaning solution for indicated time
8. Clean skin &/or stoma with cotton dipped in cleaning solution. Pat dry with gauze.
9. Brush inside of tube with cleaning solution
10. Rinse tube thoroughly with distilled water
11. Pat dry with clean gauze and replace

Replacing a Trach Tube*

Inner Cannula

1. Explain procedure to patient
2. Position patient supine or slightly elevated
3. Wash hands vigorously with soap and water
4. Apply gloves
5. Have patient take a deep breath
6. Insert inner cannula gently and lock in place
7. Position pre-cut gauze under trach tube, pulling and set up under ties

Single Tube or Outer Cannula (and accidental extubation)

1. Explain procedure to patient
2. Position patient supine or slightly elevated
3. Wash hands vigorously with soap and water; glove each hand
4. Cleanse surrounding area
5. Remove inner cannula of new tube (if present), insert obturator, and attach new ties. Check new cuff for leaks (if present).
6. Lubricate outside of tube with water-soluble lubricant
7. Oxygenate (if needed), suction trach and upper airway, re-oxygenate. Deflate cuff (if present)
8. Cut ties, have patient take a deep breath (or give deep breath with resuscitation bag), remove old trach tube gently.
9. Quickly, but gently, insert new tube (sideways, then downward) (do not force), hold tube in place and immediately remove obturator.
10. Insert inner cannula and lock in place (if present) and inflate cuff, if present.
11. Check for airflow, and observe for difficulty breathing.
12. Remove tube if cannot be placed properly or airflow is inadequate; ventilate as needed and attempt to reinsert tube.
13. Hold tube in place until urge to cough subsides.
14. Secure trach ties (leave one finger width loose).
15. Suction and oxygenate if needed. Auscultate BS.
16. Assess stoma site.
17. Wash hands vigorously with soap and water

* The frequency of tube change depends on airway size, presence of cough, secretion volume and color, malfunction, or grossly dirty or contaminated.

Commonly, adult, cuffed tubes, q 4-8 weeks; uncuffed tubes, q 6 months. Children typically require more frequent changes, due to growth changes.

Stoma Care

- The stoma site should be examined daily for secretions, signs of infection or inflammation (redness), and encrustation (granuloma formations).
- Clean stoma at least daily
- Use cotton-tipped applicator and water or 1:1 hydrogen peroxide and water or saline solution
- If skin breakdown is present, clean more frequently
- Betadine or Polysporin cream may be applied
- Change dressing at least once a day
- Trach ties (both velcro and cloth) should be changed as needed. With the flange of the trach tube secured, the dirty tie is removed and replaced with a new, properly sized one, making sure the tie is secure, but not too tight. One finger should fit beneath tie.

Choosing Humidity Therapy for Patients with Tracheostomies

	Heated Humidifier	Nebulizer	HME-HCH
Efficacy	**Good**: Efficient, temperature control preferred for long term trach ventil.	**Fair**: May be too cool, heaters not very practical, may deliver too much water	**Fair**: Not for thick, copious secretions, marginal humidity, can't use with speaking valves May be used for periods <12 hrs in pts. w/ min secretions
Safety	**Fair**: May cause burns, electrical hazard, inadvertent lavage from condensation	**Fair**: Water droplets may cause bronchospasm - may deliver too much H_2O	**Fair**: No power or condensation hazards, may occlude with secretions, ↑Raw
Cost	Expensive	Fair	Fair
Convenience	**Poor**: Complex (with heated wire), condensation (w/o heated wire), water refill > 8 hr	**Fair**: Simple, water refill < 8 hr	**Good**: Simple, no additional equipment needed

Improving Ventilation

(Correcting / Adjusting $PaCO_2$ and pH)

Goal: Maintain adequate gas exchange using safe volumes and pressures.

Principle: Adequacy of ventilation is determined by delivered $\dot{V}E$ and assessed by $PaCO_2$ and pH.

$PaCO_2$ and the resultant pH ≈ total ventilation, deadspace, and CO_2 production and are changed by altering $\dot{V}E$, $\dot{V}D$, and/or CO_2 production. ***Note: Ventilation management should be aimed at normaling pH, rather than $PaCO_2$.***

Equations	Changing $\dot{V}_E$ mech
$\dot{V}_E = \dot{V}_A + \dot{V}_D$ Total $\dot{V}_E = \dot{V}_E$ mech + $\dot{V}_E$ spont	New $\dot{V}_E$ = current $\dot{V}_E$ x (current $PaCO_2$ / desired $PaCO_2$)
$PaCO_2 \approx 1/\dot{V}_E$ $PaCO_2 \approx \dot{V}CO_2 / \dot{V}_A$ $PaCO_2 = \frac{(\dot{V}CO_2 \times 0.863)}{(\dot{V}_E \times (1 - \dot{V}_D/\dot{V}_T))}$	In VV: $\dot{V}_E = V_T \times f$ In PV: $\dot{V}_E = (PIP - PEEP) \times f$ (dependent on type of ventilation and mode being used)

Clinical Situations:

↑ $PaCO_2$ with ↓ pH (Uncompensated Respiratory Acidosis)		
Problem: ↓ $\dot{V}_E$	**In VV**	**In PV**
Solution: ↑ $\dot{V}_E$ New $\dot{V}_E$ = current $\dot{V}_E$ x ($PaCO_2$/ desired $PaCO_2$)	Increase $\dot{V}_E$ by: 1) ↑ V_T (up to 10-12 mL/kg providing P_{plat} < 30 cm H_2O) 2) ↑ f (if V_T and P_{plat} are already high)	Increase $\dot{V}_E$ by: 1) ↑ set pressure (PIP, P limit) 2) ↑ T_I (if short) 3) ↑ f (if PIP + P_{plat} are already high)

Additional Strategies

1) Increase VT_{spont}
   A) PSV
   B) Bronchodilation
   C) Increase ET tube size
   D) Respiratory muscle conditioning
   E) Improve nutritional support
2) Decrease mechanical V_D
   A) Use low compliance circuit
   B) Cut ET tube shorter
   C) Tracheostomy
3) High Frequency Ventilation
4) Permissive Hypercapnia (see below)

↑ $PaCO_2$ with ↓ pH (Despite Adequate or High $\dot{V}_E$)	
Potential Problems:	
↑ Deadspace (V_D/V_T)	**↑ CO_2 production**
Possible Causes: Air trapping High I:E ratio (e.g., 3:1) Low $\dot{V}_I$ Pulmonary emboli or hypoperfusion Uneven gas distribution (lung pathology) ***Possible Solutions:*** Increase flow Decrease I:E ratio Reposition patient	***Possible Causes:*** Burns Fever Hyperthyroidism Multiple surgeries Multiple trauma Sepsis ***Possible Solutions:*** Correct primary cause Note: Increasing $\dot{V}_E$ further may lead to air trapping and auto-PEEP PSV may be helpful to ↓WOB

Management

↓ $PaCO_2$ and ↑ pH (Uncompensated Respiratory Alkalosis)		
Problem: ↑ $\dot{V}_A$	**In VV**	**In PV**
Solution: ↓$\dot{V}_A$ by decreasing $\dot{V}_E$	↓***f***: Desired *f* = known $PaCO_2$ x (known *f* / desired $PaCO_2$) Desired $\dot{V}_E$ = known $PaCO_2$ x (known $\dot{V}_E$ / desired $PaCO_2$) **↓ V_T:** Desired V_T = known $PaCO_2$ x (known V_T / desired $PaCO_2$)	↓***f***: Desired *f* = known $PaCO_2$ x (known *f* / desired $PaCO_2$) **↓ Set pressure:** Desired set pressure = known V_T x (known set pressure / desired V_T)

Clinical Note

If patient is on A/C, decreasing *f* of mandatory breaths may have no effect. If ↓ V_T and patient increases *f* then :

1) Try PSV or SIMV
2) Sedate (esp. in patients with extreme agitation, fear, pain, or ↑WOB)
3) Add VD_{mech} (usually limited to head injury)

If pt. is hyperventilating due to hypoxemia – correct hypoxemia. Don't correct hyperventilation without 1st correcting hypoxemia.

Management

↓ $PaCO_2$ with Normal/Low pH (Compensated Metabolic Acidosis)
Problem: Hyperventilating to correct for metabolic acidosis.
Solution: Correct metabolic acidosis before correcting $PaCO_2$.

↑ $PaCO_2$ with Normal/High pH (Compensated Metabolic Alkalosis)
Problem: Hypoventilating to correct for metabolic alkalosis.
Solution: Correct metabolic alkalosis first, otherwise increasing $\dot{V}_E$ to ↓ $PaCO_2$ will worsen the metabolic alkalosis (further ↑ of pH) potentially causing cardiac dysrrhythmias, seizures, or other neurological problems.

Permissive Hypercapnia (PHY)

Definition: Deliberate limitation of ventilatory support (i.e., limiting high V_T and/or high P_{plat}) to avoid lung over-distension (either regionally or globally) and the associated VILI.

Indication: When high V_T and/or high P_{plat} are required to maintain normocapnia with a resultant $P_{plat} > 30$ cmH_2O. Examples: ARDS, status asthmaticus

Contraindications (Relative): Cerebral trauma, hemorrhage, or space occupying CNS lesions (↑CO_2 → cerebral vasodilation → ↑ ICP) and CV instability (↑ $PaCO_2$ and ↓ pH may lead to ↓ myocardial contractility, arrhythmias, and/or vasodilation).

Strategy: PHY is a "lung protective strategy": ventilate with low V_T (4 - 7 mL/kg) to keep $P_{plat} < 30$ cmH_2O, while maintaining optimal lung recruitment.

Goals: $PaCO_2$ is allowed to ↑ to 50 - 100 mmHg and pH is allowed to ↓ to 7.20 - 7.30. Gradual ↑ of $PaCO_2$ (≤ 10 mmHg/hr to allow for renal compensation) is currently under reconsideration.

Common Techniques

1) Sedate patient (mandatory breaths only) to ↓ WOB and anxiety.
2) ↓ $\dot{V}CO_2$ by cooling or paralyzing patient and/or ↓ glucose intake
3) Provide optimal PEEP to maintain lung recruitment during ↓ V_T
4) Keep pH > 7.25 (will ↓ as $PaCO_2$ ↑). Administering $NaCO_3$, THAM, or Caricarb is controversial.
5) Potential of TGI to minimize $PaCO_2$ ↑ and NO to ↓ PVR

Physiological Effects of Permissive Hypercapnia

- CNS depression (drowsiness, narcosis, coma)
- May ↑ ICP
- Proportional reduction in PaO_2 and potential hypoxemia
- Right shift of oxyhemoglobin curve (less O_2 binding)
- Stimulation of ventilation (dyspnea)
- Systemic vasodilation / pulmonary vasocontriction
- Various CV effects (hypotension, ↓ CO)

Improving Oxygenation
(Correcting / Adjusting PaO_2 and SaO_2)

Goal: To maintain adequate O_2 delivery to the tissues while ventilating with the lowest possible F_IO_2 and pressures.

Principle: PaO_2 is affected primarily by F_IO_2, $\overline{P}aw$ (V_T, PIP, PEEP, T_I, $\dot{V}I$, $\dot{V}I$ waveform) and cardiovascular disease (i.e., optimizing lung volume and V/Q matching).
Adequate O_2 delivery to tissues is dependent on F_IO_2, CO, and CaO_2.

O_2 Delivery to Tissues:
$\dot{D}O_2 = CaO_2 \times CO$ (Measure with $Ca\text{-}\overline{v}O_2$, $\dot{V}O_2$, $S\overline{v}O_2$)
$$CaO_2 = (SaO_2 \times Hgb \times 1.34) + (PaO_2 \times 0.0031)$$

Methods of Evaluating Oxygenation Status

F_IO_2	CaO_2	$C\overline{v}O_2$
PaO_2	PaO_2/PAO_2	CO
P/F ratio	$P(A\text{-}a)O_2$	Hb
SaO_2	$S\overline{v}O_2$	Shunt

(See Equations, Chapter 7)

Hypoxemia/Hypoxia – Types, Causes and Effects
See Oakes' ***Clinical Practitioner's Pocket Guide To Respiratory Care***, as well as Oakes' ***ABG Pocket Guide*** for a comprehensive summary.

Checklist for Worsening Oxygenation in Patients on MV

For Sudden Distress, see Trouble- Shooting, Chapter 5

Causes	Primary Strategies To Improve O_2†
Patient: Airway obstructions/ secretions Anemia Artificial airway problem Aspiration Atelectasis Bronchospasm Organ failure Pneumonia Pneumothorax Pulmonary edema Progression of underlying disease Sepsis Shock	Antibiotics Bronchodilators Bronchscopy CPAP/PEEP CPT Diuretics ET tube (suction, correct malposition, kinking, cuff, etc.) ↑ F_IO_2, $\overline{P}aw$, PEEP, T_I, IRV Fluids, vasopressors, inotropics Position changes (prone or continuous lateral rotation) Restore Hgb level (>10 gm/100mL) Thoracentesis / chest tube
Ventilator:	
Improper mode	Select appropriate mode
Improper settings (F_IO_2, PEEP, V_T, etc)	Correct settings
Leaks or disconnections	Find and fix
Malfunctions	Correct
Patient – ventilator asychrony	See below

† First correct primary cause, then adjust ventilator parameters (F_IO_2, $\overline{P}aw$, PEEP, T_I, modes) as needed. Unconventional methods (ECMO, HFV, hyperbaric, intravascular oxygenation, etc.) may be employed when refractory hypoxemia ($PaO_2 < 60$ on $F_IO_2 \geq 0.6$) is not responsive to conventional MV and PEEP.

Targets for Improving (Correcting) Oxygenation		
	PaO_2 (Goal)	**SaO_2/SpO_2 (Goal)**
Normal lung	≥80 mmHg	≥95%
Mild lung injury	≥70 mmHg	≥93%
Moderate lung injury	≥60 mmHg	≥90%
Severe lung injury **	≥55 mmHg	≥88%

Conventional Methods of Improving Oxygenation

F_IO_2 | $\overline{P}aw$ | IRV
PEEP (auto-PEEP) | | Patient positioning

(See Chapter 15 for some non-conventional methods)

F_IO_2

Principle: The adjustment of F_IO_2 is the main determinant of oxygenation.

Goal: Keep F_IO_2 as low as possible (< 0.5) to maintain PaO_2 60–100 mm Hg and/or SaO_2 > 90.

Clinical Note: When required, F_IO_2 > 0.5 is preferred over high Palv.
F_IO_2 (required) = PaO_2 (desired) x F_IO_2 (known) / PaO_2 (known)
(See Equations, Chapter 7)

PEEP / CPAP

Principle: The adjustment of PEEP is a key determinant of oxygenation, primarily due to the effect on $\overline{P}aw$.

Purpose of PEEP: Maintain pressures above ambient pressure during the expiratory phase of ventilation in order to help prevent collapse of the small airways and unstable alveoli.

Goals of PEEP

↑ **PaO_2** – Reduce shunt effect, ↑ FRC, and ↑ C, thereby allowing for the reduction of F_IO_2 and it's complications.

↓ **WOB** – Unload the inspiratory muscles (esp. in acute exacerbation of COPD).

Indications for PEEP / CPAP

Clinical	Physiological
Auto-PEEP- See Ch 11	PaO_2 < 60 mm Hg
Cardiogenic pulmonary edema (↑ LV preload)	on FIO_2 0.8
Hypoxemia with F_IO_2 > 0.5	PaO_2 ↑ < 10 mm Hg
Collapsing alveoli (ARDS, postop atelectasis)	with F_IO_2 ↑ of 0.2
Presence of artificial airway	$PA\text{-}aO_2$ > 300 on
Chest wall instability (chest trauma)	F_IO_2 1.0
	Shunt > 30%

Clinical Note: CPAP indication is similar to PEEP. The primary difference is that CPAP requires the patient to do all the WOB. CPAP is appropriate if patient can spontaneously maintain a normal $PaCO_2$ without much difficulty and has been shown effective in limited applications to patients with hypoxemic respiratory failure.

Contraindications for PEEP / CPAP

Absolute	Relative (may use with caution)	
Tension pneumothorax	Barotrauma	Preexisting hyperinflation (e.g. emphysema)
Untreated significant pneumothorax	BP fistula	Recent lung surgery
	Hypovolemia	Unilateral lung disorders
	Increased ICP	

Beneficial Effects of Appropriate PEEP

↑ $\overline{P}aw$ ↑ C_L ↑ PaO_2 (for a given F_IO_2) ↓ WOB

↑ V/Q (the stabilization of collapsing alveoli resulting in improved gas distribution and ↓ R-L shunting).

↑ FRC (which may include recruitment of collapsed alveoli. Exception – patients with preexisting hyperinflation such as emphysema)

↓ lung injury (minimizes shear forces associated with repetitive collapse and recruitment of alveoli.

PEEP may be beneficial in patients with CHF by ↓ preload and afterload.

Potential Adverse Effects of PEEP

Lung function-

Alveolar over-distension (volutrauma – which is proportional to lung disease, over-distension, and pressure), ↑ WOB, ↑ V_D/V_T.

Cardiovascular function-

Effects are dependent on PEEP level, C_{LT}, and CV status. The greatest effect (↓ venous return and CO) is when C_L is high, Ccw is low, and CV reserve is low.

Renal function - May ↓ renal and portal blood flow, hence ↓ UO.

ICP - When PEEP decreases venous return, ICP may ↑. Usually clinically insignificant unless ICP is already elevated. Head elevation may offset PEEP effect.

Initiating PEEP / CPAP Therapy

Start as soon as possible:

Initial PEEP = 5 cmH_2O

Increase in increments of 3 - 5 cmH_2O, q 10 - 15 min. as needed until optimal PEEP achieved (see below).

Within first few minutes:

Assess patient's vital signs (RR, HR, BP), ventilation parameters (V_T, *f*, $\dot{V}_E$, PIP, P_{plat}, BS), and appearance (color, LOC, anxiety, distress, etc.) within the first few minutes after initiation or any change (esp. CV collapse or pneumothorax).

After approximately 15 minutes:

Measure and/or calculate ABG's, oxygenation, ventilation (C_{dyn}, C_{stat}, Raw, auto-PEEP), and hemodynamic parameters, and then again 15 minutes after any changes.

PEEP Ranges

Level	Purpose
Low PEEP: 3 - 5 cmH_2O	Physiologic – to preserve patient's normal FRC
Moderate PEEP: 5 - 15 cmH_2O	Treat refractory hypoxemia caused by ↑ intra-pulmonary shunting with ↓ FRC and ↓ C. Most common range used for acute lung injury.
High PEEP: > 15 cmH_2O	Used only for severe lung injury
Optimal PEEP	See below

See also ARDS Network PEEP setting protocol, Chapter 10.

Optimal PEEP

Definition: Best PEEP, preferred PEEP, therapeutic PEEP – the level of PEEP at which O_2 delivery to the tissues is maximized.
Optimal PEEP generally correlates with the point where alveolar de-recruitment does not occur. That is:

The lowest PEEP level at which maximum beneficial effects occur:	With the least cardio-pulmonary side effects:
↑ O_2 transport (↑ PaO_2, $P\bar{v}O_2$, O_2 Sat) ↑FRC, ↓ Shunt ↑ Compliance	↓ venous return ↓ CO, ↓ BP ↑Shunt, ↑V_D/V_T Barotrauma

And all done with an F_IO_2 preferably < 0.4.

Determining Optimal PEEP

See Clinical Note on Next Page

Two Approaches:

1) *Mechanical criteria* (Best lung compliance with stable BP)

a) Use V-P curves to set PEEP/V_T combination between upper and lower inflection points. (Use conventional static approach or slow $\dot{V}_I$ approach)

b) Add small increments of PEEP and calculate C_{stat} at each level of PEEP to determine best compliance.

2) Gas exchange criteria

a) PEEP titration curve to determine lowest F_IO_2 (perform after a volume recruitment maneuver: 1 min of PEEP @ 25-40 cmH_2O, then return to optimal setting)

b) Algorithm (see below)

* See Clinical Note: Next Page

*** Clinical Note**

An optimal PEEP study is generally only done on patients requiring > 10 cmH_2O. No one single clinical parameter has been shown to be adequate for determining optimal PEEP. Instead, precise determination of optimal PEEP is best accomplished when using several parameters, including hemodynamic data. PA catheter monitoring may be recommended when using PEEP > 15 cmH_2O. PEEP effects should be monitored closely because PEEP effects may dramatically change as the pt's status changes (either improves or worsens).

See Oakes' ***Hemodynamic Monitoring: A Bedside Reference Manual***, for a thorough reference to hemodynamic changes with PEEP and zone changes.

PEEP /F_IO_2 Algorithm – *For the Algorithm used in the NIH ARDS Network MV Protocol see ARDS, Chapter 10.*

Commonly Used Parameters For Measuring and Monitoring PEEP

Ventilation		Oxygenation	
Parameter	**Desired Goal**	**Parameter**	**Desired Goal**
Breath sounds	Appropriate	PaO_2	60-100 mmHg on $F_IO_2 \leq 0.4$
V_T, f, $\dot{V}_E$	Appropriate	SaO_2	90-97% @ normal pH
PIP, P_{plat}, PEEP	Minimal	F_IO_2	Decreasing
Cdyn	Improving	PaO_2/F_IO_2	> 300 mmHg
Cstat	Improving	$P(A\text{-}a)O_2$	Decreasing
Raw	Decreasing	PaO_2/PAO_2	Increasing
$PaCO_2$, pH	Appropriate	Shunt (Q_S/Q_T)	< 15%
$Pa\text{-}etCO_2$	Decreasing		

Hemodynamics

O_2 Transport	≈ 1000 mL/min (5L x 20 vol%)
CO	Increasing or < 20% decrease
BP	Adequate or < 20% decrease
PA Pressures	Appropriate
PAOP	No change (marked ↑ may indicate over-inflation of alveoli; marked ↓ may indicate ↓ blood flow due to ↓ CO)
$P\bar{v}O_2$	Increasing and > 28 mmHg
$S\bar{v}O_2$	Increasing and > 50%
$C(a\text{-}\bar{v})O_2$	Decreasing

Using Applied PEEP in the presence of Auto–PEEP

Applied PEEP (extrinsic PEEP) may be applied up to 80% of measured auto-PEEP. Its purpose is to reduce the triggering load (ΔP required to trigger the ventilator).

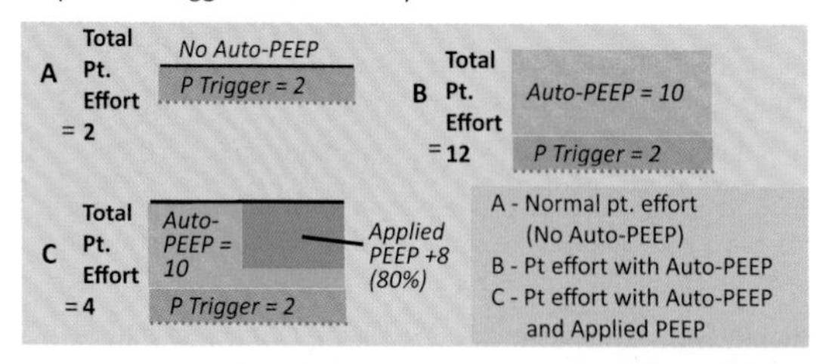

Theory: up to 80% of applied PEEP only affects the circuit and airway pressures and not alveolar pressures. It works to equilibrate trapped pressure and circuit pressure.

Note: Applied PEEP > 80% will begin to ↑ Palv with CV effects.

Two Techniques

1) Esophageal balloon
2) Trial and error

   ↑ Applied PEEP in increments of 2 - 5 cmH_2O until every patient-triggering-effort initiates a ventilator breath.

Signs of Excessive Applied PEEP

↑ dyspnea, ↓ BP, worsening signs of hyperinflation

Weaning From PEEP

There are numerous procedures and protocols listed in current literature, of which many variations exist. For ARDS, see ARDS Network Algorithm, Chapter 10. See also Chapter 13.

Top Priorities of Weaning

↓ Pplat < 30 cm H_2O, ↓ PEEP to < 15 cmH_2O, ↓ F_IO_2 to < 0.5

Do not abruptly withdraw PEEP.

↓ PEEP in increments of 2 – 5 cmH_2O, q 1- 6 hr, while step-wise decreasing Pplat and F_IO_2 to more acceptable levels.

Monitor PaO_2 or SpO_2 and hemodynamic stability very closely

When PEEP is ↓, if PaO_2 drops > 20%, return PEEP to previous level.

Complete removal of PEEP before extubation may not be necessary or advantageous.

Mean Airway Pressure ($\overline{P}aw$ or MAWP)

Principle: $\overline{P}aw$ is an important determinant of oxygenation. $PaO_2 \approx \overline{P}aw$ (until over-distension occurs, i.e., > upper inflection point on V-P curve).

Indication: ↑ $\overline{P}aw$ is indicated for patients with ↓ lung volume and refractory hypoxemia that does not respond to ↑ F_IO_2 (e.g., ARDS).

Refractory hypoxemia = $PaO_2 < 60$ mmHg on $F_IO_2 \geq 0.6$

Goal: To achieve adequate oxygenation with the lowest possible pressures and F_IO_2, without impairing CV function or injuring the lung.

Primary Factors Affecting $\overline{P}aw$ (in probable order of magnitude)

- PEEP
- PIP
- T_I
- f (↓ T_E)
- $\dot{V}_I$
- $\dot{V}_I$ waveform

Clinical Note: Limit T_I to the maximum that does not cause auto-PEEP.

If auto-PEEP present: In VV: auto-PEEP →↑Palv (V_T constant)
In PV: auto-PEEP →↓ V_T (Palv constant)

Potential Risks of ↑ $\overline{P}aw$ = barotrauma, ↓ CO

Measurement Of $\overline{P}aw$

Automatically calculated by ventilator	Manually calculated
Note: this value usually doesn't include any auto-PEEP	$\overline{P}aw$ = (PIP – PEEP) x (T_I / T_{total}) + PEEP (figuring a constant flow, VV breath and PEEP includes auto-PEEP)

Management

Inverse Ratio Ventilation (IRV)

Definition: Increasing $T_I > T_E$ (I:E ratio > 1:1)

Principle: Increasing T_I to ↑ $\overline{P}aw$ and recruit and keep alveoli open for extended periods in order to improve V/Q, without overinflating normal alveolar units.

Indication: When conventional ventilator strategies with optimal PEEP have resulted in P_{plat} > 30 cmH_2O, without providing acceptable PaO_2/FiO_2 values. Primary use is in patients with ARDS.

Strategy: ↑ T_I in 0.1 – 0.2 sec increments until either PaO_2/FiO_2 goal is achieved or air-trapping develops. When I:E ratio exceeds 1:1, patients may require sedation and paralysis.

T_I May be Lengthened by:

- ↑ Set T_I
- Decelerating $\dot{V}_I$ pattern (VV)
- ↓ $\dot{V}_I$ (VV)
- Inspiratory Pause

Note: For the interrelation of T_I, T_E, T_{tot}, $\dot{V}_I$, V_T, and f see Ch 2.

Risk of IRV

Lung Damage	Cardiovascular Compromise	Patient Discomfort or Asynchrony*
Auto-PEEP (dynamic hyperinflation) ↑ $\overline{P}aw$ ↑ PIP (in V-IRV if auto-PEEP develops)	↓ CO	↓ V_T (in P-IRV if auto-PEEP develops) ↓ $\dot{V}E$ (↓ V_T or air trapping)

* Patient may require sedation and/or paralysis.

Clinical Note: No studies to date have shown this method to improve outcome over conventional ventilation with PEEP. Because of risks and the lack of guidelines for its safe use, it should be reserved only for severe respiratory failure and applied only by skilled clinicians. Caution when using IRV in VV because of auto-PEEP.

Patient Positioning (Positional Therapy)

ARDS

Although prone positioning generally improves FRC and oxygenation, results are highly variable and no amount of time per day has been determined (at least 20 hr/day?)

Asthma/COPD

It is generally recommended that the patient be placed in the upright position.

Neuromuscular Disease

Frequent position changes are recommended.

Unilateral Lung Disease

E.g., Atelectasis, lung contusion, pneumonia, PIE in neonates.
Placing the "good side" down (lateral positioning) often improves oxygenation and may be more effective than PEEP.

Exceptions:

COPD, paralyzed patients, and unilateral pleural effusion.
"Good lung down" is contraindicated in pulmonary hemorrhage and lung abscess.

Management

Clinical Notes

Careful monitoring of ventilator parameters and patient deterioration, complications, dislodging of lines/tubes, ***is essential*** during and directly following the change.

Any improvement is likely to be seen within the first 30 minutes.

Improvement may also be sustained after turning back to supine.

Ccw may potentially ↓ with prone positioning resulting in an ↑Paw in VV, or ↓ V_T in PV.

Spinal cord instability is an absolute contraindication to prone positioning; thoraco-abdominal surgery and hemodynamic, cardiovascular instability are relative contraindications.

Continuous lateral rotation may be used before prone positioning is attempted. Lateral rotation with the correct choice of bed can be instituted even with unstable spinal injury.

Checklist for Placing a Patient in Prone Position:

- Communication amongst team of plan to prone (responsibilities)
- Check for contraindications
- Ensure patient is adequately sedated
- Check length/security of all lines and ET tube
- Preoxygenate @ 100%
- Verify vital signs and hemodynamic status
- Suction ET tube

Procedure:

- Ensure team members are in place (including 1 person in charge of monitoring secure airway/vent circuit)
- Unhook all leads/lines as necessary
- Gently place pt. on side
- Verify status of pt./equipment/lines
- Place pt. in prone position
- Turn patient's head towards the ventilator
- Reattach and verify all leads/lines - including assuring that the ET tube/head are not compressed
- Do a complete ventilator-patient check, including breath sounds
- Again verify vital signs and hemodynamic status

Patient should be monitored closely while proned.

Improving Patient-Ventilator Interaction

(Minimizing Patient-Ventilator Asynchrony or "Fighting the Vent")

Key Factors Affecting Patient-Ventilator Interaction

1) Artificial airway
2) Auto-PEEP
3) Demand valves
4) Humidifiers
5) $\dot{V}_I$
6) T_I
7) Level of vent. support
8) PEEP valves
9) Trigger sensitivity

Clinical Note: For a sudden onset of respiratory distress (apparent "fighting the ventilator") in patients who had been stable prior to the event, see Patient-Ventilator Assessment/Trouble-Shooting, Chapter 5.

1) Artificial Airway

Factors that ↑ imposed WOB	Clinical Strategies
ET tube size/bends/kinks Secretions Spontaneous rate	Use the largest ET tube size possible (8.0 men, 7.5 women). Use PSV as needed.

2) Auto-PEEP

Principle
Air-trapping increases WOB and patient-ventilator asynchrony by flattening the diaphragm, affecting respiratory muscle function, and requiring greater effort to trigger the ventilator. There is a high incidence in patients with high $\dot{V}_E$, fast rates, and ≥ 10 cmH_2O of PEEP.

Detecting and Reducing Auto-PEEP: See Chapter 11

3) Demand Valves

Principle	Clinical Strategies
Pressure-triggered mechanical demand valves often require large pressure drops to open the valves.	Use flow-triggered system or add 5 cm H_2O to a demand-flow system.

4) Humidifiers

Principle	Clinical Strategies
Bubble-through humidifiers with proximal sensitivity and water-laden HME's can increase flow resistance and WOB.	Use pass-over or wick-type humidifiers when applying partial ventilator support to patients with high $\dot{V}_E$.

Management

5) Inspiratory Flow (Flow Asynchrony) ($\dot{V}_I$ in VV)

Principle	Clinical Strategies
Inadequate $\dot{V}_I$ leads to an ↑ WOB. High demand patients may require 60-100 L/min.	Assess adequacy of machine flow by observing airway pressure waveform (see Chapter 6). Adjust $\dot{V}_I$ until airway pressure waveform is restored to normal. In PV, an inspiratory rise time too long may lead to ↑ WOB.

6) Inspiratory Time (Timing or Cycle Asynchrony)

Principle	Clinical Strategies
Most commonly, the patient attempts to exhale prior to the termination of machine inspiration. In PV: T_I is set too long In VV: The flow cycle is too prolonged	Ensure T_I (set or $\dot{V}_I$ result) is adequate to meet patient's demand.

7) Level of Ventilatory Support

Principle	Goal	Clinical Strategies
Too much support leads to atrophy. Too little support leads to fatigue.	To rest the respiratory muscles in the early phase of MV (total support). To challenge the respiratory muscles, without fatigue, in the later phases (partial support).	Provide adequate rate and depth of machine breaths to prevent tachypnea (keep f < 20/min; high demand patients may require V_T 12 –15 mL/kg). Provide adequate $\dot{V}_I$ to meet patient demand. Insure proper trigger level. *Use PSV when necessary to augment spontaneous V_T:* PSV too low → ↑ WOB PSV too high → may prompt expiratory muscle activity Titrate PSV to eupnea

Clinical Note: In reality, patients may often continue working to breath even after the initiation of full support machine breaths if the machine does not respond adequately to their demands (esp.

$\dot{V}_I$ and/or V_T).

Proper adjustment of patient-ventilator interaction is essential to insure proper level of support (i.e. without imposing any unnecessary work).

8) PEEP Valve

Principle	Signs of ↑ Expiratory Flow Resistance
All PEEP valves impose some flow resistance.	Active expiratory muscle effort ↓ $\dot{V}_E$ Prolonged T_E

9) Trigger Sensitivity (Triggering Asynchrony)

Principle	Clinical Strategies
Fine tuning the trigger sensitivity is necessary after initiating ventilatory support: Too sensitive, it will lead to auto-triggering. Too insensitive, it will lead to ↑ WOB and patient-ventilator asynchrony.	The patient's inspiratory efforts should synchronize with the machine breaths. Observe the pressure manometer or graphic display to confirm sensitivity is < 1.5 cmH_2O. Flow sensitivity preferred.

Factors that Can Cause Trigger Asynchrony

Auto-PEEP	High tubing compliance
Abdominal-rib cage paradox	Low trigger sensitivity
High bias flow in circuit	Transducer variability
High circuit dead space	Unresponsive demand valve

9 Non-Invasive Positive Pressure Ventilation (NPPV)

Chapter Contents

Other terms and abbreviations used:

Bilevel positive airway pressure
BiPAP (Brand name: Respironics)
Non-invasive ventilation (NIV)
Non-invasive positive pressure ventilation (NIPPV)

Definitions:

NPPV: Any form of ventilatory support applied without the use of an endotracheal/tracheal tube: it provides two levels of pressure (I and E) to the airway, which are triggered by the patient or by the ventilator (time) depending on the mode utilized.

Noninvasive Continuous Positive Airway Pressure (CPAP): Technically not a form of noninvasive positive pressure ventilation. It is the application of continuous positive airway pressure throughout the ventilatory cycle.

Inspiratory Positive Airway Pressure (IPAP): The higher pressure level of the two pressures of NPPV.

Expiratory Positive Airway Pressure (EPAP): The lower pressure level of the two pressures of NPPV.

Acute Care (Type I):

Indications for NPPV with Acute Respiratory Failure

Does the patient have an indication for NPPV?

1. Acute hypercapnic respiratory failure (at least two of the following should be present)
   a. Severe worsening dyspnea or
   b. Sustained respiratory rate > 25/min or
   c. Use of accessory muscles/abdominal paradox or
   d. pH < 7.35 with a $PaCO_2$ > 45 mmHg
2. Acute hypoxemia: SpO_2 < 88-90% with FiO_2 > 60% and P/F < 200

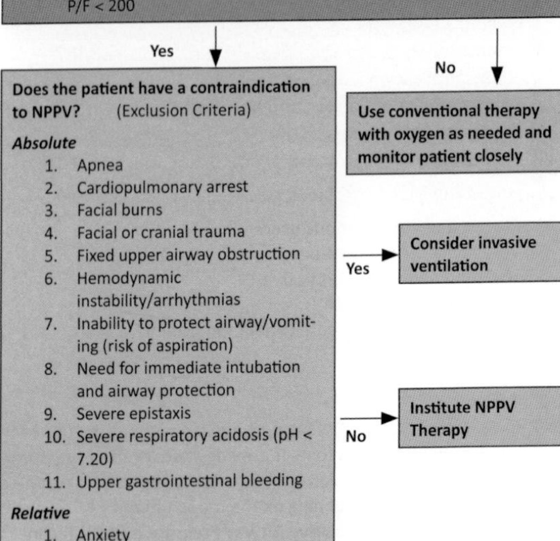

Yes ↓

Does the patient have a contraindication to NPPV? (Exclusion Criteria)

Absolute

1. Apnea
2. Cardiopulmonary arrest
3. Facial burns
4. Facial or cranial trauma
5. Fixed upper airway obstruction
6. Hemodynamic instability/arrhythmias
7. Inability to protect airway/vomiting (risk of aspiration)
8. Need for immediate intubation and airway protection
9. Severe epistaxis
10. Severe respiratory acidosis (pH < 7.20)
11. Upper gastrointestinal bleeding

Relative

1. Anxiety
2. Bowel obstruction
3. Claustrophobia
4. Copious secretions
5. Inability to clear secretions
6. Inability to cooperate or tolerate interface
7. Severe illness (high APACHE score)

No → **Use conventional therapy with oxygen as needed and monitor patient closely**

Yes → **Consider invasive ventilation**

No → **Institute NPPV Therapy**

Indications by Disease

Diagnosis	Level of evidence to support use	A = Multiple controlled trials B = A single supportive controlled trial C = Uncontrolled trials and case reports **Comments**
Acute Exacerbation of COPD	A	NPPV should be the first line of defense/intervention Most studies showed a reduction in intubations, mortality rates and length of stay Used for acute exacerbations; not mild cases Increased success when patient's pH < 7.30 IPAP assists inhalation/EPAP used to counterbalance "auto-PEEP" May be used to "buy time" while other therapies take effect
Cardiogenic Pulmonary Edema	A	Evidence for NPPV and CPAP equal May be used to "buy time" while other therapies take effect If hypercapnic, and using CPAP, switch to NPPV
Facilitation of Weaning (COPD patients)	A	Only used in patients who would otherwise be excellent candidates for NPPV Used in patients who fail multiple spontaneous breathing trials Used as a bridge to total liberation
Immuno-compromised Patients	A	NPPV should be considered early in respiratory failure episode. These patients have poor outcomes when invasively ventilated. NPPV offers an option to prevent fatal complications of NPPV such as nosocomial pneumonia

Diagnosis	Level of evidence to support use A = Multiple controlled trials B = A single supportive controlled trial C = Uncontrolled trials and case reports	Comments
Asthma Exacerbations	B	NPPV probably improves gas exchange and avoids intubations Can be used initially to reverse airway obstruction more rapidly NPPV may increase aerosol medication delivery
Extubation Failure	B	May be used as a way to avoid reintubation Patients should be monitored closely and intubated when needed if NPPV attempt has fails
Pneumonia	B	Patients with acute exacerbation of COPD If progresses to ALI/ARDS, intubate after 1 hour, if patient not improving
Postoperative Respiratory Failure	B	Used to: Prevent postoperative complications after high-risk surgeries Treat postoperative respiratory failure Prophylacticly treat obese patients following bariatric surgery Improve oxygenation in CABG patients
ALI/ARDS	C	Monitor patients closely Intubate after 1 hour if patient not improving
Cystic Fibrosis	C	Used as a bridge to transplantation in patients who deteriorate Treat acute on chronic hypercapnic respiratory failure

Diagnosis	Level of evidence to support use A = Multiple controlled trials B = A single supportive controlled trial C = Uncontrolled trials and case reports	Comments
Do-not-intubate Patients	C	Very controversial subject Cause of acute respiratory failure should be reversible such as CHF or COPD. Used to bridge through the acute illness Patients have a better prognosis if patient is awake and has a cough. Patients, family and caregivers should specifically discuss and understand therapy goals and discontinue therapy if goals are not being achieved. Goal Categories: *(SCCM 2007)* 1. NPPV without preset limits on the provision of advanced life support 2. NPPV for patients who decline ET intubation and invasive MV 3. NPPV as a comfort measure for patients who decline ET intubation
Trauma	C	May be used in some patients with chest wall injuries. Not to be used in burn patients
Upper Airway Obstruction	C	Contraindicated for patients with tight, fixed upper airway obstruction May be attempted for reversible upper airway obstruction such as post-extubation glottic edema in conjunction with heliox and/or aerosolized medication.

Overall Issues with NPPV for Treatment of Acute Respiratory Failure

Goals of NPPV in Acute Respiratory Failure	Avoid intubation and its complications Improve or stabilize gas exchange Optimize patient comfort Reduce work of breathing Relieve dyspnea
Clinical benefits of NPPV in Acute Respiratory Failure	Decreases need for sedation Improves patient comfort Preserves airway defenses/speech/swallowing Reduces incidence of nosocomial pneumonia Reduces mortality Reduces the need for intubation Shortens LOS in hospitals and ICU
Factors Associated with Predicting Successful NPPV Therapy	Ability to control secretions Air leak well controlled Good level of consciousness Hypercapnic RF (vs. Hypoxemic RF) Improvement in pH, $PaCO_2$, respiratory rate, and accessory muscle use after 1 hour of NPPV
Factors Associated with NPPV Treatment Failure	Deterioration in patient's condition Deteriorating level of consciousness Development of complications Development of new symptoms Failure to alleviate symptoms Failure to improve/deterioration in ABGs Patient refusal Poor patient tolerance
Complications of NPPV	***Minor:*** Air leaks that affect ventilation/pt. comfort Dry upper airway Eye irritation secondary to air leaks (conjunctivitis) Gastric distention General discomfort Patient ventilatory asynchrony Sinus congestion Skin reddening and breakdown ***Major:*** (infrequent) Aspiration (especially with full face masks) Hypotension Pneumothorax

Chronic Care (Type II)

Chronic conditions where ventilatory support could offer benefit (ventilatory muscle rest, lowering $PaCO_2$), but where cessation of NPPV does not cause an immediate life-threatening risk.

Indications by Disease Category

Disease	Comments
Restrictive Thoracic Disease Chronic hypoventilation syndromes secondary to: • Chest wall or spinal deformity • Idiopathic hypoventilation • Neuromuscular disease • Obesity	May respond gradually over weeks after initiating nocturnal NPPV A mouth piece interface may be tolerated by patients with severe neuromuscular disease who have very low or no Vital Capacity ALS patients with hypercapnia and orthopnea have good prediction of success using NPPV
Chronic Obstructive Pulmonary Disease (COPD)	Very controversial as far as routine use in non-acute exacerbation of COPD
Obstructive Sleep Apnea	Used for patients who cannot tolerate nasal CPAP alone.

Contraindications to Using NPPV Chronically

- Unable to protect airway due to swallowing issues or excessive secretions and a poor cough
- Unable to fit interface
- Rapidly progressive neuromuscular disease with bulbar dysfunction
- Unmotivated/uncooperative patient

Therapy Phase	Management
Initiating	Clinician must take ample time to spend with the patient for optimal success Explain therapy to patient Begin at low settings (EPAP 4-5 cmH_2O, IPAP 6-10 cmH_2O) Place mask gently on patient's face, perhaps allow patient to hold mask on his own face Do not strap mask on until patient comfortable with pressure Increase settings as needed and as patient tolerates
Managing	To increase ventilation (*to change pressure support level): Increase IPAP or Decrease EPAP To decrease ventilation (*to change pressure support level): Decrease IPAP or Increase EPAP To improve trigger dys-synchrony: *Attempt to increase EPAP (If the same PS is desired, clinician must increase IPAP the same increments as the EPAP) *If using a critical care ventilator simply change PS level to affect ventilation and change PEEP trigger dys-synchrony
Weaning	Begin by decreasing F_IO_2 and pressure as tolerated Remove NPPV from patient for short breaks and monitor for the need to restart therapy Breaks may be lengthened to wean further

Note: If using for more than 2 hours continuously, it is recommended that a passover humidifier be added to the circuit.

Monitoring for Success (Type-1)

Once NPPV is initiated, close observation is required to assess efficacy.

Rapid improvement should occur (1-2 hours) by the following signs:

Patient comfort: ↓ RR, ↓ use of accessory muscles, ↓ dyspnea, synchronization with NPPV.

Improvement in $PaCO_2$ and respiratory acidosis

Criteria for stopping NPPV attempts and initiating alternative therapy (ET intubation):

- barotrauma
- failure of indications (pg 2) to improve
- hemodynamic instability
- hypercapnia
- inability to accept any of the interfaces attempted
- inability to clear secretions
- pulmonary emboli
- sepsis
- worsening agitation
- worsening mental status
- worsening oxygenation.

Clinical effectiveness is assessed by:

Improved oximetry

Improved clinical assessment

An elevated $PaCO_2$ does not have to drop, however progressive hypercapnia with the application of NPPV indicates failure.

Choosing a Ventilator for Use in NPPV

Type of Ventilator*	Advantages	Disadvantages
Critical Care Ventilators	Any critical care ventilator can be adapted for NPPV use Multiple modes available (pressure support used majority of the time) 21-100% FIO_2 via blender Minimizes CO_2 rebreathing due to dual limb circuit Accurate tracking of V_T and $\dot{V}_E$	Confusion concerning masks and settings if clinicians are used to only using portable bilevel ventilators Limits availability of critical care ventilator Some ventilators may not be as sensitive as portable devices are for leak compensation
Portable Bilevel Ventilators	Most are excellent at leak compensation Portable and ease of use for chronic care	Unable to deliver accurate or high F_IO_2 (not including Respironic's BiPAP Vision) Only one or two modes of ventilation available not including CPAP May rebreath CO_2 due to single limb circuit

* See ventilator manufacturer's user manual for proper use and algorithms.

Choosing an Interface: Nasal vs. Full Face Masks

Interface	Advantages	Disadvantages	Sizing*
Nasal Mask	Comfort Patient compliance	Gas leaks Nasal dryness or damage Normally less efficient ventilation Not usually used for patients in acute respiratory failure	Choose a small mask over a large mask in most cases The top of the mask should be 1/3 of the way down from the bridge of the nose (too high = leaks in eyes) The bottom of the mask should rest just above the upper lip
Full Face Mask	Better ventilation Good seal	More claustrophobic Less patient tolerance Regurgitation and aspiration susceptibility Must remove to expectorate or speak	Choose a small mask over a large mask, in most cases The top of the mask should be 1/3 of the way down form the bridge of the nose The bottom of the mask should rest just below the lower lip

* See mask manufacturer's instructions for fitting details.

10 Specific Disease/Condition Management

Chapter Contents

Throughout the Chapter, an ■ indicates ACCP Guidelines from the ACCP Consensus Conference: Mechanical Ventilation; ***Respiratory Care***, vol. 38, #12, 1993.

Acute Respiratory Distress Syndrome (ARDS) and Acute Lung Injury (ALI)

*See Acute Respiratory Distress Syndrome Network Protocol; adapted from **N Engl J Med** 2000; 342(18): 1301-1308, beginning on page 10-4.*

Definition (American-European Consensus Conference on ARDS)

1. Acute onset of respiratory dsitress
2. Hypoxemia:
   ALI $PaO_2/FiO_2 \leq 300$ mmHg
   ARDS $PaO_2/FiO_2 \leq 200$ mmHg
3. Bilateral consolidation on CXR
4. Absense of clinical finding of cardiogenic pulmonary edema (PAOP < 18 mmHg or no LA hypertension)

Patient Problems

Phase 1 (first 7-10 days)	Phase 2 (> 10 days)
Intense inflammatory response resulting in: 1) Alveolar and endothelial damage 2) Increased vascular permeability 3) Increased water and protein	Extensive pulmonary fibrosis

Clinical Presentation

↓ C_L (total C < 30 mL/cmH_2O) Intrapulmonary shunting (> 20%) Marked ↑ in WOB	PCWP < 15-18 mm Hg Refractory hypoxemia (PaO_2/F_IO_2 ≤ 200) X-ray (diffuse alveolar infiltrates)

Common Causes of ARDS

Respiratory	Non-Respiratory
Aspiration Near-drowning O_2 toxicity Pneumonia (all types) Post-pneumonectomy Raised ICP (head injury) Smoke inhalation Thoracic irradiation Trauma (lung contusuion/injury) Vasculitis	Blood transfusion reactions Burns (massive) DIC Drug abuse Fat embolism Head injury Pancreatitis (acute) Prolonged cardiopulmonary bypass Sepsis Shock (severe and prolonged)

Indications for Mechanical Ventilation

Severe refractory hypoxemia
Impending acute ventialtory failure
Marked ↑ in WOB
Acute ventilatory failure

Type of Ventilation

- No evidence to date suggests that either PV of VV is better.
- Currently, no one mode of ventilation has been proven best for ARDS patients.
- The clinician should choose a mode shown to be capable of supporting oxygenation and ventilation and that the clinician has experience in using.

Notes on Volume Ventilation:

The ARDS lung is not uniformly injured. Some portions of the affected lung have ↓ C whereas other regions may retain a more normal C. Most of the V_T of a positive pressure breath is delivered to the regions of better C, resulting in over-distension of the more normal lung tissue and causing ventilator-induced lung injury (VILI). For these reasons, V_T should be kept as low as possible.

In VV, a decelerating flow pattern is often recommended to deliver the majority of V_T early in the inspiratory phase in order to minimize the difference between peak Paw and peak P_{alv}.

Initial Ventilator Settings

See also ARDS Network Protocol (next section)

V_T	*Early Phase*: 8-10 mL/kg PBW - see page 10-6 *Later Phase*: ↓ to 4-8 mL/kg to maintain Pplat ≤ 30
f	12-20/min. *Note*: V_T and *f* are selected to minimize P_{alv} and auto-PEEP. ↑ *f* to maintain $\dot{V}_E$ as V_T is ↓
T_I	0.8 - 1.2 sec *Note*: lengthen T_I to improve oxygenation only after V_T, *f* and PEEP have been optimized. ↑ in 0.1 sec increments to achieve oxygenation target (rather than a specific I:E ratio)
T_E	Allow adequate T_E to avoid auto-PEEP
F_IO_2	As needed to achieve PaO_2 target (see below)
$\overline{Paw}$	Lowest level to achieve PaO_2 target
P_{plat}	Keep ≤ 30 cmH_2O (permissive hypercapnia is allowed)
PEEP	*Early phase*: Set PEEP 2-4 cmH_2O above the UIP of the deflation limb on the V-P curve (usually 10-12 cmH_2O) *Later phase*: A lower PEEP may be tolerated
$\dot{V}_I$ waveform	Decelerating

Key Management Strategies

Lung recruitment (See Specific Ventilation Techniques, Chapter 15)

SaO_2 ≥ 90% (slightly less than 90% is reasonable when both high P_{plat} and high F_iO_2 exists.)

PaO_2: Mild ARDS ≥ 70 mmHg Moderate ARDS ≥ 60 mmHg Severe ARDS ≥ 55 mmHg	**$PaCO_2$:** 40 - 80 mmHg (if possible) **pH:** > 7.15

Permissive hypercapnia ($PaCO_2$ < 100 mmHg) is permissible to limit Palv ≤ 30 cmH_2O. It is usually a necessity once auto-PEEP develops (unless contraindicated or ↑ ICP).

↓ V_T to as low as 4 mL/kg when P_{alv} > 30 cmH_2O.

Palv > 30 cmH_2O may be acceptable in conditions with ↓ Ccw.

Sedation and paralysis are possible therapeutic measures.

Sedation is usually required because of these patients' high ventilatory drive.

Paralysis is not recommended by some clinicians, except in severe cases.

Monitoring

ABG's q. ventilator change or change in patient status Auto-PEEP (q ventilator change) Continuous SpO_2	Daily CXR Closely monitor PEEP, P_{plat}, and $\overline{P}aw$ PA catheter may be recommended to monitor hemodynamic status

Weaning

Weaning is commonly a protracted process due to lung compromise from fibrosis and prolonged ventilatory muscle disuse. No one method is proven more effective. See ARDS Network Weaning Protocol below.

Alternative Techniques for Assisting Ventilation of Refractory ARDS

APRV	HFV	Nitric oxide
IRV	IVOX	Prone positioning
ECMO CO_2	Liquid ventilation	Tracheal gas insufflation

See Chapter 15

ARDS Network Protocol

The following pages on ARDS are adapted from Acute Respiratory Distress Syndrome Network. Ventilation with lower tidal volumes as compared with traditional tidal volumes for acute lung injury and the acute respiratory distress syndrome. ***N Engl J Med*** 2000; 342 (18): 1301-1308.

Implementation

American-European Consensus Conference Criteria*

Acute onset	Bilateral infiltrates on frontal CXR
$PaO_2/FIO_2 \leq 300$ mm Hg (regardless of PEEP level)	Pulmonary artery occlusion pressure ≤ 18 mmHg (or no evidence of LA hypertension)

* The American-European Consensus Conference on ARDS. ***J Crit Care*** 1994; 9(1): 72-81.

TWO PARTS OF ARDS

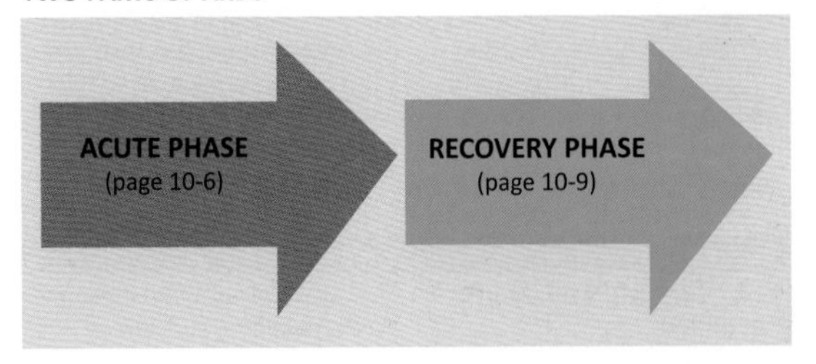

A) Acute Phase (Continuous Mechanical Ventilation Protocol)

ARDS Network Protocol Algorithm – Overview

V-ACV

↓

V_T 4 - 6 mL/kg P_{plat} 25 - 30 cmH_2O PaO_2 55 - 80 mmHg SpO_2 88 - 95 %	f 6 - 35 breaths/min Arterial pH 7.30 – 7.45 Specific F_IO_2 and PEEP relationship

Initiation of Mechanical Ventilation

Step 1:	Step 2:
V_T is set at 8 - 10 mL/kg (PBW) PBW (predicted body weight) = Male (kg): 50 + 2.3 (Ht in inches – 60) Female (kg): 45.5 + 2.3 (Ht in inches – 60) ——— Male (kg): 50 + 2.3 [(Ht in cm – 152) / 2.54] Female (kg): 45.5 + 2.3 [(Ht in cm –152) / 2.54]	V_T is corrected for compression volume loss: performed automatically by some ventilators or calculated. Compression volume = ventilator circuit compliance x (PIP – PEEP) Corrected V_T = V_T (set) + compression volume (See Initial Settings, Ch 4)
Step 3:	**Step 4:**
V_T is reduced to 6 mL/kg over a 4 hr period. Further reductions may be made by 1 mL/kg over a 2-3 hr period. As V_T is reduced, $\dot{V}_E$ is maintained by increasing set f ($\dot{V}_E = V_T \times f$). Set f is limited to 35 breaths/min Permissive hypercapnia is allowed as needed. I:E ratio is set between 1:3 and 1:1 $\dot{V}_I$ and $\dot{V}_I$ pattern is at clinician's discretion.	The effect of set V_T on Pplat and oxygenation is considered. V_T is aggressively reduced to keep P_{plat} between 25 – 30 cmH_2O. Pplat is measured using a 0.5 sec end-inspiratory hold. Insure patient is not coughing, inspiring, or actively expiring during the hold.
F_IO_2/PEEP: F_IO_2 for any given PEEP is given in table below.	

Relationship between PEEP and F_IO_2 Settings in the ARDS Net Protocol

Low PEEP Approach		High PEEP Approach**	
F_IO_2	PEEP	F_IO_2	PEEP
0.3	5	0.3	12
0.4	5	0.3	14
0.4	8	0.4	14
0.5	8	0.4	16
0.5	10	0.5	16
0.6	10	0.5	18
0.7	10	0.5-0.8	20
0.7	12	0.8	22
0.7	14	0.9	22
0.8	14	1.0	22-24
0.9	14		
0.9	16		
0.9	18		
1.0	18		
1.0	20-24		
1.0	26-34*		

F_IO_2 and/or PEEP are adjusted in intervals of 5-15 min until values are compatible with the table. As PEEP is increased, P_{plat} is re-measured to see if V_T is to be reduced below 6 mL/kg.

*When PaO_2 < 55 mmHg or SpO_2 < 88% on F_IO_2 1.0 and PEEP = 24 cmH_2O, then I:E is ↑ to 1:1 and PEEP is ↑ in increments of 2 cmH_2O until a maximum of 34 cmH_2O or until PaO_2 > 55 mmHg or SpO_2 > 88%. If no improvement occurs by 4 hrs, then PEEP is ↓ to 24 cmH_2O.

NHLBI ARDS Clinical Trials Network. Higher versus lower positive end-expiratory pressures in patients with the acute respiratory distress syndrom. ***N Engl J Med* 351: 327-336, 2004

Protocol Ranges: PaO_2 55 – 80 mmHg, SpO_2 88 – 95%

Note: Mild hypoxemia is preferred over high levels of F_IO_2 and PEEP. Therefore, promptly reduce F_IO_2 and PEEP levels when upper levels of protocol ranges are reached.

In the presence of severe hypoxemia or severe acidosis:
Pplat limit of 30 cmH_2O may be temporarily suspended.

When severe patient-ventilator asynchrony occurs:
V_T may be ↑ to 7 - 8 mL/kg as long as Pplat ≤ 30 cmH_2O.
Set *f* is adjusted between 6 - 35 breaths/min to maintain pH 7.30 – 7.45. High levels of sedation are often necessary to control the restlessness and anxiety associated with low V_T and/or hypercapnia.

ARDS NET Protocol Adjustments

Condition	Recommended Adjustment
P_{plat} > 30 cmH_2O	↓ V_T by 1 mL/kg every 2-3 hr, down to a minimum of 4 mL/kg ↑ *f* to maintain $\dot{V}_E$
Pplat < 25 cmH_2O and V_T < 6 mL/kg	↑ V_T to 6 mL/kg and ↓ *f* to maintain $\dot{V}_E$
Mild Acidosis: pH 7.15-7.30	↑ *f* to 35 breaths/min or until pH ≥ 7.30 with $PaCO_2$ ≥ 25 mm Hg. If pH remains < 7.30 and $PaCO_2$ < 25 mm Hg, consider treatment with $NaHCO_3$.
Severe Acidosis: pH < 7.15	↑ *f* to 35 breaths/min and consider treatment of pH with $NaHCO_3$. If pH remains < 7.15, ↑ V_T by 1 mL/kg until pH > 7.15. Pplat > 30 cm H_2O is acceptable Upper limits of V_T and Pplat are suspended until pH = 7.20.
Severe Hypoxemia: PaO_2 < 55 mm Hg (SpO_2 < 88%) on F_iO_2 1.0 and PEEP 24 cmH_2O	Upper limits of V_T and P_{plat} are suspended during PEEP trial between 26 and 34 cmH_2O. I:E is set at 1:1
Severe Patient-Ventilator discoordination: The failure of the ventilator to pressurize the circuit above PEEP during inspiration, or double-triggering the ventilator during inspiration (> 3/min).	↑ *f* and ↓ I:E to ↑ $\dot{V}_I$ Maximize trigger sensitivity If available on VV, use decelerating flow pattern to ↑ $\dot{V}_I$. If above measures ineffective and Pplat < 30 cmH_2O, ↑ V_T by 1 mL/kg up to 8mL.

Clinical Notes

Hemodynamic response to low V_T ventilation (including hypercapnia, respiratory acidosis, sedation, low V_T, high PEEP, patient's underlying disease, etc.) is complex and varied. Careful attention to hemodynamic monitoring is indicated.

Low V_T ventilation is disadvantageous to pulmonary hygiene and ↑ the risk of retained secretions. Adequate humidification is essential and transient hyperinflation to promote secretion clearance (esp. with suctioning or CPT) should be considered when secretions are thick.

B) Recovery Phase (Weaning Protocol)

Two ARDS Network Weaning Protocol Algorithms:

1) Overview
2) Weaning from A/C Ventilation to Unassisted Breathing

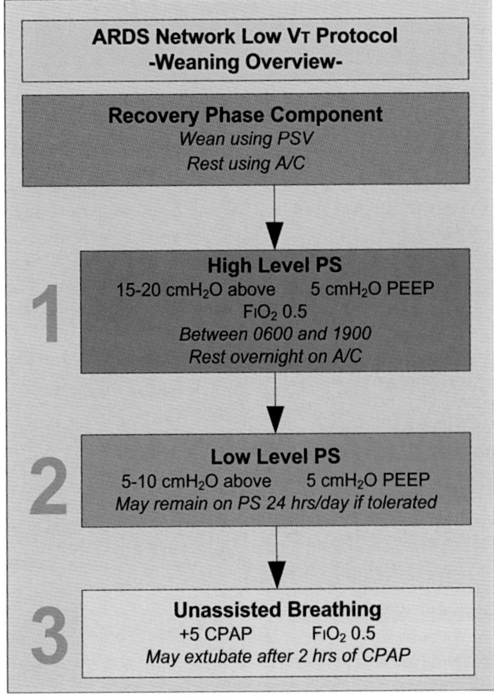

Algorithms on this page and next, adapted from Kallet RH, Corral W, Silverman HJ, Luce JM. Implementation of a Low Tidal Volume Ventilation Protocol for Patients with Acute Lung Injury or Acute Respiratory Distress Syndrome. ***Resp Care*** 2001; 46(10): 1024-1037

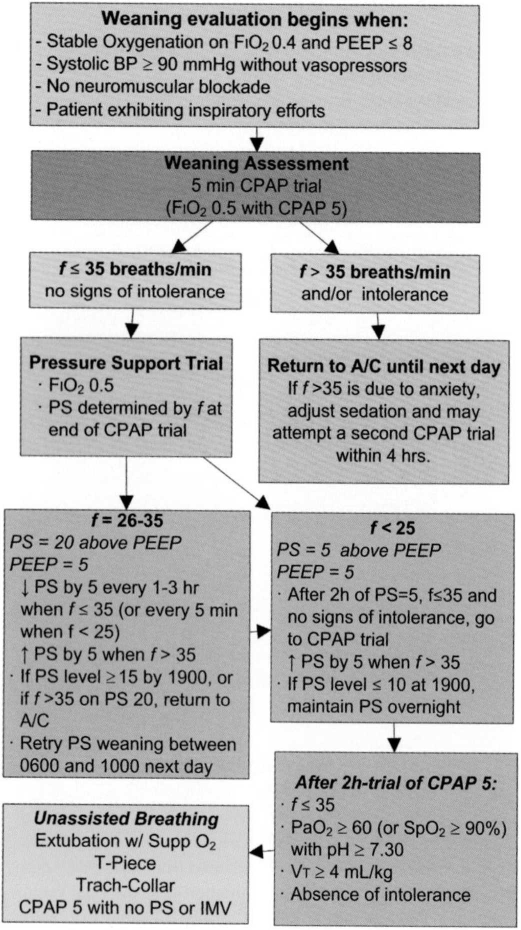

Weaning evaluation begins when:
- Stable Oxygenation on FiO_2 0.4 and PEEP ≤ 8
- Systolic BP ≥ 90 mmHg without vasopressors
- No neuromuscular blockade
- Patient exhibiting inspiratory efforts

↓

Weaning Assessment
5 min CPAP trial
(FiO_2 0.5 with CPAP 5)

↓

***f* ≤ 35 breaths/min**
no signs of intolerance

↓

Pressure Support Trial
- FiO_2 0.5
- PS determined by *f* at end of CPAP trial

↓

***f* = 26-35**
PS = 20 above PEEP
PEEP = 5
- ↓ PS by 5 every 1-3 hr when *f* ≤ 35 (or every 5 min when f < 25)
- ↑ PS by 5 when *f* > 35
- If PS level ≥ 15 by 1900, or if *f* >35 on PS 20, return to A/C
- Retry PS weaning between 0600 and 1000 next day

→

***f* < 25**
PS = 5 above PEEP
PEEP = 5
- After 2h of PS=5, f≤35 and no signs of intolerance, go to CPAP trial
- ↑ PS by 5 when *f* > 35
- If PS level ≤ 10 at 1900, maintain PS overnight

↓

After 2h-trial of CPAP 5:
- *f* ≤ 35
- PaO_2 ≥ 60 (or SpO_2 ≥ 90%) with pH ≥ 7.30
- V_T ≥ 4 mL/kg
- Absence of intolerance

→

Unassisted Breathing
Extubation w/ Supp O_2
T-Piece
Trach-Collar
CPAP 5 with no PS or IMV

***f* > 35 breaths/min**
and/or intolerance

↓

Return to A/C until next day
If *f* >35 is due to anxiety, adjust sedation and may attempt a second CPAP trial within 4 hrs.

Clinical Notes

F_IO_2 and PEEP have either ↓ or remained stable during previous day. Dopamine or dobutamine infusions of ≤ 5 μg/kg/min are not considered vasopressor support.

Evaluate for weaning between 6:00 and 10:00 AM

If patient is not triggering breaths, reduce mandatory *f* by 50% for 5 min. If still no triggering, then patient does not meet weaning criteria. (May re-evaluate after any sedation is ↓).

Criteria Used to Assess Weaning Tolerance

Total $f \leq 35$ breaths/min (>35 breaths/min for ≤ 5 min is allowed)

$SpO_2 \leq 88\%$ (< 88% for < 15 min is allowed)

No respiratory distress, defined as *2 or more* of the following:

- HR > 120% of 6:00 AM value (> 120% for 5 min is allowed)
- Pronounced accessory muscle use
- Abdominal paradox
- Diaphoresis
- Pronounced subjective sense of dyspnea

Asthma

Patient Problems

↑ Raw – bronchospasm and mucosal edema with ↑ secretions resulting in ball-valving and long time-constants

Air-trapping (auto-PEEP) – ↑ FRC and ↓ CL resulting in ↑ WOB and barotrauma

Large intrathoracic pressure changes – resulting in altered gas distribution and altered perfusion

Progressive hypoxemia and anxiety

Indications for Mechanical Ventilation

Acute respiratory failure Air-trapping on CXR BS absent and chest hyperresonant to percussion Exhaustion (↑ or ↓ RR and altered consciousness)	Impending respiratory failure (rising $PaCO_2$ and falling pH) Life threatening arrhythmias Respiratory or cardiac arrest Severe refractory hypoxemia

Clinical Note: The respiratory distress in these patients is generally due to hypoxemia, which in turn results in hypocarbia ($PaCO_2$ < 40 mm Hg). MV is generally instituted when the $PaCO_2$ climbs back to normal (40 mmHg), which is now indicative of impending respiratory failure due to fatigue. At this point, full ventilatory support should not be delayed because severe hypercarbia and acidosis will develop rapidly.

Type of Ventilation

Although no one type of ventilation is superior, patients generally don't tolerate assisted ventilation, and PV is commonly preferred for severe asthma. Advantages of PV: A change in V_T is a good indicator of change in resistance and air-trapping, T_I is not prematurely terminated by a high pressure limit, and flow will adjust automatically.

National Asthma Education Guidelines*

Signs of Impending Respiratory Failure:

Altered mental state	Inability to speak
Worsening fatigue	Intercostal retractions
$PaCO_2 \geq 42$	

Intubation: DO NOT DELAY ONCE DEEMED NECESSARY (see Near-Fatal Asthma below for intubation indications and procedure.) Heliox (Heliox-driven Albuterol treatments) or MgSO4 may be considered to avoid intubation).

Mechanical Ventilation - Initial Settings

V_T	6 - 10 mL/kg (VV) (↓ V_T to keep PIP < 35 cmH_2O)
PV:	keep PIP ≤ 30 - 35 cmH_2O
f	12 – 25 breaths/min
PEEP	4 - 10 cm H_2O
FiO_2	1.0
T_I	Keep short enough to ensure expiration ends before next inspiration.

Clinical Notes: Immediately assess for chest rise, BS, airflow, and T_E. Watch for auto-PEEP and barotrauma. Monitor with end-tidal CO_2

Permissive hypercapnia is the recommended strategy, but it is not uniformly successful. Minimize high airway pressures and barotrauma.

*Adapted from the ***Guidelines for the Diagnosis and Management of Asthma, the National Asthma Education Program's Expert Panel: Report 2, 1998, and EPR-3, 2007***; Nation Heart Lung, and Blood Institute; National Institutes of Health, Bethesda, MD.

Key Management Strategies

1) ↑ Raw – aggressive treatment with bronchodilators and steroids
2) Avoid or reduce air-trapping (includes permissive hypercapnia)

Clinical Notes:

Auto-PEEP is a major concern in these patients, hence the mechanical ventilation approach should focus on minimizing air-trapping with small V_T and slow *f* (long T_E and short T_I). Permissive hypercapnia is often required to accomplish this. The risks of VILI and barotrauma far outweigh the risk of ↓ pH.

Care must be taken NOT to manually ventilate the patient at a rate higher than 10 - 12 (adult) or 16 - 20 (child) after intubation. The patient MAY benefit from a clinician-applied period of apnea of up to 60 seconds, until either the patient has fully exhaled, or SpO_2 has dropped.

The application of applied PEEP is a major controversy in asthma management. It is generally recommended to not apply more than 80% of the measured auto-PEEP. Applied PEEP is not additive to auto-PEEP when the auto-PEEP is due to airflow limitation. If PIP increases with applied PEEP, decrease PEEP.

Minimize PIP and Pplat (keep Pplat < 30 cmH_2O).

Sedation and/or paralysis may be necessary if patient is fighting the ventilator. Many clinicians avoid paralysis if possible.

Near-Fatal Asthma[1]

Intubation

Indications:

Obtunded, diaphoretic (profusely), "Floppy" muscle tone, severe agitation, confusion, and fighting.

Clearly rising $PaCO_2$ (not just elevated)

Procedure:

Sedation with ketamine or barbituate (ketamine – bolus 0.5 - 1.5 mg/kg, repeated in 20 min or infusion 1 - 5 mg/kg/hr. Provide atropine (0.01 mg/kg, 0.1 mg minimum) for bronchial secretions.

Paralyze patient with succinylcholine or vecuronium.

Immediately after intubation: inject 2.5 - 5.0 mg albuterol directly into ET tube. Confirm correct placement – both primary and secondary.

Ensure ET tube in correct position and patent (correct immediately, if needed).

Troubleshooting: Hypotension or Desaturation After Intubating

Check for tension pneumothorax:

- Unilateral chest expansion
- Tracheal shift
- Subcutaneous emphysema
- Decompression – insert 16 gauge needle into 2nd IC space, mid-clavicular line. Insert chest tube if air is emitted.

Massive auto-PEEP

(the most common cause of profound hypotension):

Stop ventilation for < 1 min to allow auto-PEEP to dissipate. Observe oxygenation.

Ventilation - Permissive Hypercapnia

Sedate and paralyze to allow $PaCO_2$ to rise as high as 80 mmHg (control ↓ pH with bicarbonate if necessary).

FiO_2	1.0
V_T	5-7 mL/kg
f	8-10/min (to avoid auto-PEEP)
$\dot{V}_I$	60 LPM with decelerating pattern

If airway is difficult to ventilate, perform the following in order until ventilation is adequate: ‡

1) Ensure passive patient-ventilator interaction (sedated or paralyzed).
2) Check ET tube for patency.
3) Ensure adequate V_T: ↑ T_E, ↓T_I and ↑ PIP
4) ↓ Rate to 6 - 8/min (to ↓ auto-PEEP to ≤ 15 cmH_2O)
5) ↓ V_T to 3 - 5 mL/kg (to ↓ auto-PEEP to ≤ 15 cmH_2O).
6) ↑ $\dot{V}_I$ to > 60 LPM (may use 90 - 120 LPM to further shorten T_I and ↑ I:E ratio).

Monitoring

Careful monitoring for auto-PEEP & barotrauma (P_{plat}, $\overline{Paw}$, V_T)

Weaning

Once the acute episode is reversed and the patient is alert, oriented, and cooperative, the mechanical ventilation can usually be simply discontinued and the ET tube removed, provided there are no secondary pulmonary complications.

‡ *Synopsis of the Guidelines 2000 for Cardiopulmonary Resuscitation and Emergency Cardiovascular Care: International Consensus on Science. American Heart Association and the International Liaison Committee of Resuscitation, Circulation, 2000; 102 (Suppl I): I-1-384, and 2005 Update; Circulation, 2005, Vol 112, No. 24.*

Broncho-Pleural Fistula (B-P Fistula)

Common Causes

Trauma Surgery Invasive procedures	Diffuse lung disease (ARDS, Pneumocystis carinii, necrotizing pneumonia, etc.; esp. with MV)

Type of Ventilation

- No single mode or approach has been shown more effective.
- A ventilator capable of delivering high $\dot{V}_I$ and large V_T may be required where there is a large air leak.

PV is often recommended due to the ability to control peak P_{alv}.

Avoid PSV – if BP fistula leak is > than the flow level required to terminate inspiration, then the ventilator will not cycle from I to E.

Allowing spontaneous ventilation is dependent on the severity of the disease and patient hemodynamics.

Note: Non-conventional approaches include ILV and HFV. Neither have been shown to improve outcome.

Indication for Mechanical Ventilation

B-P fistula in itself is not an indication for MV. Rather, its presence is often in conjunction with other pulmonary problems.

Initial Ventilator Settings

V_T	4-8 mL/kg
f	6 - 20 (depending on underlying disease)
T_I	≤1.0 sec
$\dot{V}_I$ waveform	decelerating
PEEP	0-10 cmH_2O

Key Management Strategies

- The goal is to minimize inflation pressures and V_T.
- Use a mode that minimizes transpulmonary pressures (PIP, P_{alv}, PEEP) to minimize air leak through the fistula.
- Use the lowest V_T that allows adequate ventilation.
- Ventilatory support should provide adequate inflation for the uninvolved areas of lung.
- Consider permissive hypercapnia to minimize inspiratory pressures and volumes.

Minimize T_I and chest tube suction

Note: The flow through a fistula is proportional to the magnitude and duration of the pressure gradient (e.g., Palv 30 cmH_2O and chest tube suction - 20 cmH_2O = 50 cmH_2O pressure gradient).

Management of oxygenation is often difficult because most maneuvers which ↑ PaO_2 (↑ PEEP, ↑ $\overline{P}aw$, ↑ T_I) also ↑ leak.

- Consider ILV or HFV in cases of severe leak. (Early intervention with HFV is considered best by some).

Monitoring

Careful monitoring of pressures and the volume of air leak (inspired V_T - expired V_T).

Weaning

Weaning approach is based on the underlying disease process and closure of the air leak.

Burns and Smoke Inhalation

Two Types: 1) Surface Burns;
2) Inhalation (Thermal, Parenchymal, Systemic Toxins)

Complications Associated with Burns and Smoke Inhalation:

ARDS Airway obstruction CO poison Pneumonia Pulmonary edema	Pulmonary embolism Sepsis Upper airway/ bronchial obstruction

Indications for Mechanical Ventilation

Surface Burns:	***Thermal Injury:***
ARDS due to sepsis, or hyper-metabolism. Chest restriction due to severe burns. Respiratory depression from pain medication.	Most common effects are upper airway edema, spasm, and ↑ secretions. Immediate intubation is indicated due to risk of complete airway obstruction. MV may not be required if there is no lower airway injury.
Parenchymal Injury:	***Systemic Toxins:***
Smoke inhalation induces bronchospasm and ↓ mucociliary transport. These patients commonly develop ARDS (see ARDS section).	Respiratory depression due to CO poisoning, cyanide, and/or nitrogen oxides.

Type of Ventilation

VV is commonly used. PV may be better if ↑ Raw or ↓ CL.
Full ventilatory support is often required, at least initially.
HFV may be of benefit.

Initial Ventilator Settings

V_T	4 - 12 mL/kg
f	6 - 20 /min (<10 if auto-PEEP present)
T_I	1.0 sec
PEEP	5 cmH_2O
FiO_2	1.0 (esp. with CO poison)

Disease Management

Key Management Strategies

Many patients require sedation and paralysis.

If patient develops ARDS, see ARDS section.

Patients who are hypermetabolic may require high $\dot{V}_E$ to maintain normocarbia.

PaO_2 is often normal or ↑, but an F_IO_2 of 1.0 is mandatory for the treatment of CO poison until the measured carboxyhemoglobin level is < 10%. Hyperbaric O_2 therapy is useful if available.

Monitoring

Pulse oximetry may be unreliable if a high carboxyhemoglobin level is present.

Closely monitor for auto-PEEP if high $\dot{V}_E$ is used or patient exhibits bronchospasm and/or ↑ secretions.

Weaning

Reversal of the acute process usually leads to early and quick weaning, provided there are no secondary complications, such as ARDS, sepsis, or pulmonary infections.

Chronic Obstructive Pulmonary Disease (COPD)

Patient Problems

Airway obstruction (inflammation and hyperreactivity) and loss of structural integrity of lung parenchyma (commonly due to hyperinflation):

Resulting in:	Iatrogenic Problems:
Accessory muscle use Air trapping (dynamic hyperinflation) Flattened diaphragm ↑ FRC, ↑ TLC ↑ Raw (with ↓ expiratory flow) ↑ WOB, Possible ↑ C_L	Aspiration Barotrauma (volutrauma) Cardiac (↓ CO) Nosocomial infections

Indication for Mechanical Ventilation

Acute exacerbation of COPD

! **Note**: NPPV is now considered a first choice of ventilation to avoid the morbidity associated with invasive ventilation.

Selection and Exclusion Criteria for NPPV †

Selection Criteria (At least two should be present)	Exclusion Criteria (Any may be present)
pH 7.30 – 7.35 and $PaCO_2$ 45 – 60 mmHg Respiratory rate > 25/min Moderate to severe dyspnea (accessory muscle use and paradoxical abdominal motion)	CV instability (↓ BP, arrhythmias, MI) Craniofacial trauma, fixed nasopharyngeal abnormalities Extreme obesity High aspiration risk; viscous or copious secretions Recent facial or gastroesophageal surgery Respiratory arrest Somnolence, impaired mental status, uncooperative patient

Indications for Invasive Mechanical Ventilation †

NPPV failure (or exclusion criteria, see above)

$PaO_2 < 40$ mmHg or $PaO_2/F_IO_2 < 200$ mmHg

pH < 7.25 and $PaCO_2 > 60$ mmHg

Respiratory arrest

Respiratory rate > 35/min

Severe dyspnea (accessory muscle use and paradoxical abdominal motion)

(continued next page)

Somnolence, impaired mental status
CV complication (↓ BP, shock, heart failure)
Other complications: barotrauma, embolism, massive pleural effusion, metabolic abnormalities, pneumonia, sepsis.

† Adapted from the ***GOLD Executive Summary***, NHLBI and WHO, Respiratory Care, Vol 46, #8, August 2001 & 2007 Update. (See GoldCOPD.org)

Type of Ventilation

Either PV or VV may be used effectively.

■ Use of V-ACV in the initial treatment of awake COPD patients may result in hyperinflation (auto-PEEP) and should be avoided.

PV is well suited for these patients due to: 1) flow on demand to meet patient's needs, 2) set TI, 3) back up rate and, 4) patient triggering is allowed.

Full ventilatory support is recommended for the first 24-48 hrs because most patients are completely exhausted after several days of ↑ WOB.

■ Currently no one mode of ventilation has been proven best for initial management of COPD patients.

■ The clinician should choose a mode he or she is familiar with and has used successfully in this setting.

Clinical Notes

A/C: ↑ spontaneous ventilation may result in alkalosis and auto-PEEP.

SIMV: ↑ spontaneous ventilation may result in ↑ WOB and auto-PEEP.

May use low level PS (5-10 cmH_2O) to minimize WOB.

Keep backup rate high enough so that spontaneous ventilation is not necessary during sleep time.

Initial Ventilator Settings

V_T	5-10 mL/kg
f	8-16 /min
T_I	0.6-1.2 sec (minimize to allow longer T_E)
T_E	Lowest $\dot{V}E$ and the longest T_E that produces an acceptable gas exchange (including permissive hypercapnia)
I:E	1:4 or longer
PaO_2	60 - 70 mm Hg is generally acceptable
$PaCO_2$	Maintain at patient's baseline (generally 50 -

	60 mmHg) or that required to maintain a pH > 7.30. Permissive hypercapnia is acceptable. Avoid hyperventilation.
PEEP	≥ 5 cmH2O or 50% of Auto-PEEP. Adjust up to 80% of Auto-PEEP
$\dot{V}_I$	≥ 60 LPM (high enough with VV to meet inspiratory demand and ↓ T_I to allow more time for expiration)
$\dot{V}_I$ flow pattern	A decelerating flow pattern is recommended because patient inspiratory demand is greatest at the beginning of inspiration, plus the lower end-inspiratory flow improves gas distribution to the long time-constant regions.

Key Management Strategies

↓ WOB (unload and rest ventilatory muscles)

↓ $PaCO_2$ to patient's baseline

Treat hypoxemia

Maintain $P_{plat} \leq 30$ cmH_2O. (Permissive hypercapnia is acceptable if needed to keep $P_{alv} < 30$ cmH_2O). *See Chapter 8.*

↓ Raw (bronchodilators and corticosteroids)

Minimize air-trapping and auto-PEEP – use the least $\dot{V}_E$ (↓ V_T and slow f) that produces an acceptable gas exchange and the greatest T_E. (Note: ↑ Raw requires a greater T_E to expel all the air).

Applied PEEP may be helpful to ↓ WOB when auto-PEEP exists.

Maximize patient-ventilator synchrony.

↓ patient anxiety

Provide adequate secretion hydration, mobilization, and removal.

Provide adequate nutrition.

Monitoring

Closely monitor for:

Auto-PEEP (for signs of auto-PEEP see Ch 11).

Clinical signs of cardiopulmonary distress (RR, BS, retractions, etc)

Patient-ventilator asynchrony

Systemic and pulmonary hemodynamic Δ's (pulse, BP, PAP)

Weaning

To date, there is no definitive best approach. NPPV and weaning protocols have been shown to shorten weaning time (GOLD Executive Summary, ***Respiratory Care***, Vol 46, #8, August 2001)

See Chapters 9 and 13.

Drug Overdose

Common Symptoms

Obtunded Stuporous Respiratory depression	Ineffective spontaneous breathing (either hyper/hypoventilation) CV compromise (hypotension and/or arrythmias)

Indications for Mechanical Ventilation

Apnea, acute respiratory failure, or impending respiratory failure

Type of Ventilation

Any type is acceptable.

Initial Ventilator Settings

V_T	10 - 12 mL/kg
f	8 - 12 /min
T_I	0.8 - 1.2 sec
PEEP	usually not indicated (or 3 - 5 to maintain FRC)

Note: The majority of patients are young and healthy, and without underlying lung disease, but care must be taken to assure that pre-hospital aspiration did not occur.

Monitoring

Monitor closely for:

Aspiration, hemodynamic stability, LOC, patient-vent synchrony

Weaning

Discontinuation is indicated when the drug is cleared and adequate spontaneous ventilation is restored.

Be aware, when possible, of underlying drug/ETOH addictions in many overdose patients, where withdrawals complicate the weaning process.

Myocardial Infarction (MI) and Congestive Heart Failure (CHF)

Patient Problems

Severe heart failure leads to hypoxemia, ↑ WOB, and ↑ work of myocardium.

Precipitating Causes: Acute MI, fluid overload, ↑ BP, tachycardia with ↓ fill time, valve disease.

Indications For MV: ↑ WOB, ↑ work of myocardium, refractory hypoxemia

Type of Ventilation

The first method of choice for LVF with pulmonary edema is CPAP 5 - 10 cmH_2O with FiO_2 1.0. Do not use if mask CPAP further agitates patient.

- In the presence of myocardial ischemia, choose modes that ↓ WOB.
- Modes that ↑ WOB will ↑ O_2 demand and detrimentally affect myocardial O_2 supply and demand.
- Spontaneous ventilation in patients with myocardial ischemia and high lung resistance and/or poor respiratory muscle function is likely detrimental.

Full ventilatory support with 100% FiO_2 is recommended initially, until ABG data is obtained to support lowering.

Initial Ventilator Settings

V_T	5-10 mL/kg
f	8 - 12 /min
T_I	1 - 1.2 sec
$\dot{V}_I$	> 60 LPM (VV)
PEEP	5 - 10 cmH_2O
FiO_2	1.0

Key Management Strategies

Select a mode of ventilation that minimizes WOB.

↓ Preload and afterload (vasodilators)

↓ Vascular load (diuretics)

Improve cardiac contractility (positive inotropic agents)

↑ Myocardial oxygenation (vasodilators)

- Consider the potentially beneficial effects of PPV on decreasing venous return and improving oxygenation in patients with severe CHF and life-threatening hypoxemia.

Note: PPV and PEEP may have variable effects on myocardial function and oxygenation depending on whether the LV is normal or failing.

Monitoring

Careful monitoring and assessment of the effects of PPV on hemodynamics, as well as fluid and electrolyte balance is essential.

Weaning

Any technique is suitable.

The process is dependent on any underlying pulmonary problems.

Caution with PEEP titration because of complex effects on myocardial function.

CV function can change dramatically as intrathoracic pressure changes with the withdrawal of PPV and PEEP, especially the LV preload and potential pulmonary edema. The removal of PEEP is usually one of the last steps in the process.

Fluid balance and inotropes must be titrated to insure maximum myocardial contractility.

Neuromuscular Disorders

Two Types

Rapid Onset (days to weeks)	Gradual Onset (months to years)
Botulism	ALS
Cervical spinal cord injury	Muscular dystrophy
Guillian Barré	Post polio syndrome
Myasthenia gravis	Progressive thoracic deformities (scoliosis, kyphosis, kyphoscoliosis)
Poliomyelitis	
Tetanus	

Patient Problems

Aspiration from airway muscle weakness

Atelectasis from inadequate lung inflation.

Pneumonia from impaired cough and mucociliary clearance.

Indication for Mechanical Ventilation

Progressive ventilatory muscle weakness leading to acute respiratory failure. Best initiated before the onset of acute respiratory acidosis.

Types of Ventilation

There is no evidence that either positive pressure or negative pressure ventilation is superior.

When appropriate and possible, noninvasive ventilation (positive or negative pressure) is preferred, especially in acute care setting where lung volume is normal. Initial ventilator settings are consistent with invasive settings, making allowances for air leaks.

Full or partial ventilatory support is dependent on the patient's capabilities and disease process.

VV is most commonly employed, yet no one type has been proven best.

Initial Ventilator Settings

Setting	Pt. with Normal Lung Volumes	Pt. with Reduced Lung Volumes
V_T	7-15 mL/kg	4-8 mL/kg
f	8-12 /min	12-20 /min
T_I	≤ 1.5 sec	≤ 1.0 sec
$\dot{V}_I$	≤ 60 LPM (VV)	≥ 60 LPM (VV)
$\dot{V}_I$ waveform	--	Decelerating
PEEP	*Usually unnecessary :* 3-5 cmH_2O for FRC 5-10 cmH_2O to relieve dyspnea	*Usually unnecessary:* 3-5 cmH_2O for FRC

Key Management Strategies

The main needs of these patients are adequate lung inflation and aggressive airway management. Provide support based on the patient's inherent ventilatory muscle strengths.

Psychologically, many of these patients desire or demand large V_T, high flow, fast rates, and long T_I (more than needed). Adjust to satisfy patient's inspiratory needs. Mechanical deadspace may be used to maintain normocarbia and prevent hypocarbia/alkalosis.

Monitoring

Daily monitoring of spontaneous V_T, *f*, VC, P_{Imax}, and ventilatory pattern. Less frequent ABG's are required.

Weaning

Primary neuromuscular deficit must be reversed.

Goal is independence during the day with support at night.

Retraining of ventilatory muscles is frequently needed.

Organ Donor (Lung)

Designation:
- Patient/Guardian wishes
- Family wishes
- Age ≤ 65 years
- No history of significant lung disease
- Smoking history: Pack Years < 30
- Clear lung fields on CXR
- PIP < 30 @ V_T 15 mL/kg + 5 PEEP
- Satisfactory Gross Appearance and bronchoscopic inspection

Determination of (Brain) Death (2-5 min observation):

Lack of circulation
Lack of spontaneous respiration
Unresponsive

Mechanical Ventilation Settings

V_T	8-10 mL/kg
PEEP	5 cmH2O
FiO_2	≤ 0.4
Maintain:	
P_{plat}	< 30
pH	7.35-7.45
PaO_2	> 100
$PaCO_2$	35-40 torr
CVP	6-8 torr
PCWP	8-12 torr

Strategies:
- Identify potential donor early
- Prevent atelectasis with use of suction, percussion, postural drainage and recruitment maneuvers
- Bronchoscopy goals include: evaluation of anatomy; assess for FBO and remove; collect sample for microbiological analysis; clearance of secretions
- Use of antibiotic agents based on Gram Stain results
- Family support should be securely in place to meet emotional needs, with obvious considerations for ethical/religious/moral factors

Post-Operative Patients

Indications For MV

Apnea – from unreversed anesthesia (esp. due to hypothermia)
Complicaions of phrenc nerve or diaphragmatic injury
Compromised cardiopulmonary reserve – due to pre-existing lung disease
Post-op cardiopulmonary stress (esp. heart and lung transplants)
Note: Prophylactic use is not an indication for post-op MV.

Type of Ventilation: No one type or mode has been proven best.

Initial Ventilator Settings

Patients With No Prior Pulmonary Disease	Patients With Prior Obstructive Lung Disease (See COPD)	Patients With Prior Restrictive Lung Disease (See Restrictive)
V_T 10 - 12 mL/kg f 8 - 12 /min T_I 1 - 1.2 sec PEEP ≤ 5cmH$_2$O $\dot{V}_I$ waveform Decelerating	V_T 5-10 mL/kg f 8-16 /min T_I 0.6 - 1.2 sec PEEP ≤ 5 cmH$_2$O (to offset auto-PEEP) $\dot{V}_I$ waveform Decelerating	V_T 4 - 8 mL/kg f 12 - 30 /min T_I ≤ 1.0 sec PEEP 5 cmH$_2$O $\dot{V}_I$ waveform Decelerating

Exception: Patients with reduced body temperature:
$\dot{V}_E$ must be reduced to avoid decreasing $PaCO_2$ and increasing pH.
(↓ temperature → ↓ metabolic rate → ↓ CO_2 production)
Initial rate may need to be as low as 5 - 6 /min and gradually ↑ as temperature rises.

Key Management Strategies

The greatest concern for the clinician is to avoid iatrogenic complications of ventilatory support, including infection, ↓ cardiac output, unnecessary sedation, hyperventilation, inspissated secretions, and unnecessary exposure to high F_IO_2.

Monitoring

Close monitoring of LOC, fluid balance, hemodynamics, and pulmonary mechanics (esp. ability to breathe deeply and cough).

Weaning

Weaning is commonly quick and easy, but dependent on underlying problems.

Usually the patient can be extubated when the patient is alert, oriented, able to lift head, and able to take a deep breath.

- Residual anesthetic effects may require a variable period for MV.

Restrictive Pulmonary Lung Disease

Similar to COPD except:

Initial Ventilator Settings	
V_T	4 - 8 mL/kg
f	12 - 30 /min (increased to maintain ↑ $\dot{V}_E$)
T_I	≤ 1.0 sec
$\dot{V}_I$	≥ 60 L/min
$\dot{V}_I$ waveform	Decelerating
PEEP	5 cmH_2O

Note: Auto-PEEP is generally not a concern in this disease process.

Trauma (Chest)

Two Types

Blunt chest trauma

Penetrating chest trauma

Indications for Ventilation

Blunt Chest Trauma:

Rib fracture (flail chest) – Many patients with flail chest are now managed without intubation and MV. MV is now generally instituted only if the patient also has:

- Shock
- Closed head injury
- Deteriorating respiratory status
- Need of immediate operation
- Severe pulmonary dysfunction
- Respiratory depression from pain medications

Pulmonary contusion – Although clinically similar to ARDS, the localized damage often lends itself to treatment by O_2, CPAP, and positioning. If ARDS develops, see ARDS section.

Penetrating Chest Trauma

MV is usually post-op.

Type of Ventilation

VV is most commonly employed initially. PV may be more appropriate in patients with air leaks and/or barotrauma.

Full ventilatory support is usually required initially.

Initial Ventilator Settings	
V_T	10-12 mL/kg (normal compliance)
	4 – 8 mL/kg (pulmonary contusion and ARDS)
f	8-12 /min
T_I	1.0 sec (↑ if ARDS develops)
$\dot{V}_I$ waveform	decelerating
PEEP	5 cmH_2O (no PEEP if severe air leak present)

Key Management Strategies

Ventilate at the lowest possible mean airway pressures due to risks of pulmonary air leaks (pneumothorax).

Use PEEP with caution due to barotrauma (esp. unilateral contusion) and hemodynamic instability due to blood loss and/or head injury.

Many patients require initial sedation or paralysis.

Permissive hypercapnia may be employed provided no accompanying head trauma with ↑ ICP.

Monitoring

Monitor closely for signs of air leak, pulmonary embolism, and hemodynamic stability.

Weaning

Discontinuation often occurs early and rapidly unless ARDS develops or severe chest wall or diaphragm injury is present.

Trauma (Head)

Patient Problems: Cerebral edema and/or ↑ ICP

CPP = MAP – ICP	Normal CPP = (90-95) – (< 10) = 80-85
	CPP < 60 = poor perfusion

Common Causes

Stroke (CVA)	Surgery (post craniotomy)
Hepatic failure	Trauma
Post-resuscitation hypoxia	

Indications For MV

Central respiratory depression from injury or drugs used to treat acute head injury (barbituate coma, sedation, paralysis)
Glascow Coma Score < 8
Impending or actual cardiac arrest
Neurogenic pulmonary edema

Type of Ventilation

Either volume or pressure ventilation can be used.
Full ventilatory support should be used initially, hence PS is generally not appropriate.

Initial Ventilator Settings

V_T	8 - 12 mL/kg
f	10 - 15 /min (15 - 20 for hyperventilation, provided no auto-PEEP present)
T_I	≤ 1.0 sec
$\dot{V}_I$	High (to keep TI short)
$\dot{V}_I$ waveform	Decelerating
$\overline{P}aw$	Keep as low as possible
PEEP	Keep as low as possible
PaO_2	Use F_IO_2 1.0 initially until ABG obtained. Keep PaO_2 80 - 100 mmHg (to avoid hypoxemia and minimize ICP increase).

Key Management Strategies

Protect the airway. Patients with head injury are at ↑ risk of vomiting and aspiration.
Maintain patient's head in neutral position and 30 degree elevation.
Maintain a normal CPP by maintaining a normal MAP + normal ICP.

Management of MAP = Hemodynamic control of BP
Management of ICP

The Brain Trauma Foundation currently recommends[1]:

1. Avoid hyperventilation in the first 24 hours after injury
2. Prophylactic hyperventilation ($PaCO_2 \leq 25$) is not recommended
3. Hyperventilation is recommended as a temporizing measure for lowering increased ICP.
4. If hyperventilation is used, monitor O_2 delivery with jugular venous O_2 Sat (SjO_2) or brain tissue O_2 tension ($PbrO_2$)

[1] Brain Trauma Foundation's Guidelines for the Management of Severe Traumatic Brain Injury, 3rd Edition, 2007. BrainTrauma.org.

- If hyperventilation is used to ↓ ICP, gradually return to normocarbia over 24 - 48 hrs.
- Maintain normocarbia in patients with normal ICP. There is no evidence to support prophylactic hyperventilation in patients with head injury who do not have raised ICP.
- PPV and PEEP can ↑ ICP because Palv is easily transmitted to vascular space in patients with normal lungs: A large ↑ in Paw, (due to ↑ $\dot{V}E$ to cause hyperventilation and ↓ ICP) may cause a paradoxical ↑ in ICP.

PEEP < 10 cmH_2O will rarely adversely affect ICP and any effect can usually be offset by head elevation.

Suctioning and CPT can dramatically ↑ ICP. Therefore, perform bronchial hygiene with extreme caution.

Patients with Normal ICP: Maintain normal gases

Interventions for Patients with Increased ICP:

Barbituates: Decreases cerebral O_2 consumption and ↓ ICP

Diuretics: Decreases fluid resulting in ↓ MAP and ↓ ICP

Mannitol: Increases osmotic pressure resulting in ↓ ICP

Sedation and paralysis: Suppresses agitation, coughing, and pain that causes ICP to rise.

Iatrogenic hyperventilation: $PaCO_2$ 25 - 30 mmHg (Maintain PaO_2 90 - 100 mmHg) (Controversial).

Normalize $PaCO_2$ ASAP. If ICP levels permit, allow $PaCO_2$ to gradually return to normal over 24 - 48 hrs (before CSF pH normalizes). If $PaCO_2$ rises too rapidly, ICP may rebound to unacceptably high levels.

Neurogenic pulmonary edema

Acute head injury with ↑ ICP may cause neurogenic pulmonary edema, which is clinically indistinguishable from ARDS. Treat similar to ARDS with extra caution on increasing ICP (See ARDS).

Monitoring

- Effective monitoring should be instituted to allow a rapid ↑ in ventilation and oxygenation should hypoxemia or ↑ ICP occur.

Monitor closely for: Hypoxemia, auto-PEEP, ↑ ICP (during suctioning, CPT, and following ventilator changes), and pulmonary emboli and infections.

Weaning

Criteria for weaning: Normalized $PaCO_2$, no respiratory depressant drugs in use, and ventilatory drive intact.

11 Ventilator Effects, Cautions and Complications

Chapter Contents

Pulmonary

Airway Obstruction

Causes		Signs & Symptoms	
Patient	**Circuit**	**Patient**	**Machine**
Bronchospasm Inadequate suctioning and/or bronchial hygiene	ET tube displaced, kinked, or cuff herniation H_2O in circuit	Adventitious sounds ↓ PaO_2 ↑ WOB	↑ PIP (VV) Patient-ventilator asynchrony

Atelectasis

Causes		Signs & Symptoms	
Patient	**Machine**	**Patient**	**Machine**
Inadequate turning and postural drainage ↑ Secretions/obstructions	High F_IO_2 (> 70%) Low V_T	↓ BS Crackles ↓ PaO_2	↑ PIP (VV) ↓ V_T (PV)

Auto-PEEP (Air-Trapping)

Causes		Signs & Symptoms	
Patient	**Machine**	**Patient**	**Machine**
↑ expiratory Raw or airway collapse on expiration: Ball-valve obstructions, bronchospasm, COPD, mucosal edema, secretions. *Active exhalation* (auto-PEEP) without air-trapping ↑ $\dot{V}_E$ *(pain, fever, ARDS)*	*Short T_E:* Long T_I, slow $\dot{V}_I$, high rates, high $\dot{V}_E$, high or inverse I/E ratio. *Mechanical expiratory Raw*: ET tube, expiratory valve, PEEP valve	↑ A-P diameter ↑ radiolucency on CXR ↑ resonant percussion ↑ WOB	Expiratory flow fails to return to zero before next inspiration on F-T curve ↑ PIP (VV) and P_{plat} Patient-ventilator asynchrony

Definition: Unintentional PEEP during MV when inspiration begins before expiration is complete, resulting in air trapped in the lungs at end-exhalation and leading to alveolar over-distension, ↑ WOB (difficult to inhale), and potential lung injury.

Also called: Air-trapping, breath stacking, dynamic hyperinflation, inadvertent PEEP, intrinsic PEEP, occult PEEP.

Auto-PEEP = intrinsic PEEP ($PEEP_I$) and is unintentional
PEEP = extrinsic PEEP ($PEEP_E$) and is pre-selected
Total PEEP = $PEEP_I + PEEP_E$

Clinical Effects of Auto-PEEP

- Alveolar over-distension
- Flattened diaphragm
- Hemodynamic compromise
- Patient-ventilator asynchrony
- ↓ Compliance
- ↓ Efficiency of the respiratory muscles
- ↓ V_T (PV)
- ↑ Effort to trigger the ventilator
- ↑ FRC
- ↑ Risk of volutrauma
- ↑ WOB

Identifying Auto-PEEP

Auto-PEEP Present	
Flow / time curve: Expiratory flow fails to return to zero before next inspiration begins.	*Respirometer*: Connect a respirometer to patient's ET tube. The needle is still moving when the next inspiration begins.

Auto-PEEP Suspected	
Ventilator: ↑ PIP and P_{plat} Transient ↓ in exhaled V_T's High ventilator rates (AC)	*Patient*: Accessory muscle use ↓ BS ↓ chest wall movement Dyspnea ↑ resonant percussion ↑ radiolucency on CXR Inspiratory efforts do not trigger ventilator Patient still exhaling when ventilator delivers next breath Prolonged TC Patient's RR > ventilator response rate (assuming sensitivity is set properly) *

* *Clinical Note*: Auto-PEEP increases the pressure gradient needed to trigger an assisted breath. The above is a sign that the patient is unable to overcome the auto-PEEP and trigger the ventilator.

Measuring Auto-PEEP

End-expiratory pause	Braschi valve
The exhalation valve is occluded for 1 – 2 sec. (some up to 4 sec) just prior to next inspiration; inspiration is delayed. As Palv equilibrates with the proximal Paw, the level of auto-PEEP is reflected on the pressure gauge during the pause (accuracy is questionable). Auto-PEEP = total PEEP – set PEEP $PEEP_I = PEEP_{tot} - PEEP_E$	A T-piece adaptor with a one-way valve and cap. The cap is removed during expiration. While the next mechanical breath is diverted out the uncapped hole, the pressure equilibrates between the patient's lungs and circuit. Auto-PEEP pressure is read on a manometer proximal to the patient.
Clinical Note: Measuring auto-PEEP by end-expiratory pressure requires a quiet patient on controlled ventilation (i.e., no spontaneous breathing) and a circuit with no leaks. Newer ventilators may directly measure auto-PEEP.	**Pplat Estimate** Measure P_{plat} during VV (P_{plat} #1) Place on CPAP for 30 sec Return to VV and measure P_{plat} on 1st or 2nd breath (P_{plat} # 2) P_{plat} 1 – P_{plat} 2 = rough estimate of auto-PEEP

Methods to Reduce Auto-PEEP

1) ↑ T_E by: ↓ f (↑ T_E) ↓ V_T (↓ T_I) ↓ T_I ↑ $\dot{V}_I$ (↓ T_I)	2) ↓ airflow obstruction: Aggressive bronchodilation, larger ET tube, remove secretions, steroids 3) ↓ $\dot{V}_E$: ↓ pain or fever
4) Lower resistance exhalation valve	5) Allow as much spontaneous breathing as possible (SIMV, PS, CPAP)
6) Apply PEEP/CPAP (up to 80 % of auto-PEEP). Carefully ↑ applied PEEP in increments of 1 cmH_2O until the patient's rate and the ventilator rate are equal. (Applied PEEP > auto-PEEP may lead to further hyperinflation and complications).	

Clinical Note: Permissive hypercapnia is sometimes recommended when auto-PEEP cannot be reduced due to high $\dot{V}_E$ demand and/or severe airway obstruction.

Oxygen Toxicity

Causes	Signs & Symptoms
FiO_2 > 0.6 for > 48 hrs PaO_2 > 80 mm Hg (in premature or newborn babies)	$\downarrow$ PaO_2; $\uparrow$ $PA\text{-}aO_2$ $\downarrow$ C $\uparrow$WOB $\uparrow$ V/Q mismatch

Pulmonary Vascular Resistance (PVR)

PVR changes are complex and dependent on the patient's pathophysiology, and the level and mode of MV – which is beyond the scope of this book.

Respiratory Drive Decreased

Causes	Signs & Symptoms
Overventilation CO_2 narcosis	Absence of breathing $\downarrow$ $PaCO_2$ $\uparrow$ $PaCO_2$/ $\downarrow$ PaO_2

V/Q Imbalances

Causes	Signs & Symptoms
V/Q imbalances are complex and dependent on the patient's pathophysiology and the level and mode of MV – which is beyond the scope of this book.	Abnormal ABG's

Ventilator Associated Lung Injury (VALI) or Ventilator Induced Lung Injury (VILI)

A) Over-distension Injury

High ventilating pressures (esp. $\overline{P}aw$) can produce high distending volumes, leading to alveolar over-distension in areas of high lung C. This over-distension (volutrauma) and shearing may cause acute lung injury (ALI), biotrauma (release of anti-inflammatory mediators) and/or air leaks (pneumothorax, pneumomediastinum, PIE, and/or subcutaneous emphysema) (barotrauma). See Ventilator Graphics, Chapter 6.

Causes		Signs & Symptoms	
Patient	**Machine**	**Patient**	**Machine**
ARDS (late stage) ↑ C_L (bullous or necrotizing lung disease, emphysema) Rt mainstem intubation	High airway pressures [high V_T, PIP, Palv (PPlat) PEEP] *	Arrhythmias ↓ BP ↓ BS ↑ Chest expansion (affected side) ↓ PaO_2 ↑ WOB	↑ PIP (VV) ↑ PPlat

* ***Clinical Note***: Over-distension is primarily a factor of transpulmonary pressure (Palv – Ppl). The higher the transpulmonary pressure, the greater the alveolar distention.

Ways to Minimize Over-distension

Use low V_T ↓ V_T as ↑ PEEP Keep P_{plat} < 30 cmH_2O Avoid Rt mainstem intubation Use PEEP cautiously	Minimize/correct auto-PEEP Do not use inflation hold (VV) Do not use sigh breaths with high V_T Use permissive hypercapnia as needed

B) De-recruitment Injury

Alveolar collapse at end-expiration (de-recruitment) leads to repeated opening and closing of alveoli, resulting in shear force injury (atelectrauma).

WOB Increase

Causes		Signs & Symptoms	
Patient	**Machine**	**Patient**	**Machine**
↓ C_L (various) High inspiratory flow demand (various) ↑ Raw (various)	Inadequate $\dot{V}_I$ Insensitive trigger Inadequate demand valve (SIMV) High resistance circuits, ET tubes, humidifiers, PEEP, and/or exh. valves.	Accessory muscle use ↑ Spontaneous rate Restlessness / anxiety Nasal Flaring Diaphoresis Retractions	Asynchrony ↑ PIP

Reducing WOB

1) *Patient-ventilator synchronization:*
   $\dot{V}_I$ to match patient demand (usually 60 – 100 L/min)
   Proper machine sensitivity (most sensitive possible without auto-triggering)
   Proper $\dot{V}_I$ pattern
   Proper mode
2) ↓ *Raw*: Larger ET tube
   Keep ET tube free of secretions and kinks
   Use of bronchodilators
3) ↑ *C_L*:
   Diuretics to reduce lung H_2O
   Pleural drainage to eliminate pleural fluid or air
   Semi-Fowler position
4) ↓ $\dot{V}_E$ *requirement*:
   Reduce or eliminate – agitation, anxiety, fear, fever, pain, seizures, shivering
5) *PSV and/or PEEP*:
   To reduce any WOB not corrected by above.

Arterial Blood Gases

Hypoxemia

Causes		Signs & Symptoms
Patient	**Machine**	**Patient**
Various*	Low F_IO_2 Ventilator/circuit malfunction	↓ PaO_2 ↑ WOB

For a detailed explanation of types, causes and effects of Hypoxemia, see Oakes ABG Pocket Guide.

Hypoventilation

Causes		Signs & Symptoms
Patient	Machine	Patient
↑ $\dot{V}_E$ demand	↓ $\dot{V}_E$ delivered	↑ $PaCO_2$, ↓ pH ↑ WOB

Hypoventilation can lead to:

Potential hypoxemia (in absence of supplemental O_2):

Rt shift of O_2-Hgb dissociation curve (↓ Hgb binding of O_2)

↑ $PaCO_2$ leads to ↓ PaO_2

Hyperkalemia (cardiac dysrhythmias)

↑ ICP in patients with cerebral disorders

Clinical Notes: Hypercapnia with moderate acidosis is not as harmful as high level ventilation to maintain normocapnia.

Rapid ↑ $PaCO_2$ and ↓ pH can lead to coma.

Hyperventilation

Causes		Signs & Symptoms
Patient	Machine	Patient
↓ $\dot{V}_E$ demand	↑ $\dot{V}_E$ delivered	↓ $PaCO_2$, ↑ pH

Hyperventilation can lead to:

ALI, ↓ CO

Hypokalemia (cardiac dysrrhythmias)

Lt shift of O_2-Hgb dissociation curve (↑ Hgb binding resulting in less O_2 available at tissue level)

Clinical Notes: Prolonged, severe hypocapnia can lead to tetany and ↓ cerebral perfusion. Normocapnia in chronic CO_2 retainers is indicative of relative hyperventilation.

Artificial Airway (ET Tube)

Aspiration
Communication problems
Cuff herniation, or rupture
Esophageal intubation
Inadvertent extubation
Infection
Kinked
Laryngeal edema/spasm
Loss of adequate humidification
Loss of effective cough
Obstruction from secretions
Right mainstem intubation
Tracheal mucosa trauma (edema, necrosis, stenosis, malacia)
Vagal stimulation

Masks: Gastric insufflation, leaks, skin breakdown

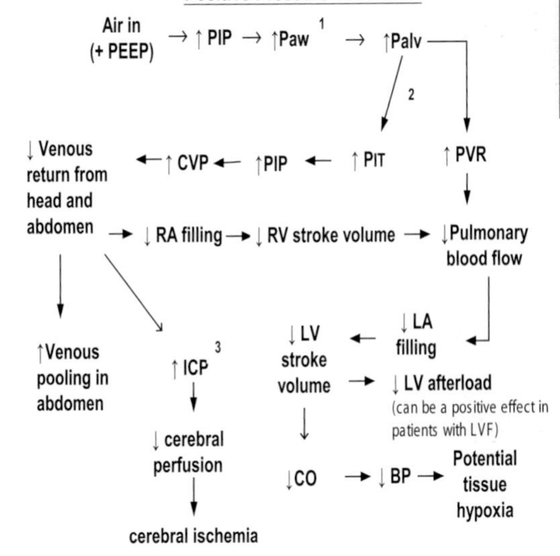

Note- These effects are either minimal or of no effect in normal subjects due to compensatory responses. They are commonly magnified in patients with cardiopulmonary disorders. Prevention /correction--use lowest possible Paw and maintain CO with circulatory loading volume and vasopressors.

1. This transference of pressure may be minimized with ↑ Raw.
2. This transference of pressure may be minimized with ↓ C_L (ARDS) or maximized with ↑ C_L (emphysema) or ↓ C_{CW} (kyphoscoliosis).
3. Only in patients with pre-existing cercbrovascular problems.

For a detailed overview of ventilatory effects on hemodynamic pressures (including, "Estimating "true" hemodynamic values while on PEEP", "PEEP and zone changes", and "Measuring PAWP while on PPV and PEEP", see ***Oakes' Hemodynamic Monitoring: A Bedside Reference Manual***.

Gastrointestinal

Positive pressure to abdomen:
- ↓ splanchnic venous outflow → gastric mucosal ischemia → GI bleeding and stress ulcers
- Fecal impaction, stress, ↓ mobility.

Gastric distention due to mask ventilation, leaks around ET tube, or aerophagia.

Hepatic

↓ CO, plus the downward movement of the diaphragm, leads to a ↓ portal blood flow leading to potential liver ischemia or impaired function.

Infection

Causes		Signs & Symptoms
Patient	Machine	Patient
↓ resistance	Unsterile technique	Cough, diaphoresis, fever, ↑ HR, ↑ WBC, possible CXR infiltrates, sputum production

Ventilator-Associated Pneumonia (VAP)

Nosocomial pneumonia in a patient on MV, with ET tube or tracheostomy, for ≥ 48 hrs. Commonly caused by aspiration of gram-negative bacteria from the oropharynx, GI tract, and circuit condensate around the artificial airway.

Diagnostic Criteria

Core Temperature > 38.3 ºC
WBC > 10,000 per mm³
Purulent tracheal secretions
Presence of a new and/or persistent X-ray infiltrate
Occurs within 48-72 hrs of intubation

Prevention

A. Ventilator Bundle*

1. Elevation of the head of the bed to between 30 and 45 º
2. Daily "sedation vacation" and daily assessment of readiness to extubate
3. Peptic ulcer disease (PUD) prophylaxis
4. Deep venous thrombosis (DVT) prophylaxis

* Institute for HealthCare Improvement, 100,000 Campaign (www.IHI.org)

B. Prevent bacterial colonization of upper airway
- Avoid unnecessary antibiotic use
- Chlorhexidine oral rinse in high-risk patients
- Isolation precautions (pts infected with high-risk pathogens)
- Oral hygiene and decontamination
- Routine hand washing (with alcohol rubs) and glove

C. Prevent aspiration of contaminated secretions into the lower airways
- Avoid unnecessary use of sedation
- Avoid gastric overdistention
- Discontinue NG/ET tubes ASAP
- Drainage of ventilator circuit condensate
- ET tube cuff pressure > 20 cmH_2O
- Limit saline instillation with suctioning
- Subglottic drainage

D. Other

Avoid paralytics when possible
Change ventilator circuit only when soiled or non-functioning
Immunize healthcare workers for influenza
Maintain patient's immune defenses and nutritional status
Noninvasive ventilation
Use HME or heated wire circuit instead of active humidifier.

Mechanical

Ventilator Malfunction

Alarm/equipment failure or disabled
Loss of/disconnection from electrical power
Loss of/disconnection from gas pressure

Patient-Ventilator Asynchrony – See Chapter 8

Circuit/Humidifier Problems

Improper circuit assembly
Disconnection/leaks (loose assembly, patient movement, high pressures)
Inadequate humidification (mucosal drying/obstruction)
Under/over heated air (hypo/hyperthermia, fluid overload, burns)
Water in circuit draining into patient's airway

Note: See AARC Clinical Practice Guideline, in Appendix.

Neurological

↑ P_{IT} → ↓ venous return from head → ↑ intracranial blood volume → ↑ ICP → ↑ cerebral edema and ↓ CPP leading to potential hypoperfusion.

Clinical Note: ↑ ICP does not generally occur in patients with normal cerebral dynamics, but rather in patients with head injury, cerebral tumors, or post-neurosurgery.

Signs & Symptoms: ↓ Mental status, headache, ↑ ICP

To decrease ICP: Hyperventilation → ↓ $PaCO_2$ and alkalosis → cerebral vasoconstriction → ↓ ICP → improved cerebral perfusion.

(Note: this effect only lasts for 24 – 36 hrs and is controversial).

Nutritional

Malnutrition due to: Pre-existing chronic disease, inadequate intake, hypermetabolism

Effects of Malnutrition

↓ Surfactant production (atelectasis) Electrolyte imbalance Impaired cell immunity Muscle wasting/atrophy	Potential pulmonary edema (low serum albumin) Slow healing Weight loss

Underfeeding leads to:	***Overfeeding leads to***:
Respiratory muscle catabolism ↑ pneumonia risk ↑ pulmonary edema risk	↑ metabolic rate → ↑ CO_2 production (esp. with carbohydrates) and ↑ ventilatory need (↑ WOB).

Psychological

- Aging
- Alcohol/drug withdrawal
- Anxiety
- Depression
- Drug response
- Emotional response to situation
- Fear of failure of ventilator
- Fear of future health and abilities
- Fear of personnel/incompetence
- Helplessness
- Hopelessness/despair
- Impending death
- Loneliness/isolation
- Loss of control of body functions
- Loss of privacy/modesty
- Loss of speech and mobility
- Pain response
- Sleep deprivation
- Total dependence on others

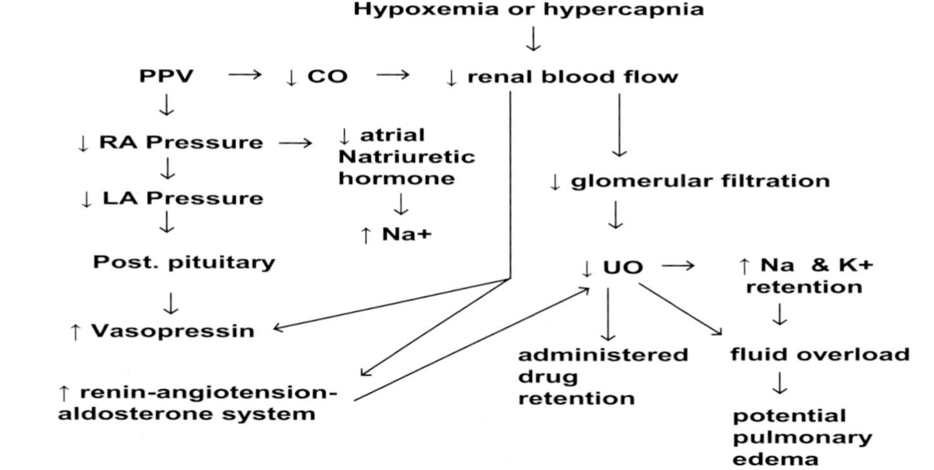
Renal Overview of PPV Effects
Hypoxemia or hypercapnia
PPV → ↓ CO → ↓ renal blood flow
↓ RA Pressure → ↓ atrial Natriuretic hormone
↑ Na+
↓ LA Pressure
Post. pituitary
↑ Vasopressin
↑ renin-angiotension-aldosterone system
↓ glomerular filtration
↓ UO → ↑ Na & K+ retention
administered drug retention
fluid overload
potential pulmonary edema

12 Drug Management

Chapter Contents

Aerosol Administration - Bronchodilators

Factors Affecting Aerosol Delivery During MV

Delivery Method	*SVN*: Neb type, cycling, gas flow, duration, position in circuit, volume *MDI*: Position in circuit, spacer type, timing of actuation
Drug	Aerosol particle size, dose, duration of action, target site
Patient	Airway obstruction (type and severity), disease type, dynamic hyperinflation, spontaneous ventilation
Ventilator	*f*, I:E ratio, mode, trigger, $\dot{V}_E$ and waveform, V_T,
Circuit	ET tube size, humidifier type, relative humidity

Optimal Drug Delivery Techniques*

SVN (Small Volume Nebulizer)	MDI (Metered-Dose Inhaler)
Check order, identify patient, assess need. Establish dose (2 - 5x normal) Fill SVN 4-6 mL (drug + diluent) Place SVN in inspiratory line 12" from patient wye. Turn off flow-by/contin. flow. Remove HME	Check order, identify patient, assess need. Establish dose (e.g., 4 puffs) Shake MDI, warm to hand temperature. Place MDI in spacer chamber adapter in circuit. Remove HME

(continued on next page)

Set gas flow at 6 - 8 LPM: use the ventilator if flow appropriate and cycles on inspiration, otherwise, use external source of continuous flow. When possible adjust vent for optimal delivery (↑ V_T, ↑T_I, ↓f, ↓$\dot{V}_I$) Adjust ventilator and alarms to compensate for added flow Tap SVN periodically until all medication is nebulized. Monitor patient for response. Remove SVN, rise with sterile water, run dry, store in safe place. Reconnect HME, return vent settings to prior settings. Document.	Actuate MDI at beginning of inspiration - coordinate with initiation of spontaneous breath if patient can inspire ≥ 500 mL and encourage to hold breath for 4 - 10 sec. Wait ≥ 20 sec between puffs. Administer total dose. Assess response, titrate dose for effect. Remove MDI Reconnect HME Document.

* Adapted from ***Egan's Fundamentals of Respiratory Care***, 9th Ed., by Wilkins, R. et. al., Mosby, 2009

SVN Disadvantages	SVN Advantages
Potential infectious source Continuous flow may ↑ V_T (VV) or PIP (PV) and/or effect ventilator functioning, F_IO_2, triggering, expiratory filters, or flow sensors. Most papers show that an MDI with a spacer is much more efficient than the SVN in ventilated patients.	May be more effective than MDI if high doses are required (e.g., status asthmaticus) May be more time efficient if large numbers of MDI puffs are required.

Clinical Notes: ET tubes obstruct much of the aerosol from reaching the lower airways, hence dosages may need to be substantially larger (generally at least 2X) in intubated patients (no established criteria).

Humidity in the circuit diminishes aerosol delivery and passive humidifiers will filter out the aerosol particles.

Assessing Response To Bronchodilator Therapy

Assess BS and patient comfort.

Watch for ↓ in PIP, P_{plat}, PIP - P_{plat}, Raw, WOB, auto-PEEP, and expiratory F-V curve.

See AARC CPG in Appendix for Indications, Contraindications, etc.

Analgesics

Primary Indication: Pain relief

Primary Effects: Relieve pain, ↓ stress response, ↓ cough reflex, improve tolerance to MV (↓ pt-vent asynchrony *), ↓ pain associated with invasive procedures, and ↓ O_2 consumption.

* *Should not be used in lieu of appropriate ventilator strategies or as an alternative to appropriate doses of sedatives.*

Two Categories: Narcotics + Non-narcotics

Narcotics (Opiates, Opioids) ***Affect CNS, and are used for moderate to severe pain***
Main Drugs *Fentanyl (Sublimaze)* ACCP preferred drug when CV instability exists. SCCM preferred for rapid onset in acutely distressed patients. *Hydromorphone (Dilaudid)* Acceptable alternative to morphine; recommended for patients in renal failure *Meperidine (Demerol)* No longer recommended; avoid in renal failure patients due to ↑ risk of seizures. *Morphine* ACCP preferred drug unless CV instability (hypotension effect)
Clinical Notes: Secondary effects – respiratory depression, drowsiness but not sedation, mood changes, mental clouding, and potential ↑ ICP in traumatic brain injury, paradoxical excitation, esp. in the elderly. Naloxone (Narcan) is a narcotic antagonist (used for drug overdoses, not to reverse prolonged analgesic use). Use with caution in patients taking narcotics chronically.

Non-narcotics ***Affect peripheral pain receptors, used for mild to moderate pain***
Salicylates (e.g., aspirin) Aniline derivatives (e.g., acetaminophen (Tylenol)) Non-steroidal antiinflammatory drugs (e.g., ibuprofen, ketorolac, etc.)

Algorithm for Analgesia Use in Mechanically Ventilated Patients

See Sedatives below

Assessment of Inadequate Pain Control *

(In patients who cannot communicate)

Diaphoresis	Grimacing
Dilated pupils	Guarding
↑ BP, ↑ HR	Restlessness

* Note: Narcotic and sedative withdrawal may mimic the signs and symptoms of inadequate pain control. Patients should be evaluated appropriately to determine the cause of the patient's clinical presentation.

Clinical Note: Analgesics do not ↓ awareness or provide amnesia

Assessment – Use NRS Scale (Numeric Rating Scale) or refer to in-house clinical practice guideline scale.

Neuroleptics

Primary Indication – Delirium – e.g., ICU psychosis

Altered consciousness and sensory perception, disorganized thinking/confusion/delusion, disorientation, incoherent / irrelevant/ rambling speech

Primary Effects: Organizes thought process

Assessment – Use CAM-ICU (Confusion Assessment Method for the ICU) or refer to in-house clinical practice guideline scale. SCCM recommends the CAM-ICU as a promising tool for assessing delirium.

SCCM Drug of Choice: Haloperidol (Haldol)

Sedatives

Primary Indications: Reduce anxiety, produce amnesia and muscle relaxation, hypnotic (sleeping aid).

Primary Effects: Helps improve tolerance to MV (↓ patient-ventilator asynchrony*) and invasive procedures, decreases O_2 consumption, and protects patient from self-injury, decreases anxiety and antegrade amnesia for current procedure or illness.
* *Should not be used in lieu of appropriate ventilator strategies.*

Main Types

Benzodiazepines:	**Barbituates**:
Diazepam (Valium) – Slow elimination may hinder ventilator discontinuation. Used mainly for peri-procedure amnesia and to ↓ peri-procedure anxiety. *Lorazepam (Ativan)* – ACCP recommended for prolonged use in critically ill patients. More appropriate for weaning due to short half-life (10 - 20 hr) *Midazolam (Versed)*- Although, SCCM recommends for short-term use only, it may be used for long-term sedation. Midazolam is more water soluble than lorazepam.. ——— Although, SCCM recommends diazepam or midazolam for rapid sedation of acutely agitated patients, all Benzodiazepines are equally effective for this indication.	*Phenobarbital (Luminal)* *Pentobarbital (Nembutal)* *Thiopental (Pentothal)*: may be used for "rapid sequence intubation". Note: Limited use with MV due to respiratory and CV depression ——— ***Propofol*** *(Diprivan)*- Short-term sedative Sedative of choice for rapid induction of anesthesia in ICU or when rapid awakening (e.g., extubation) is important. Preferred agent for daily awakening and weaning assessment protocols

Two Different Sedation Scales (Both preferred by the SCCM)

Ramsay Scale for Assessment of Sedation

Level/Score	Clinical Description
1	Anxious, agitated, restless
2	Cooperative, oriented, tranquil
3	Responds only to verbal commands
4	Asleep, brisk response to light stimulation
5	Asleep, sluggish response to stimulation
6	Unarousable

Note: This scale is not suitable for paralyzed patients. In paralyzed patients, ↑ HR, ↑ BP, diaphoresis, or lacrimation may suggest inadequate sedation.

Riker Sedation-Agitation Scale (SAS)

Level	Description	Explanation
1	Unarousable	Minimal to no response to noxious stimuli
2	Very Sedated	Arouses to physical stimuli. Doesn't communicate or follow commands. May move spontaneously.
3	Sedated	Difficult to arouse. Awakens to verbal stimuli or gentle shaking, but drifts off again. Follows simple commands.
4	Calm/ Cooperative	Calm, awakens easily, follows commands
5	Agitated	Anxious or mildly agitated. Attempts to sit up. Calms with verbal instructions.
6	Very Agitated	Doesn't calm despite frequent verbal reminding of limits. Requires physical restraints. Bites ET tube.
7	Dangerous Agitation	Pulling at ET tube. Tries to remove catheters, climb over bedrail, strike at staff, and/or thrashing side-to-side.

Clinical Notes

Most patients on MV require some level of sedation.

The SCCM recommends the use of sedation guidelines, algorithm, or protocol. They also recommend that sedatives be administered intermittently or "as needed" and should be started only after providing adequate analgesia and treating the underlying causes.

Cautious use of sedatives/analgesics is recommended for patients not yet intubated because of the risk of respiratory depression.

Watch for metabolic acidosis or arrhythmias in pts. on Propofol.

Flumazenil (Romazicon) is a benzodiazepine antagonist (overdoses)

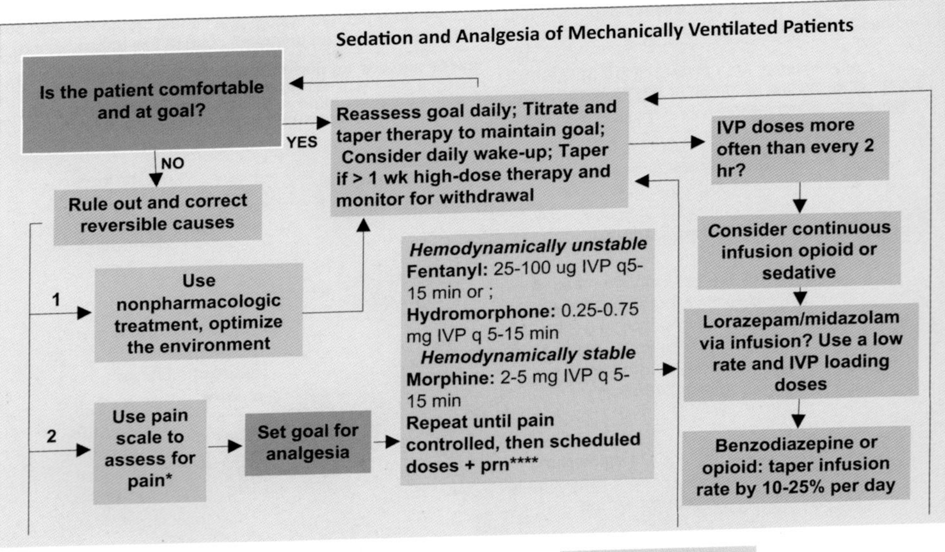
Sedation and Analgesia of Mechanically Ventilated Patients
Is the patient comfortable and at goal?
YES
NO
Reassess goal daily; Titrate and taper therapy to maintain goal; Consider daily wake-up; Taper if > 1 wk high-dose therapy and monitor for withdrawal
IVP doses more often than every 2 hr?
Consider continuous infusion opioid or sedative
Lorazepam/midazolam via infusion? Use a low rate and IVP loading doses
Benzodiazepine or opioid: taper infusion rate by 10-25% per day
Rule out and correct reversible causes
1
Use nonpharmacologic treatment, optimize the environment
2
Use pain scale to assess for pain*
Set goal for analgesia
Hemodynamically unstable
Fentanyl: 25-100 ug IVP q5-15 min or ;
Hydromorphone: 0.25-0.75 mg IVP q 5-15 min
Hemodynamically stable
Morphine: 2-5 mg IVP q 5-15 min
Repeat until pain controlled, then scheduled doses + prn****

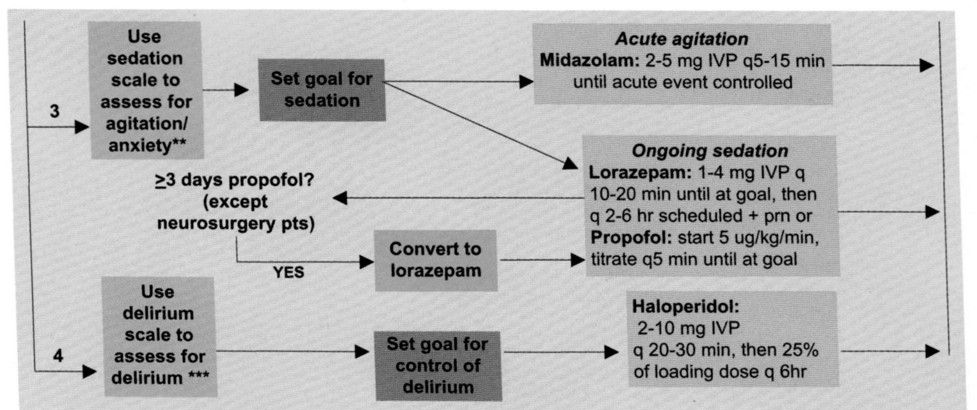
3
Use sedation scale to assess for agitation/ anxiety**
Set goal for sedation
Acute agitation
Midazolam: 2-5 mg IVP q5-15 min until acute event controlled
Ongoing sedation
Lorazepam: 1-4 mg IVP q 10-20 min until at goal, then q 2-6 hr scheduled + prn or
Propofol: start 5 ug/kg/min, titrate q5 min until at goal
≥3 days propofol? (except neurosurgery pts)
YES
Convert to lorazepam
4
Use delirium scale to assess for delirium ***
Set goal for control of delirium
Haloperidol:
2-10 mg IVP
q 20-30 min, then 25% of loading dose q 6hr

* Numeric rating scale or other pain scale
** Riker Sedation-Agitation Scale or other sedation scale
*** Confusion Assessment Method for the ICU
**** See Guidelines for intermittent dosing for specific agents

Adapted from Jacobi J, et al. Clinical Practice Guidelines for the Sustained Use of Sedatives and Analgesics in the Critically Ill Adult. ***Critical Care Medicine*** 2002; 30(1):124.

 # This algorithm is a general guideline for the use of analgesics and sedatives. Refer to the guidelines for clinical and pharmacologic issues that dictate optimal drug selection, recommended assessment scales, and precautions for patient monitoring. Doses are approx. for a 70 kg adult. IVP = intravenous push.

Paralytics (Neuromuscular Blocking Agents)

Primary Indications

Achieve patient-ventilator synchrony (e.g., inverse ratio modes, permissive hypercapnia, ↑ T_E for COPD)

Intubation

Minimize WOB, O_2 consumption, and PIP

Restrain restless/uncooperative patients after all other methods of control have failed. Paralytics may be administered only after the pt. has received appropriate doses of sedatives and analgesics.

Manage patients with head trauma or tetanus

Primary Effects: Block neuromuscular transmission

Two Types (specific drugs and doses pg 12-12 and following):

Depolarizing: Succinylcholine (Used primarily for intubation) (Contraindicated in many critically ill patients: Use rocuronium, vecuronium, atracurium or cisatracurium, a non-depolarizer).

Non-depolarizing (Used primarily for MV and surgery)

Monitor level of paralysis (Esp. to prevent overdose)

Precise assessment –	***General assessment –***
"Train-of-four" (TOF)(motor nerve response), q 15-30 min initially then q 4-8 hr or in-house clinical practice guideline.	Spontaneous breathing efforts, chewing on ET tube, coughing, moving (all may indicate inadequate level).

Disadvantages of NMBA

Masking of patient's complaints (pain, anxiety, etc.), eliminates cough and airway clearance, and prolonged paralysis/weakness following prolonged use. (Discontinue NMBA use ASAP).

Reversal Agents

Depolarizing: There is no reversal agent for Succinylcholine

Non-depolarizing: Edrophonium (Tensilon), Neostigmine (Prostigmin), or Pyridostigmine.

Clinical note: Give atropine or glycopyrrolate to offset ↑ bronchial secretions caused by non-depolarizing reversal agents.

Signs of Adequate Paralysis Reversal

Adequate ABG's	Normal VC
Hand grip	PImax > 25 cmH_2O
Head lift five seconds	Tongue protrusion for five seconds

NMBA USE IN THE ICU

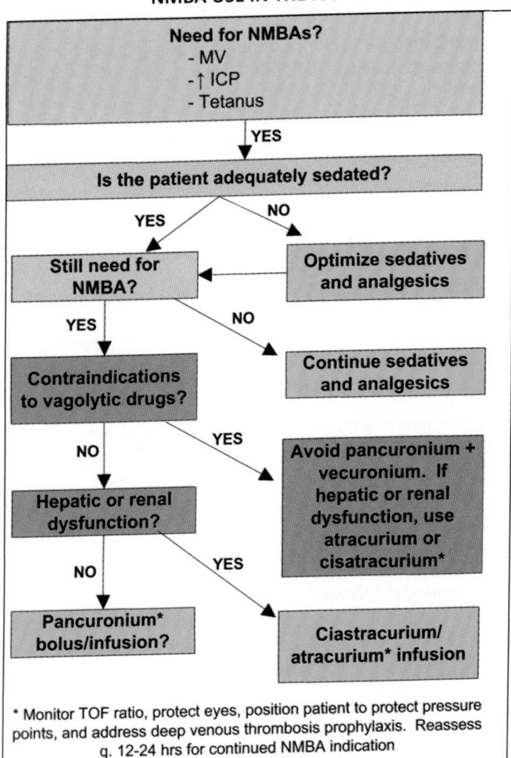

Need for NMBAs?
- MV
- ↑ ICP
- Tetanus
YES
Is the patient adequately sedated?
YES
NO
Still need for NMBA?
Optimize sedatives and analgesics
YES
NO
Continue sedatives and analgesics
Contraindications to vagolytic drugs?
YES
NO
Avoid pancuronium + vecuronium. If hepatic or renal dysfunction, use atracurium or cisatracurium*
Hepatic or renal dysfunction?
YES
NO
Pancuronium* bolus/infusion?
Ciastracurium/ atracurium* infusion
* Monitor TOF ratio, protect eyes, position patient to protect pressure points, and address deep venous thrombosis prophylaxis. Reassess q. 12-24 hrs for continued NMBA indication

Adapted from Murray MJ, et al. Clinical Practice Guidelines for Sustained Neuromuscular Blockade in the Adult Critically Ill Patient. ***Critical Care Medicine*** 2002; 30(1):145.

See Clinical Notes next page

Clinical Notes

SCCM recommends the use of NMBAs, as indicated, only after all other means have been tried without success.

Adequate airway control and ventilator support is mandatory prior to and during paralytic drug use.

During use, close patient and machine monitoring, with proper alarms in place, is essential to prevent hypoventilation, hypoxemia, or warn of accidental disconnection.

NMBAs do not have analgesic or amnestic effects. Sedatives/narcotics and analgesics must always be given in conjunction with paralytics for patient comfort. Administer sedatives/analgesics until patient appears not to be conscious, then administer NMBA.

↑ HR, ↑ BP may indicate anxiety caused by inadequate sedation or pain control.

Drug Dosage Tables

Drug	Initial Dose	Maintenance Bolus Dose*	Infusion Rate*	Onset	Duration
Narcotic Analgesics					
Fentanyl (Sublimaze) Hydromorphone Morphine	25-50 µg 1- 4 mg 2-10 mg	25-75 µg q1-2hr 1-4 mg q4-6hr 2-10 mg q1-2hr	50-100 µg/hr 1-2 mg/hr ≥ 4-6 mg/hr	rapid fast fast	0.5-2 hr 2-3 hr 4-5 hr
Non-narcotic Analgesics (Nonsteroidal Agents)					
Ketorolac	15-60 mg IV	15-30 mg IV q6h max 5 days of	N/A	30-60 min	4-6 hr
Ibuprofen	400 - 800 mg po	IV/PO therapy 400-800 mg po tid-qid	N/A	30 min	4-6 hr
Neuroleptic					
Haloperidol (Haldol)	Acute delerium: 2-10 mg every 10 to 15 min-utes as needed until calm	Once calm, determine total dose and give this dose divided into four doses every 6 h	1-10 mg/hr (monitor QTc interval)	30-60 min	N/A

Drug	Initial Dose	Maintenance Bolus Dose*	Infusion Rate*	Onset	Duration
Sedatives					
Benzodiazepines:		2.5-10 mg q2-4hr	N/A	1-3 min	1-2 hr
Diazepam (Valium)	0.1 - 0.2 mg/kg	0.5-2 mg q1-4hr	0.02-0.1 mg/kg/hr	3-5 min	1-6 hr
Lorazepam (Ativan)	0.04 mg/kg	0.025-0.35 mg q1-2hr	0.05-5 µg/kg/min	1-3 min	0.5-3 hr
Midazolam (Versed)	0.025-0.35 mg/kg				
Barbituates:		2-5 mg/kg/day	N/A	N/A	N/A
Phenobarbital	15 mg/kg	N/A	1-4 mg/kg/hr	< 1 min	15 min
Pentobarbital	5-20 mg/kg	N/A	N/A	10-20 sec	5-15 min
Thiopental	3-4 mg/kg				
Others					
Propofol (Diprivan)	0.5-2 mg/kg	N/A	5-50 µg/kg/min	1 min	5-10 min
Dexmedetomidine (Precedex)	1 µg/kg over 10 min	N/A	0.2-0.7 µg/kg/hr	< 10 min	< 60 min

Drug	Initial Dose	Maintenance Bolus Dose*	Infusion Rate*	Onset	Duration
Paralytics *Note: Maintenance doses and infusion rates should be adjusted to achieve the desired Train-of-Four response.					
Depolarizing:		N/A	N/A	0.5-1 min	3-10 min
Succinylcholine (Anectine)	0.3-1.1 mg/kg				
Non-depolarizing:					
Atracurium (Tracrium)	0.4-0.5 mg/kg	0.08-0.1 mg/kg	5-9 µg/kg/min	2 min	30-40 min
Cisatracurium (Nimbex)	0.15 mg/kg	0.03 mg/kg	1-3 µg/kg/min	2 min	30-40 min
Mivacurium (Mivacron)	0.15 mg/kg followed in 30 sec by 0.1 mg/kg	0.01-0.1 mg/kg	9-10 µg/kg/min	1-5 min	15 min
Pancuronium (Pavulon)	0.06-0.08 mg/kg	0.01-0.015 mg/kg	1 µg/kg/min	3-7 min	45-60 min
Rocuronium (Zemuron)	0.3-1.2 mg/kg	0.1-0.2 mg/kg	1 µg/kg/min	1-4 min	30-40 min
Vecuronium (Norcuron)	0.1- 0.28 mg/kg	0.01-0.15 mg/kg		1-2 min	> 30-40 min

Drug	Initial Dose	Maintenance Bolus Dose*	Infusion Rate*	Onset	Duration
Reversal Agents					
Edrophonium	500 - 1000 μg/kg			30-60 sec	10 min
Neostigmine	25 - 75 μg/kg			3-8 min	40-60 min
Pyridostigmine	100 - 300 μg/kg			2-5 min	90 min
Atropine	10 μg/kg				
Glycopyrrolate	5 - 15 μg/kg				

13 Discontinuation/Weaning

Chapter Contents

Definitions

Discontinuation	The permanent removal from the ventilator
Liberation	The ability to breathe without the assistance of the ventilator
Weaning*	The gradual reduction of ventilator support and its replacement with spontaneous ventilation
Progressive withdrawal	Refers to the gradual (weaning) approach of discontinuation
Readiness Testing	The initial period of minimal ventilatory support for evaluation of abrupt discontinuation
Spontaneous Breathing Trial (SBT)	A period of up to 30 - 120 minutes in which a patient breathes with little or no help from the ventilator. A successful trial lasts 30-120 minutes, and implies no further need for mechanical ventilation.
Ventilatory Demand	≈ CO_2 production/retention
Ventilatory capacity	≈ Drive to breath (CNS) and muscles ability to breathe (strength and endurance)
Ability to wean	Ventilatory capacity > ventilatory demand
Inability to wean	Ventilatory capacity < ventilatory demand
Discontinuation failure	The need to re-institute ventilatory support
Ventilator-dependent	Patients who need MV beyond 24 hours or those who have failed discontinuation attempts.
Extubation	The removal of the artificial airway

* Note: The term weaning has become ambiguous. Although it primarily refers to the gradual reduction of ventilator support, it is used by some authors to describe the collective process of removing a patient from the mechanical ventilator. However, the new ACCP/AARC/SCCM recommendations define "Discontinuation" as the encompassing term referring to the removal of the ventilator, abrupt or gradual.

Discontinuation Assessment

Note: Each factor should be optimized before attempting the discontinuation process. Although every problem need not be resolved before discontinuation, major problems should be corrected and the other areas need to be assessed as to their cumulative effect on inhibiting the discontinuation process. Approximately 80% of patients can be abruptly discontinued when the "Indications for Mechanical Ventilation" are reversed (See Chapter 1).

Primary Pathology

Resolution of the acute phase of the cause (disease) is the most important indicator of readiness for discontinuation.

Vital Signs

Parameter	RR	HR	BP	Temp
Desired Value	≤ 30	≤ 140	stable with no/minimal pressors	Normal (< 38° C)

Respiratory Assessment

Below, plus see Chapter 5 for Patient - Ventilator Assessment and Trouble-Shooting.

Predictive Indices (see chapter 7 for Equations)

Oxygenation

Parameter	Desired/Threshold Value
$PaO_2 \leq 0.4\text{-}0.5\ FiO_2$	>60 mmHg
SaO_2 on FiO_2 up to 0.4	>90%
PaO_2/FiO_2 ratio	>200
PaO_2/PAO_2	>0.35
$P(A\text{-}a)O_2$	<350 mmHg on FiO_2 = 1.0
Qs/QT (shunt %)	< 0.2 (20%)
Hgb	>8-10 g/dL
Low PEEP	< 8 cmH_2O

Discontinuation

Ventilation

Parameter	Desired/Threshold Value
$PaCO_2$	< 50 mmHg
$\dot{V}_E$ (spont.)	< 10 to 15 L/min
V_D/V_T	< 0.6
V_T	> 5 mL/kg
Respiratory rate (spont.)	< 35/min or > 6-10/min
Respiratory pattern	Regular

Mechanics

Parameter	Desired/Threshold Value
P_{IMAX} (MIF)	≤ - 15 to - 30 cmH_2O
VC	> 10 - 15 mL/kg
MVV	≥ 2 x spontaneous $\dot{V}_E$ (resting) or > 20 L/min
C_{dyn}	≥ 22 mL/cmH_2O
C_{stat}	≥ 33 mL/cmH_2O
$P_{0.1}$	≤ 6 cmH_2O

Integrated Indices

Parameter	Desired/Threshold Value
RSBI (f/V_T)	< 105 breaths/min/L
SWI (Simplified Weaning Index)	< 9/min
CROP index	> 13 mL/breaths/min
$P_{0.1}/P_{IMAX}$	< 0.9

Acid-Base Balance (Desired pH Value: 7.35 - 7.45)

Imbalance	Causes	Effects
Respiratory Acidosis	Hypoventilation	↑ ventilatory demand
Respiratory Alkalosis	Hyperventilation	↓ ventilatory drive ↑ Hgb affinity for O_2
Metabolic Acidosis	Lactic acidosis Ketoacidosis	↑ ventilatory demand Confusion Pulmonary edema Arrhythmias (severe)
Metabolic Alkalosis	↓ K^+, CL^- Nasogastric tube Vomiting	↓ ventilatory drive ↑ Hgb affinity for O_2

Airway

Airway Factors	Note
Inadequate gag reflex and cough Obstruction: anatomical, bronchospasm, secretions	The inability to protect or maintain the airway is a factor affecting extubation, but not necessarily discontinuation.

Chest X-ray: Should be resolving.

Ventilatory Muscles: Decreased strength and endurance

↓ Capacity	↑ Load
Drugs (See Pharmacological Assessment)	*Airway*: ↑ Raw (bronchospasm, secretions) ↓ ET tube size Obstruction
Hypothyroidism (See Metabolic Assessment)	*Lungs*: ↓ C_L (ARDS, atelectasis, edema, fibrosis, pneumonia) Auto-PEEP
Neuromuscular disorders / disease / injury / blockers	*Thorax (↓ C_L)*: Chest Restrictions Abdominal distension, ascites, obesity, surgical dressings. *Ventilator* ↓ Inspiratory flow (flow starvation) Inadequate triggering
Neuromuscular fatigue: Disease/atrophy Electrolyte imbalance (See Renal Assessment) Malnutrition Sleep deprivation	

Ventilatory Drive:

Factors that ↑ Ventilatory Drive	Factors that ↓ Ventilatory Drive
Acidosis (respiratory or metabolic), agitation, anxiety, closed head injury, drugs (stimulants), dyspnea, fear, hypoxia, pain.	Alkalosis (respiratory or metabolic), CNS injury or disease, drugs (depressants), electrolyte imbalance, fatigue, ↓ metabolism, sedation.

See also Acid-Base Balance, Pharmacological, Metabolic and Neurologic Assessments

Ventilatory Demand

Factors that Increase Ventilatory Demand:	↑ Ventilatory drive (see above) ↑ $\dot{V}CO_2$ (See Metabolic Assessment) ↑ V_D: Anatomical, mechanical

Cardiovascular Assessment

Below, plus see also chapter 5, *Patient - VentilatorAssessment and TroubleShooting*.

Cardiovascular Factors	
Angina BP requiring pressors and inotropes Fluid imbalance Hgb/Hct (anemia) Myocardial ischemia	Hemodynamic stability: Cardiac output (high or low) Presence of shock Poor left ventricular function Excessive preload Impaired contractility

Discontinuation

Electrolyte Assessment

Imbalance	Effect
↓ PO_4, ↓ K^+, ↓ Mg^+	↓ ventilatory drive

Metabolic Assessment

Acid-Base Balance (See also Acid-Base Balance above)

Imbalance	Effect
Metabolic acidosis	↑ ventilatory demand
Metabolic alkalosis	↓ ventilatory drive

Metabolism

↑ Metabolism (↑ $\dot{V}CO_2$)		↓ Metabolism (↓ $\dot{V}CO_2$)
Agitation Excessive caloric intake (See Nutritional Assessment) Fever	Seizures Sepsis Shivering Tremors ↑ WOB	Malnutrition Starvation (↓ ventilatory drive and muscles)

Neurologic Assessment

Neurologic Factors	
CNS drive (See "Ventilatory Drive" in the Respiratory Assessment section) Mental Status (See Psychological Assessment) Muscles (See "Ventilatory Muscles" in the Respiratory Assessment section)	Neurologic Injury / Disease: ICP > 20 mmHg CPP < 60 mmHg Seizures

Nutritional Assessment

Nutritional Factors	
Excessive nutrition (↑ CO_2 production) High carbohydrate load (↑ $\dot{V}_E$ requirements) Poor nutritional status	Low PO_4 (less than 1 mg/dL): Muscle weakness Diaphragmatic weakness ↓ Ventilatory drive ↑ Susceptibility to infections

Appropriate caloric intake

- Appropriate nutrition-caloric intake: 1.5 - 2 x REE (resting energy expenditure)
- Appropriate protein intake: 1 - 1.5 gm/kg/day
-

Pharmacological Assessment

Drug	Effect
Hypnotics Sedatives Narcotics Tranquilizers	↓ Ventilatory drive and/or mental response
Stimulants	↑ Ventilatory drive
Aminoglycosides (potentiates NMBs) Corticosteroids Muscle Relaxants Neuromuscular blockers (NMB)	↓ Ventilatory muscle function

Psychological Assessment

Psychological Factors To consider:

Age
Agitation
Attitude
Denial
Depression
Disease (severity/duration)
Drugs
Electrolytes
Fear and Anxiety (abandonment, burden, dying)
Hypoxemia
LOC (delirium, coma)
Mental status
Motivation
Nutrition
Personality
pH abnormal
Psychological dependence on the ventilator
Sleep deprivation: (anxiety, irritability, psychosis)
Stress factors (↓ communication, dependence, disorientation, isolation, loss of memory, pain, discomfort)
Traumatizing procedures

Renal Assessment

Renal Factors	Comments
Acid-base abnormalities	Affects drive and load
Fluid imbalance / I & O	Overload impairs pulmonary gas exchange and leads to pulmonary edema
Renal Insufficiency	(Adequate output > 1000 mL/day and equal to intake)
Electrolyte imbalance	Causes ventilatory muscle weakness

Miscellaneous Factors

Exercise tolerance
Gastrointestinal (stress-related hemorrhage, inability to take enteral nutrition, bowel obstruction, ascites)
Hyperglycemia
Infection/sepsis (↑ $\dot{V}CO_2$ + $\dot{V}O_2$)
Impending surgical procedures requiring general anesthetics
Malpositioning

Procedural factors -
Improper weaning procedures:
- Time of day (avoid evenings, nights, and shift change)
- Inadequate staffing
- Interruptions and disruptions

Improper technical factors:
- Inappropriate support level
- Inappropriate sensitivity level
- Inappropriate PEEP level

Discontinuation Methods*

Method	Description	Technique/Procedure	Comments
Abrupt			
Spontaneous Breathing Trial (SBT) ***Readiness Testing***	A period of 30 - 120 minutes in which patients breathe with little or no help from the ventilator.	Off Ventilator: T-piece with or without low level CPAP (e.g., 5cmH_2O). Use adequate continuous flow. On Ventilator: 1) Spontaneous breathing through a flow-triggering ventilator with or without low level CPAP (e.g., 5cmH_2O) 2) Spontaneous breathing with low level PSV. Use minimal PS to offset ET tube resistance.	Most recommended method for the majority of patients. If the patient is not extubated, rest at night on non-fatiguing ventilatory support.
Gradual: Weaning			
1) PSV	Reducing the PS level as the patient's respiratory muscles strengthen	Begin with a PS level at which the respiratory rate and V_T are close to full (PS_{MAX}) or partial ventilatory support (maintain minute volume). Gradually ↓ the PS level as tolerated. The most appropriate level is that just high enough to prevent activation of accessory muscles. Continue to a minimal level (~5-10 cmH_2O) to overcome resistance of the artificial airway and ventilator circuit. Discontinue when the patient can maintain this minimal level.	Most preferred method of gradual weaning. It works best for short-term weaning (< 72 hours). If it is used in long-term weaning, increase support at night to near maximum to allow patient to rest and sleep.

Method	Description	Technique/Procedure	Comments
2) SIMV	Volume or pressure machine breaths synchronized with the patient's spontaneous breaths.	Decrease the mandatory (machine) breaths as tolerated, requiring the patient to assume more of the responsibility for the minute volume. Discontinue when the patient can maintain for 1-2 hours at a rate of 4 breaths/minute.	Related to the poorest weaning outcomes due to the fatiguing load of the mandatory breaths. Patient/ventilator asynchrony may occur at low rates. Works best for short-term weaning. If used for long-term weaning, increase support at night to near maximum to allow the patient to rest and sleep. PS at low levels (5-10 cmH_2O) is commonly added to help overcome resistance of the ET tube.

Method	Description	Technique/Procedure	Comments
3) SBT On or off the ventilator (*T-Piece*)	Gradually increasing period of time (length of time and number of times/ day) off ventilatory support.	*Same as SBT above*: Start with 5 minutes of spontaneous breathing Work up to 20-30 minutes with appropriate rest intervals on the ventilator. Gradually increase the amount of time of spontaneous breathing plus decrease the rest intervals. When using the ventilator, PS and/or CPAP can be added.	Patients should not be required to breathe through a ET tube for > 30-60 minutes due to ↑ WOB. Any patient who can last 30 minutes is probably ready to be discontinued and possibly extubated. (See Abrupt)
4) NPPV (Non-invasive Positive Pressure Ventilation)	The method used when a patient no longer requires an artificial airway, but does need ventilatory support.	As a patient is extubated, NPPV may be needed to ventilate the patient noninvasively to prevent reintubation. A mask covers the nose or full face in which positive pressure is delivered.	Prevents the complications of invasive ventilation. See Chapter 9.

* **Clinical Notes**: Any combination of the above gradual weaning methods may also be used.

Automated weaning approaches (MMV, VS, VAPS, etc) may be an option. There is currently no evidence that these modes improve weaning outcomes.

The method chosen should be based on careful patient assessment, clinical experience, and a sound protocol, which should be individualized for that particular patient. See Page 13-13.

ACCP Discontinuation/Weaning Guidelines

General Guidelines (Regardless of method)

Provide explanation and encouragement to the patient.
Preferably done during the day to allow the patient to rest at night; avoid weaning during shift change
Do not fatigue the patient's ventilatory muscles (i.e., do not "wean to exhaustion"). Monitor clinical signs closely.

Clinical Recommendations of ACCP 1993*

Do not begin weaning until evidence of significant improvement in the initial precipitating illness.
Routinely evaluate pt's ability to sustain spontaneous ventilation
Stop/modify weaning process if insufficiency and/or distress appear, persist, or worsen.
Avoid ↑ WOB imposed by breathing circuits, demand valves, and small ET tubes.
SIMV weaning should be guided by pH, $PaCO_2$, total RR, HR, and signs of distress.
Know the signs of ↑ ventilatory insufficiency and patient distress:

↑ Tachypnea (> 30 - 35 breaths/min)	↑ HR	↓ pH (< 7.25 –7.30) and ↑ $PaCO_2$
Diaphoresis	Pain	Unrelieved agitation

* Adapted from ACCP Consensus Conference: Mechanical Ventilation, ***Respiratory Care***, Vol. 38, #12, 1993.

Clinical Recommendations of ACCP 2001 †

Start discontinuation or weaning of MV soon after initiation, by developing a protocol that assesses readiness.
Regardless of the technique used, a non-physician, healthcare professional-driven protocol significantly expedites safe weaning.
For cardiac surgery, a rapid protocol allows early extubation.
The role for computerized protocols has not been established.
No weaning parameters (predictors) have been proven. However, some do have better predictive power than others, such as RSBI (f / V_T), CROP, and PaO_2/FiO_2.
SBT and PSV techniques are superior to IMV.
Early identification of readiness (followed by extubation or extubation with NPPV) is beneficial and prevents MV complications related to unnecessary delays.

† Adapted from ACCP/AARC/SCCM Evidence-Based Guidelines for Weaning and Discontinuing Ventilatory Support, ***Chest***, Vol. 120, # 6, supplement, 2001.

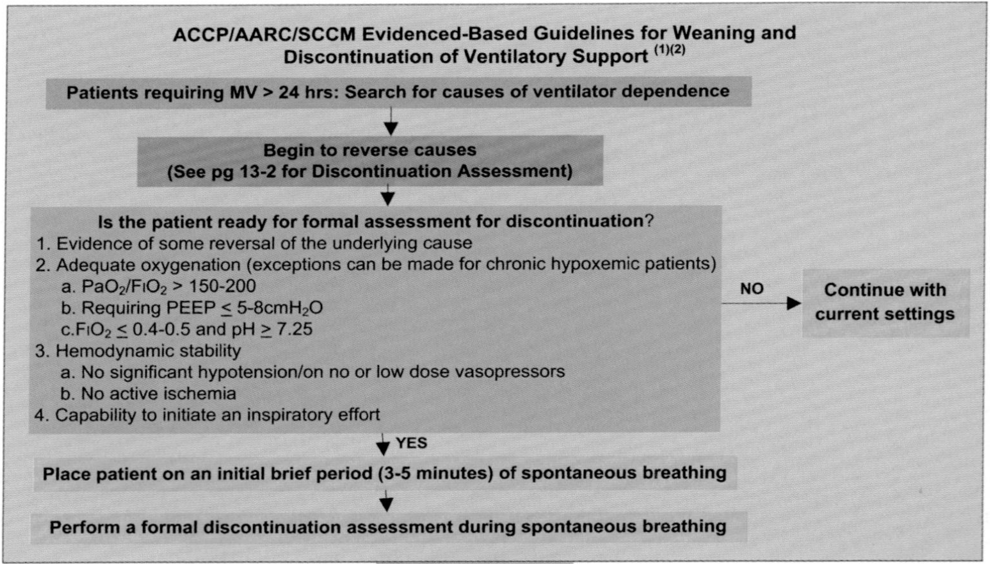

ACCP/AARC/SCCM Evidenced-Based Guidelines for Weaning and Discontinuation of Ventilatory Support [1][2]

Patients requiring MV > 24 hrs: Search for causes of ventilator dependence

↓

Begin to reverse causes
(See pg 13-2 for Discontinuation Assessment)

↓

Is the patient ready for formal assessment for discontinuation?

1. Evidence of some reversal of the underlying cause
2. Adequate oxygenation (exceptions can be made for chronic hypoxemic patients)
   a. $PaO_2/FiO_2 > 150-200$
   b. Requiring PEEP $\leq$ 5-8cmH_2O
   c. $FiO_2 \leq 0.4-0.5$ and pH ≥ 7.25
3. Hemodynamic stability
   a. No significant hypotension/on no or low dose vasopressors
   b. No active ischemia
4. Capability to initiate an inspiratory effort

NO → **Continue with current settings**

YES ↓

Place patient on an initial brief period (3-5 minutes) of spontaneous breathing

↓

Perform a formal discontinuation assessment during spontaneous breathing

Did the patient tolerate the initial brief period of spontaneous breathing? (3-5 minutes)

I. Objective measurements indicating tolerance/success
- 1. Acceptable gas exchange
  - a. Oxygenation
    - i. $SpO_2 \geq 85\text{-}90\%$
    - ii. $PaO_2 \geq 50\text{-}60$ mmHg
  - b. Ventilation
    - i. Increases in $PaCO_2 \leq 10$ m Hg
    - ii. $pH \geq 7.32$
- 2. Hemodynamic stability
  - a. HR < 120-140 beats/min or < 20% change
  - b. Systolic BP < 180-200 and > 90 mmHg, BP not changed > 20% and no pressors required
- 3. Stable ventilatory pattern
  - a. RR< 30-35 breaths/min and change < 50%

II. Subjective clinical assessments indicating intolerance/failure
- 1. Change in mental status (e.g., somnolence, coma, agitation, anxiety)
- 2. Onset or worsening of discomfort
- 3. Diaphoresis
- 4. Signs of increased WOB
  - a. Use of accessory muscles
  - b. Thoracoabdominal paradox

YES

NO

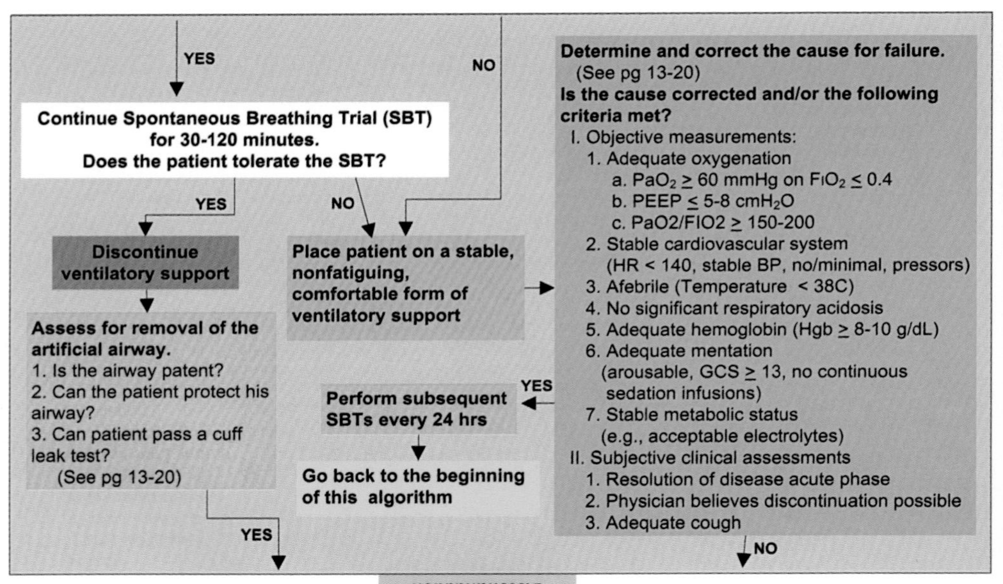
YES
Continue Spontaneous Breathing Trial (SBT)
for 30-120 minutes.
Does the patient tolerate the SBT?
YES
NO
NO
Discontinue ventilatory support
Place patient on a stable, nonfatiguing, comfortable form of ventilatory support
Assess for removal of the artificial airway.
1. Is the airway patent?
2. Can the patient protect his airway?
3. Can patient pass a cuff leak test?
(See pg 13-20)
YES
Determine and correct the cause for failure.
(See pg 13-20)
Is the cause corrected and/or the following criteria met?
I. Objective measurements:
1. Adequate oxygenation
a. $PaO_2 \geq 60$ mmHg on $FiO_2 \leq 0.4$
b. PEEP $\leq$ 5-8 cmH_2O
c. PaO2/FIO2 $\geq$ 150-200
2. Stable cardiovascular system
(HR < 140, stable BP, no/minimal, pressors)
3. Afebrile (Temperature < 38C)
4. No significant respiratory acidosis
5. Adequate hemoglobin (Hgb $\geq$ 8-10 g/dL)
6. Adequate mentation
(arousable, GCS $\geq$ 13, no continuous sedation infusions)
7. Stable metabolic status
(e.g., acceptable electrolytes)
II. Subjective clinical assessments
1. Resolution of disease acute phase
2. Physician believes discontinuation possible
3. Adequate cough
YES
NO
Perform subsequent SBTs every 24 hrs
Go back to the beginning of this algorithm

Extubate
(See pg 13-19)

In post surgical patients, anesthesia/ sedation strategies and ventilator management should aim for early extubation.

Gradual discontinuation methods may be attempted. Weaning to approximately half-support as the causes of failure are gradually corrected.

Tracheotomy should be considered when it becomes apparent the the patient will require prolonged ventilatory assistance.
Tracheotomy should then be performed when the patient appears likely to gain one or more of the benefits of this procedure:

Early tracheotomy is considered in :

1. Those requiring high levels of sedation to tolerate translaryngeal tubes
2. Those with marginal respiratory mechanics (often manifested as tachypnea) in which a tracheostomy tube, having lower resistance, might reduce the risk of muscle overload
3. Those who may derive psychological benefit from the ability to:
   a. Eat orally
   b. Communicate by articulated speech
   c. Experience enhanced mobility
4. Those in whom enhanced mobility may assist physical therapy efforts

Weaning strategy in the prolonged mechanical ventilated patient should:
Be slow paced, then at half-support, switch to gradual lengthening self-breathing trials

Go back to the beginning of this algorithm

Critical care practitioners should familiarize themselves with facilities in their communities or units in their hospital that specialize and have success in managing patients who require prolonged dependence on mechanical ventilation.

Unless the disease is irreversible, a patient requiring prolonged ventilatory support for respiratory failure should not be considered permanently ventilator-dependant until 3 months of weaning attempts have failed.

When medically stable for transfer, patients who have failed ventilator discontinuation attempts in the ICU should be transferred to those facilities that have demonstrated success and safety in accomplishing ventilator discontinuation.

[1] Adapted from the ACCP/AARC/SCCM Evidence-Based Guidelines for Weaning and Discontinuing Ventilatory Support (2001) From: *Chest* 2001;120(6)375S-395S)

[2] Protocols designed for non-physician health care professionals should be developed and implemented by ICUs: a. Weaning/discontinuation; b. Optimizing of sedation

See AARC Clinical Practice Guidelines: ACCP MV Weaning Protocols (www.RCJournal.com/cpgs/index.cfm)

Monitoring of Success/Failure

Clinical Indicators of Discontinuation/Weaning Failure

Monitor	Signs of Failure
Respiratory	
RR	> 30 - 35 breaths/min or < 10 breaths/min or > 50% change
V_T	< 5 mL/kg (< 250cc in adults)
↑ WOB	↑ Accessory muscle use Thoracoabdominal paradox
RSBI	> 105 breaths/min/L
ABGs/Oxygenation	
PaO_2	< 50-60 mmHg
SaO_2	< 85-90%
$PaCO_2$	↑ > 10 mmHg from baseline or > 55 mmHg (except in CO_2 retainers)
pH	↓ > 0.10 from baseline or < 7.30
Cardiovascular	
HR	Change by 20% or < 60/min or > 120 - 140/min
BP	Change > 20% systolic or 10% diastolic or < 90 mmHg or > 180 mmHg systolic > 90 mmHg diastolic
EKG	Significant arrhythmias, angina, ↑ PAWP
Other	
Δ in Mental Status	Agitation, anxiety, coma, somnolence
Diaphoresis	Present
Discomfort	Increased or pain or dyspnea

RSBI Procedure *

1. Remove the patient from ventilatory support.
2. Allow patient's spontaneous breathing pattern to stabilize.
3. Measure expired $\dot{V}_E$ and RR for one minute with respirometer (May stay on ventilator using ventilator rate of 0 and pressure support level of 0).
4. Divide $\dot{V}_E$ by frequency f to obtain average V_T.
5. Divide f by V_T to obtain RSBI (f / V_T)
   (Shortcut calculation: $f / V_T = f^2 / \dot{V}_E$)

(See Examples next page)

RSBI example:	RSBI shortcut calculation example:
$\dot{V}_E$ = 10 L	$\dot{V}_E$ = 10 L
f = 20 breaths/min	f = 20
$\dot{V}_E / f$ = 10 L/20 breaths/min	$f^2 / \dot{V}_E$ = 20 x 20
= 0.5L	= 400/10
f / V_T = 20 breaths/min/0.5L	= 40 breaths/min/L
= 40 breaths/min/L	

* Adapted from Ely EW, Baker AM, Dunagan DP, et al: Effect on the duration of mechanical ventilation of identifying patients capable of breathing spontaneously. ***N Engl J Med***, vol. 335, pp. 1864-9, 1996

Common Causes for Discontinuation Failure

Reasons for failure are the same reasons for not beginning the discontinuation process (See Discontinuation Assessment and Predictive Indices in this Chapter).

Weaning (Gradual Reduction of Ventilatory Support)

Advantages Over Abrupt Discontinuation for Some Patients

May be tolerated better in patients who have been ventilated for long periods (> 1week).

Fewer risks of CV instability in patients with impaired CV system.

Gradually increasing muscle loads in relation to the patient's ventilatory muscle recovery.

Optimal Criteria for Ventilatory Support Weaning

Proper muscle loading (↓ ventilatory support must not lead to fatigue).

Maximal patient-ventilator synchrony is essential.

Frequent assessments and readjustments.

See sample protocols at the end of this chapter.

Extubation

AARC Clinical Practice Guideline

Removal of the Endotracheal Tube (See Appendix)

Assessment for Removal of the Artificial Airway

Is the airway patent?

Can the patient protect his lower airway?
(Gag reflex, adequate cough)

Can the patient pass a cuff leak test?
If the leak test is "negative", consider:
Pre-extubation: Steroids
Post-extubation (if stridor is occurring):
Cool aerosol with supplemental oxygen via mask
Nebulized epinephrine
Helium-oxygen mixture (60% helium and 40% oxygen) delivered with a nonrebreathing mask

Cuff Leak Test †

Assess the patient to ensure that he can breathe spontaneously off the ventilator.
Suction the mouth and upper airway.
Deflate the cuff
Briefly occlude the ET tube.
If the patient is unable to breathe around the occluded ET tube with the cuff deflated, laryngeal edema should be suspected (negative test).

† From Sharar S: Weaning and extubation are not the same, ***Respiratory Care***, Vol. 40, pp.239-43, 1995.

SEE EXTUBATION PROCEDURE NEXT PAGE

Parameters to be Monitored Post-Extubation

Stridor	Diaphoresis	Chest pain
Cyanosis	Paradoxical breathing	↓ Mental status
Dyspnea		

Consider Re-intubation or NPPV if:

RR	> 35 breaths/min or < 6 breaths/min
$\dot{V}_E$	>10 L/min
HR	Tachycardia (>100beats/min) Bradycardia (< 60 beats/min)
BP	Hypotension (BPsys < 90 mmHg) Hypertension (BPsys >170 mmHg) or↑ > 20 mmHg ↑ baseline
ECG	New arrhythmias & ischemia

Causes for extubation failure: Upper airway obstruction, inability to protect the airway, inability to remove secretions.

Note: *Extubation failure can occur for reasons distinct from discontinuation failure.*

Extubation Procedure

Equipment Needed:

- Manual resuscitation bag with reservoir for 100% F_IO_2 with mask
- Oxygen source
- Oxygen mask or cannula (hooked up and running)
- High-volume suction source and equipment (appropriately sized catheter, large bore oral suction device)
- Oral and pharyngeal airways
- Reintubation equipment (if needed)
- A 10cc syringe (for cuff deflation)
- Disposable "Chuck"

Procedure:

- Choose an appropriate time of the day (preferably AM) and not during shift change.
- Explain the procedure to the patient.
- Consider removal of NG/OG tube simultaneously with ET tube.
- Monitor patient throughout and after procedure (EKG, SpO_2).
- Sit patient in semi- or high Fowler's position.
- Pre-oxygenate patient with 100% F_IO_2.
- Suction the mouth and pharynx.
- Give large breath with hold as the cuff is being deflated to force secretions above the cuff (repeat until clear).
- Loosen the tape or ET Tube holder.
- Instruct patient to cough as ET tube is being removed (or hyperinflate patient).
- Remove tube (including OG/NG if appropriate) quickly and smoothly as pt. coughs.
- Instruct the patient to cough directly after the ET tube is removed.
- Have patient speak a word or two.
- Administer the same (or slightly higher) F_IO_2 as prior to extubation.
- Auscultate for BS, auscultate throat for stridor
- Encourage the patient to take deep breaths and cough.
- Monitor the patient closely.
- Obtain ABG after 1 hour (optional).

Terminal Discontinuation (Withdrawing from Life Support)

Primary Concerns: Patient's informed consent, medical futility, reduction of pain and suffering. Each medical facility should have its own protocol.

Sample Weaning Protocols

PSV Trial *

Reduce PSV to induce RR of 25 - 30 breaths/min.
Continue trial as tolerated for 30 - 45 minutes.
D/C trial and rest if RR > 35 or patient becomes unstable.
To rest the patient:
- Return to PSV level that slows RR to 10 - 15 (20's acceptable).
- Repeat PSV Trial after 3 - 4 hours of rest.
- Continue PSV Trial so that the patient totals 1-2 hours of PSV Trial between 0600-2200.
- Patients should not have PSV Trials during activity such as PT and transports, etc.
- Patients are to be completely rested from 2200-0500 using PSV.

---

* Adapted from the "Ventilator Liberation Protocol", Dartmouth-Hitchcock Medical Center, Lebanon, NH).

Gradual T - Tube Weaning †

Psychological preparation of the patient.
Manual ventilation with resuscitation bag.
Oxygen/aerosol apparatus set at 10% above the F_IO_2 setting on the ventilator with the Briggs (T - tube) adapter.
D/C ventilator and place patient on oxygen/aerosol apparatus with T - tube adapter.
Monitor the patient's appearance, RR, HR, SpO_2, and BP. Observe cardiac monitor for arrhythmia.
Start with 5 minutes off the ventilator (or less if the pt does poorly).
Work up to 20 - 30 minutes, with appropriate rest intervals on the ventilator as necessary. At the end of 20 or 30 minutes, obtain an ABG, reassess the pt's condition while breathing spontaneously.
The weaning schedule would be stopped during the night so that the patient may rest and sleep.
Another option is to keep the patient on the ventilator with a rate of zero. PS and/or CPAP may then be added.

---

† Adapted from ***Egan's Fundamentals of Respiratory Care***, 9th Ed, Wilkins, R, et. al., Mosby, 2009.

14 Neonatal/Pediatric Ventilation

Chapter Contents

Neonatal Ventilation

Neonatal Physiology Affecting Ventilation

- Compliant chest wall (excessive inspiratory efforts will collapse upper airway and compliant chest wall and lungs, decreasing V_T)
- Horizontal ribs and flatness of diaphragm reduce potential lung expansion and V_T
- Possible R-L shunting (PDA and/or foramen ovale) (L-R shunt through PDA increases the risk of pulmonary edema)
- Increased risk of atelectasis and airway closure due to paucity of collateral ventilation between alveoli.
- Surfactant deficiency (↓ C_L, ↓ FRC; may grunt and/or shorten T_E to maintain FRC)
- Postnatal clearance of lung liquid and ↑ pulmonary interstitial fluid
- High metabolic rate
- ↓ Muscle mass, ↓ oxidative capacity, ↓ Type 1 (slow twitch) muscle fibers

Initial Management Plan for the Neonate with Pulmonary Disease*

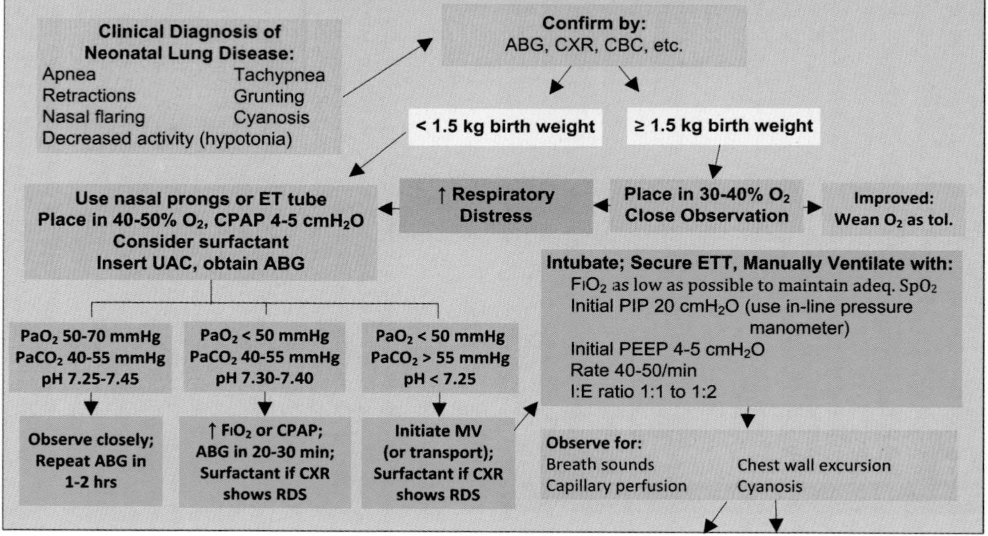

Clinical Diagnosis of Neonatal Lung Disease:

- Apnea
- Tachypnea
- Retractions
- Grunting
- Nasal flaring
- Cyanosis
- Decreased activity (hypotonia)

→ **Confirm by:** ABG, CXR, CBC, etc.

< 1.5 kg birth weight → **Use nasal prongs or ET tube**
Place in 40-50% O_2, CPAP 4-5 cmH_2O
Consider surfactant
Insert UAC, obtain ABG

≥ 1.5 kg birth weight → **Place in 30-40% O_2**
Close Observation

- → **Improved: Wean O_2 as tol.**
- → **↑ Respiratory Distress** → Use nasal prongs or ET tube (as above)

After ABG:

PaO_2 50-70 mmHg $PaCO_2$ 40-55 mmHg pH 7.25-7.45	**PaO_2 < 50 mmHg $PaCO_2$ 40-55 mmHg pH 7.30-7.40**	**PaO_2 < 50 mmHg $PaCO_2$ > 55 mmHg pH < 7.25**
Observe closely; Repeat ABG in 1-2 hrs	**↑ FiO_2 or CPAP; ABG in 20-30 min; Surfactant if CXR shows RDS**	**Initiate MV (or transport); Surfactant if CXR shows RDS**

Initiate MV → **Intubate; Secure ETT, Manually Ventilate with:**

- FiO_2 as low as possible to maintain adeq. SpO_2
- Initial PIP 20 cmH_2O (use in-line pressure manometer)
- Initial PEEP 4-5 cmH_2O
- Rate 40-50/min
- I:E ratio 1:1 to 1:2

→ **Observe for:**

- Breath sounds
- Chest wall excursion
- Capillary perfusion
- Cyanosis

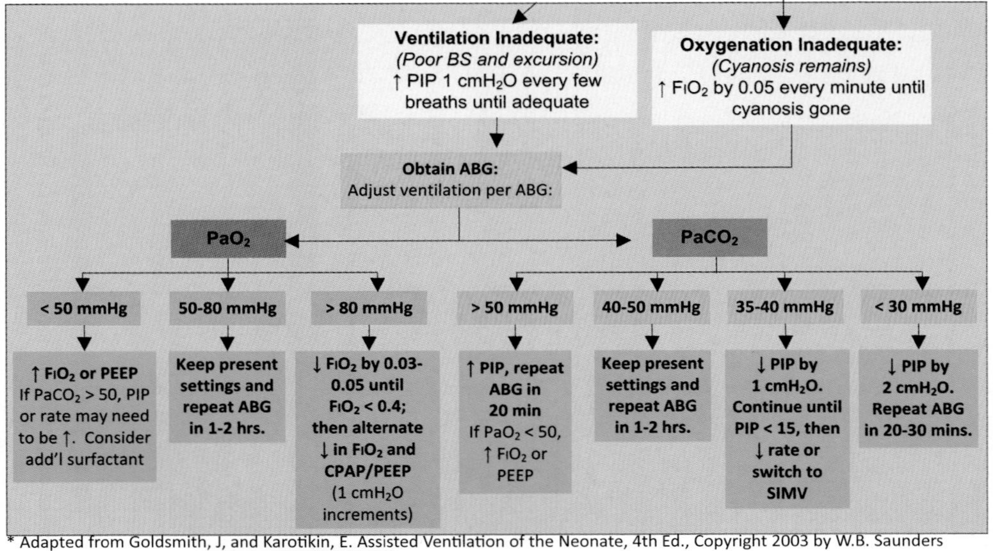
Ventilation Inadequate:
(Poor BS and excursion)
↑ PIP 1 cmH_2O every few breaths until adequate
Oxygenation Inadequate:
(Cyanosis remains)
↑ FiO_2 by 0.05 every minute until cyanosis gone
Obtain ABG:
Adjust ventilation per ABG:
PaO_2
$PaCO_2$
< 50 mmHg
50-80 mmHg
> 80 mmHg
> 50 mmHg
40-50 mmHg
35-40 mmHg
< 30 mmHg
↑ FiO_2 or PEEP
If $PaCO_2$ > 50, PIP or rate may need to be ↑. Consider add'l surfactant
Keep present settings and repeat ABG in 1-2 hrs.
↓ FiO_2 by 0.03-0.05 until FiO_2 < 0.4; then alternate ↓ in FiO_2 and CPAP/PEEP (1 cmH_2O increments)
↑ PIP, repeat ABG in 20 min
If PaO_2 < 50, ↑ FiO_2 or PEEP
Keep present settings and repeat ABG in 1-2 hrs.
↓ PIP by 1 cmH_2O. Continue until PIP < 15, then ↓ rate or switch to SIMV
↓ PIP by 2 cmH_2O. Repeat ABG in 20-30 mins.

* Adapted from Goldsmith, J, and Karotikin, E. Assisted Ventilation of the Neonate, 4th Ed., Copyright 2003 by W.B. Saunders

Neonatal CPAP

Indications - (See *AARC Clinical Practice Guideline in Appendix*)

Diseases causing a PaO_2 < 50 - 60 mmHg on F_IO_2 0.6 Disease examples: Atelectatic disease (RDS, pneumonia) Meconium aspiration syndrome** Patent ductus arteriosus (PDA) Persistent pulmonary hypertension (PPHN)** Pneumonitis (inhalation or chemical) Post-op thoracotomy or major bowel procedure Pulmonary edema**	Apnea of prematurity Tracheobronchomalacia Differential diagnosis of cardiac vs. pulmonary cyanosis in newborn – Give CPAP trial: If PaO_2 ↑ > 20 mmHg and ↓ or no change in $PaCO_2$ = pulmonary disease If PaO_2 ↓ and $PaCO_2$ ↑ = congenital heart disease or PPHN Weaning from MV

Clinical Notes

Some clinicians do not recommend ET-CPAP for infants < 1500 gm, except during weaning from ventilator support, due to the ↑ WOB and high O_2 consumption. They proceed directly to low rate SIMV, then to extubation.

Other clinicians prefer "early CPAP" (PaO_2 < 50 mmHg on F_IO_2 ≥ 0.4) in premature infants (esp. < 1500 gm).

** Use with caution in these diseases.

*Advantages And Disadvantages Of Early CPAP or High PEEP in Infants with RDS**

Advantages	Disadvantages
Alveolar recruitment and stability	CV impairment
↑ Alveolar volume and FRC	CO_2 retention
Improved V/Q matching	Over-distension and ↓ CL
Redistribution of lung water	↑ Risk of air leaks
	May ↑ PVR

*Adapted from Mariani and Carlo, Ventilator Management in Neonates, in ***Clinics in Perinatology***, March 1998.

Contraindications

See AARC Clinical Practice Guideline in Appendix.

Methods Of Administration and Physiological Effects Of CPAP

See Oakes' ***Neonatal/Pediatric Respiratory Care: A Critical Care Pocket Guide***

AARC Clinical Practice Guideline: Application of Continuous Positive Airway Pressure to Neonates via Nasal Prongs (NCPAP) or Nasopharyngeal Tube (NP-CPAP). See Appendix

Initiation and Management of CPAP

Clinical Note: The following are only general guidelines and must be applied with flexibility for each patient.

Initiation: Initial CPAP 4 - 6 cmH_2O (when PaO_2 < 50 - 60 mmHg on F_IO_2 0.6 and stable $PaCO_2$ and pH)

Adjusting: Adjust CPAP by the following steps for continued hypoxemia (PaO_2 < 50 mmHg):

1) ↑ CPAP by 2 cmH_2O increments up to 10 - 12 cmH_2O
2) ↑ F_IO_2 by 0.05 - 0.1 increments up to 1.0
3) Insert ET tube (if not already used)
4) Mechanical ventilation if CPAP failure (see below)

Appropriate CPAP level	Optimal CPAP level
↑ PaO_2 / SpO_2 , ↓ RR towards normal (RR may ↑), ↓ WOB, and CXR: improved aeration.	Highest PaO_2 / SpO_2 without significant change in $PaCO_2$, pH, or CV status (or) Point of initial rise in esophageal pressure (3 - 6 cmH_2O)

Attempt to maintain PaO_2 50 - 80 mmHg (SpO_2 85 - 95% ; may use higher SpO_2 in infants > 35 wks gestation).

Assess patient after each change: BS, BP, RR, WOB, SpO_2.

Obtain ABG 10- 15 min after Δ or use continuous SpO_2.

Worsening hypoxemia, hypercapnia, respiratory distress, ↓ BP, and/or active abdominal expiratory effort may indicate excessive CPAP or CPAP failure. ↓ CPAP and consider MV.

Rule of Thumb

↑ CPAP if oxygenation is main problem.	↓ CPAP if CO_2 retention is not improving at 6 - 8 cmH_2O.

Parameters To Monitor During CPAP Administration

Patient		CPAP setup
Abdominal distention,	Skin color	CPAP pressure
ABG's,	CXR	Gas temperature, humidity, and $\dot{V}_I$ ($2\text{-}3 \times \dot{V}_E$)
CNS (lethargy or unresponsiveness)		
Vital signs (HR, RR, BP)		
WOB (RR, pattern, grunting, retractions)		

CPAP failure (Any one of the below)

$PaO_2 < 50$ mmHg on FIO_2 1.0 and CPAP 10 - 12 cm H_2O pH < 7.20 (respiratory)	Apnea and bradycardia Patient becomes lethargic and unresponsive

Common Causes of CPAP Failure

Apnea Atelectasis not overcome ↑ VD and ↑ $PaCO_2$ before ↑ PaO_2 IVH	Muscle fatigue (inadequate nutrition, severe prematurity) Metabolic acidosis Pulmonary edema

Complications To Watch For

Air leaks (esp. during weaning phase) Aspiration Excessive CPAP (esp. during weaning phase) (↑ $PaCO_2$, ↓ PaO_2, ↓ BP or CO, ↑ WOB, ↑ PVR) Gastric distention/ rupture Hypothermia Increased ICP (IVH)	Infection (esp. ET tube) Muscle fatigue (esp. small infants) Necrotizing enterocolitis PDA PPHN Pulmonary edema Recurrent apnea	Renal dysfunction Respiratory failure Sepsis Tube/prong obstruction, dislodgment, irritation, necrosis of nose Under or over hydration or gas temperature

Weaning From CPAP

Initiation

ABG's improving (SpO_2 ≥ 90% or PaO_2 ≥ 70 mmHg) and/or ↑ esophageal pressure	CXR improving No apnea or respiratory distress Vital signs stable

Adjustments

1) ↓ FIO_2 by 0.03 - 0.05 increments, down to 0.4
2) ↓ CPAP by 1 - 2 increments, down to 3 - 4 cm H_2O
3) Remove CPAP when FIO_2 ≤ 0.4, CPAP 3 - 4 cm H_2O, and no respiratory distress for several hours (several days for BPD patients)

Note: In babies with apnea of prematurity; keep CPAP at 4 cm H_2O and lower FIO_2 to 0.21 - 0.3 before removing CPAP.

4) Extubate ET tube when discontinuing CPAP, due to the high resistance of small ET tubes.
5) Place patient in slightly higher FIO_2 then was on with CPAP.

Clinical Notes:

Maintain SpO_2 ≥ 90%, PaO_2 50 - 70 mmHg, $PaCO_2$ < 55 mmHg, and pH > 7.25.

Move to next step as SpO_2 > 90% or PaO_2 > 70 mmHg.

Incremental changes may be made as often as q 2 hrs.

Obtain CXR to assess for adequate lung inflation.

Stop wean if PaO_2 < 50 mmHg or retractions increase.

May use Vapotherm™ 2000i (up to 8 Lpm for neonates).

Neonatal Ventilation

Indications For MV (See also Chapter 1)

Apnea (prolonged unresponsive apnea associated with bradycardia or cyanosis).

Respiratory failure in newborns:

$PaO_2 < 50$ mmHg on $FIO_2 \geq 0.6$

$PaCO_2 > 60 - 65$ mmHg (> 55 in infants < 1500 gm)

pH < 7.20

Impending ventilatory failure (worsening oxygenation and/or respiratory distress [↑ RR > 70 infants; > 40 children], retractions, grunting, nasal flaring even when ABG values are within acceptable ranges).

Neonatal Considerations

There are no well defined criteria for when to initiate MV in infants and children. Many clinical factors come into play and must be individualized for each patient's problem.

Early intubation and MV is recommended in many situations:

- Congenital anomalies affecting ventilatory function (diaphragmatic hernia)
- Infants with low Apgar scores and responding poorly to resuscitation efforts
- Infants with severe sepsis or compromised pulmonary blood flow (PPHN)
- Premature babies < 1000 gm
- Progressive atelectatic disease

Blood Gas Scoring System For Assisted Ventilation

	Points *			
	0	1	2	3
PaO_2 (mmHg)	< 60	50 - 60	< 50 **	< 50 **
$PaCO_2$ (mmHg)	< 50	50 - 60	61 - 70	> 70
pH	> 7.30	7.20 - 7.29	7.10 - 7.19	< 7.10

* A score of 3 or more indicates the need for CPAP or IMV.

Ambient O_2 failure → CPAP

CPAP failure (10 cm H_2O & FIO_2 1.0) → IMV

** May indicate the need for CPAP or IMV by itself, if cyanotic heart disease not present.

---

* Adapted from Goldsmith, J, and Karotkin, E. ***Assisted Ventilation of the Neonate***, 4th Ed. Copyright 2003 by W. B. Saunders Co.

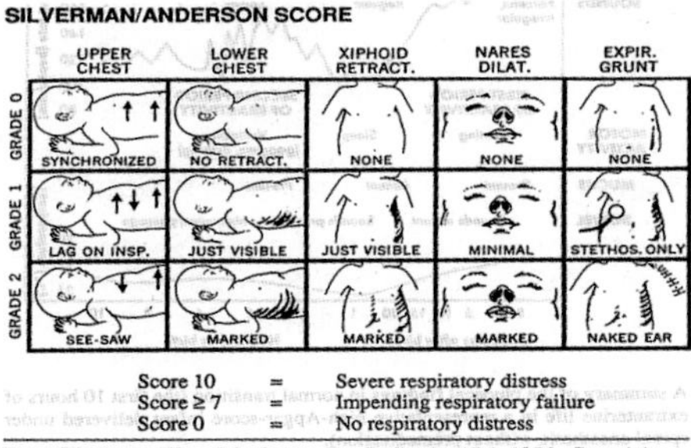

SILVERMAN/ANDERSON SCORE
UPPER CHEST
LOWER CHEST
XIPHOID RETRACT.
NARES DILAT.
EXPIR. GRUNT
GRADE 0
GRADE 1
GRADE 2
SYNCHRONIZED
NO RETRACT.
NONE
NONE
NONE
LAG ON INSP.
JUST VISIBLE
JUST VISIBLE
MINIMAL
STETHOS. ONLY
SEE-SAW
MARKED
MARKED
MARKED
NAKED EAR
Score 10 = Severe respiratory distress
Score ≥ 7 = Impending respiratory failure
Score 0 = No respiratory distress

From Silverman, W. and Anderson, D.: *Pediatrics* 17:1, 1956. Copyright American Academy of Pediatrics.

Clinical Note: Newborns tolerate hypoxemia and acidosis better than children and adults.

Types Of Ventilation

Notes: The actual practice of MV of infants varies widely between centers. The vast majority of neonatal ventilation is PV, however VV is gaining in popularity due to improved ventilators. No clinical evidence supports the superiority of one over the other.

Patient-Triggered Ventilation (PTV): Newer ventilators have improved abilities to detect and respond to infant ventilatory demands, making possible newer modes of assisted and synchronized ventilation. Because of this, synchronized and assist/control ventilation are becoming common choices as an initial mode of ventilation in acute respiratory failure of the neonate.

Pressure Ventilation (PV)

Neonatal Pressure Support

PS for the neonate is gaining in clinical use and popularity and is now commonly used in combination with V-SIMV and P-SIMV.

Clinical Notes: PS levels < 10 cmH_2O are not recommended due to the high resistance of the small neonatal ET tube. Extra care must be taken to observe triggering, synchrony, T_I, and V_T.

Volume Ventilation (VV)

Conventional Indications

- Infants > 1.5 kg without significant lung disease
- BPD patients requiring long term ventilation
- Post-cardiothoracic or abdominal surgery

Clinical Notes:

VV is becoming widely used on smaller and smaller infants as ventilator technology improves. Some of the newer ventilators are now capable of ventilating babies as small as 500 - 600 gms.

A consistent V_T may be beneficial in diseases with constantly changing C_L (e.g. BPD).

Cautions: The consistent V_T of VV may over-distend normal lung units and volume loss around uncuffed ET tubes must be accounted for, as well as compressible volume loss in the circuit.

Initial Settings *

* There are no absolute rules or definitive guidelines – only suggestions. All settings are variable and must be modified based on the disease state, ventilation type, gestational age, postnatal age, and weight.

Parameters associated with optimal tissue oxygenation and ventilation are often associated with detrimental side effects (pulmonary toxicity, BPD, barotrauma, IVH, CV instability, etc.). The benefits of any type or mode of MV must be carefully weighed against the risks.

One general rule is to employ values and modes which minimize complications and risks.

Over the last 5 - 7 years, neonatologists have moved more towards "gentle ventilation" and permissive hypercapnia.

Initial V_T, PIP, T_I, and *f* may be estimated by observing response to manual bagging, using an in-line manometer.

Summary Overview of Initial Settings (See guidelines next pg)

Parameter	*Infant Setting*	*Parameter*	*Infant Setting*
V_T	4 - 6 mL/kg	T_I	0.3 - 0.5 sec
PIP (P/L)	15 - 20 cmH_2O	$\dot{V}_I$	8 - 12 L/m
$\overline{P}aw$	5 - 15 cmH_2O	T_E	0.5 - 1.5 sec
PEEP	4 - 7 cmH_2O	I:E	1:1 to 1:3
f	20 - 40 breaths/min	FIO_2	0.4 - 0.5

Parameter	Clinical Notes	Cautions
V_T 3 - 5 mL/kg (low-birth weight infants) 4 - 6 mL/kg (term infants) 6 - 10 mL/kg (children)	V_T can be measured or estimated by BS, chest excursion, ABG's, and respiratory reflexes (e.g., Hering-Breuer). *Measured:* V_T monitor (V_T should be measured at ET tube) *Note*: V_T monitor can measure % leak % leak = V_T delivered – V_T expired × 100 / V_T delivered Up to a 20% leak is common, acceptable, and desired around cuffless ET tubes used in neonates. The presence of a leak assures tracheal inflammation is minimal.	
PIP 15 - 25 cm H_2O	The lowest PIP that adequately ventilates the patient in usually appropriate. PIP should remain < 30 cm H_2O in infants and children and higher PIP's should be avoided, if possible, but may be necessary in some patients with ↓C_L or for intentional hyperventilation. It is a misconception that PIP should be proportional to gestational age or weight. Appropriate PIP can usually be assessed by BS, chest movement, and ABG's and adjusted for ventilating open or partially open alveoli. When high PIPs are used to open closed alveoli, the open alveoli may over-distend, resulting in volutrauma.	***In PV, PIP and $\overline{Paw}$ must often be decreased quickly when surfactant is administered.*** Rapidly changing (increasing) C_L and FRC places the patient at high risk for lung over-distension and resultant air leaks. V_T should be continuously monitored.

Selecting Initial PIP:

1) Initial PIP may be determined by manual ventilation with a pressure gauge by taking the average PIP required to obtain bilateral chest movement, good BS, color, and SpO_2.
2) When a V_T monitor can be placed in line, the PIP may be adjusted to obtain the desired V_T.
   Note: V_T = PIP – PEEP (approx). Hence, V_T will vary when changing PEEP as well as PIP (↓ PIP and/or ↑ PEEP results in ↓ V_T).
3) Volume – Pressure Loop: Adjust PIP to point where there is little or no flattening of loop.

Low PIP < 25 cm H_2O		High PIP > 25 cm H_2O	
Advantages	***Side Effects***	***Advantages***	***Side Effects***
Fewer side effects (esp. BPD, PAL) Normal lung development may occur more rapidly.	Insufficient ventilation (may not control $PaCO_2$) Generalized atelectasis may occur (may be desirable in air leaks)	May re-expand atelectasis ↑ PaO_2 ↓ $PaCO_2$ ↓ PVR	Associate with PAL, BPD. May impede venous return. May ↓ cardiac output

Parameter	Clinical Notes	Cautions
$\overline{P}aw$ 5 - 15 cm H_2O	$\overline{P}aw$ is often the most critical factor in determining optimal gas exchange (oxygenation) as it correlates with lung volume. Generally, there is a linear rise in PaO_2 with ↑ $\overline{P}aw$ until over-distension occurs, then a ↓ PaO_2 (and ↑ $PaCO_2$) occurs. Best correlation occurs with RDS. *Factors affecting $\overline{P}aw$ (in probable order of magnitude):* PEEP, TI, PIP, *f* (↓TE), $\dot{V}$I, and pressure waveform. *Optimal level:* The lowest level in which gas exchange is most efficient and beyond which alveolar over-distension occurs.	***In PV, PIP and $\overline{P}aw$ must often be decreased quickly when surfactant is administered.*** $\overline{P}aw$ > 12 cm H_2O in infants < 1500 gms is associated with BPD. Consider HFV. Rapidly changing (increasing) CL and FRC places the patient at high risk for lung
PEEP 4 - 7 cm H_2O	PEEP is used to prevent alveolar collapse and establish FRC, but is not usually used to recruit atelectatic lung units in newborns. A PEEP titration study may be performed to determine appropriate PEEP level: Start low and ↑ PEEP in 1 - 2 cm H_2O increments q 20 min, until achieve best SpO_2, CL and hemodynamics. ***Optimal Level*** = Lowest level producing the best gas exchange and the largest end-expiratory volume without over-distension.	Excessive PEEP may cause ↓ CO, ↓ O_2 transport, ↓ CL, ↑$PaCO_2$ (↓ PIP – PEEP difference), ↑ PVR, and air-leak syndromes (e.g., PIE). Always maintain PEEP level while hand bagging. (May be accomplished with Neopuff®).

Parameter	Clinical Notes	Cautions
	Minimum PEEP (3 - 4 cm H_2O) is usually employed to help overcome ET tube resistance and prevent lung collapse, esp. in newborns. < 3 cm H_2O **<u>should not</u>** be used unless indicated (PPHN). Infants with surfactant deficiency require low to moderate PEEP. Infants with abdominal distention may require high PEEP. PEEP > 5 - 6 cm H_2O may begin to worsen C_L and > 10 cm H_2O is rarely used in newborns. PEEP > 7 cm H_2O should be used with caution in infants with airway obstruction, such as meconium aspiration or bronchiolitis.	See Oakes' *Neonatal/ Pediatric Respiratory Care: A Critical Care Pocket Guide* for a table listing the advantages and side effects of low, medium, and high PEEP levels.

Rule of Thumb

Infant on O_2%:	Requires a PEEP:
100	5-8
90	5-8
80	5-8
70	5-7
60	4-6
50	4-6
40	3-4

Monitoring PEEP Effects

1) Increased PaO_2
2) CXR is commonly employed to monitor effect of PEEP by determining lung under/over inflation.
3) Volume – Pressure Loop
   Beneficial effects of PEEP = shift of loop to left (↑ V_T at same PIP)

Parameter	*Clinical Notes*	*Cautions*
***f* (Rate)** 20 - 40 breaths/min	Rate is the parameter used most commonly to adjust $PaCO_2$ and pH (i.e., $\dot{V}_E$) Best rate is highly variable depending on the disease state, complications, infant size, ventilator capabilities, and clinical response. ***General rule of thumb***: The worse the C_L (↓ TC), the faster the rate. High rates are commonly used in PPHN to induce mild respiratory alkalosis and ↓ PVR; and in PIE and barotrauma - to reduce PIP and V_T. Also, permissive hypercapnia is well tolerated in infants and children.	High rates may lead to ↓ T_E, and auto-PEEP. See Oakes' *Neonatal/Pediatric Respiratory Care: A Critical Care Pocket Guide* for a table listing the advantages and side effects of slow and rapid ventilator rates.
T_I 0.25 - 0.5 sec (VLBW infants) 0.35 - 0.5 sec (term infants) 0.5 - 0.75 sec (toddlers) 0.5 - 1.5 sec (children)	Select T_I for patient comfort and synchronous breathing. Considerations include lung TC (time constant), patient age, and breathing pattern. Infants with ↓ C_L (e.g., surfactant deficiency) have a short TC (use short $T_I \approx 0.35$ sec. initially). Infants with ↑ Raw (e.g., chronic lung disease; BPD) have a long TC (use long $T_I \approx 0.5 - 0.7$ sec. May lead to air-trapping.	The longer the TI (esp. > 1.0 sec), the greater the risk of barotrauma and/or CV effects.

Parameter	Clinical Notes	Cautions
$\dot{V}_I$ 5 – 8 L/m (LBW infants) 6 – 10 L/m (term infants)	***In VV***, set to lowest value that will generate the desired PIP and pressure waveform. Minimum flow should be 2 × $\dot{V}_E$ (normal neonatal $\dot{V}_{Espont}$ = 0.2 - 1.0 L/m). Ideal $\dot{V}_I = 3 \times \dot{V}_E$. High flows may be needed to maintain V_T when T_I is shortened. However, flows > 10 L/m may result in ↓V_T due to ↑ turbulence in small ET tubes and are associated with an ↑ risk of air-leaks. Slower $\dot{V}_I$'s are used for patients with ↑ Raw and/or poor gas distribution. ***In PV***, the flow will be patient determined.	***Signs of Insufficient Flow*** Desired PIP not reached with mandatory breaths. ↑ WOB (retractions, etc.) Pressure fluctuations on pressure manometer around baseline PEEP setting. Ventilator asynchrony
T_E 0.5-1.5 sec	T_E is most commonly the result of a desired rate and T_I.	0.2-0.3 sec is commonly the lower limit. Shorter T_E's may result in auto-PEEP, ↓ V_T, and worsening oxygenation.

Parameter	Clinical Notes	Cautions
I:E 1:1 to 1:3	Today, more emphasis is on selecting appropriate TI and TE than a specific I:E ratio. I:E ratio is not as effective as PIP or PEEP in altering PaO_2, and $PaCO_2$ is usually not altered by changes in I:E. Waveform monitoring is preferred for setting TI and TE. See TI.	Inverse ratios carry a high risk of auto-PEEP and the potential of hyperinflation, barotrauma, ↓ CO, and cerebral injury. See Oakes' ***Neonatal/Pediatric Respiratory Care: A Critical Care Pocket Guide*** for a table listing the advantages and side effects of different I:E ratios.
FIO_2 0.4 - 0.5 (or as previously established)	***PaO_2 known*** – use same FIO_2 as adequate for spontaneous ventilation or bagging. Caution: initial MV may dramatically ↑ PaO_2, monitor closely and ↓ FIO_2 accordingly. ***PaO_2 unknown*** – use minimum dosage necessary to keep neonate or infant pink until ABG can be obtained. See target PaO_2 values below.	Inadequate FIO_2 may lead to hypoxemia and severe neurologic injury. Excessive FIO_2 may lead to ROP in infants < 1500 gms (≈ PaO_2 > 100 mmHg) or BPD in infants (≈ FIO_2 >0.4 for prolonged periods).

Ventilator Management Strategies *

* The most important aspect of proper ventilatory management is the continuous presence of skilled personnel.

Oxygenation	*Ventilation*
The primary controls for oxygenation are FiO_2 and $\overline{P}aw$ (PIP, I:E, PEEP, $\dot{V}_I$, and waveform). Aggressive efforts should be employed to keep FiO_2 and $\overline{P}aw$ as low as possible (esp. $FiO_2 < 0.5$ and $PaO_2 < 90$ mmHg in premature infants. During increasing MV, FiO_2 is first ↑ to 0.6 before additional increases in $\overline{P}aw$. See target PaO_2 values below.	Primary controls for ventilation are PIP/V_T and *f*. 1) Adjust PIP/V_T to achieve appropriate lung inflation (assess by BS, chest excursion, exhaled V_T, and CXR). 2) Adjust *f* to achieve target $PaCO_2$ and pH values (see below). ***$PaCO_2$:*** Aggressive conventional MV to reduce $PaCO_2$ is discouraged. Permissive hypercapnia is well-tolerated in infants and children.

Arterial Blood Gases (ABG's)

Target Values

Peripheral artery puncture or peripheral/UAC	Heel or finger stick (appropriately done)	Pulse Oximeter
PaO_2 50 - 80 mmHg (infants) 70 - 100 mmHg (children) SaO_2 85 - 92 % $PaCO_2$ 35 - 55 mmHg pH 7.25 - 7.45	PaO_2 usually not accurate (measurement of blood oxygenation should be with pulse oximeter) $PaCO_2$ 35 - 55 mmHg pH 7.25 – 7.45	SpO_2 ≥ 85% (with an upper limit of 94% for very low birth-weight)

Neonatal/Pediatric

*Exceptions **

Infants < 28 wk gestation	***Infants 28-40 wk gestation***	***Term infant with PPHN***	***Infant with BPD***
PaO_2 45 - 65 mmHg $PaCO_2$ 40 - 55 mmHg pH > 7.25	PaO_2 50 - 70 mmHg $PaCO_2$ 40 - 60 mmHg pH > 7.25	PaO_2 80 - 120 mmHg $PaCO_2$ 25 - 40 mmHg pH 7.40 - 7.55	PaO_2 60 - 80 mmHg $PaCO_2$ 45 - 70 mmHg pH 7.30 - 7.40

* Adapted from Goldsmith, J, and Karotkin, E. ***Assisted Ventilation of the Neonate***, 4th Ed. Copyright 2003 by W. B. Saunders Co. and personal communication.

Clinical Notes

The pulmonary circulation of infants and children is highly sensitive to changes in oxygenation. PVR increases due to hypoxemia can become life threatening.

O_2 delivery to tissues is highly dependent on hematocrit level. Maintain ≥ 35% in infants and children.

O_2 delivery and tissue perfusion may be assessed by capillary refill.

Tissue oxygenation may be assessed by observing skin and mucous membrane color.

Permissive Hypercapnia

Permissive hypercapnia is now widely used in newborns, as well as adults, in order to minimize lung injury. $PaCO_2$ values up to 65 mmHg and pH values down to 7.20 are accepted.

One Approach To Ventilator Management

See Page 2 of this Chapter. *Note:* This is only one of many approaches available. Numerous other strategies have been successfully employed by experienced clinicians.

Overall Balance Of Ventilatory Support Parameters*

O_2 %	PIP (< 1500 gm)	PIP (> 1500 gm)	PEEP	Rate
100	20-30 cmH_2O	25-35 cmH_2O	5-8	40-60
90	20-30	25-35	cmH_2O	40-60
80			5-7	
70	20-25	25-32		35-55
60			5	
50	20-25	22-30		30-45
40	18-25	18-25	4	20-35
30	15-20	15-22	3-4	< 30
			2-3	(wean)

Notes: If a patient's ventilator settings differ significantly from the overall pattern across any one row, then a ventilator strategy should be incorporated to return the settings to a more appropriate combination.

An I:E ratio of 1:1 to 1:3 and an initial rate of 40 - 60 breaths/min is assumed.

Normal ABG values for this table are: PaO_2 50 - 80 mmHg, $PaCO_2$ 40 - 50 mmHg, pH 7.25 - 7.45.

If $\overline{Paw}$ cannot be maintained at < 12 cmH_2O (esp in VLBW), consider HFV.

---

* Adapted from Goldsmith, J, and Karotkin, E. ***Assisted Ventilation of the Neonate***, 4th Ed. Copyright 2003 by W. B. Saunders Co. and personal communication.

Making Parameter Changes, Troubleshooting, and Ventilator Management Of Specific Diseases:

See Oakes' *Neonatal/Pediatric Respiratory Care: A Critical Care Pocket Guide,* for How Parameter Changes Generally Affect ABG's.

Weaning From MV:

See Chapter 13 and Oakes' ***Neonatal/Pediatric Respiratory Care: A Critical Care Pocket Guide,*** for a detailed explanation of weaning in infants.

Pediatric Ventilation

Pediatric CPAP

Clinical Notes:

CPAP in pediatric patients follow closely the same guidelines as adults. It is used primarily during weaning to evaluate the patient's ability to adequately ventilate and oxygenate before extubation and its use in acute lung disease has been primarily replaced by forms of NPPV (BiLevel, BiPAP, or APRV).

It is usually less well tolerated then in adults, especially toddlers between 1-3 years of age.

Pediatric Ventilation

Clinical Notes:

There are few controlled studies indicating which methods or modes of ventilation are superior in pediatric patients.

After the first few months of life, the pediatric ventilatory strategy and techniques more closely resembles that of adult patients, than the newborn population.

Historically, because of the limitations of ventilators that were available, patients < 10 kg were ventilated with PV, whereas those > 10 kg were ventilated with VV. Modern ventilators make this distinction unnecessary, although there may be reasons to consider one method over another, as noted below.

The most common mistakes made in iatrogenic causes of inadequate oxygenation or ventilation are:

1) ***Inadequate TI*** – for *significant* lung disease, start with a TI of 0.8 sec.
2) ***Inadequate distending pressure*** – for *significant* lung disease, PIP may need to reach 30 - 35 cm H_2O to adequately recruit alveoli for adequate ventilation and/or oxygenation. This should be evaluated by chest rise, BS, chest x-ray, and ABGs.

Note: This may also be applicable upon weaning. As pediatric patients in the first few years of life may have airways that close in the V_T range (closing volumes), it is not infrequent that during weaning lowering the PIP < 30 cm H_2O, may lead to atelectasis in those patients with the most severe disease.

Indications For Mechanical Ventilation

The same as for adults, see Chapter 1.

Initial Settings

Parameter	Child Setting	Parameter	Child Setting
V_T	6 - 10 mL/kg	T_I	0.5 - 1.5 sec
PIP (P/L)	25 - 30 cmH_2O	$\dot{V}_I$	2 - 3 × MV
$\overline{P}aw$	5 - 15 cmH_2O	T_E	0.5 - 1.5 sec
PEEP	4 - 10 cmH_2O	I:E	1:1 to 1:4
f	12 - 25 breaths/min	FIO_2	0.4 - 0.5

Target ABG Values *

PaO_2 70 - 100 mmHg	$PaCO_2$ 35 - 45 mmHg
SaO_2 > 92 %	pH 7.3 - 7.45

* Excluding permissive hypercapnia or permissive hypoxemia

Pressure Ventilation (PV)

Indication

PV is considered, as in adults, when the patient is at ↑ risk for ventilator-induced lung injury. Criteria used by some clinicians for children who are difficult to oxygenate:

PIP > 35 cm H_2O, PEEP > 8 cm H_2O, PaO_2/FIO_2 < 100

Advantage

Immediate rise to PIP permitting extended time for gas distribution within the lung.

The decelerating flow wave pattern favors this method as a lung protective strategy (↓ PIP, ↑ $\overline{P}aw$) compared to VV with a constant flow.

PV may also compensate better than VV for leaks around uncuffed ET / trach tubes used in small children.

Common Problems In Pediatric PSV

Small ET tube:

1) Premature Pressure Support Termination (PPST) – is common when small ET tubes (esp. < 4.5 mm) offer excessive resistance. The ventilator circuit pressurizes before sufficient flow enters the airway causing a premature termination of the inspiratory phase with a resultant ↓ in delivered V_T.
2) Failure of flow-cycle due to ET tube leaks.

15 Specific Ventilation Techniques*

Chapter Contents

* The following descriptions are meant to be introductory; it is beyond the scope of this book to describe the complete management procedures.

Extracorporeal Gas Exchange

Description	Indications	Comments
Invasive forms of providing cardiopulmonary bypass by removing blood from the body and exchanging gas through a specialized membrane before returning the blood to the body. **Techniques**: 1. Extracorporeal Membrane Oxygenation (ECMO) 2. Extracorporeal CO_2 removal ($ECCO_2R$) 3. Intravascular Membrane Oxygenation (IVOX)	Differ from center to center Usually done in the neonatal setting. Used in children post cardiac surgery as a bridge from pump; also severe pneumonia (RSV), near drowning. Use in adults with ARDS is pending final results of CESAR study.Used after other therapies attempted are maximized ***<u>Common neonatal criteria</u>*** 1. Reversible disease process 2. > 32 wks gestational age 3. > 2 kg 4. < 7 - 10 days on mechanical ventilation 5. No significant immunosuppression 6. Absence of IVH 7. No severe neurologic dysfunction 8. No significant chromosomal abnormality ***<u>Other criteria</u>*** 1. Persistent air leak 2. Oxygen Index > 40 3. P_{A}-aO_2 (A-a DO_2) > 500 × 4 hours	Provides adequate gas exchange with less ventilatory support FRC is maintained by PEEP Lungs inflated with low respiratory rates (4 - 8/min) May use either VA (veno-arterial) or VV (veno-venous) approach. <u>Hazards include</u>: Clot formation Extensive bleeding Technical failure

Helium-Oxygen Therapy (Heliox; He/O_2)

Description	Indications	Comments
A gas mixture of He and O_2 (usually 70:30 or 80:20) delivered to the patient. He is less dense than nitrogen O_2, resulting in a more laminar flow. This improves flow past upper airway and/or lower airway (asthma) obstructions by decreasing the pressure gradient. Used with spontaneously breathing non-intubated patients or cautiously via a ventilator.	**Airway Obstrucive Disorders such as:** **Spontaneously breathing patients:** Acute severe asthma Post extubation stridor Tracheal stenosis **Intubated patients*** Severe asthma * He/O_2 ventilation may be recommended for patients with a severe condition who have failed to respond to other validated treatments.	**Potential Positive Effects:** ↑ $\dot{V}_I$, ↓ respiratory muscle fatigue, ↓ $PaCO_2$, ↓ pulsus paradoxus, ↓ Raw, ↓WOB ***Delivery to spontaneously breathing patients:*** Face mask with reservoir bag, keep bag inflated ***Intubated patients:*** Delivered V_T can be affected Exhaled V_T, not always accurate Use pressure ventilation (pressure sensors are not affected by He). Heliox regulator is attached to the ventilator's air hose. If $FIO_2 > 0.4$ is required, He/O_2 may have little clinical benefit. Clinicians should be familiar with the ventilator's capability and the procedure to properly administer He/O_2 therapy. *Flow conversions:* 70:30 = 1.6; 80:20 = 1.8 (Multiply flow to the mask by the conversion factor to estimate total flow) (i.e., 10L × 1.8 = 18L He/O_2)

High-Frequency Ventilation (HFV)

Note: Medical facilities providing HFV will or should have their own protocols for initiation and management.

Definition: Ventilation occurring at rates > 2 x the upper limit of normal. (*FDA Definition: Rates > 150 breaths/min or 2.5 Hz*)

Adults = Rates 60 breaths/min or 1 Hz

Neonates = Rates > 120 breaths/min or 2 Hz

Types

High-Frequency Positive Pressure Ventilation (HFPPV)	Conventional ventilation delivered at a rapid rate (≥ 60/min) and low V_T (≤ 5 mL/kg).
High-Frequency Jet Ventilation (HFJV)	Delivers a high-pressure pulse of gas via a special ET tube or adapter augmented by a conventional ventilator.
High-Frequency Flow Interruption Ventilation (HFFIV)	Delivers rapid gas pulses to the airway by periodically interrupting a high-flow gas stream.
High-Frequency Oscillation Ventilation (HFOV)	Piston driven or microprocessor operated machine that applies a "to and fro" pressure utilizing a bias flow of gas.

Techniques for High-Frequency Ventilation

	HFPPV	HFJV	HFFIV	HFOV
Exhalation	Passive	Passive	Passive	Active
P waveform	Variable	Triangular	Triangular	Sine
V_T	$> V_D$	$< V_D$	$>$ or $< V_D$	$< V_D$
Frequency	60-150/ min	60-600/ min	300-900/ min	180-3000/ min

Overall advantages for using HFV

Lung protective strategy:

Limits over-distension with smaller V_T and lower PIP.

Alveolar recruitment with PEEP (set and auto).

Improved gas mixing and improved V/Q matching from the rapid flow pattern.

High-Frequency Ventilation Overview

Indications		Theoretical Advantages	Contraindications /Cautions	Potential Hazards
Clinical Criteria: Any condition not controlled by conventional MV, including situations where high airway pressures and high FiO_2 are required. Heterogenous lung disease with $\overline{P}aw$ on MV >15 cmH_2O. Premature neonates requiring surfactant administration (before high MV settings are used). Air-leak syndrome (before high MV settings are used) Oxygen Index of > 13	**Disease Examples:** Air-leak/PIE ARDS Aspiration Syndromes Bronchoscopy and airway-thoracic surgery Congenital diaphragmatic hernia Impaired cardiac function PPHN Pneumonia Pulmonary hemorrhage Pulmonary hypoplasia Respiratory distress syndrome Restrictive lung disease Sepsis	↓ Barotrauma (air leaks & BPD) ↓ CO compromise ↓ ICP ↓ PIP ↑ $\overline{P}aw$ ↑ Gas exchange	No absolute contraindications. **Cautions:** Obstructive lung disease Elevated intracranial pressure Hypovolemia	Air trapping Adverse hemodynamic effects Inadequate alarms and pressure monitoring IVH Inadequate humidification (jet) Mucous plugging Tracheal injury (jet) (high flow velocity or inadequate humidity)

Independent Lung Ventilation (ILV)

Description	Indications	Comments
A method of ventilating (with two different ventilators) each lung separately utilizing two small ET tubes or more commonly, a specially designed double-lumen ET tube (DLT).	Used to ventilate asymmetric lung disease that requires different ventilatory strategies after conventional therapies have failed (i.e., lateral positioning). **Anatomic:** 1. Intrabronchial aspiration 2. Massive unilateral hemoptysis 3. Pulmonary alveolar proteinosis (lung lavage) **Physiologic:** 1. Bronchopulmonary fistula 2. Single lung transplant 3. Unilateral lung disease: a) Hypoxia refractory to high FIO_2 and generalized PEEP b) Overinflation of noninvolved lung c) $PaO_2/FIO_2 < 150$ d) PEEP induced deterioration in oxygenation e) Significant deterioration in hemodynamics in response to PEEP	Bronchoscopy should be used to place DLT. Each ventilator should be clearly labeled. Only experienced personnel at all levels should administer and manage ILV. Ventilators do not have to be synchronous with each other, except in children under 8 yrs, due to the "pendaluft" phenomenon. **Complications:** Bronchial trauma Laryngeal trauma Obstruction/malpositioning of DLT

Liquid Ventilation

Description	Indications	Comments
Methods of ventilating patients by replacing gas in the lungs with a gas-soluble, inert liquid (Perfluorocarbon). This liquid has 2 times the density of water and allows the transport of various chemicals and diffusion of gases. The heavier liquid may reach atelectatic areas more effectively than gas. **Techniques:** 1. Partial Liquid Ventilation (PLV) 2. Total Liquid Ventilation (TLV)	Conditions of ↓ C where conventional therapies are not effective and could cause lung injury: 1. Severe ARDS 2. Infant respiratory distress syndrome	***Effects:*** Improves gas exchange in atelectatic areas Improves V/Q Reduces lung injury Reduces surface tension Frequent readministration is required Liquid ventilation is considered experimental only. Spontaneous breathing should be avoided due to ↑ WOB from the heavy liquid. Very expensive procedure.

Lung Recruitment Maneuver (LRM or RM)

Description: Method of reestablishing ventilation to collapsed or partially collapsed lung units, using a sustained ↑ in P in the lungs

Indications	Contra-indications	Hazards	Techniques	Monitoring During RM
ARDS/ALI; ↓ FRC: On a low V_T, lung-protective strategy. After vent disconnection. Hypoxemia caused by a true shunt and V/Q mismatch Hypoxic respiratory failure Post-op tx of atelectasis Post-Suctioning of vented pts Ventilated patients with evidence or risk of atel ectasis and ↓ FRC who: Have impaired oxygention Are refractory to standard therapy Whenever a sustained (≥ 5 min) ↓ in SpO_2 is observed.	Bronchospasm Bullous emphysema Head trauma and ↑ ICP Hemodynamic instability Untreated pneumothorax	Acute desaturation Barotrauma or volutrauma Hemodynamic instability: ↓ BP from ↓ CO	Recruitment with CPAP Recruitment with Pressure Control Recruitment with Sighs Open Lung Concept *Numerous other variations exist.*	*Abort RM if:* MAP < 60 mm Hg or decreases by > 20 mm Hg SpO_2 < 85% HR > 140/min or < 60/min New arrhythmias develop

LRM Techniques

The following techniques are adapted from the LRM procedures from *Lung Recruitment* by Kacmarek, R.M. and Schwartz, D.R., in ***Respiratory Care Clinics of North America***. Volume 6: No 4, 597-623. December 2000.

Recruitment with CPAP Technique	*Recruitment with Pressure Control Technique*	*Sigh Breaths During Reduced Tidal Volume Ventilation Technique*
Ensure hemodynamic stability Set F_IO_2 at 1.0 Wait 10 minutes Recruit with 30 cm H_2O CPAP for 30 - 40 sec. If unresponsive, recruit with 35 cm H_2O CPAP for 30 - 40 sec.* If unresponsive, recruit with 40 cm H_2O CPAP for 30 - 40 sec.* *Allow 15-20 minutes recovery period between RM.	Used in cases refractory to Recruitment with CPAP. *Experimental* approaches: PC 20 cm H_2O (Pressure Control level above PEEP; PCLAP) PEEP 30 cm H_2O; I:E 1:1; Rate 10/min. Duration 2 min.* *If still unresponsive:* PC 20 cm H_2O (PCLAP) PEEP 40 cm H_2O; I:E 1:1; Rate 10/min. Duration 2 min.* *Allow 15-20 minutes recovery period between RM	"Sigh" Breaths usually ≈ 150% of set V_T or Pplat ≈ 45 cm H_2O. Usually several events/hr. Consecutive sighs (2 sighs Q 10 min) may be more beneficial.

Open Lung Concept (Used in patients > 12 years old)

Preconditioning Period			
Bedside workup: Adequate vital signs Optimize patient-ventilator synchrony Auscultate - Suction if needed Establish mean arterial pressure clinical limit (If MAP ↓ > 30%, abort proc. and give fluid/inotropes).	**Monitoring devices:** Set alarm limits Setup graphic screen *Servo I* ventilator has an *"Open-Lung Tool"* for monitoring.	**Ventilator setup:** Mode = PV (control) FIO_2 to obtain 92 - 94 % RR = 15/min PEEP = 10 cm H_2O T_I for zero flow at end I Rise time = 1%	**Procedure:** Progressively ↑ PIP to obtain V_T 8.0 mL/kg or PIP 35 - 40 cm H_2O over a 5 minute period. Monitor vital signs Q minute for 10 minutes.

Opening Maneuver	Closing Maneuver	Reopening Maneuver	Keep the lung open
Set pressure level above PEEP (now ↑ to 12 cm H_2O) to obtain PIP 35 cm H_2O. ↑ PIP by increments of 2 - 4 cm H_2O up to 40 cm H_2O or until substantial ↑ in V_T- this corresponds to the <u>opening pressure</u>. If > 40 cm H_2O of PIP is needed, ↑ pressure level above PEEP (PCLAP) by increments of 1 - 2 cm H_2O. **Clinical Limits:** PIP < 60 cm H_2O; PEEP < 20 cm H_2O	↓ PCLAP by increments of 4 cm H_2O to obtain a V_T of 10 mL/kg. ↓ PEEP by increments of 1 cm H_2O until substantial ↓ in V_T – this corresponds to the <u>closing pressure</u>.	Set PEEP at 2 - 3 cm H_2O above <u>closing pressure</u>. Set peak pressure at <u>opening pressure</u>. Maintain the opening pressure for 4 - 5 ventilations.	Mode = PRVC or PC V_T = 6 - 8 mL/kg PEEP = 2 - 3 cm H_2O above the closing pressure Perform maneuvers each time derecruitment occurs.

Nitric-Oxide Inhalation (NO)

Description	Indications	Comments
An inhaled gas that is administered directly to the lungs via a ventilator and becomes a selective pulmonary vasodilator. It decreases PVR without affecting SVR. NO improves blood flow to ventilated alveoli, which improves oxygenation.	ARDS in adults and pediatric (not FDA approved) PPHN or hypoxemic respiratory failure in neonates (on label use) $\geq$ 34 weeks gestational age OI > 15 Echocardiogram = no evidence of congenital heart disease	Lungs must be ventilated optimally for NO to be effective. Withdrawal from NO therapy should be gradual. *Contraindications:* Congenital heart disease High baseline methemoglobin (> 5%) levels *Side effects:* Methemoglobinemia ↑ NO_2 levels (>0.5ppm)

Tracheal Gas Insufflation (TGI)

Description	*Indications*	*Comments*
A technique using a low (6 – 10 L/min) flow of fresh gas that is delivered via a small bore catheter to the distal end of the ET tube. The flow of gas can be continuous, or intermittent during exhalation only. The purpose is to reduce dead space and improve gas mixing due to the turbulent flow of gas. This may enable the enhanced removal of CO_2 and the reduction of V_T and ventilating pressures.	Patients who cannot tolerate, but need permissive hypercapnia such as: ARDS with head injury Severe cardiovascular dysfunction During a surgical procedure of the lung. Patients who are risk for lung injury secondary to conventional therapy. May prove beneficial in difficult-to-wean patients (↓ V_D and ↓ WOB)	Pressure ventilation is recommended with TGI due to ↑ V_T, peak alveolar pressures and $\overline{P}aw$. TGI is still experimental.

A Appendix

Chapter Contents

Abbreviations

AARC	American Association of Respiratory Care
A/C	Assist/control
ACCP	American College of Chest Physicians
ADH	Anti-diuretic hormone
ABG	Arterial blood gas
APRV	Airway pressure release ventilation
APV	Adaptive pressure ventilation
ARDS	Adult respiratory distress syndrome
ASV	Adaptive support ventilation
ATC	Automatic tube compensation
BiPAP	Bi-level positive airway pressure
BP	Blood pressure
BPD	Bronchopulmonary dysplasia
BPdia	Diastolic blood pressure
BPsys	Systolic blood pressure
B-P	Broncho-pleural
BSA	Body surface area
CABG	Coronary artery bypass graph
CaO_2	Arterial oxygen content
$Ca\text{-}\bar{v}O_2$	Arterial –mixed venous O_2 content difference
Ccw	Compliance of the chest wall
Cdyn	Dynamic compliance
CF	Conversion factor
CI	Cardiac index
CL	Compliance of the lung
CLT	Compliance of the lung and thorax
cm H_2O	Centimeters of water
CNS	Central nervous system
CO	Cardiac output
CO	Carbon monoxide
COPD	Chronic obstructive pulmonary disease
CPAP	Continuous positive airway pressure
CPG	Clinical Practice Guideline
CPP	Cerebral perfusion pressure
Cstat	Static compliance
Ctubing	Compliance of the tubing
CV	Cardiovascular
CVA	Cerebrovascular accident
CVP	Central venous pressure
CXR	Chest x-ray
E	Expiration
ECMO	Extracorporeal membrane oxygenation
EKG	Electrocardiogram
EPAP	Expiratory positive airway pressure
et	End-tidal
ET	Endotracheal
f	Frequency (ventilator rate)
FIO_2	Fraction of inspired oxygen
FRC	Functional residual capacity
F-T	Flow-time
GI	Gastrointestinal
Hgb	Hemoglobin
HME	Heat moisture exchanger
HR	Heart rate
I	Inspiration
ICP	Intracranial pressure
I:E	Inspiratory/expiratory ratio
IPAP	Inspiratory positive airway pressure
IRV	Inverse ratio ventilation
J	Joule
JVD	Jugular vein distention
kg	Kilogram
LBW	Low birth weight
LIP	Lower inflection point
LOC	Level of consciousness
LV	Left ventricle
MAP	Mean arterial pressure
MDI	Metered dose inhaler
MIF	See PImax
MIP	See PImax
mmHg	millimeters of mercury
MV	Mechanical ventilation
NIF	See PImax
NO	Nitric oxide
NPPV	Noninvasive positive pressure ventilation
O_2	Oxygen
O_2ER	Oxygen extraction ratio
P	Pressure
$PA\text{-}aO_2$	Alveolar-arterial oxygen partial pressure difference
$PaCO_2$	Partial pressure of arterial carbon dioxide
P-ACV	Pressure-assist/control ventilation
PAPD	Pulmonary artery diastolic pressure
Palv	Alveolar pressure
PAMP	Pulmonary artery mean pressure
PaO_2	Partial pressure of arterial oxygen

ventilation

- PAO_2 — Partial pressure of alveolar oxygen
- PAOP — Pulmonary artery occlusion pressure
- PAP — Pulmonary artery pressure
- Paug — Pressure augmentation
- PAV — Proportional assist ventilation
- Paw — Airway pressure
- $\overline{P}aw$ — Mean airway pressure
- Pawo — Pressure at airway opening
- PASP — Pulmonary artery systolic pressure
- PAWD — Pulmonary artery wedge pressure
- PCWP — Pulmonary capillary wedge pressure
- PB — Barometric pressure
- PBW — Predicted body weight
- PEEP — Positive end-expiratory pressure
- pH — Negative log of hydrogen ion concentration
- PIE — Pulmonary interstitial emphysema
- PImax — Maximal inspiratory pressure
- PIP — Peak inspiratory pressure
- P-IRV — Pressure-inverse ratio ventilation
- PIT — Intrathoracic pressure
- P-MMV — Pressure-mandatory minute ventilation
- PMI — Point of maximal impulse
- PP — Pulse pressure
- Ppl — Intrapleural pressure
- Ppeak — Peak inspiratory pressure
- PPHN — Persistent pulmonary hypertension of the newborn
- Pplat — Inspiratory plateau pressure
- PPV — Positive pressure ventilation
- PRVC — Pressure regulated volume control
- P-SIMV — Pressure-synchronized intermittent mandatory ventilation
- PSV — Pressure support ventilation
- $PtcO_2$ — Transcutaneous partial pressure of oxygen
- PV — Pressure ventilation
- $P\overline{v}O_2$ — Partial pressure of oxygen in mixed venous blood
- PVR — Pulmonary vascular resistance
- Qs/Qt — Physiological shunt
- Raw — Airway resistance
- RHF — Right heart failure
- ROP — Retinopathy of prematurity
- RR — Spontaneous respiratory rate
- SaO_2 — Saturation of arterial oxygen
- SCCM — Society of Critical Care Medicine
- SpO_2 — Saturation of arterial oxygen by pulse oximeter
- $S\overline{v}O_2$ — Saturation of oxygen in mixed venous blood
- SVR — Systemic vascular resistance
- TE — Expiratory time
- T-E — Tracheo-esophageal
- TGI — Tracheal gas insufflation
- TI — Inspiratory time
- Ttot — Total cycle time
- UAC — Umbilical artery catheter
- UIP — Upper inflection point
- UO — Urinary output
- V — Volume
- $\dot{V}$ — Flow
- VA — Alveolar volume
- $\dot{V}A$ — Alveolar ventilation
- V-ACV — Volume-assist/control ventilation
- VAPS — Volume assured pressure support
- VCO_2 — Volume of carbon dioxide production
- VD — Deadspace volume
- ΞD — Deadspace ventilation
- VD/VT — Deadspace/tidal volume ratio
- $\dot{V}E$ — Minute ventilation
- $\dot{V}Emech$ — Minute ventilation mechanical
- $\dot{V}Espont$ — Minute ventilation spontaneous
- VILI — Ventilator-induced lung injury
- V-IRV — Volume-inverse ratio ventilation
- V-MMV — Volume-mandatory minute ventilation
- $\dot{V}O_2$ — Volume of oxygen consumption
- VPC — Variable pressure support
- V-P — Volume-pressure (curve)
- VS — Volume support
- V-SIMV — Volume-synchronized intermittent mandatory ventilation
- VT — Tidal volume
- Vtubing — Volume loss to tubing
- V/Q — Ventilation/perfusion ratio
- WOB — Work of breathing
- VV — Volume ventilation

Conversion Table

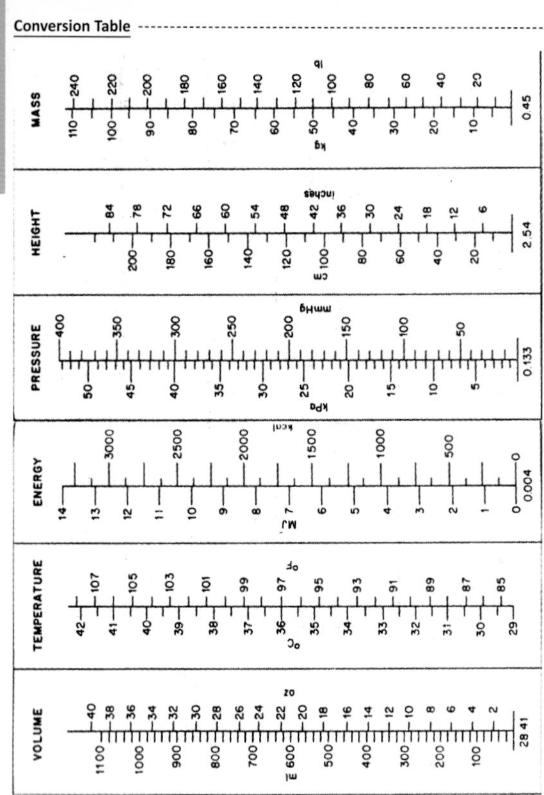

SI = Standard International Unit

Pressure Unit: kPa = mmHg × 0.133; kPa = cm H_2O × 0.098

Compliance Unit: L/kPa = L/cm H_2O × 10.2

Radford Breathing Nomogram

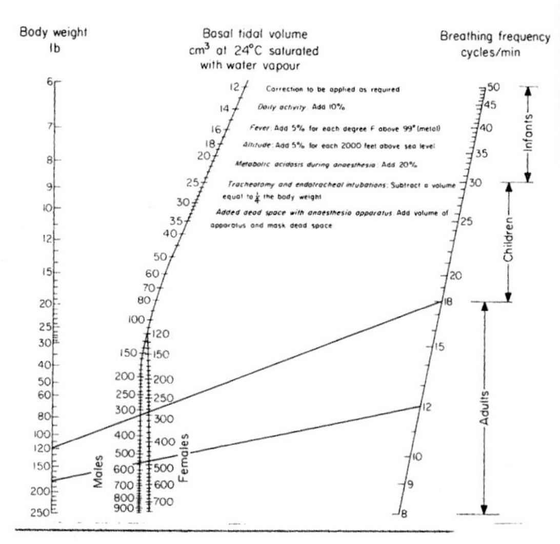

Reprinted with permission from Radford, E.P.: J. of Appl. Physiol. 7:451, 1955.

Body Surface Area Nomogram

BODY SURFACE AREA FROM HEIGHT AND WEIGHT

(DUBOIS - MEEH)

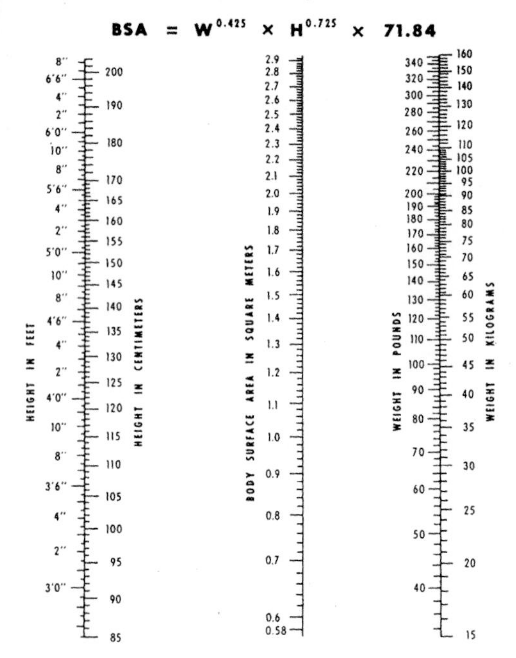

$$BSA = W^{0.425} \times H^{0.725} \times 71.84$$

In the above formula, weight is in kgm and height is in cm, giving body surface area in cm^2.

Application of Continuous Positive Airway Pressure to Neonates via Nasal Prongs (NCPAP), Naso-pharyngeal Tube (NP-CPAP), or Nasal Mask (NM-CPAP) – 2004 Revision & Update * (AARC CPG)

Description

The application of positive pressure to the airways of a spontaneously breathing patient throughout the respiratory cycle via nasal prongs, nasopharyngeal tube, or mask attached to a suitable ventilator, set in the CPAP mode, or a gas source delivering a continuous or variable flow of warm, humidified gas.

CPAP maintains inspiratory and expiratory pressure above ambient pressure resulting in:
- ↑ $\overline{P}$aw, FRC, VT/ΔP, CL
- ↑ WOB, Raw, & O2 requirement Stabilization of $\dot{V}$E
- Improved V/Q

CPAP may also expand or stent the upper airway preventing collapse and obstruction.

Monitoring

Continuous monitoring: Airway pressures (proximal, $\overline{P}$aw, PEEP), CO_2 ($PetCO_2$), O_2 ($PtcO_2$ and SpO2), ECG, FIO_2, RR.

Periodic monitoring: ABG's (arterial, capillary or venous), BS & WOB, chest X-rays, patient-ventilator checks (q 2-4 hrs), nasal septum.

Frequency

Continuous use

Indications

ABG's inadequate: $PaO_2 \leq 50$ mmHg on $FIO_2 \geq 0.6$ (with adequate $\dot{V}$E: $PaCO_2 < 50$ mmHg, pH ≥ 7.25)†

Chest radiograph: Poorly expanded or infiltrated lung fields

Physical exam abnormalities: ↑ WOB: agitation, grunting, nasal flaring, ↑ RR > 30% above normal, retractions (sub/supra-sternal), skin color (pale or cyanotic).

Certain conditions associated with one of the above indications: Apnea of prematurity, atelectasis, extubation (recent), pulmonary edema, RDS, tracheal malacia, TTN. Early intervention with surfactant admin. for VLBW infants at risk of RDS.

Administration of NO in spontaneous breathing infants.

Contraindications

Bronchiolitis

Congenital diaphragmatic hernia

Need for intubation and MV: CV instability (impending arrest), respiratory drive unstable (frequent apnea), upper airway abnormalities

Limitations Ineffective during mouth breathing Difficult to secure in place ***Hazards / Complications*** *Equipment Related:* Insufficient gas flow (↑ WOB) Excessive gas flow (overdistention, auto-PEEP) Decannulation or malpositioning of prongs or tube Mucous plugging or kinking of prongs/tube. *Alarm inactivation*: Low airway pressure/disconnect – due to ↑ resistance from turbulent flow; low or high airway pressure – due to complete obstruction resulting in continued pressurization. Manual breath activation causing gastric insufflation and discomfort. *Patient Related:* Gastric insufflation (potential aspiration) Lung overdistention leading to: air leaks, CO_2 retention, impeded pulmonary blood flow, V/Q mismatch, ↑WOB. Nasal irritation or mucosal damage (drying) Skin irritation and pressure necrosis	(choanal atresia, cleft palate, TE fistula), ventilatory failure ($PaCO_2 \geq 60$ mmHg and pH < 7.25).† ***Assessment of Outcome*** Initiate CPAP at 4 - 5 cm H_2O and gradually ↑ up to 10 cm H_2O to provide: Chest radiograph improvement FIO_2 stabilized ≤ 0.6 with: PaO_2 > 50 mmHg, SpO_2 clinically acceptable, $PaCO_2 \leq 50$ - 60 mmHg, pH ≥ 7.25 Patient comfort improvement ↓ WOB (evidenced by): ↓ RR 30 - 40%, ↓ retractions, grunting, and nasal flaring ↓ Apnea, bradycardia, and cyanosis episodes ***Infection Control*** Employ Standard Precautions 104 (CDC) Sterile suctioning procedures Ventilator: Do not change circuits/humidifiers routinely with humidity other than aerosol; clean external surfaces according to manufacturer recommendations. Disposable nasal CPAP kits recommended

* Adapted from AARC Clinical Practice Guideline, *Respiratory Care*, Vol. 49, #9, 2004.

† $PaCO_2$ 60 mmHg and pH 7.20 is more concurrent with today's "gentile ventilation" and permissive hypercapnia.

Capnography/Capnometry during Mechanical Ventilation[1, 2] (AARC CPG)	
Indications Evaluation of exhaled CO_2 (esp. $PetCO_2$ to assess alveolar ventilation or metabolic rate) Intubation (verify ET tube placement – tracheal vs. esophageal) [3] Monitor pulmonary disease: Adequacy of pulmonary, systemic and coronary blood flow, response to therapy, and severity of disease. Therapeutic administration of CO_2 gas Ventilatory support: Monitor circuit integrity (including airway), efficiency ($PaCO_2$ – $PetCO_2$ diff), patient-ventilator interface (graphics). **Contraindications**: None	**Hazards / Complications** ↑ V_D, ↑ weight on artificial airway or line **Monitoring** Ventilatory variables: V_T, f, PEEP, I/E, PIP, FIO_2 Hemodynamic variables: BP (sys & pulm), CO, shunt, V/Q imbalances **Frequency:** PRN, during intubation **Limitations** Is not a substitute for assessing $PaCO_2$ Reliability may be affected by: resp. gas mixture, RR, Freon, secretions/condensate, filters, leaks, low CO or V_T.

1) Evaluation of CO_2 in respiratory gases on MV patients.
2) Adapted from AARC Clinical Practice Guideline: Capnography / Capnometry during Mechanical Ventilation, 2003 Revision and Update, ***Respiratory Care***, Vol. 48, #5, 2003.
3. Low CO may negate its use for this indication.

Endotracheal Suctioning of Mechanically Ventilated Adults and Children * †
(AARC CPG)

Indications

Atelectasis (from secretion retention)
Maintain airway patency
Obtain sputum specimen
Remove accumulated secretions: Evidenced by – ABG deterioration, coarse BS, ↑ WOB, X-ray changes, suspected aspiration, ineffective cough, ventilator changes (↑ PIP, ↓ VT, change in flow), visible secretions in airway.

Contraindications

Relative: Adverse reaction or worsening clinical condition from the procedure.

Frequency: PRN

Hazards/Complications

Atelectasis
Bronchospasm/constriction
Cardiac arrhythmia/arrest
Hemorrhage/bleeding
Hypo/hypertension
Hypoxia/hypoxemia
↑ ICP
Infection (patient or caregiver)
Interruption of MV
Mucosal trauma
Respiratory arrest

Monitoring

ABGs/SaO_2, BS, cough effort, CV parameters (BP, HR, EKG), ICP, RR and pattern, skin color, sputum prod (color, volume, consistency, odor), ventilator parameters (PIP, Pplat, VT, graphics, FIO_2).

Clinical Goals

Improvement in: ABGs/SaO_2, BS, ventilator parameters (↓ PIP, ↓ Raw, ↑ VT, ↑ Cdyn), removal of secretions

* A component of bronchial hygiene therapy involving the mechanical aspiration of pulmonary secretions from a patient with an artificial airway.

† Adapted from the AARC Clinical Practice Guideline: Endotracheal Suction of Mechanically Ventilated Adults and Children with Artificial Airways, ***Respiratory Care***, Vol. 38, #5, 1993.

Humidification during Mechanical Ventilation[1] (AARC CPG)	
Indication Continuous gas therapy: high flow or bypassed upper airway. **Contraindication** None except HME when: Body temperature < 32°C, concurrent aerosol therapy, expired VT < 70% of delivered VT, spont $\dot{V}E$ > 10 L/min, thick, copious, or bloody secretions. **Monitoring** *Check*: alarm settings (30 – 37ºC) (HR), humidifier temp setting (HR), inspired gas temp (33 ± 2°C) (HR), water level and feed system (HR), sputum quantity and consistency Remove condensate in circuit Replace HMEs contaminated with secretions **Frequency**: Continuous during gas therapy	**Hazards/Complications** Burns (patient or caregiver) (HR) Electrical shock (HR) Hypo/hyperthermia Hypoventilation (HME → ↑VD) ↑ Resistive WOB through humidifier Infection (nosocomial) Tracheal lavage (pooled condensate or overfilling) (HR) Underhydration (mucous impaction or plugging of airways → air-trapping, hypoventilation, ↑ WOB Ventilator malperformance: pooled condensate → ↑ airway pressures or asynchrony with patient (HR) HME → ineffective low pressure alarm during disconnection **Clinical Goal** Humidified and warmed inspired gases without hazards or complications.

1) Adapted from AARC Clinical Practice Guideline: Humidification during Mechanical Ventilation, ***Respiratory Care***, Vol. 37, #8, 1992.
HR = heated reservoir, HME = heat moisture exchanger

In Hospital Transport of the Mechanically Ventilated Patient [1] (AARC CPG)

Indications Following a careful evaluation of the risk-benefit ratio ***Contraindications*** All members of transport team are not present.. *Inability during transport to:* Adequately monitor CV status Maintain acceptable hemodynamic performance Maintain airway control Provide adequate O_2 and ventilation ***Monitoring*** Same as during stationary care. *Continuous:* EKG, HR, BP (if invasive line), SpO_2 *Intermittent:* BS, RR, BP (no invasive line), PIP, VT	***Hazards/Complications*** Accidental extubation or removal of IV access due to movement CV instability Equipment failure Hyperventilation (manual ventilation) Inadvertent disconnection of IVs or MV support Loss of O_2 supply Loss of PEEP/CPAP Position changes causing ↓ BP, ↓ PaO_2, and/or ↑ $PaCO_2$ VAP ***Assessment of Need:*** Risk vs. benefit ***Assessment of Outcome:*** Safe arrival ***Infection Control:*** Universal Precautions, disinfection of equip between patients, CDC recommendations for TB risk.

1) Adapted from AARC Clinical Practice Guideline: In-Hospital Transport of the Mechanically Ventilated Patient, ***Respiratory Care***, Vol. 47, #6, 2002.

IPPB [1,2]
(AARC CPG)

Indications

Lung expansion

Atelectasis (when not responsive to other therapies or patient cannot/will not cooperate)

Secretions (inability to clear)

Short-term ventilation (alternative form of MV for hypoventilating patients, consider NPPV)

Delivery of aerosolized medication [3]

Used when other aerosol techniques have been unsuccessful. [4]

Patients with fatigue, severe hyperinflation or during short-term ventilation.

Assessment of Need

Acute, severe, unresponsive bronchospasm or exacerbated COPD.

Impending respiratory failure

NM disorders

PFT (FEV_1 < 65% pred, FVC < 70% pred, MVV < 50% pred, VC < 10 mL/kg) without effective cough.

Significant atelectasis

Contraindications

Absolute – untreated tension pneumothorax

Relative – active hemoptysis, active untreated TB, air swallowing, bleb, hemodynamic instability, hiccups, ICP > 15 mmHg,
nausea, recent oral, facial, esophageal or skull surgery, TE fistula.

Monitoring

Patient: RR, V_T, HR, rhythm, BP, BS, response (mental function, pain, discomfort, dyspnea), skin color, O2 Sat, sputum, ICP, chest x-ray.

Machine: *f*, VT, peak, plateau, PEEP pressures, sensitivity, flow, F_IO_2, T_I, T_E.

Clinical Goals (desired outcome)

For lung expansion: a V_T of at least 33% of IC predicted

↑FEV_1 or PF

More effective cough, enhanced secretion clearance, improved chest x-ray and BS, good patient response.

Frequency	*Hazards/Complications*
Critical care: q 1-6 hrs as tolerated, re-evaluate daily *Acute care*: bid, qid per patient response, re-evaluate q 24 hrs	Air trapping (auto PEEP), barotrauma, ↓ venous return, exacerbation of hypoxemia, gastric distention, hemoptysis, hyperoxia (with O2), hypocarbia, hypo / hyperventilation, ↑Raw, V/Q mismatch, infection, psychological dependence, secretion impaction.

1) Intermittent positive pressure breathing (IPPB) is intermittent, or short-term mechanical ventilation for the purpose of augmenting lung expansion, assisting ventilation, and/or delivering an aerosolized medication (not the therapy of first choice) (Does not include NPPV).
2) Adapted from the AARC Clinical Practice Guideline: IPPB, 2003 Revision + Update, ***Respiratory Care***, Volume 48, #5, 2003.
3) Efficacy is technique dependent (coordination, breathing pattern, VI, PIP, inspiratory hold), device design, and patient instruction.
4) MDI or nebs are devices of choice for aerosol therapy to COPD or stable asthma patients.

Management of Airway Emergencies[1] (AARC CPG)

Indications

Conditions requiring general airway management: airway compromise, protection, respiratory failure.

Conditions requiring emergency tracheal intubation, surgical placement or alternative techniques (see the AARC guideline for a list of numerous specific conditions).

Contraindications

Patient's documented desire not to be resuscitated.

Monitoring

Patient:

Clinical signs – airway obstruction (blood, foreign objects, secretions, vomitus), BS, chest movement, epigastric sounds, LOC, nasal flaring, retractions, skin color, upper airway sounds (snoring, stridor), ventilation ease.

Physiologic variables – ABG, pulse ox., CXR, $PeCO_2$, HR, rhythm, f, V_T, Paw.

Tube positioned in trachea:

Confirmed by – chest x-ray, endoscopic visualization, exhaled CO_2

Suggested by – BS (bilateral), chest movement (symmetrical), condensate upon exhalation, epigastrium (absence of ventilation sounds), esophageal detector devices, visualization of passage through vocal cords.

Precautions/Hazards/ Complications

Emergency Ventilation: barotrauma, gastric insufflation/rupture, hypo/hyper ventilation, hypotension, O_2 delivery (inadequate), unstable cervical spine, upper airway obstruction, ventilation (prolonged interruption), vomiting, aspiration.

Trans-Laryngeal intubation, Cricothyroidotomy:

Aspiration, bronchospasm, laryngospasm, bradycardia, tachycardia, dysrhythmia, hypo/hypertension.

ET tube problems –

Cuff herniation, perforation, extubation (inadvertent), pilot tube valve incompetence, size inappropriate, tube kinking, occlusion.

Failure to establish patient airway, intubate the trachea

Intubation of bronchi, esophagus

Pneumonia

Trauma – airway, cervical spine, dental, esophagus, eye, nasal, needle cricothyroidotomy (bleeding, esophageal perforation, subcutaneous emphysema), vocal cords.

Ulceration, stenosis, malacia

1) Adapted from the AARC Clinical Practice Guidelines: Management of Airway Emergencies, ***Respiratory Care***, Volume 40, #7, 1995.

Patient-Ventilator System Checks * (AARC CPG)	
Objectives Assure proper ventilator operation Evaluate/document patient's response *Verify/document*: alarms are activated, circuit properly connected to patient, inspired gas heated/humidified, FIO_2, and ventilator settings comply with orders ***Indications*** *Regularly scheduled interval* (institutional-specific) plus: Prior to obtaining: ABG, hemodynamic data, PFT data (bedside) *Following:* Any change in ventilator setting Any time ventilator performance is questionable ASAP after any acute deterioration in patient's condition	***Contraindications:*** None (see hazards) ***Hazards/Complications*** *Disconnection may result in*: ↓ HR, ↓ BP, hypoxemia, hypoventilation (preoxygenation/hyper-ventilation may minimize these hazards) Some ventilators: high circuit flow may aerosolize contaminated circuit condensate ***Frequency:*** Same as indications ***Clinical Goals*** Assure proper ventilator settings Prevent untoward incidents Warn of impending events

* Adapted from the AARC Clinical Practice Guideline: Patient-Ventilator System Checks, ***Respiratory Care***, Vol. 37, #8, 1992.

Removal of the Endotracheal Tube - 2007* (AARC CPG)

Indications

Airway control no longer necessary and patient is able to maintain patent airway & adequate spontaneous ventilation (i.e. adequate neuro drive, muscle strength, cough)

Artificial airway obstruction (not able to be cleared rapidly)

Discontinuance of further medical care

Contraindications:

No absolute

Hazards/Complications

Hypoxemia (aspiration, atelectasis, bronchospasm, hypoventilation, laryngospasm, low O_2, pulmonary edema)

Hypercapnia (bronchospasm, excessive WOB, muscle weakness, upper airway edema)

Death (discontinuance of medical care)

Assessment of Readiness

Artificial airway no longer needed as indicated by reversal of cause, adequate spontaneous ventilation and meet readiness criteria:

Maintain adequate PaO_2:

- $PaO_2/F_IO_2 > 150\text{-}200$,
- PEEP $\leq$ 5-8 cm H_2O and
- $FIO_2 \leq 0.4\text{-}0.5$
- Maintain appropriate pH > 7.25 and $PaCO_2$
- Cthorax > 25 mL/cmH_2O
- f < 35/min (adult)
- Modified CROP $\geq$ 0.1-0.15 mL.mmHg/breaths/min/mL/kg
- MVV > 2x$\dot{V}E$ (resting)
- NIP > - 20-30 cm H_2O
- O_2 cost of breathing < 15% total
- P0.1 < 6 cm H_2O
- PEF $\geq$ 60 L/min
- RSBI $\leq$ 105 (modified RSBI $\leq$ 8-11 breaths/min.mL.kg)
- SMIP > 57.5
- Successful SBT (30-120 min) with low CPAP (5 cmH_2O) or low PS (5-7 cmH_2O) (i.e., adequate respiratory pattern, gas exchange, hemo stability and comfort)
- VC > 10 mL/kg (ideal)
- $V_D/V_T < 0.6$
- $\dot{V}_E$ (spont) < 10 L/min
- WOB < 0.8 J/L.

(continued from previous page)	
Assessment of Outcome/ Monitoring Assess/monitor: ABGs, adequate spontaneous ventilation & oxygenation, airway patency, chest X-ray, complications, hemodynamics, neuro status, VS, WOB Note: Attentive monitoring, prompt ID of respiratory distress and maintaining patent airway is essential. **Infection Control** Follow CDC Standard Precautions	**Resolution of need for airway protection:** Adequate airway protective reflexes Easily managed secretions Normal consciousness **Other Considerations** Electrolytes Hemodynamics Nutrition Prophylactic meds (lidocaine, steroids) Reintubation need Risk factors Upper airway obstruction/ edema

* Adapted from AARC Clinical Practice Guideline: Removal of the Endotracheal Tube – 2007 Revision & Update, ***Respiratory Care***, Vol. 52, #1, 2007.

Selection of Device, Administration of Bronchodilator, and Evaluation of Response to Therapy in Mechanically Ventilated Patients *	
Indications Bronchoconstriction or ↑ Raw during MV ***Contraindications*** Certain medications in some patients Some assessment maneuvers in extremis (e.g., prolonged inspiratory pause for patients with high auto-PEEP). ***Limitations of Device or Procedure*** Refer to original Guideline for details beyond the scope of this book. ***Assessment of Need.*** *Need for bronchodilator:* Previous positive response to bronchodilator Presence of auto-PEEP (not eliminated with ↓ *f*, ↑ $\dot{V}_I$, or ↓ I:E ratio) ↑ Raw (evidenced by ↑ PIP - Pplat diff, wheezing or ↓ BS, retractions, pt-vent asynchrony)	***Hazards/Complications*** Bronchospasm/irritation of airways by medication, propellant, or cold, dry gas. Complications of specific medications Device, adaptor, and/or technique may affect ventilator performance (↑ V_T, $\dot{V}_I$, PIP), and/or alter alarms or trigger sensitivities. Device malfunction Failure to return any adjusted ventilator settings back to pre-treatment levels. Some assessment procedures may have inherent hazards. Underdosing (inappropriate device, use and/or technique) ***Frequency.*** *Acute, unstable patient:* Full assessment with first treatment Assess all appropriate monitored variables before and after, and VS, BS, and side effects during therapy. Frequency of PIP - Pplat diff and physical exam is based on patient status. Continuous SpO_2. *Stable patient:* PIP - Pplat diff before and after therapy

(continued from previous page)	
Monitoring Patient observation (general appearance, VS, subjective response, adverse response to drug, presence of tremor, use of accessory muscles, pt-vent asynchrony). Percussion/auscultation (wheezing) Changes in patient (dyspnea, ABGs, SaO_2/SpO_2, sputum clearance) Changes in ventilator variables (PIP - Pplat diff, Raw, expiratory flow, F-V loop, auto-PEEP).	***Assessment of Outcome.*** *Evaluate need and response:* Prior to, during, and following therapy Check for lack of or adverse responses and any change from baseline values Identify need to modify dose, therapy or frequency *Document:* Patient response (VS, PIP, Pplat, auto-PEEP, etc) Medication (type, dose, time)

Infection Control

CDC Standard Precautions

Nebulizers should not be used between patients without disinfection. Nebs should be changed or sterilized at end of dose administration, q 24-hr for continuous admin. or when soiled. Nebs should not be rinsed with tap H_2O between treatments.

Handle meds aseptically.

Multidose sources in acute care settings should be discarded after 24 hrs.

Synopsis

Ventilator Settings: An external gas source to power neb may affect V_T, F_IO_2, and triggering.

Humidifier: An external gas source to power neb may cause heated circuit malfunction. Remove artificial nose or HME prior to therapy. Keep heated humidifier in place. Med dose may be ↑ to compensate for loss due to humidified gas.

MDI: Actuation should be manually, synchronized with beginning of inspiration. Use a chamber device. Greater doses may be required if patient response incomplete or inadequate.

(continued from previous page)

Nebulizer: If possible, place neb 30 cm from proximal end of ET tube. Do not leave inline between treatments. Do not rinse with tap H_2O. Change q 24 hrs. An expiratory limb filter may be needed to maintain expiratory flow-sensor accuracy.

Patient Monitoring: For VV, monitor PIP-Pplat diff. For PV, monitor V_T. Monitor BS, auto-PEEP and PEF or F-V loop for both VV and PV.

* Adapted from AARC Clinical Practice Guideline: Selection of Device, Administration of Bronchodilator, and Evaluation of Response to Therapy in Mechanically Ventilated Patients, ***Respiratory Care***, Vol 44, #1, 1999.

Ventilator Circuit Changes *	
Indications Determined by: Appearance of circuit Length of time existing circuit in use Type of circuit and humidifier Presence of malfunction or leak ***Contraindications*** Absence of a clean and functional replacement circuit Disconnection from MV hazardous to patient (CV or Neuro intolerance) Inability to safely and effectively ventilate or maintain patient during change ***Limitations of Procedure*** Changing more frequently than 48 hrs provides no infection control advantage	***Hazards/Complications*** *Patient predisposed to harm or injury:* Airway obstruction Contamination of patient or staff from exposure to material in circuit ET tube displacement Hemodynamic instability Hypo/hyperoxia Hypo/hypercarbia *Patient unsafely maintained during disconnect:* Airway obstruction Inappropriate/inadequate V_T, *f*, FiO_2, PEEP, WOB Replacement circuit unsafe (malfunctioning, improperly reconnected) or not properly disinfected Risk of patient infection from condensate in circuit spilling into airway

* Adapted from AARC ***Clinical Practice Guideline***: Ventilator Circuit Changes, *Respiratory Care*, Vol. 39, #8, 1994.

Bibliography

Books and Texts:

Aloan, C. and Hill, T.	*Respiratory Care of the Newborn and Child*, 2nd Ed., 1997. Lippincott-Raven Publishers
American Heart Association	*Guidelines 2005 for Cardiopulmonary Resuscitation and Emergency Cardiovascular Care: International Consensus on Science*. AHA and the ILCR, *Circulation*, 2005; 112, #24.
Burton, G. et al.	*Respiratory Care: A Guide to Clinical Practice*, 4th Ed., 1997. Lippincott-Raven Publishers
Cairo, J. and Pilbeam, S.	*Mosby's Respiratory Care Equipment*, 7th Ed., 2004. Mosby, Inc.
Chang, D.	*Clinical Applications of Mechanical Ventilation*, 3rd Ed., 2005. Delmar Publishers
Chang, D.	*Respiratory Care Calculations*, 2nd Ed., 1999. Delmar Publishers
Chatburn, R.	*Fundamentals of Mechanical Ventilation*, 2003, Mandu Press
Goldsmith, J. & Karotkin, E.	*Assisted Ventilation of the Neonate*, 4th Ed., 2003. W.B. Saunders Co.
Hess, D. & Kacmarek, R.	*Essentials of Mechanical Ventilation*, 2nd Ed., 2002. McGraw-Hill Co., Inc.
MacIntyre, N. & Branson,R.	*Mechanical Ventilation*, 2009. Saunders/ Elsevier
NHLBI	*Guidelines for the Diagnosis and Management of Asthma, The National Asthma Education Program's Expert Panel: Report 2*, 1998 and 2002; National Heart, Lung, and Blood Institute; NIH
Oakes, D.	*Clinical Practitioners Pocket Guide to Respiratory Care*, 7th Ed., 2008. Health Educator Publications

Oakes, D.	*Hemodynamic Monitoring: A Bedside Reference Manual*, 4th Ed., 2005. Health Educator Publications.
Oakes, D.	*Neonatal/Pediatric Respiratory Care: A Critical Care Pocket Guide*, 6th Ed., 2009. Health Educator Publications.
Ouellet, P.	*Waveform and Loop Analysis in Mechanical Ventilation*, 1997. Siemens-Elema
Papadakos, P. and Lachmann, B.	*Mechanical Ventilation: Clinical Application and Pathophysiology,* 2007, Saunders/ Elsevier
Pilbeam, S., and Cairo, J.	*Mechanical Ventilation: Physiological and Clinical Applications*, 4th Ed., 2006. Mosby, Inc.
Raoof, S. and Khan, F.	*Mechanical Ventilation Manual*, 1998. American College of Physicians
Sinha, S. and Donn, S.	*Manual of Neonatal Respiratory Care*, 2000. Futura Publishing Co., Inc.
Tobin, M.	*Principles and Practice of Mechanical Ventilation*, 2nd Ed., 2006. McGraw-Hill Professional.
Waugh, J. et al.	*Rapid Interpretation of Ventilator Waveforms*, 1999 Prentice-Hall, Inc.
Wilkins, R. et al.	*Egan's Fundamentals of Respiratory Care*, 9th Ed., 2009. Mosby, Inc.

Clinics:

Clinics in Chest Medicine, W.B. Saunders Co. Clinics Editor: Donley, S.

Guest Editor(s)	Title, Vol:No, Date
MacIntyre, N	Controversies in Mechanical Ventilation, 2008
Nahum, A. and Marini, J.	Recent Advances in Mechanical Ventilation, 17:3, Sept., 1996

Clinics in Perinatology, W.B. Saunders Co. Clinics Editor: Davis, C.

Guest Editor(s)	Title, Vol:No, Date
Goldsmith, J. and Spitzer, A.	Controversies in Neonatal Pulmonary Care, 25:1, March, 1998
Wiswell, T. and Donn, S.	Mechanical Ventilation and Exogenous Surfactant Update, 28:3, Sept., 2001

Critical Care Clinics, W.B. Saunders Co. Clinics Editors: Carlson, R. and Geheb, M.

Guest Editor(s)	Title, Vol:No, Date
Papadakos, P and Dooley, J	Mechanical Ventilation, 2007
Tharratt, R.	Mechanical Ventilation, 14:4, Oct., 1998
Vender, J.	Respiratory Procedures and Monitoring, 11:1, Jan., 1995

Respiratory Care Clinics of North America, W.B. Saunders Co. Clinics Editors: Branson, R. and MacIntyre, N.

Guest Editor(s)	Title, Vol:No, Date
Blanch, L.	Adjuncts to Mechanical Ventilation, 8:2, June, 2002
Brown, S.	Acute Respiratory Distress Syndrome, 4:4, Dec., 1998
Fein, A. et al.	Oxygen Therapy, 6:4, Dec., 2000
Heffner, J. and Petty, T.	Chronic Obstructive Pulmonary Disease, 4:3, Sept., 1998
Hill, N. and Bach, J	Noninvasive Mechanical Ventilation, 2:2, June, 1996
Iotti, G.	Closed-Loop Control Mechanical Ventilation, 7:3, Sept., 2001
Manthous, C.	Liberation from Mechanical Ventilation Part I & II, 6:2, June, 2000 & 6:3, Sept., 2000

Salyer, J.	Pediatric Mechanical Ventilation, 2:4, Dec., 1996
Stewart, T.	High-Frequency Ventilation, 7:4, Dec., 2001
***Update in Intensive Care and Emergency Medicine*, Springer-Verlag**	
Guest Editor(s)	**Title, No, Year**
Mancebo, J. et al.	Mechanical Ventilation and Weaning, 36, 2002
Slutzky, A. and Brouchard, L.	Mechanical Ventilation (Update), 40, 2004

Consensus Conferences, Standards and Guidelines:

Mechanical Ventilation (In General)

AARC

Consensus Conference: Noninvasive Positive Pressure Ventilation, ***Respiratory Care*** 1997; 42(4): 364-369.

AARC Clinical Practice Guidelines, ***Respiratory Care***, See Appendix for the various Issues.

Consensus Statement on the Essential of Mechanical Ventilators, ***Respiratory Care*** 1992: 37(9): 1000-1008.

ACCP

Mechanical Ventilation, American College of Chest Physicians' Consensus Conference, ***Chest*** 1993; 104:1833-1859 or ***Respiratory Care*** 1993; 38(12).

AHA

Guidelines 2005 for Cardiopulmonary Resuscitation and Emergency Cardiovascular Care: International Consensus on Science. American Heart Association and the International Liaison Committee of Resuscitation, ***Circulation***, 2005; 112, #24.

ARDS

The ARDS Network, ***The New England Journal of Medicine*** 2000; 342 (18): 1301-1308; and 2004, 351(4):327.

The American-European Consensus Conference on ARDS, ***American Journal of Respiratory and Critical Care Medicine*** 1994; 149: 818-824.

Asthma

Guidelines for the Diagnosis and Management of Asthma, The National Asthma Education Program's Expert Panel: Report 2, 1998 & 2002; ***National Heart, Lung, and Blood Institute***; National Institutes of Health, Bethesda, MD.

Near-Fatal Asthma :

See AHA, Mechanical Ventilation In General, below.

COPD

GOLD Executive Summary, ***American Journal of Respiratory and Critical Care Medicine*** 2001; 163(5): 1256-1276; or ***Respiratory Care*** 2001; 46(8): 798-825. And 2003 and 2004 Updates, www.goldcopd.org.

Discontinuation/Weaning

ACCP/AARC/ACCM Evidence-Based Guidelines for Weaning and Discontinuing Ventilatory Support, ***Chest*** 2001; 120(6): 375S-395S.

Non-Invasive Positive Pressure Ventilation

International Consensus Conferences in Intensive Care Medicine: Noninvasive Positive Pressure Ventilation in Acute Respiratory Failure. ***Am J Respir Crit Care Med*** 2001; 163: 283-291.

Consensus Statement: Noninvasive Positive Pressure Ventilation. ***Respiratory Care*** 1997; 42(4): 365-367.

Index

A

B

C

D

E

F

G

H

I

K

L

M

N

O

P

Q

R

S

T

U

V

W

Z

Table of Contents

at-a-glance

Turn to Page 1 of each chapter for a DETAILED TABLE OF CONTENTS

Preface

Ventilator management is one of the fastest changing applications of advanced medical care today. The level of knowledge and clinical skill required for ventilatory support clinicians have increased dramatically over the past decade.

Today more than ever, it is critical for clinicians to have a clear understanding of:

- Mechanical ventilator capabilities and limitations, including modes, principles of operation, hazards and complications;
- The strategic clinical application of those capabilities and limitations to highly variable patient pathophysiology;
- The resultant physiological effects; and
- The continual appropriate matching of management strategies to a patient's ever-changing therapeutic and ventilatory needs.

The older, classic concept of "clinician-controlled" ventilation is rapidly being overtaken with the newer concept of "patient-controlled" ventilation, making today's ventilator care both a "science" and an "art". Profound technological advances in microprocessor ventilators marks the new science, while the competency required to custom fine-tune these ventilators to meet continually changing patient needs, indeed, marks a new art.

This new era in ventilation has made it more imperative than ever for the competent clinical specialist at the controls of the ventilator to have a complete understanding of the above, plus considerable clinical experience and skill in patient-ventilator assessment and management.

With the vast amount of knowledge now required, and the speed at which this information changes, it has become obvious that today's clinician needs quick and easy access to the current schools of thought on ventilator management strategies, as well as the new national standards and guidelines.

The purpose of this book is to help bridge the gap between the vast amount of knowledge available and the appropriate (and timely) clinical application of that knowledge. Principles and practices of the current literature have been boiled down to their basic tenets, providing the user with a quick and easy, comprehensive bedside reference for use within the clinical setting.

The hope is that this book will help empower the ventilatory support clinician to provide a comprehensive, confident, precise, and safe approach to patient-ventilator management.